Education
Policy
Implementation

SUNY Series, Educational Leadership
Daniel L. Duke, Editor

Education Policy Implementation

Edited by
Allan R. Odden

State University of New York Press

Published by
State University of New York Press, Albany

For information, address State University of New York
Press, State University Plaza, Albany, N.Y. 12246

Production by Diane Ganeles
Marketing by Bernadette LaManna

Library of Congress Cataloging-in-Publication Data

Education policy implementation / edited by Allan R. Odden.
      p.   cm. — (SUNY series, educational leadership)
     Includes bibliographical references and index.
     ISBN 0-7914-0665-2 (alk. paper). — ISBN 0-7914-0666-0 (pbk. :
alk. paper)
     1. Education and state—United States—History. 2. Education-
-United States—History. I. Odden, Allan. II. Series: SUNY series
in educational leadership.
LC89.E27   1991
379.73—dc20   90-43395
                                              CIP

10 9 8 7 6 5 4 3 2 1

Contents

Preface

I would first like to thank all the authors who helped me produce the materials for this book. The chapters include writings from the country's top analysts of education policy implementation, as well as policy implementation in fields outside of education. As most of these authors know, implementation research is time consuming and requires hours in the field collecting and then analyzing qualitative data. It is easy to do an average job and hard to do excellent work. These authors all have produced excellent work and as a result have helped improve our understanding of the local process of government policy implementation.

I would also like to thank my research assistant, Nancy Kotowski, who helped edit these materials, tracked down references, and secured reprint permissions. She also raised questions about key analytic points and helped draw conclusions. Without her continuous hard work, this book would not have been completed.

Thanks also are due to Cindy Stuehler who with great speed and unequaled accuracy entered each chapter into the computer and then modified them with each round of editorial changes. Without her extraordinary skill, the book also would be in some middle stage of production.

Finally, I hope this book proves to be useful to those studying education policy implementation as well as useful to the policy community that makes education policy. The fact is that local educators are highly skilled in implementing higher level governmental programs. Now that we have ambitious education goals, the issue in the 1990s is not just whether programs can be implemented, but also whether the right programs are enacted and whether supports are provided for the implementation processes that facilitate full and complete implementation.

Chapter 1

The Evolution of Education Policy Implementation

Allan R. Odden

When implementation research began to analyze local response to the 1960s "War on Poverty" programs, the findings were sobering. Most studies found misuse of governmental funds, services provided to the wrong clients, and in some cases, outright local resistance to these new governmental initiatives. In education, for example, early research showed that there was a lack of both capacity and will at all levels of government—the U.S. Office of Education, state departments of education, local district offices and local schools—to develop and implement newly created governmental programs, particularly Title I of ESEA, which was enacted to provide educational services to selected groups of students. Research showed not only that most local educators did not want to implement such programs (the will was not there), but also that they did not know how to implement them (the capacity was not there).

Subsequently, a large body of implementation research emerged that essentially argued that federally (or state) initiated programs, for education or other social services, were doomed to failure on the beaches of local implementation resistance, and that the priorities, orientations, and pressures of local governments (school districts in the case of education) were simply at odds with those of higher level of governments (Pressman and Wildavsky, 1973; Derthick 1976).

When regulatory structures were created during the 1970s to give greater clarity to the intent and acceptable operations of the new federal and state governmental programs, there was considerable analysis that showed the initial weak impact these regulations had on local behavior and the continuing dominance of local priorities (Barro 1978). Astute analysts realized that "street level bureaucrats" (those local educators

1

who had to implement admittedly grandiose state or federal programs usually without sufficient resources) made the key policy decisions because what they did in the school and classroom constituted the program as implemented, despite legislative intent or regulatory requirements (Weatherly and Lipsky 1977). And in the early 1980s, seasoned implementation researchers concluded that it was difficult, if not impossible, for state or federal government programs to garner the interest, effort, and commitment of local educators to the higher level government's objectives (Elmore and McLaughlin 1981).

A complementary line of research—on the local educational change process—concluded that it was difficult to get new programs (created or designed outside the local school district) implemented (Sarason 1982) unless there was a "mutual adaptation" process in which local educators could tailor (adapt, change and mold) the program to meet their unique, local needs and circumstances (McLaughlin 1976). In short, early implementation research findings coupled with somewhat later research findings on the local educational change process concluded that local response was inherently at odds with state (or federal) program initiative. If higher level governments took policy initiatives, it was unlikely that local educators would implement those policies in compliance with either the spirit, expectations, rules, regulations or program components.

These tenets of "conventional wisdom" led to great skepticism about the efficacy of the state education reform movement that began in 1983 with publication of *A Nation at Risk* and large numbers of subsequent state commission reports calling for major overhauls in the country's elementary and secondary schools. Boyd (1987) provided one of the most elegant critiques of state education reform initiatives, invoking both the early implementation research findings and the early local educational change findings to argue that the top-down nature of state education reforms rendered them unlikely to accomplish their goals of improving local educational practice. Peterson (1983) criticized both the reform report rhetoric and the reform proposals themselves as largely without research support and thus doomed to failure.

Moreover, Cuban (1984b) was articulate in voicing his skepticism of the probability that new state education standards and mandates would make local school districts, schools, and classrooms better. Through a series of local newspaper articles, Cuban took issue with California's chief state school officer, Bill Honig (a major designer of California's 1983 education reform and a rapidly rising state education leader) and strongly questioned the efficacy of that state's efforts to improve the quality of local districts, schools, and curriculum and instruction in classrooms.

Further, since state political leaders and the business community had designed education reforms with little input from the education community, there was concern that resistance would form simply because local educators had been denied participation in the education reform process. Finally, there was widespread concern that the new policy push for excellence and quality might "smother" and push aside the two decade-old focus on improving equity in the nation's schools. In short, state education reformers appeared to face an army of skeptics and a consensus—at least among many educators and educational researchers—that state education reform and other efforts to improve fundamentally local education systems "would not work."

But several other indicators at that time, largely ignored by state education reform critics, provided hope that state education reform initiatives might not be dashed by local implementation resistance. First, several state education policy initiatives created during the 1970s—school finance reform, collective bargaining, minimum competency testing—not only spread across the states at a faster diffusion rate than traditional political science predicted (McDonnell and Fuhrman 1986) but also appeared to have at least some success (Odden, McGuire, and Belsches-Simmons 1983). Second, while almost totally ignored by state education reformers, several states in the early 1980s had enacted a variety of school improvement programs (Dougherty and Odden 1982), often based on the emerging effective teaching and schools research (Cohen 1983). Studies showed that several of these early state efforts had substantial impact on local school operations (Anderson et al. 1987). Third, there were indications from several other sources that local educators were beginning, on their own initiative, to improve the regular curriculum and instruction program, so that new state programs in those same areas at least had a chance of reinforcing and strengthening local priorities rather than pushing them in different directions (which clearly was a major characteristic of governmental programs in the 1960s and 1970s).

1. The Evolution of Implementation Knowledge and Theory

As the following chapters show, policy implementation has evolved through several stages during the past twenty five years. The first two stages primarily addressed macro-implementation issues of whether and how policies initiated at higher levels of government get implemented at lower levels of the system, i.e., penetrate school districts and schools. Stage one began with the expansion of intergovernmental grant programs in the 1960s and is characterized by early implementation problems and "inherent conflict" in federal (or state) initiated but locally implemented programs. Stage two, which began about a decade later, showed that programs ultimately get implemented, but through a mutual adaptation process. Stage three has just begun. It includes various attempts to improve local education systems rather than just create new categorical programs at the margin, including such diverse policy initiatives as comprehensive state education reforms, teacher professionalism proposals, major curriculum change and school restructuring. As the latter chapters in this volume show, these policies do penetrate local districts and schools and also create a new set of implementation challenges, more difficult than the simpler problems created by the newness and redistributive character of the early 1960s War on Poverty education programs.

A key message throughout the book is that the realities of policy implementation are no longer entrenched in the simple "lack of capacity and will" problems unearthed by early implementation research on such programs as Title I of the Elementary and Secondary Education Act (ESEA). The policy objectives today are grander, the programs more comprehensive, and implementation challenges more complex. A second message is that state and federal initiatives rather quickly affect local practice—the system is a bit more tightly coupled than previously thought. Another key message is that the understandings about effective implementation processes for the 1960s and 1970s categorical education programs, while providing a more sophisticated base of knowledge for addressing current education policy issues, nevertheless fall quite short of describing effective strategies for restructuring the curriculum, the teaching profession and schools—the policy goals of today. Thus, the chapters show that, in the early 1980s, just as local educators and researchers solidified understandings of how to cope effectively with governmental initiatives to create narrow categorical programs for specific groups of people or to change single curriculum programs, the policy focus shifted to improving the overall education system, a much tougher substantive implementation challenge for which more knowledge is still needed.

2. The First Stage of Education Policy Implementation

The first stage of implementation research was based mainly on late 1960s and early 1970s research on several programs (for education as well as several other functions), and concluded that there was inevitable conflict between local orientations, values, and priorities and state or federally initiated programs. New governmental programs met hostility at the local level. Most research showed that local governments had neither the capacity nor the will to implement initiatives designed by higher level governments (Murphy, chapter 2). The expectations and hopes of state and federal program designers were dashed on the shoals of local resistance and ineptness (Derthick 1976; Pressman and and Wildavsky 1973). At best, higher level governmental programs created opportunities for continuous bargaining with local governments over the values, foci, and substance of the new programs (Ingram 1977). But according to expectations at this stage, conflict would continue, bargaining would never abate and programs would rarely get implemented.

Early implementation research showed that implementation problems not only emerged from faulty program design but also, and even more importantly, from the policy's relationship to the local institutional setting. Indeed, much early implementation research showed that local governments often used new program fiscal resources for purposes other than those for which the programs were designed (Murphy, chapter 2). As a result, regulations were developed to constrain noncompliant local behavior and to force correct use of funds (Barro 1978 and Peterson, Rabe, and Wong, chapter 4). Theories addressing both policy design (including needed regulations) and, in part, local institutional settings were developed to improve policy implementation (Sabatier and Mazmanian 1979). Yet, conventional wisdom held that ongoing and continuous conflict was inevitable, that higher level government programs simply did not work, and that local governments would never implement them faithfully. Indeed, these understandings of implementation undergirded many criticisms of the 1980s state education reforms (Boyd 1987 and Timar and Kirp 1988).

3. The Second Stage of Education Policy Implementation

Changes in understanding the workings of government program implementation began to emerge with publication of several studies that investigated late 1970s and early 1980s implementation realities of policies designed in the 1960s and early 1970s. These studies focused on program implementation after the initial start-up years and addressed the question of whether, after fifteen years of effort, programs in compliance with legislative design and accompanying regulations could be implemented.

Kirst and Jung (chapter 3) produced the first second stage synthesis of federal education program implementation, focusing on Title I of ESEA. They claimed that late 1970's research showed that early Title I implementation problems had essentially abated by the late 1970s. A combination of new rules and regulations that "tightened up" Title I, a political support system of extreme interest groups, and Title I program protectors in the Congress helped shape a clear Title I program structure. By the close of the decade, local school districts had not only learned how to administer Title I in compliance with rules and regulations but also had even begun to sanction the education priorities embodied in Title I.

Their claim was substantially strengthened by publication of a series of research products that emerged from several federally sponsored studies. These research efforts, conducted between 1981 and 1983, investigated the state level interaction and local implementation of several similar federal and state categorical programs including compensatory education, special education, bilingual education, vocational education, and other civil rights rules and regulations (Moore, Goertz and Hartle, chapter 5; Knapp et al., chapter 6). These studies found, at both state and local levels, that the federal (and state) programs: (1) were being implemented in compliance with legislative intent and accompanying rules and regulations; (2) were providing extra services to students who needed them and who probably would not get them if the state and federal programs did not exist; (3) did not cause curriculum fragmentation in local schools and, in fact, allowed local educators to create a set of relatively integrated services for eligible students; and (4) were, in the minds of local educators, worthwhile because they provided needed extra services, despite extra paper work.

A few years later, additional Title I (then changed to Chapter I of ECIA) research showed that even when rules and regulations were waived (but subsequently reinstated) state and local district implementation practices maintained behaviors that had been required by the rules and regulations (Farrar and Milsap 1986). These studies showed that, over time, the grand expectations and rigid regulations of federal and state program designers were adapted to a program that could work locally, that local opposition was transformed into support for new program initiatives for targeted students, that local capacity was developed to run the programs in compliance with rules and regulations, and that eligible students were provided appropriate services (Jung and Kirst 1986).

Peterson, Rabe, and Wong (1986) produced a book about this implementation stage that provided both a new theory of program implementation and empirical data for programs in education and for other functions to support the theory. Peterson et al., chapter 2, identified two types of higher level governmental programs—developmental and redistributive—and argued that the implementation process differed for each.

Developmental programs, such as community development, transportation, and, in education, curriculum, instruction and vocational education, are those in which most local governments are involved anyway. Thus, federal and state policies in these areas tend to reinforce local initiatives and program priorities as well as provide extra resources for them, usually with marginal new program requirements. Based on several case studies of such programs, Peterson et al. showed that developmental programs typically get implemented fairly quickly and with a relatively uncontentious implementation process.

Redistributive programs, such as compensatory education, special education, and desegregation assistance in education, require local governments—school districts in the case of education—to engage in activities in which they had not been involved and to provide more service to some clients—students—than to others. Through an analysis of multiple case studies of a number of these programs, Peterson et al., chapter 2, concluded that redistributive programs experience a relatively contentious initial implementation process but that, over time, get fully implemented in compliance with legislative intent, rules, and regulations. Initial grandiose redistributive program goals and initial local resistance get tailored through a mutual adaptation process that produces a workable program for both local and higher level governments. This process is aided by the interaction of two other processes: the development of internal professional expertise and an external political support structure. The internal professionals write rules and regulations to define the program, use them to administer the program, and discover classroom practices to use in delivering the program's services. The professionals are undergirded by the external political community of special interest groups and congressional or state legislator program fixers. The professional and political communities work formally and informally over time to put a workable program into place.

Over time, then, most governmental programs, even redistributive programs, eventually become implemented, but the implementation process is different and more contentious for redistributive than for developmental programs. Hargrove (1983) provides both a theory about and empirical data for the politics of redistributive program implementation. The important overall conclusion from stage two implementation research is that higher level government programs eventually get implemented locally, that the initial conflict gets worked out over time, and that the opportunity for bargaining ultimately produces a workable program for both parties. Another conclusion is that state and federal initiatives do impact local practice: there may be questions about the impact, but impact occurs.

4. The Third Stage of Education Policy Implementation

Claiming that programs get implemented, however, is not the same as claiming that they are effective, i.e., that they solve the problems for which they were created. At about the same time as stage two implementation research knowledge emerged, so also did the realization that many programs were not having their desired impact. Students receiving extra services did better than similar students who did not receive services, but the impact was small and often eroded over time (Odden, chapter 7). Indeed, as the 1980s began, several analysts argued that there were direct trade-offs between compliant implementation and program quality, and noted that efforts to develop rules and regulations to get programs implemented had overlooked issues of program substance, quality and impact (Elmore and McLaughlin 1981; Elmore and McLaughlin 1983; Hargrove 1983).

Thus, a focus for stage three implementation research was to determine not only how to get programs implemented but also how to make them "work." Several approaches have been suggested for this twin objective. McDonnell and Elmore (chapter 9) suggest that new research should focus less on specific programs and more on policy instruments such as mandates, regulations, incentives, funds, etc. They argue that the underlying policy instruments used in any new program may be the most important element for program impact and that more needs to be known about how different policy instruments work across different types of programs.

McLaughlin (chapters 8 and 10) takes a different tack and suggests that program quality and impact issues are most promisingly analyzed by focusing on local, micro-implementation issues, and the connections between micro- and macro-implementation concerns. McLaughlin argues that program impact depends on focusing those who deliver services— teachers in education—on the substance of the particular program and in having those professionals apply state-of-the-art knowledge in the delivery of appropriate new services. McLaughlin sees this task as a micro-organizational/implementation issue that is informed more by the local educational change literature (Fullan 1982; Huberman and Miles 1984) than by political science literature. Indeed, in assessing the findings of the Rand Change Agent Study after fifteen years, she argues that the "problem" is still one of how to enhance the professional expertise of local educators (chapter 8).

Given the problem for which the program has been developed, the implementation issues are, according to McLaughlin: (1) what is known about effective practice at the service delivery level; (2) how local practitioners can be influenced to apply their energies and attentions to that problem; (3) what strategies can be used to make local practitioners experts in the effective practices they need to apply; and (4) how higher-level policy at the district, state, and/or federal level can be designed to help local practitioners put these practices into local use. Thus, McLaughlin suggests an approach closer to Elmore's (1979–80) "backward mapping" that emphasizes intra-organizational implementation issues and a local change orientation.

There is an additional issue, related to the nature of the program itself, to consider in deciding how to approach analysis of education policy implementation today. The 1980s education reforms, and likely the 1990s reforms as well, are substantively different from the education reforms of the 1960s and 1970s. The earlier reforms targeted special programs to particular types of students. Even when there was overlap between the types of students who could be served in the various programs, the implementation issue was whether services could be delivered to the targeted students. Rarely did a categorical program from the 1960s and 1970s focus on the regular curriculum program or the overall local education system. By contrast, current state education reforms are being created to improve the regular curriculum and instruction program—to change the quality of the local education system. Thus, the implementation issue is not just whether some or all of the programs were implemented but also whether they worked together to improve local schools and districts. The remaining chapters present implementation findings of several policy strategies designed to accomplish that goal.

Fuhrman, Clune, and Elmore (chapter 11) show that the early 1980's education reform implementation was quite different from what skeptics predicted. Indeed, these authors found that many local districts not only quickly and faithfully implemented the key elements of state education reform programs but also went beyond state requirements and standards. Rather than the lack of capacity and will and implementation resistance found in the first round of research after the War on Poverty Programs (and predicted by many for education reform policies), this study found sufficient capacity and will and, further, several "active user" districts (Firestone 1989) who latched onto new state initiatives and went beyond them (i.e., used them to reinforce local initiatives with similar objectives). Odden and Marsh (1988) found the same pattern for several California districts actively responding to California's comprehensive 1983 state education reform program. Odden and Marsh (1989) further made the point that education reforms were developmental (i.e., reinforced activities in which local districts already were engaged) and not redistributive programs and, thus, implementation should have been relatively swift, relatively uncontentious, and strongly linked to extant local priorities.

If education reform implementation findings confounded most pundits, subsequent findings about other 1980s policy initiatives began to raise a series of new and more complex issues. While education reform generally was a strategy to intensify conventional notions of education excellence and in the main did not require substantial change in teacher pedagogical practices (Fuhrman, Firestone, and Kirst 1989), the next reforms calling for major curriculum change, teacher professionalism, and school restructuring entailed fundamental change in teacher and administrator behavior and school organizational structures. Chapters 12, 13, and 14 show that these initiatives have experienced several dimensions of effective implementation as well as raised a host of new issues about both the types of program designs and combinations of implementation strategies that are needed to change dramatically local education systems.

Marsh and Odden (chapter 12) report on implementation realities of California's major curriculum reform initiatives, a bold set of reforms broader than the curriculum reforms outlined in the *Nation at Risk* (National Commission on Excellence in Education 1983) report but somewhat less grandiose than the total school restructuring outlined in *Caught in the Middle* (Superintendent's Middle Grade Task Force 1987). Noting the less than optimistic findings from the previous NDEA post-Sputnik curriculum changes attempted during the 1960s and 1970s (Atkin and House 1981; Ravitch 1984), this study identifies how the current California curriculum reforms are substantively different from the NDEA curricula and outlines advances in knowledge of curriculum change learned from research in the thirty years between 1960 and 1990 (see Crandall 1982 for example). One key finding from this curriculum implementation study is that changing one curriculum area at a time is much easier than changing several simultaneously, which is what California is attempting to accomplish. Further, the study notes that local efforts to change fundamentally the curriculum runs into the central dilemma outlined by McLaughlin (chapter 8) of how to enhance the professional expertise of local teachers and administrators. The findings confirm McLaughlin's hunches that infiltrating local professional networks is a powerful strategy for accomplishing this goal. Nevertheless, the results show that fundamental curriculum change is a hard and slow process, akin to what Elmore and McLaughlin (1988) call the "steady work" of American education reform.

McDonnell (chapter 13) outlines quite clearly how teacher professionalism proposals raise fundamental issues about who controls American education: the public or professional educators. She shows how several implementation snags with different state approaches to professionalizing teachers are linked more to this fundamental political dilemma than to traditional notions of local capacity and will. Her chapter thus adds a new dimension to implementation research—how issues beyond technical feasibility and local capacity and will affect implementation. McDonnell argues and shows from implementation research that policy implementation may be difficult when a governmental initiative fundamentally challenges traditional notions of who governs schools.

Marsh and Crocker (chapter 14) report on a study of California middle school reform that not only focuses on the difficulties of restructuring an entire school organization but also on the role that two types of state policies can play in that process. In the mid-1980s California synthesized knowledge about effective schools for early adolescents into a report entitled *Caught in the Middle,* which outlined a vision for what a good middle school should be. The vision included a restructured curriculum, changes in teacher and administrator roles, instructional strategies, changes in student activities, and changes in school organization. The report was disseminated as a stimulus for middle school change but was not mandated. Simultaneously, however, the state's School Improvement Program (see Marsh and Bowman 1989, for a description) was expanded for middle schools to provide planning and implementation funding with the requirement that the *Caught in the Middle* vision was the program to implement. Marsh and Crocker's results show some of the positive impacts as well as shortcomings of these twin policy initiatives as well as document the difficulties of dramatically restructuring a school—even when a clear and substantively strong vision exists and there is money both to plan and carry out implementation.

Finally, Wohlstetter (chapter 15) describes new mechanisms that states have devised to monitor education policy implementation for the variety of wide ranging policies they enacted in the 1980s. Indeed, the existence of these oversight initiatives themselves show how sophisticated the states have become about the implementation process. In the late 1960s, there were no such entities. Even in the 1970s few states established mechanisms to track formally the implementation of broad new education policies. But across the country during the 1980s states created a variety of different implementation monitoring mechanisms, from a broadly based committee of business, political, and education leaders in South Carolina who were sanctioned to monitor reform implementation as well as suggest changes in the strategic directions of policy, to technical and program specific "watch dog" committees in several other states. Wohlstetter is not overly sanguine about the ulti-mate impact of these oversight strategies. She found that the political payoffs for legislative involvement in oversight are pretty small. She nevertheless suggests that some oversight is better than none at all and hopes that these fledgling beginnings could mature into yet another element of the implementation structure of the 1990s that make policy implementation both more interesting, more sophisticated, and more complex in this decade.

The last chapter attempts to synthesize key points in the entire book and emphasizes findings in chapter 12 through 15. Chapter 16 shows how yet another stage of implementation began to emerge in the late 1980s post-"Wave I" education reform era as states began efforts to alter dramatically the curriculum, the teaching profession, and traditional school organization. This chapter shows how successful implementation of these ambitious efforts entail both an antecedent stage of teacher development and new dominant teachers' roles in advanced implementation stages. This chapter also argues that well designed state policies and programs can both inform the local visions of good curriculum, instruction, and school organization and reinforce several key aspects of the implementation process needed to put those visions into practice. While all facets of successful local implementation strategies are not identified, the chapter shows that the effective imple-mentation processes used to implement "Wave I" education reform are relevant and need to be augmented as districts, states and schools seek fundamentally to restructure curriculum, the teaching profession, and school organizations in the 1990s. Additional research will be needed for these topics in order to firm-up and deepen the implementation knowledge base required for the country's education systems to meet the bold education goals outlined by the President and state governors in the early 1990s.

Chapter 2

Title I of ESEA: The Politics of Implementing Federal Education Reform*

Jerome T. Murphy

If there was a single theme characterizing the diverse elements of the 1965 Elementary and Secondary Education Act (ESEA), it was that of reform. The Act was designed to stimulate innovation, to strengthen the states, to link research with the schools, and to make the problems of the poor the nation's number one education priority. In short, ESEA was the first step toward asking whether this spirit of reform has been translated into educational practice. Has state and local administration reflected these new priorities? Has the U.S. Office of Education (USOE) asserted leadership? What are the political and bureaucratic impediments to reform? How can implementation be improved?

Answers to these questions are important for two reasons. First, they will provide useful information about the limits of federally initiated reform. After all, the extent to which states and localities meet the new priorities is a measure of the balance of power within the federal system as well as of the central government's capacity to execute reform. Second, a better understanding of the problems of implementation can lead to improvement in ESEA's operation. That understanding can best be achieved, I believe, by viewing key administrators at the federal, state, and local level as primarily political figures—rather than educators—subject to the demands of their constituencies and to the constraints of their bureaucracies.

*Reprinted from Jerome T. Murphy, "Title I of ESEA: The Politics of Implementing Federal Education Reform," *Harvard Educational Review*, vol. 41, no. 1, February 1971, pp. 35–63. Copyright © 1971 by the President and Fellows of Harvard College. All rights reserved. Reprinted by permission.

To answer these questions, I have focused on Title I, aid to the disadvantaged. This program, the heart of ESEA, provides a good test of the limits of federal reform. It is the largest program by far and called for the greatest change at the local level—a new focus on the needs of the poor. This chapter, then, examines the origins of Title I, the nature of the agencies administering it, and the working relationships between one state department of education (Massachusetts), the USOE, and local school districts. Finally, it describes some recent efforts to make the program more responsive to the program's clients, the poor.[1]

Federal Legislation for the Disadvantaged

The central thrust of ESEA is to eliminate poverty. The underlying notion was familiar—poor children given the opportunity to do well in school will do well as adults—and it was embodied in the Act's first and most important Title. By allocating extra funds to schools with high concentrations of poor families, federal reformers sought better education and improved opportunity.

In this, Title I expressed the political atmosphere prevailing in mid-sixties Washington. The Economic Opportunity Act of 1964 had just been passed, and high government officials believed that poverty soon would be eliminated. It was only natural, then, that they would try to extend the President's "unconditional war" on poverty by providing quality education for poor children. This attitude also reflected the influence of what Daniel P. Moynihan (1969, p. 23) calls the professionalism of reform:

> (President Kennedy's) election brought to Washington as officeholders, or consultants, or just friends, a striking echelon of persons whose profession might justifiably be described as knowing what ails societies and whose art is to get treatment underway before the patient is especially aware of anything noteworthy taking place ...

This predisposition was translated into law in the 1965 ESEA, mainly through the work of Commissioner of Education Francis Keppel, a strong advocate of concentrating resources on disadvantaged children. He was aided by a bill (S.2528), introduced by Senator Morse (D–Oregon) in 1964, which suggested a formula for concentrating funds on cities and rural areas at the same time, thus helping to assure a coalition of northern urban and southern rural Congressmen.

Through negotiations with key individuals and interest groups, the details of ESEA were hammered out prior to the bill's introduction, successfully avoiding major amendments during Congressional debate (Bailey and Mosher 1968; Meranto 1967; Guthrie 1967).

It is important to understand that the reform was not a response to public pressure. Unlike the great national programs passed during the New Deal, Title I did not arise from public demand. The poor were unorganized and had made no demands for such legislation. Nor was Title I a natural outgrowth of tried and tested programs at the local level. At the time it was developed, only three states (California, Massachusetts, and New York) had passed legislation specifically geared to disadvantaged children, and those laws funded only small pilot projects. Other local efforts were new, few, and concentrated in a limited number of cities (U.S. Congress 1965). Nor was Title I the creature of the established educational organizations or educational administrators. The "old guard" bureaucracy in USOE viewed its job as providing technical assistance to the states and local schools when requested. They saw USOE more as a consulting firm than a focal point for leadership or initiative; the guiding principle was deference to the states and the local schools, and they had reservations about Title I (Bailey and Mosher 1968). The attitude of the professionals who staff the state and local school systems was little different. They were "dismayed" to learn that ESEA was not general aid (Bailey and Mosher 1968), and in a national survey of school administrators in May 1966, approximately seventy percent stated that Title I funds should not be allocated on the basis of poverty (Bailey and Mosher 1968). As far as the educational associations in Washington were concerned, their primary interest was general support for ongoing public school activities (Bailey and Mosher 1968). Although they accepted the poverty theme as a necessary compromise to achieve aid for the public school system, their emphasis was on breaking barriers to federal aid, on the ground that this would be a major step toward general support at a later date. As one observer put it:

> Having passed the Senate seven times and the House twice since the 1960s, a large-scale school aid measure had yet to reach the President's desk for signature . . . 'Getting the law on the books' was the objective uniting perhaps the widest constellation of interest groups ever assembled on a domestic issue (Halperin 1970, p. H8492).

In sum, Title I was not a reflection of pressure from the poor and had little support among educational administrators. Some urban school officials saw the need for categorical aid, but most support from within the profession was based on the notion that Title I was the first step toward general aid. The objective was a law, not reform. The main thrust for aid to poverty schools came from reformers in the Executive Branch who had a double objective: the establishment of the principle of federal aid to schools and a redirection of local priorities.

The Allocation of Responsibility

The successful implementation of reform depends heavily on the distribution of power. Given USOE's historically weak role in American education, the reformers saw the need for additional federal leverage. The legislative record, however, was mixed on this point. While the reformers were anxious to use federal power to improve schooling for the poor, they were acutely aware of their limitations. Federal control of schools was a major issue when the bill was drafted, and every increment in federal power meant a corresponding decrease in the states' authority.

The result was a complicated and highly significant compromise. The formula-grant mechanism was used to bypass the states and localities in determining roughly on whom the money should be spent. Funds were to be distributed among school districts based on the relative incidence of poverty, and within each school district they would be spent on educationally deprived (not necessarily poor) children in areas of high concentration of poverty.[2] The poverty formula is simply a device to get the money to those geographic areas of greatest need based on the premise that there is a high correlation between poverty and educational deprivation. The formula grant system cuts both ways; however, while it bypasses state and local governments, it establishes a virtual entitlement for each state and locality, once the total amount of federal appropriation is known. This absence of competition for program funding combined with the local view that the money is rightfully theirs immensely weakens the ability of federal officials to bargain with the states over the improvements in administration.[3]

Initiative as to program content and character was left with the states and localities. The local school districts identify eligible educationally deprived children, determine their needs, design programs to meet them, and apply to the appropriate state department of education for approval. The state departments approve projects of sufficient "size, scope, and quality," monitor them, and submit fiscal reports and evaluations of the effectiveness of the local projects to USOE. The federal role in this respect was minimal—it consisted of little more than approving applications submitted by the state departments of education for participation in the program. This application is simply a two-page letter signed by a state official stating, in effect, that the law will be followed.

The only counterweight to this almost complete delegation of programmatic responsibility was an effort to reserve federal authority to establish "basic criteria," which could be used to guide administration of Title I at the state and local level. Although this provision in the draft legislation emerged unchanged from Congress, it caused considerable controversy in both houses (U.S. Congress, 1965). It was viewed as a threat to local control of the schools and was hotly contested during Congressional debate. The resistance portended future obstacles to the exercise of the federal quality control authority.

In summary, Title I provides influence for each level of government but at the same time sets limits. The USOE bypasses the state departments of education in determining the allocation of grants and establishes basic criteria which must be met by local districts, but it has no operating control over the projects. The states have the responsibility for approving projects, but they must apply federal criteria in carrying out this responsibility. Local districts have access to earmarked funds and latitude in designing projects circumscribed only by the effectiveness of state supervision and federal criteria. Thus, even on paper, the local school districts had the greatest say in how Title I funds were to be spent. Other factors, discussed below, also tend to favor local interests over state and federal.

The Administration of Title I: Federal Efforts

It is beyond the scope of this chapter to describe in detail the administration of Title I by USOE. The initial problems of reorganizing the agency, recruiting "new blood," staffing the programs, and writing the regulations and guidelines have been amply and adequately covered by Bailey and Mosher in their book, *ESEA: The Office of Education Administers a Law* (Bailey and Mosher 1968). Some observations, however, are in order.

After nearly one hundred years of effort to obtain general federal support for elementary and secondary schools, it is not surprising that passage of ESEA was viewed as a tremendous breakthrough. The much tougher job, however, was to implement the reform. But the problem of administrative niceties was not the focus of the reformers. As former U.S. Commissioner of Education Harold Howe (1970) explains:

ESEA was the only type of Federal activity in education which was
likely to be politically viable in 1965 . . . I doubt that anyone could
have dreamed up a series of educational programs more difficult to
administer and less likely to avoid problems in the course of their
administration, but ESEA was not designed with that in mind.

Also, the reformers involved in the development and passage of ESEA
for the most part were not involved in its implementation. They went
on to the development and passage of additional legislation while federal administration of ESEA was turned over to lower levels in the
ninety-eight-year-old USOE. This staff had virtually no impact on the
development of Title I and would have preferred more traditional
approaches or general aid. The agency had no experience with grants-
in-aid of the size and scope of Title I nor had it ever been called on to
write "basic criteria" governing the approval of projects. Herculean
efforts were made to bring in new blood and make the agency responsive to its new and different responsibility, and the agency did change.
Nevertheless, the "old guard," if not always controlling policy, were the
ones who for the most part staffed the program and made the day-to-
day decisions setting the tone of the federal operations.

Furthermore, USOE has not had enough people to effectively
monitor the program. Title I is administered by the Division of Compensatory Education in the Bureau of Elementary and Secondary Education of the USOE. Monitoring is carried out by area desk officers in
the Operations Branch. Although Title I policy is usually set at higher
levels, the area desk officers are the link with the states and have day-
to-day responsibility to assure that the states are following the law, regulations, guidelines, and basic criteria.

While as recently as January 1970, there were some thirty professionals working on all facets of Title I—technical assistance, accounting, program support—there were only three area desk officers for the
entire nation.[4] The one[5] dealing with Massachusetts had responsibility
for twenty-three other states, the District of Columbia, Puerto Rico, and
the Virgin Islands. In addition to his Title I responsibilities, he spent
approximately two-thirds of his time working on other projects at the
Bureau level having practically nothing to do with Title I. The desk
officer had no assistants and spent a substantial part of his Title I time
drafting replies to Congressional mail. He felt that he could use at least
four assistants to provide adequate technical assistance to the states.

In addition, the USOE staff has traditionally taken a passive role
with respect to the states. The Massachusetts desk officer described his
relationship with the Massachusetts Title I Director as "very nice." In the

six months preceding the interview, they had met together once and talked occasionally on the telephone. The area desk officer viewed his job as one of trouble-shooting, answering complaints, and providing service. He did not want to provide leadership, nor did he view himself as a program "monitor" in the sense of being an enforcement officer. He readily admitted that he did not have the time to know what was going on in his states and thus was dependent on information supplied by state officials as to whether they were enforcing the law. He found the limited staff situation frustrating, not because he was unable to monitor the states, but because he could not give them assistance.

The prevailing *modus operandi* was succinctly described by an official in the Division of Compensatory Education who has been with the program since its start:

> Title I is a service-oriented program with predetermined amounts for the states. This sets the framework where the states are entitled to the money. Other than making sure states got their money and making sure it was spent, there was no role for the Office of Education. I don't know anyone around here who wants to monitor. The Office of Education is not investigation-oriented, never has been, and never will be.

During the last few months, however, the Title I staff has grown significantly. As of October 1970, there were some fifty professionals, including fifteen new desk officers, on the Title I staff.[6] While this increase gives the appearance of greater control of the program, it is too early to assess its full impact at the state and local level. It seems fairly clear, though, that USOE's service-oriented attitude toward the states has not changed significantly. After all, changing the style of a bureaucracy rooted in tradition cannot be accomplished overnight. Furthermore, as one USOE official commented: "Most of the new people are state-oriented."[7]

But why the sudden jump in staff size? The underlying cause can be traced to the fall of 1969 and the release of the report, *Title I of ESEA: Is it Helping Poor Children?* (Martin and McClure 1969). The so-called Martin–McClure Report (named after its authors Ruby Martin of the Washington Research Project and Phyllis McClure of the NAACP Legal Defense and Educational Fund, Inc.) charged flagrant violations of the law. USOE responded with a high level Title I task force. This focus of attention on an obviously understaffed program combined with continuing pressure from the report's authors led to the increase in staff.

But the report's importance goes far beyond its identification of problems; its release may well mark a turning point in the administration of Title I. The report represents the first major effort by spokesmen of the poor to bring significant pressure to bear on USOE. Later in the chapter we shall see that a growing new Title I constituency, largely triggered by the report, has also had some impact on Title I guidelines and is tenaciously tugging at the established powers in education.

The area desk operation is not the only respect in which federal administration of Title I has been weak. Since the beginning of the program, evaluation has been high on the list of federal rhetorical priorities but low on the list of actual USOE priorities. The reasons for this are many. They include fear of upsetting the federal–state balance, recognition of that little expertise exists at the state and local levels to evaluate a broad-scale reform program, and fear of disclosing failure. No administrator is anxious to show that his program is not working.

The matter is further complicated by the lack of agreement on what would prove whether Title I is "working." This confusion stems from covert disagreements over the relative importance of Title I's several purposes. These include breaking the federal aid barrier, raising achievement, pacifying the ghettos, building bridges to private schools, and providing fiscal relief to school districts. Depending on one's perspective and priorities, Title I may or may not be working. If one views the program primarily as a vehicle to provide fiscal relief for a city school system, achievement test scores are hardly an appropriate way to measure success; the program is successful if fiscal collapse is avoided. The legislation, however, calls for objective measures, and if they show that children are not gaining in achievement it makes it difficult for Congressmen to justify their continued support of the program. At the same time, it is politically dangerous to be opposed to program evaluation. Therefore, inconclusive evaluations are politically acceptable, although they may provoke rhetorical wrath in the Congress and exasperation in the Executive agencies.

Another important area of federal responsibility involves the federal audit reviews. These are conducted by the HEW Audit Agency, and their purpose is to determine whether funds are being spent in accordance with the legislation, regulations, and guidelines. These reviews are fairly comprehensive—in fact, they are the only full-scale investigations of Title I operations at the state and local level which HEW undertakes. Since 1965, audits have been conducted in twenty-four states and the District of Columbia; two have been conducted in Massachusetts (Martin and McClure 1969). The results are always referred to the Division of Compensatory Education for action. According to the Martin–McClure (1969, p. 52–53) study of Title I:

The audit reports have brought to light numerous violations of the law and have recommended that millions of dollars be recovered by the Federal government. Yet in only three cases has the Office of Education sought and received restitution of funds illegally spent . . . Even in the most flagrant cases of unlawful use of the money—the two swimming pools in Louisiana for example—the Office of Education has failed to act.

The fundamental question is why has USOE not been more aggressive in managing the program and following up on the audits. Limited staff and a service orientation are only part of the answer. There are several other interrelated factors which help to explain USOE's attitude. First, in the early days there was pressure to get the program moving quickly and to get federal–state relations off on the right foot. There was a natural tendency to overlook alleged misuses and accentuate the positive. Second, there was tremendous pressure on program administrators to generate statistics on the number of schools involved, the number of children affected, and so forth, so that the Administration could demonstrate the program's success to the public and the Congress. Third, there was fear that if USOE pushed too hard the Congress would replace categorical programs with general aid, in which case USOE would have even less influence.

Another factor is that it is one thing to try to persuade a state to follow certain criteria, but an altogether different thing to accuse it of misusing funds which it views as its money. While Congressmen abhor waste and never tire of abusing bureaucrats who countenance waste, these are general principles which do not necessarily apply to individual cases, particularly if alleged misuses occur in their own districts. Top federal officials recognize the political nature of their jobs and know that they need Congressional support to survive. Thus, they are not anxious to arouse Congressional wrath—especially when there is a high probability that they will not get the money back. USOE staff remembers well the Presidential veto in October 1965 of Commissioner Keppel's attempt to cut off funds from Chicago for civil rights violations (Bailey and Mosher 1968). The basic problem, then, is political, and Morton Grodzins (1966, p. 270) describes the situation neatly:

The undisciplined (political) party system impels administrators to seek political support for their programs. The parties do not supply this support, and administrators and their programs cannot survive without it . . . (This situation makes) the administrator play a political role.

Finally, USOE's behavior has in part been adapted to take advantage of its strategically weak bargaining position. It is virtually impossible for USOE to cut off funds which the states view as their rightful entitlement under the law. The states know this and so does USOE; thus, orders or demands by USOE are bound to be ineffective since they cannot be backed up with action. Furthermore, demands might alienate the states and result in loss of communication. Since USOE's influence comes mostly from the power of persuasion and since it is presently almost totally reliant on the states for information about local programs, it is absolutely essential that USOE maintain cordial relations with the states. Under these bargaining conditions, the states are in a position to exact a price for their good will. As a result, USOE will be willing to sanction (perhaps covertly) deviations from the statute in exchange for open communications. Thus, the agency's service orientation and deference to local officials can be understood in part as rational behavior, designed to achieve the greatest possible influence from a weak bargaining position. USOE's problem, then, is not simply the lack of will or lack of staff, but lack of political muscle. And like other politicians, many key federal administrators are unwilling to take risks unless pressured.

There are some examples, however, where the USOE has attempted to assert leadership. For the most part these efforts have been unsuccessful. This is best exemplified in USOE's attempts to establish two basic criteria—one calling for the establishment of local parent advisory councils and the other governing the concentration of funds. Since the beginning of the program, USOE has sought to involve parents in local Title I programs on the theory that the more parents were involved the better their children would do in school. In general, however, USOE has been unable to enforce this notion on the states. In 1969, three out of five school districts did not have Title I local parent advisory councils (Brown and Rosendahl 1970).

The first set of basic criteria issued by the USOE responded to what the memorandum described as a "definite need" (Hughes 1967, p. 1) for states to apply specific criteria in approving local projects. It called for parent participation in Title I programs, but was not specific on the nature of this participation other than to say that it should be "appropriate" (Hughes 1967, p. 7). The second set of basic criteria (Howe 1968a) went a step further. It called for the involvement of parents "in the early stages of program planning and in discussions concerning the needs of children in the various eligible attendance areas" (Howe 1968a, p. 4). Four months later (Howe 1968b), the USOE issued a separate memorandum focusing on community and parent involvement calling for the establishment of a formal mechanism for their involvement. The memorandum (Howe 1968b, p. 1) stated that :

> each Title I applicant must have an appropriate organizational arrangement. This means, in effect, that *local advisory committees will need to be established* for the planning, operation, and appraisal of a comprehensive compensatory educational program. (Emphasis added.)

This aroused considerable concern. It was one thing to discuss parent involvement, but quite another to call for formal committees which could be identified, counted, and perhaps exert some influence over the program's direction. Many educators viewed these committees as a threat to professional control.

Seventeen days later, under pressure from interest groups, local educators, and the Congress, a clarifying memorandum was sent to the Chief State School Officers, retreating from the previous position. The new memorandum (Howe 1968c, p. 1) stated:

> In most instances it will be advantageous for a local educational agency to establish a local advisory committee . . . In some instances, however, local conditions may favor other arrangements . . . Whatever arrangement is decided upon, it should be one which your office, in the light of its understanding of the local situation, finds likely to be effective.

In effect, USOE told the states to do as they pleased. When asked about the status of local advisory committees in Massachusetts, the USOE area desk officer for Massachusetts stated: "Frankly, I've heard nothing about them. Haven't heard any complaints."

In frustration over the apparent lack of implementation of local advisory committees, the Division of Compensatory Education convinced the Nixon Administration to recommend that local advisory committees for Title I be explicitly included in the law.[8] The recommendation was made and the provision added by the House Committee on Education and Labor. It was dropped, however, during floor debate by the House of Representatives on the 1969 amendments to ESEA because of strong opposition, particularly from Southern Congressmen. The bill that emerged from the Congress (April 13, 1970) further confused the matter with unclear language on the extent of USOE's authority.[9]

During the following six months, USOE once again worked to devise a guideline covering local parent advisory councils. At one point a draft was circulated requiring parent councils for each Title I project area. Representatives of the public school lobby met with USOE officials and flatly asserted that requiring councils was unacceptable. Unlike the past, however, USOE was also under pressure from the other side. Groups coordinated by the Washington Research Project were pushing USOE to promulgate strong requirements. As a spokesman for the National Education Association stated: "USOE has been getting pressure from some groups I've never heard of. I don't know whether they represent a constituency or not." Finally on October 30, 1970, a compromise emerged from USOE (Bell 1970c, p. 2) requiring "system-wide" parent councils.

This guideline represents a small but significant victory for groups representing the poor. After all, it is not very often that the public school lobby is forced to compromise, particularly on a matter related to the control of the public schools. But the story may not be over yet. It remains to be seen whether the requirement survives Congressional scrutiny.

A similar pattern exists in federal efforts to require concentration of funds. One of the critical issues addressed in the original draft guidelines was the concentration of limited resources for a limited number of students. USOE officials believed that if Title I was to have any impact, the money could not be spread thin. The original provision in the draft guidelines (Fall 1965) stated that the number of children served could be no greater than the number of children in the district counted under the poverty formula. This effort to concentrate funds met with strong disapproval from both the Congress and professional interest groups who argued that the standard was not consistent with Congressional intent. Strong opposition also was expressed about other provisions of the guidelines and regulations. In November 1965, the word came down from Commissioner Keppel to "slenderize" the documents.[10] The concentration provision was removed from the guidelines. This defeat set the stage for the determination of future standards.

USOE's first set of basic criteria proposed twelve criteria and included "a supporting statement of the types of evidence or indications that the applicant's proposal should contain in order to show that it meets the criterion" (Hughes 1967, p. 1). The criterion regarding concentration simply stated: "Title I services will be programmed so that the services provided will be concentrated on a limited number of children" (Hughes 1967, p. 4). The supporting discussion, however, established a new standard:

> The investment per child on an annual basis for a program of compensatory educational services which supplement the child's regular

school activities should be expected to equal about one-half the expenditure per child from State and local funds for the applicant's regular school program (Hughes 1967, p. 4).

Exactly ten days later, under Congressional pressure, the USOE issued a "clarifying" memorandum, retreating from the thrust of the original memorandum (Hughes 1967, p. 1). It read in part:

> The criteria statements are the requirements to be met, whereas the discussion matter *provides guidance* in meeting the criteria. It should be expected, of course, that the discussion guides *may not be fully applicable to every project application.* (Emphasis added.)

Under the terms of the "clarifying" memorandum, then, the new concentration standard provided only "guidance" and was not "fully applicable to every project application." Thus, within ten days the new standard had been rendered impotent.

Not satisfied that funds were being adequately concentrated, USOE issued another memorandum on November 20, 1968 focused specifically on improving the quality of Title I. The draft memorandum that went to Commissioner Howe's desk for signature specifically called for the implementation of the concentration standard by 1970. At the last minute, under political pressure, the draft was pulled back by the USOE Bureau of Elementary and Secondary Education and revised (Hughes 1967). The concentration standard was replaced by the hastily drawn statement: "Plan the program so that by 1970 the average Title I expenditure per child in high priority areas is *raised to a significant level*" (Howe 1968d, p. 2). (Emphasis added). Nowhere in the memorandum is "significant level" discussed or defined and nowhere is the previous standard mentioned. Thus, a memorandum which had begun in the Division of Compensatory Education as an attempt to accomplish greater concentration of resources emerged from the bureaucracy with no standard even as "guidance." Meanwhile, dollar expenditures per Title I child have been decreasing each year, and thirty percent of the students participating in 1968 were not disadvantaged while millions of eligible students went unaided (U.S. Office of Education, 1970).

This chronology of federal efforts to establish strong basic criteria points to USOE's weakness in influencing local priorities. Time after time local and state educators, mainly through Congressional intervention, were able to have their priorities recognized in federal directives, diluting federal attempts to gain leverage. But local pressure is not limited to efforts to prevent USOE from asserting leadership. It also is used to initiate federal guidelines backing up local priorities. This allows local and state authorities to "pass the buck" and claim that they are constrained by federal directives, when in fact federal action is a result of local pressure. This can be seen clearly in a recent controversy surrounding the use of Title I funds for clothing.

Last summer, the National Welfare Rights Organization, with the encouragement of the Washington Research Project, started a drive to increase Title I expenditures for clothing. The organizers saw the effort as a way for parents to gain greater political control over the program. The first incident took place in Providence, Rhode Island, with welfare mothers reportedly demanding a clothing allowance of $48 per Title I child (National School Public Relations Association, 1970). To neutralize this pressure, the Rhode Island Title I coordinator urged the USOE to promulgate a strong guideline restricting Title I expenditures for clothing. USOE complied with a guideline (Burns 1970) setting forth numerous requirements. During the next few weeks, however, similar pressure for clothing grew in New York City; Cleveland, Ohio; and Norfolk, Virginia (National School Public Relations Association 1970). As a result, USOE was pressured by Chief State School Officers, school superintendents, and state Title I coordinators to come out with even more stringent guidelines. USOE officials were sympathetic to the schoolmen's concern; they viewed the demands of the welfare mothers as a threat to Title I's "integrity" and the whole operation as a "raiding party." On September 15, 1970 a new guideline stated that Title I is "an educational program, not a welfare program" and that funds could be used for clothing "only in emergency situations" (Bell 1970a, p. 1). Furthermore, the guideline prohibited "any increase over previous years" in the proportion of local Title I expenditures for clothing. Enraged by what they viewed as repressive and illegal restrictions, representatives of the National Welfare Rights Organization and the Washington Research Project met with Secretary of Health, Education, and Welfare Richardson. Shortly thereafter, on October 5, 1970, a third guideline on clothing was issued which repealed the ceiling on clothing expenditures (Bell 1970b). Nevertheless, the other restrictions in the previous two guidelines were confirmed.

The merits of the clothing demands are not at issue here. What is important for my discussion is the fact that schoolmen apparently were able to get USOE to issue immediately strong guidelines reflecting local priorities. By contrast, it is interesting to note that the flagrant violations of Title I alleged in the Martin–McClure Report evidently were not viewed as a threat to the programs integrity, although they were viewed as a serious problem. The response was the establishment of a

Task Force which a year later has yet to issue its report. No doubt changes will result—I have pointed out some—but the different responses to the clothing issues and the Martin–McClure Report simply reflect the obvious—USOE is mainly responsive to its major constituency, the public school system. Nevertheless, the clothing episode also demonstrates that counter-pressure can have some impact on USOE, in this case through pressure brought to bear on the Secretary of Health, Education, and Welfare.

These descriptions of guidelines and of program management illustrate the context in which USOE officials operate. They are indisposed to compliance activities to begin with, but even if this were not the case, the staff to operate an effective compliance program has not existed. Furthermore, even if both the staff and the will were present, they lack the political support to assert leadership. Most federal legislators are sure to be more responsive to the wishes of state and local school officials than to the desires of bureaucrats in the Executive Branch. As a result, the Title I program administrators act as though their main constituency lies in the Congress and the state and local school officials, rather than among the poor people whose children the legislation is supposed to assist. Only recently are there some signs that this is changing. But as long as these counter-pressures—in the Congress and at the state and local level—remain relatively weak, federal officials will be almost powerless to enforce their standards on state and local school systems. Either they will not try to enforce federal standards, or their efforts at enforcement will be continually challenged and frustrated.

The Administration of Title I: State Efforts

The problems, of course, do not lie only within the USOE, or between it and the Congress. There are important barriers to implementing the legislative priorities at the state level, and in the relations between federal, state, and local school government. These problems appear in Massachusett's efforts to monitor the program and in the state's response to federal initiatives.

One important problem lies in the fact that many state departments of education provide little educational leadership, and Massachusetts has been no exception. In 1965, a report characterized its Department as "a conglomerate historical institution trying earnestly and valiantly to become an organization" (Commonwealth of Massachusetts, 1965, p. 130). Following the recommendations of this report, the legislature the same year passed a bill calling for a major overhaul of the Department, reorganizing it into five manageable divisions. Five years later, however, a follow-up study (Gibson 1970, p. 95) found:

> The Department of Education, for many reasons, continues to carry out a wide variety of mandated functions, most of which have little to do with educational leadership or which have any visible impact on improving quality of education for students in our schools.

In part this is a problem of personnel. For one thing, it is extremely difficult for the Department to staff its activities; in January 1970 there were seventy professional positions funded but vacant (Commonwealth of Massachusetts, 1965, p. 130). Low salaries are a major reason for this difficulty. The remuneration for professionals in the Department is simply not competitive with that for other educators in the state with comparable credentials. But even apart from this, the staff is not varied in background, training, or experience. A 1969 study found a striking degree of homogeneity in the backgrounds and career patterns of the top officials in the Massachusetts Department. For example, the eight who responded to the study questionnaire all had prior experience as teachers and school administrators, and none was born, raised or had been a teacher or administrator in a city with a population of more than one hundred thousand (Buckley 1969). Homogeneity, of course, is not the same as incompetence. It may tend, however, to establish an inbred, insular attitude and approach which probably are resistant to new ideas, innovation or acceptance of employees from different backgrounds.

These personnel problems carry over into the state's Title I unit of five professionals. Of the four responding to my questionnaire on their careers, all had past experience as teachers, and three of the four worked as school administrators. All were white. Although the state Title I director[11] has been unsuccessfully trying to hire two additional staff members, his problem is not money. For several years the state has been returning federal funds earmarked for state administration of the program; almost $100,000 was returned in 1969 (Jordan and Spiess 1970). The Title I director argues that a major problem is finding competent people willing to work for the Department.

A second problem is staff size. Even if the two new professionals were added, this would leave seven people to monitor some 420 projects, with a total cost of $16 million.[12] Furthermore, the Title I unit is responsible for state management of seven other federal programs related to the disadvantaged (Jordan and Spiess 1970). Considering this work load, it would appear impossible to even visit each Title I project once a year, let alone understand what is being done with the money.

The third problem is that the state Title I staff is not oriented toward compliance activities. They view themselves as professional educators, and the idea of enforcement or regulation is simply incompatible with their view of public education. The state Title I director views his job as providing technical assistance and service, and he strives for cordial and cooperative relationships with local school districts. When they employ questionable practices, he tries to discourage them through friendly persuasion. In effect, the Title I director expresses the same reluctance to interfere with local prerogatives that federal officials express about interfering with state prerogatives. Moreover, he sees his role vis-a-vis local districts—technical assistance and service—the same way that his federal counterparts perceive their role toward Massachusetts. To paraphrase one student of federalism (Elazar 1966), what usually happens is that federal, state, and local educators, working in the same program, trained in the same schools, and active in the same professional associations, think along the same lines and have relatively little trouble in reaching a meeting of minds.

These personnel problems, of course, have an enormous impact on Massachusetts' management of Title I. This is evidenced in the state's efforts to monitor Title I, mainly through meetings with local educators, project audits, and program evaluation. Much of the state Title I office staff time is spent in consultation with local Title I coordinators. In fact, a good part of the approval process is handled informally through telephone conversations and visits to the state office prior to the submission of formal applications. This is supplemented by visits to local projects, with emphasis placed on those districts receiving more than $100,000 a year under Title I. Recently, task forces have been set up to visit the six largest cities. In addition to the visits, regional conferences and workshops are held to discuss matters of mutual concern to Title I coordinators. These visits, conversations, and conferences, however, are very time-consuming and provide virtually no opportunity for a limited staff to see whether the Title I funds are spend in accordance with the law.

The Department's financial management procedures are even weaker. The second HEW audit report on Massachusetts concluded that "significant improvements in procedures and practices are needed at both the State and local levels . . . " (U.S. Department of Health, Education, and Welfare 1969, p. 3). The audit found that for the fiscal years 1966, 1967, and 1968 the Department allowed Title I allotments of

more than $1 million to lapse each year because of ineffective manage-
ment (U.S.Department of Health, Education, and Welfare, 1969).

The situation in Boston dramatizes the problem (U.S. Department
of Health, Education, and Welfare, 1969, p. 20):

> Even though the amount of $263,000 was unused by the City of
> Boston in fiscal year 1968, we found that certain eligible attendance
> areas with high concentrations of children from low-income families
> in the City of Boston were receiving minimal services for meeting the
> special educational needs of these children . . . We are advised by City
> of Boston program directors that the limited availability of funds pre-
> cluded them from providing additional services in these areas.

Although three auditors are paid with Title I funds, only one actually audits local projects. The others do some bookkeeping for the program but also spend much of their time on non-Title I activities. The
Title I director states that the Department is developing a team
approach for auditing all federal programs although no date has yet
been set for implementation. The second HEW audit report (U.S.
Department of Health, Education, and Welfare, 1969, p. 5) states:

> We found that (1) the SEA (State Department) does not have any writ-
> ten procedures, audit guidelines, and/or audit standards for conduct-
> ing audits, . . . (2) no audits of LEA's (local districts), however inade-
> quate, were performed on any fiscal year 1968 projects; and less than
> one-third of fiscal year 1967 projects at LEA's were reviewed as of
> November 1968 . . .

The only audit report local districts are required to submit is a
one-page sheet which breaks down Title I expenditures by educational
categories such as instruction, food, administration, and divides the
expenditure into salaries, contracted services, and other expenses. It is
absolutely useless in efforts to determine whether funds were spent in
accordance with the law.

The HEW auditors examined four school districts in depth. They
found inadequate time and attendance records, lack of substantiation
of overtime pay to teachers, inadequate accounting procedures covering contractual services, inadequate equipment controls and unremitted
unused funds. One school district was found with inaccurate financial
reporting (U.S. Department of Health, Education, and Welfare, 1969).
The Title I coordinator of this school district stated that he knew about
the audit discrepancies because he met with the auditors before they
left the school system. He said, however, that he had never heard from
the State Department about correcting the matter.

The State Title I director does not believe that money is being misused in Massachusetts but admits that he has no way of proving this. He would like to have more auditors for Title I but again argues that it is difficult to get competent people to work for the Department.

A similar pattern exists in the state's execution of its responsibilities for program evaluation. Title I requires local districts to make annual evaluation reports to the states, including "appropriate objective measurements of educational achievement."[13] Unlike previous federal programs, this provision called for the public display and disclosure of information which schoolmen knew could be used against them in the enforcement of new priorities. The evaluation provisions also put strain on the many local school districts and state departments of education which had little evaluation experience. It is no wonder that from the start there has been reluctance and resistance toward fully implementing this provision of Title I, and a tendency toward obfuscation. After all, to the extent that evaluations do not disclose meaningful information on program results, local districts can meet their own priorities without being subject to challenge based on evidence of failure.[14] Evaluation activities in Massachusetts have produced very little useful data. According to Cohen and Van Geel (1970, p. 231):

> The analysis in the (Massachusetts Title I) state (evaluation) report is meaningless, then, because the data it collected could serve no conceivable evaluative purpose. Collecting this information was, in the strict sense of the word, futile . . .

The approach of the Massachusetts Department to local districts on this point corresponds to the federal approach to the states—little direction. This is apparent from a recent internal memorandum. Referring to fiscal year 1971, the Title I director's office states: "*Next year,* all projects will be expected to show evidence of evaluation and to indicate how the evaluation contributes to modifications in project activities" (Jeffrey 1969, p. 11). (Emphasis added.) Apparent frustration with Massachusetts' commitment to Title I evaluation is also expressed in the memorandum (Jeffrey 1969, p. 12):

> *If we are serious* about obtaining meaningful information about the impact of these projects and these funds and about fostering continued improvement in Title I, we must devote substantial effort to the immediate and long-range approaches that state and local communities take in the area of productive and useful evaluation (Jeffrey 1969, p. 12). (Emphasis added.)

There are signs, however, after years of virtual inaction, that the Department is attempting to improve the situation. Consultants have been hired and the Title I director would like an evaluation expert for his permanent staff. In addition, conferences were held last spring announcing the state's intention to require evidence of success or progress before a project can be refunded. Some of the motivation for this strong stand, no doubt, came from the release in March 1970 of a comprehensive study of Title I, sponsored by the Massachusetts Advisory Council on Education (Jordan and Spiess 1970). The study found that less than half of the local projects sampled had an evaluation design and two of every three made little or no effort to analyze their evaluation data (Jordan and Spiess 1970). Despite the conferences and the report, the Title I director admitted that no projects were turned down this year because of failure to show success. Furthermore, apparently none of the study's recommendations has yet been carried out and the Department is now in the process of choosing an outside group to make recommendations on the study's recommendations. Prospects for improvement remain gloomy. Cohen and Van Geel (1970, p. 234) conclude:

> At a minimum, improving the state department's evaluation capacity would add between $150,000 and $200,000 a year to the budget. And supporting the experiments required for effective research and development (assuming no reallocation of funds within the Title I budget) would require a huge increase in that budget. If state education revenues are the sole source, neither step will be easy to arrange.

This description of Massachusetts' management of Title I highlights the devastating impact of personnel problems on all phases of monitoring—state-local consultation, project auditing, and program evaluation. But major obstacles to implementing the federally-initiated reform would remain even if the Massachusetts Department hired additional competent staff. The reasons for this are basically political. In the federal system, states have no inherent reason for following federal directives, such as basic criteria, unless they are rewarded or penalized for their action. Since states receive their full entitlement for mere participation in Title I—as opposed to producing some specified result, or doing a good job—there are virtually no reasons to follow federal directives. State officials know that there would not be any major repercussions for ignoring federal directives, even with USOE's knowledge. As we saw earlier with the HEW audits, USOE has been quite reluctant to take any action even when the purported violations were blatant. In fact, not only are incentives missing, but federal efforts to persuade the states to follow the federal directives have been almost nonexistent. The Massachusetts Department for the most part does not hear from USOE except for occasional memoranda, and USOE is looked upon mainly as a consultant. The Massachusetts Title I director states: "USOE provides technical and administrative assistance. They are helpful . . . They won't come out flatly and say what you can't do. I don't feel any kind of control. It just isn't there." As an example, last spring USOE sent a team to Massachusetts to review the state management of the program. The Title I director described the visit as "helpful" but half a year later the Department is still in the process of examining USOE's recommendations. Furthermore, the Title I director stated that the recent increase in the USOE Title I staff has not yet resulted in any new pressure from Washington. Thus, Massachusetts is fairly free to ignore federal directives conflicting with state priorities. The state Title I director passes the federal memoranda on to the local districts if he thinks they are "significant," but the Department does not take them (or the audit reports) too seriously. For example, it took Massachusetts nine months to respond to the second HEW audit report. The Title I director attributed the delay to "bureaucratic lag." This casual attitude, however, is not without grounds; USOE, a year later, has still not replied to Massachusetts (Jeffrey 1969). The matter remains unresolved.

Another illustration is evidenced in Massachusetts' response to the previously discussed federal efforts to concentrate resources on a limited number of children. Although sympathetic to the idea of concentration, the Department disagreed with the standard contained in the original basic criteria and simply did not enforce it. The final memorandum—dropping the standard—was passed on to the local districts (Jeffrey 1969). One local district's Title I coordinator stated that he had never been encouraged to concentrate Title I resources on fewer children until the summer of 1969, and, as far as he knew, no standard was ever adopted by Massachusetts. In the summer of 1970, however, the Department issued a memorandum calling for $200 per Title I child (Bongiovanni 1970). Nevertheless, new project applications falling below this standard continue to be approved by the state.

When state priorities are consistent with federal priorities, on the other hand, the states can use the federal priorities to back up their efforts to influence local policy. The Massachusetts Department happened to favor the establishment of local advisory councils, and therefore welcomed the federal criterion of July 2, 1968 requiring them. To encourage implementation at the local level, the Department distributed the memorandum to all participating school districts. The July 19, 1968 USOE memorandum, which weakened the requirement, was not distributed. Thus, the Department was in a position to push its own priority by arguing with local districts that the reason to establish local advisory committees was the federal pressure, when in fact the USOE had already retreated from that position. Despite Massachusetts' urging, more than half of the Title I projects in 1969 did not have parent councils (Jordan and Spiess 1970).

This reliance on a federal criterion to support a state priority reflects in part the historical balance of power between state and local prerogatives in Massachusetts. This balance can be further illustrated by one recent example. In 1969 the Department sent a memorandum to the Boston Public Schools regarding program modification which previously had been discussed with local officials. In the directive the Department stated that Boston "must" rather than "should" make certain modifications. The matter was brought to higher levels and was resolved by the staff of the Massachusetts Chief State School Officer and the staff of the Superintendent of Boston Public Schools: "must" was changed to "should."

Just as USOE is unable to dictate to the states, similarly the Massachusetts Department is in general unable to impose state priorities on local districts. Part of the explanation lies in the historical commitment in Massachusetts to local control of the schools and the resultant concentration of power at the local level. The Title I director characterized local control as "'The Battle Hymn of the Republic' of New England educators." But part of the explanation, as noted earlier, stems from the formula grant system. The absence of competition for Title I funds weakens the state's bargaining position as it does USOE's. Districts receive fixed amounts almost regardless of their programs. Few applications for funds have ever been rejected, and funds have never been withheld. Because of these political factors and its serious personnel problem, the Massachusetts Department is deprived of its leverage to control local expenditures. As a result, even when federal priorities are consistent with state priorities, implementation depends on local priorities which often may be different. A recent study of Title I evaluation (Cohen and Van Geel 1970, pp. 31, 34) in Boston points out the conflict:

> Looking back over this period of five years since Title I evaluation was brought to Boston, we can see there has been a clear absorption of all federal and state attempts (especially state attempts) to improve the quality of the evaluation ... not only has the federal thrust toward reform been absorbed by the school system, it has been turned to the advantage of Boston to serve Boston's own needs.

Conclusion

This discussion of bureaucracy and politics reveals some of the pitfalls in implementing federally initiated reform and suggests the present limited capacity of federal and state agencies to carry through the hoped for reform. Translating an Act into action is marked by marginal changes, not sudden great leaps forward.

Whose priorities are being met, then?

The answer is that local schools are fairly free to meet their own priorities. Local autonomy is respected by the Massachusetts Department of Education, and state persuasion is no more effective on important decisions affecting local programs than is federal pressure on the state. That is not to say that the local school districts blatantly violate the law, only that they are in control of the situation and are able to stretch the law to meet the needs of their constituencies which include more than the poor. The Department and USOE exercise little effective direction and have only superficial knowledge of how the money is being spent.

Why has Title I been administered in this way?

To blame the problems on timidity, incompetence, or "selling out" is to beg the question. I have identified a number of contributing causes: the reformers were not the implementors; inadequate staff; a disinclination to monitor; a law and tradition favoring local control; and absence of pressure from the poor. The primary cause, however, is political. The federal system—with its dispersion of power and control—not only permits but encourages the evasion and dilution of federal reform, making it nearly impossible for the federal administrator to impose program priorities; those not diluted by Congressional intervention, can be ignored during state and local implementation. Grodzins (1966, p. 274) describes the situation:

> [This dispersion of power and control] compels political activities on the part of the administrator. Without this activity he will have no program to administer. And the political activity of the administrator, like the administrative activity of the legislator, is often turned to representing in national programs the concern of state and local interests, as well as of other interest group constituencies . . . always [the administrator] must find support from legislators tied closely to state and local constituencies and state and local governments. The administrator at the center cannot succeed in his fundamental political role unless he shares power with these peripheral groups.

What can be done?   Several steps can be taken to improve Title I. At a minimum, the program needs better administration at the federal and state level. This will require more people trained in management, evaluation, and program development. But additional manpower may have only limited impact unless federal and state agencies gain greater leverage over local school districts. The problems of improving Title I administration are complicated and cannot be totally resolved outside the context of political change.

Creation of countervailing *local* forces to prod federal, state, and local officials to act more forcefully may be the most important step. Efforts to establish strong local parent advisory councils under the new federal guidelines could help produce more local responsiveness to the educational needs of the poor. Their demands for public accountability and a role in the development of programs could increase the influence of the poor at the local level. But if strong local councils are an important first step, greater organizing efforts aimed at the state and federal levels are also necessary. In Massachusetts, for example, the State Welfare Rights Organization, community action agencies, the Harvard Center for Law and Education, and other groups have recently banded together to encourage the Department to issue strong guidelines governing local councils. On October 23, 1970, Massachusetts approved the most far-reaching guidelines of any in the country (Sullivan 1970). They require each school district to set up election procedures immediately for as many parent councils as necessary to ensure representation from every Title I school. Furthermore, the guidelines provide local advisory council chairmen with the right of appeal to the State Commissioner of Education on questions of Title I implementation. Such pressure may result not only in the establishment of local councils, but also in the strengthening of the state's bargaining position with local school districts. No longer will the state be totally beholden to the wishes of local public schoolmen.

Similarly, community groups could band together on a nationwide basis, to bring pressure to bear on USOE and Congress. Until recently, whenever USOE attempted to exert any influence, the only people they heard from were spokesmen for public educators trying to protect their own interests; typically USOE responded positively to this constituency. In the last few months, as we have seen, pressure has been coming from such groups as the Washington Research Project, the NAACP, the National Welfare Rights Organization, and they have had some success. But additional organization will probably be needed if such pressure is going to have a significant long term effect; many more poor will have to be organized for national pressure. In fact, chances of success may be greatest at the national level. Federal officials share with poor parents the distinction of being on the outside of our nation's school system.

Assuming that some desire for reform remains in USOE, it is not inconceivable that it could work with the poor on some issues to force change on recalcitrant public school systems. For example, USOE and the poor probably have a mutual interest in increasing public school accountability for Title I. USOE has never used its broad authority to require good evaluation at the local level. Given a strong push for an effective lobby, USOE would be in a better bargaining position to impose this priority on public school educators.

This strategy of countervailing power, however, is not without its problems. For one thing, organizing effective parent lobbies around the fuzzy issue of "good education" is a formidable task. For another, there are many unresolved questions about the most productive relationship between professional educators and parents. How much parent control should there be? Who should make what decisions? What arrangements are in the best interests of school children? Finally, how would the Congress react if a lobby for the poor really threatened the established powers in education? Could the strategy backfire and result in the replacement of Title I with more general support for the schools? Merely raising these questions points out the risks and uncertainties involved in the development of countervailing local power. These uncertainties, however, must be contrasted with the near certainty of continued dilution of reform under the present balance of power. The expansion of local counter-pressures appears necessary and worth the risks if we are serious about translating the spirit of Title I reform into educational practice.

Chapter 3

The Utility of a Longitudinal Approach in Assessing Implementation: A Thirteen-Year View of Title I, ESEA*

Michael Kirst and Richard Jung

What directions should public policy implementation research take in the 1980s? Certainly the embryonic and interdisciplinary field of implementation research will benefit from experimentation with and evaluation of numerous research approaches. Still largely unexplored are cross-program comparative case studies and statistical prediction models of implementation. There is also much to be learned from macrocase study analyses tracing implementation from policy formation through the measurement of a program's impact on intended recipients at a single point in time. We also are benefitting from an increased number of in-depth descriptions of individual subunits within the implementation scenario.

1. A Longitudinal Approach to Implementation Analysis

One largely overlooked direction, however, appears to hold considerable promise in the eighties. We believe a longitudinal case study approach (ten years or more) merits serious consideration. An extended time line of ten years or more seems especially necessary in

*Reprinted from Michael W. Kirst and Richard Jung, "The Utility of a Longitudinal Approach in Assessing Implementation," *Educational Evaluation and Policy Analysis*, vol. 2, no. 5, September–October 1980, pp. 17–34. Copyright 1980 by the American Educational Research Association. Reprinted by permission of the publisher.

an implementation context where responsibilities and powers are shared among federal, state, and local agencies. We also contend that evidence for a long-run implementation perspective needs to be collected from a confluence of sources. We base our contention on an inspection of previous implementation case studies, "meta-implementation" analyses, political and organizational theory, and primarily our current investigation of federal efforts to implement the largest federal program in elementary and secondary education.

Relying largely on our present implementation research of Title I of the Elementary and Secondary Education Act (ESEA), a program which to date has funnelled over $26 million to state and local educational agencies with high concentrations of low-income families, we will detail theoretical and empirical arguments for the utility of a longitudinal case study approach. Moreover, we will outline procedural considerations for conducting such investigations, and in the process, make explicit some of the limitations and problems inherent in such an approach.

A Theoretical Rationale for a Longitudinal Approach

Less than a decade ago, implementation research pioneers such as Pressman and Wildavsky (1973) complained that "except for a few pieces mentioned in the body of this book, we have been unable to find any significant analytic work dealing with implementation" (p. 166). That statement was debatable in 1973; it certainly is not the case today.

Within the last ten years, implementation research of federal domestic programs has passed through two distinct, although overlapping, periods. The first period began in the late 1960s and peaked in the mid 1970s. It was characterized by a flurry of case studies describing the initial few years of implementation for a variety of specific Great Society social service and regulatory programs in education, civil rights, urban development, employment opportunity, health services, and environmental protection. (For a summary of the most frequently cited of these first generation's case studies, see Sabatier and Mazmanian 1979, footnotes 2–7; March 1980, footnotes 2–5.)

In aggregate, these initial, predominantly descriptive case studies represented the first state of theory development, a stage Eckstein (1975) has called "probability probes" (p. 14). These early case studies begin identifying variables, mapping relations among variables, and formulating preliminary research assertions before more rigorous theory building and hypotheses testing was initiated.

Case studies.   The most widely cited of these "first generation" short-run case studies:

- were factually dense accounts, usually lacking explicit theory or conceptual frameworks;

- found more failure than success during the initial phases of implementation;

- underscored the wide scope of political, organizational, and socioeconomic factors which influenced the implementation process;

- used multiple sources of evidence; and

- concentrated primarily on the first one to three years of implementation (Yin 1979).

Although this type of case study continued to proliferate in the late 1970s, these earlier analyses, along with conceptual models drawn from a variety of disciplines, served as fodder for a new type of implementation analysis in the mid and late 1970s, a meta-implementation literature.

Meta-analyses.   Some of these meta-implementation analyses were primarily concerned with setting out conceptual maps for subsequent case studies (Bardach 1977; Elmore 1978; Sabatier and Mazmanian 1979; Van Horn and Van Meter 1976), while others gleaned methodological lessons and gaps in the first generation case studies (Meyer 1979; Williams 1976; Yin 1979). These first attempts to conceptualize the implementation process ranged from Bardach's metaphoric concept of a "fixer" who "watch-dogged" the implementation "game," to prototypes of multistaged, recursive causal models (Sabatier and Mazmanian 1979). Generally agreeing that at least some generalizable propositions can be formulated about the implementation of legislated public policy, these researchers and theoreticians still differ on fundamental issues such as:

- the factors most affecting the implementation of legislated social programs;

- the linkages among these factors;

- procedures and scales for measuring variations within proposed explanatory "variables";

- appropriate sources and uses as well as limitations of existing data sources and research methodologies; and even

- how to describe or measure implementation.

Certainly, the most comprehensive of the implementation perspectives to date is Sabatier and Mazmanian's (1979) attempt to integrate several previous conceptualizations (Bardach 1977; Lowi 1969; Van Horn and Van Meter 1976) into a broad-scoped systems model that emphasizes the legal, political, and socio-economic variables structuring the implementation process. They postulate that four variables most affect a program's first 3 to 5 years of implementation:

- The "strength" of the statutes and ensuing regulations, including both how precisely and consistently the objectives are specified and ranked, and how clearly authority is delegated to organizational subunits;

- The presence of a "fixer", i.e., a key legislator or administrator ideologically attuned to program requirements who controls resources important to crucial actors and who has the status, desire, and staff to monitor closely the implementation process;

- The resources of various constituency groups—the salience of an issue, the solidarity, the access to policy channels and information, and availability of side payments for representatives from implementing agencies and intended target group recipients;

- The commitment and leadership of agency officials, including the direction and ranking of statutory objectives in officials' preference ordering, and the skills in realizing these preferences.

Yet Sabatier and Mazmanian concede implicitly for the first three factors and explicit for their most important explanatory factor—the commitment and leadership skills of implementing officials—that these variables are essentially "elusive concepts" (pp. 21–22).

The two factors they hypothesize to have the most significant effect in the long run (after five years), changing socioeconomic conditions, and the ability of supportive constituencies to intervene effectively, are equally difficult to quantify. The slippery and global nature of such factors and the inextricably complex dynamics of their interactions lead Yin (1979) to conclude that "the research-measure, research-design approach, even in its modified quasiexperimental form, may not readily be applicable to the study of organizational processes" (p. 9).

A new perspective. We are not quite so pessimistic. Instead, we recognize the limitations of the present social science technology expressed in Tukey's (1962) research caveat; "Far better an approximate answer to the right question, which is often vague, than an exact answer to the wrong question, which can always be made precise" (pp. 13–14). One pervasive feature of implementation case studies is that they have

concentrated almost exclusively on the first three to fives years of implementation and this preoccupation with short-time lines continues in the
face of growing empirical and theoretical evidence and that a long-run
perspective may reveal quite different patterns. Although the methodology for longitudinal analyses is not particularly exact, it appears that
such an approach will broach at least the right questions.

Organizational theorists and researchers have observed that when
power is distributed widely among a variety of administrative units, legislative factions, and interest groups, one center of power can rarely
impose its policies on others (Lindblom 1959; Lindblom and Braybrooke
1963; Sharkansky 1970; Wildavsky 1975). In such a situation, policies
that are the outcomes of bargaining among these actors are likely to
reflect only a small degree of change over existing procedures. Incre-
mentalism typically dominates the federal budgetary process (Wildavsky
1974, chap. 3) and although perhaps more difficult to measure precisely,
regulatory outputs are also likely only to change marginally over the
short haul. Cyert and March (1963) have noted in their study of various
large private and governmental organizations that (1) goals are often
vaguely stated initially to attain consensus, (2) that incrementally these
goals are operationalized in standard operating procedures through bargaining and compromise and; (3) over time, "(m)inor changes can lead
to more fundamental ones" (March 1980, p. 23).

Salamon (1979) provides additional theoretical justification for a
longitudinal approach in assessing the effects of Title I. Using a review
of previous evaluation research and primarily his analysis of New Deal
land reform experiments, he argues that programs which call for the
alteration of established social structures are likely to have delayed
effects that could be systematically ignored by evaluation designs with
short-run time lines (pp. 178–180).

Our preliminary research findings in studying the implementation
of Title I from a thirteen-year perspective reinforce these theoretical
arguments for using a longitudinal time line. Specifically we have
found:

- given the pluralist nature of the groups responsible for policy setting and implementation of Title I within a highly political and
  bureaucratic setting of decentralized power, changes in established
  administrative policies and procedures have been dominated by
  incremental change;

- when aggregated, these incremental changes have resulted in significant structural and substantive changes in implementation policies and practices;

- the direction of these changes over the long haul has been toward a more aggressive federal rule-setting, monitoring, and enforcement role in implementing some of the Program's crucial categorical requirements, and more congruence with key provisions in the law;

- the following set of interrelated factors have most affected the pace and directions of these changes.

(a) a shifting interest group scenario—from one which was initially dominated by professional education lobbies to one with an orientation toward compliance with federal mandates, including categorical program personnel, beneficiaries of Title I services, and lobby groups championing the recipients' causes;

(b) broad social movements and socio-economic conditions;

(c) specific feedback mechanisms, especially reports and exposes produced by external research organizations and activists group as well as procedures including audits and law suits; and,

(d) the political dynamics of a three-tiered (federal/state/local) structure of administration.

We have traced in-depth two pivotal Program requirements across time: targeting of funds to disadvantaged pupils and program design regulations that result in interventions for target pupils (discussed in more detail further on). Although in the short run, improvements in the operationalization, monitoring, and enforcement of the requirements have occurred slowly and intermittently, when viewed from a thirteen-year perspective, one observes a dramatic shift in the implementation of these two Program regulations. In effect, the standard operating procedures are much closer to federal intent in 1979 than in 1965.

2. The Passage of ESEA, Title I

The Elementary and Secondary Education Act was primarily crafted by a handful of top-level assistants from the Johnson Administration and by Francis Keppel, then Commissioner of Education who oversaw the operation of the Unites States Office of Education (now the Department of Education). They had two primary purposes which were not totally complementary. First, they wanted to find a legislative strategy that would successfully attain what almost every other Congress since World War II had futilely attempted: a strategy that would establish the precedent of federal aid to elementary and secondary schools. Second, they wanted this education legislation to serve as the cornerstone of President Johnson's "War on Poverty" program. To realize the first objective, the legislative and administrative strategists devised an ESEA "package" to satisfy "perhaps the widest constellation of interest groups ever assembled on a domestic issue" (Halperin 1970, H.8493). The original legislation contained five titles with multiple and even conflicting goals. The political viability of the bill was, in fact, enhanced by promising something for most major interest groups and by circumventing, often through obfuscation of statutory language, the issues which had historically contributed to the defeats of previous efforts to increase federal involvement in elementary and secondary education. The three major obstacles revolved around (1) the debate over whether federal aid should support private schools, either directly or indirectly; (2) the politically volatile issue of providing federal dollars to racially segregated schools; and, (3) a traditional antagonism toward most efforts for federal control over public education.

Title I was and still is by far the largest financial component of the ESEA package with an appropriation for 1979 of over $3 billion. The purpose of the Program, as stated in the bill's "Declaration of Intent" is "to provide financial assistance to local educational agencies serving areas with high concentrations of children from low-income families to expand and improve their educational programs by various means" (P. L. 89–10).

Some read this language to mean that the Program's top priority was to begin reform of the entire fabric of American education. Reform in this context meant restructuring of state and local educational agencies allocation priorities which traditionally spent more per child in those schools with high concentrations of students from high income families (Barro 1974; Mundell 1975; Owen 1972). Others saw Title I as a cleverly disguised general aid program. These individuals recognized the political expediency of using the "disadvantaged child" as a symbolic rallying point to get the bill passed, and believed that Title I was designed to provide general aid to districts with limited property tax bases. Unlike the reform interpretation, the assumption here is that the present institutions are functioning as well as can be expected, and they just need more money to better address the problem of educating poor children.

These two interpretations call for two very different implementation scenarios. The reformist would accept a strong federal involvement in the development, implementation, and evaluation of state and local projects, whereas the other interpretation would limit federal involvement to determining the size of entitlements and signing checks (Stoner 1976). The two priorities (1) the reform agenda of some of the program's original designers, and (2) the maintenance of state and local control over federal funds, form the underlying ideological tension for the implementation of Title I over time.

The Program had two other objectives as well: accelerating the pace of desegregation in the South and strengthening federal-state relations by increasing the capacities of state departments of education. Hundreds of southern school districts received an increment of thirty percent to their total operating budget. This influx of funds was a "sugar solvent" designed to melt southern resistance to quick desegregation in order not to forfeit the windfall funds. Title I also initially provided one percent of its $1.3 billion for state agencies (now two percent of its $3.08 billion) for state agencies to administer the Program. In effect, ESEA represents a deliberate policy of underwriting the growth and reorientation of state departments of education that had historically been independent of, and in part, antagonistic to increases in federal administrative control (Wirt and Kirst 1972).

Compromise and ambiguity were evident in the distribution of administrative responsibilities as well as in the Program's objectives. The United States Commissioner of Education shared with state and local educational agencies (SEA's and LEA's) responsibilities for administering Title I projects. In summary, the responsibilities were distributed in the following manner:

- The United States Office of Education (a) develops and disseminates regulations, guidelines, and other materials regarding the approval of Title I projects; and (b) reviews and assesses the progress under Title I throughout the nation.

- State Education Agencies (a) approve proposed local projects in accordance with federal regulations and guidelines; (b) assist local educational agencies in the development of projects; and, (c) submit state evaluation reports to USOE.

- Local Education Agencies (a) identify the educationally deprived children in the areas where there are high concentrations of low-income families and determine their special educational needs and, (b) develop and implement approved projects to fulfill the intent of Title I (Wirt and Kirst 1972).

The inclusion of these multiple objectives and overlapping governance responsibilities, indeed, facilitated a speedy congressional affirmation of the Act. Only during the implementation process did the categorical priorities evolve and the jockeying for administrative control of the Program begin.

In order to maintain a manageable analytic scope for a longitudinal analysis, we compared across time changes in two of the fourteen major Program requirements (or Program administrative outputs): targeting and program design requirements.

If a program is to be successful, monies must first reach the intended beneficiaries. Targeting requirements detail the criteria for the selection of eligible schools and children who are to participate in the Program within these schools. Once the monies reach the targeted schools and students, some reporting mechanisms are necessary for federal officials to determine how the schools are spending Title I monies. Program design requirements set forth that each Title I school must identify their project's objectives and detail the activities and services used to realize these stated goals. We have chosen these two requirements for cross-time comparisons as representatives of the two major categories of Title I requirements; funds allocation requirements and program development requirements. (These are discussed in more detail further on.)

3. An Empirical Rationale for a Longitudinal Perspective

The evaluations of Title I's administration during the first five years splashed horror stories of weak federal administration and even malfeasance (Martin and McClure 1969; Murphy 1973; Wargo 1972); early impact studies consistently found negligible educational impacts of the Program on Title I students (Glass 1970; Hawkridge 1968; Picariello 1969). After four years of the Program's operation (1965–1969), the first comprehensive evaluation of Title I's administration by an external research group concluded that "many of the misuses of Title I funds were so gross that even non-experts can readily spot them" (Martin and McClure 1969, p. 104). All other early studies of Title I administration by external research agencies or individuals have reinforced this first negative assessment of wide-scale misallocation of Title I funds during the first 4 years of the Program.

Title I Administration

The major analysis of Title I administration conducted by a contracted research agency during the middle years of the Program, from 1972 to 1973, used extensive interviews with USOE area desk personnel responsible for the monitoring practices of SEAs, site visits to five states, and questionnaire data from a sample of ten states and thirty-six LEAs. Their general conclusion was that "the administration of the program in the Division of Compensatory Education is far more effective than the critics would have one believe" (The Planar Corporation 1973, pp. 16–18). However, they described the administrative efficiency and effectiveness as "quite depressing." Their major findings were that: (1) regulations published by USOE were inadequate for LEAs and basically worthless for SEAs; (2) criteria used by the DHEW Audit Agency to determine noncompliance were drawn directly from the statutes because the regulations were inadequate; (3) USOE did not take into account LEA reporting burden; (4) evaluations of Title I educational impact were not satisfactory; and (5) enforcement of sanctions for noncompliant behavior identified in DHEW audits were virtually nonexistent.

More recent assessments of Title I management by external research organizations depict a strikingly different scenario. Using essentially the same major data source as the first compliance study of Title I (Health, Education, and Welfare Audit Agency audit reports), but covering eleven years rather than just the first four, Stanford Research International (SRI, 1977a) noted among its "most important trends" that "most states have developed adequate to good procedures for reviewing LEA (local education agencies) applications for Title I funds. These systems have greatly reduced many of the initial problems. However, more subtle problems remain"; and "at the LEA level, blatant misallocation of funds which clearly violated the intent of Title I have been substantially reduced" (pp. iii). Based primarily on the findings of three other external analyses of Title I administration using data from 1972 to 1977, a long-time analyst of Title I with the Syracuse University Research Corporation, Robert Goettel, contends:

> The common view of Title I administration may be overly pessimistic and unjustified. A more current "end of the decade" view of the federal–state–local partnership could provide a good deal more confidence in the ability of the federal government to influence the operation of categorical programs in local school systems (1978, p. 156).

Targeting Dollars

Over time, for example, our research reveals that federal efforts to target more Title I dollars to each participating student have been particularly successful. The ambiguous statutory language requires that Title I projects must be "of sufficient size, scope, and quality" to ensure that monies are not spread too thinly and thereby threaten to diminish the effectiveness of the projects. In the early years of the Program, there was a strong tendency for districts to use Title I as general aid by allowing more students to participate than were actually eligible to receive Title 1 funds. Table I indicates, for instance, in 1966, approximately 5.5 million students met Title I's eligibility criteria for poverty. Yet, more than an estimated 8.2 million students actually participated in the Program, almost one-and-a-half times the number of eligible students. In contrast, in 1978, while about nine million students were counted for local entitlements, only five million actually participated in the Program, or less than sixty percent of the eligible students. This contributed to an increase in per pupil expenditure from $116 to 1966 to $378 in 1979. Discounting for the effects of inflation (Row V), this translates into a sixty-two percent increase in per pupil expenditure over these thirteen years.

Table 1   Percentage of Children in Compensatory Reading Programs, by Status and Program, 1976[a]

Program	Poor, Low Achievers[b]	Not Poor, Low Achievers	Poor, High Achievers	Not poor, High Achievers
Title I	32.7	20.4	4.9	2.7
Other Compensatory Services	14.4	14.9	8.1	6.3
Nonparticipants	52.9	64.7	87.0	90.9

Source: Mary M. Kennedy, Richard K. Jung, and Martin E. Orland, *Poverty, Achievement and the Distribution of Compensatory Education Services,* interim report from the National Assessment of Chapter 1, Office of Educational Research and Improvement (U.S. Department of Education, January 1986), p. 88.

[a]Columns may not total 100 percent because of rounding.

[b]Bottom 50 percent in reading.

It is important to note that during this same time when per pupil expenditures were increasing by sixty-two percent in real dollars, the total appropriations for Title I in dollars adjusted for inflation actually declined by five percent (Row VII). Therefore, larger per pupil expenditures were due to increased targeting of funds by local district rather than additional appropriations.

Longitudinal studies aggregating more recent implementation data are also needed to partially abate the tendency by some researchers, even those quite knowledgeable in public policy literature, to cite dated, short-run analyses as if these accounts still applied today (Berman 1980; McLaughlin 1978). For instance, a prominent economist (Levin 1977) who has written prolifically on educational equity issues and specifically on Title I, concludes: "The ostensible inability of Title I Programs to create even a nominal impact on student scores in basic skills seems to be endemic to the program" (p. 156). The studies on which he bases his conclusion, however, contain achievement data collected between 1965 and 1969, the first four years of the Program. More than a decade of changes have occurred since then. Substantial changes have been documented in the Program's legal framework (Lawyer's Committee for Civil Rights Under Law 1977), federal and state monitoring procedures, (SRI 1977b; Planar Corporation 1973), and federal enforcement efforts (Demerest 1977; "OE Collecting" 1980; Pollen 1975). In fact, the most recent impact study for Title I argues for an extension of Title I programs into the summer months to maintain the increases in reading and math attained during regular school year Title I programs (SRI 1977b). While the evidence on pupil achievement is mixed, we contend the evidence on implementation congruence with federal objectives is more conclusive.

Explanatory Forces—The Development of an Iron Triangle

We have found that an interest group framework integrated with a social movement perspective provides a useful model of explanation for longitudinal implementation research.

Interest groups. In the context of Title I, an interest group perspective couches explanations in the political interplay among what has been called the "iron triangle" consisting of:

- Congress, and more specifically the Congressional subcommittees responsible for educational legislation;

- implementing agencies; and,

- professional education and special interest lobbies.

In the tradition of educational federalism, the symbolic language of the legislation accorded to each level of administration a potential for substantial power. The law gave to the Commissioner of Education the responsibility to develop "basic criteria" which the states were to use in their review of local applications. The states were reserved the power to approve or disapprove these projects. The local districts had wide latitude in planning, implementing, and evaluating the actual programs, be they for school construction or remedial programs for a highly selective group of students.

Overall, incremental change in the direction of more federal control has been characterized by an ongoing series of sallies, retreats, and parleys by (1) growing internal and external constituencies who see ESEA as a vehicle for changing schools and who favored or at least accepted a strict interpretation of the categorical intent of Title I, and (2) traditional education lobbies, most Congressmen, and local and state as well as a large number of federal administrators who preferred general aid and minimum federal involvement.

Early in Title I's history the lobby group scenario was almost exclusively dominated by interest groups representing established professional educational constituencies. These lobbies included, for instance: (1) National Education Association; (2) Council of Chief State School Officers; (3) National School Board Association; (4) American Association of School Administrators; (5) National Association of State Boards of Education; and (6) National Congress of Parents and Teachers. These six major educational lobbying blocks, known in Washington circles as "The Big Six," have rarely joined forces to form a unified lobbying front; however, they, in general, share an ideological preference for protecting local and state control of education and minimizing federal regulations. Other active lobbies, usually with strong general aid preferences, have been producers of educational materials and supplies. Another general aid educational lobby group more active in the later part of the Title I implementation history is the Council of Great City Schools.

Over the years, the one lobby group promoting categorical restrictions on Title I funds during the initial enactment of Title I, the National Catholic Welfare Board, has been joined by a number of other groups concerned with resisting efforts to turn Title I into a general aid program. These interest groups generally represent special or focused interests of the providers or recipients of Title I funds and include: National Advisory Council for the Education of Disadvantaged Children, the National Welfare Rights Organization, the Legal Standards and Education Project of the NAACP, the Lawyers Committee for Civil Rights Under Law, the National Association of Administrators of State and Federally Assisted Education Programs, and the Education Commission of the States. Some of the lobbying, technical assistance, and other advocacy processes of the special focused pressure groups have received financial or consultative support from such organizations as the Ford Foundation and the Harvard Center for Law and Education.

In 1965, before these interest groups coalesced, Commissioner Keppel attempted to withhold all Title I funds from the Chicago schools until a civil rights investigation was completed. Illinois State School Superintendent Page informed Chicago's Mayor Daley of the impending loss of funds, and Daley in turn complained to President Johnson of unlawful federal intrusion into the local domain of providing public education. Under pressure from Johnson, Keppel rescinded the withhold ruling within five days. USOE's first attempt to flex its jurisdictional muscle resulted in a precedent that for a time reduced its autonomy in the implementation of Title I (Hughes and Hughes 1972). The battle, however, had just begun.

A handful of new, middle-level staff members gave initial impetus to continued attempts from several quarters at translating ambiguous statutory language into a more tightly monitored program. This small band of reformers, in effect, formed an internal constituency group within the largely traditional USOE bureaucracy. They had two basic strategies.

First, they persisted in pushing for an expansion of the "basic criteria" powers relegated to the Commissioner by making more explicit the regulations guiding states' approval of local applications. The criteria they initially developed were to a large degree successfully resisted by more traditional elements within USOE and opposed by state and local administrators. After the widely publicized release of the Martin and McClure report (1969), other task forces again recommended tougher restrictions on the allocation of Title I funds, increased monitoring, and improvements in the resolutions of complaints by outside groups. As might be expected, the traditional forces were partially successful in watering down these recommendations, but when compared to the initial requirements and monitoring practices, substantial changes had accumulated through year-by-year incremental movement toward a more active federal involvement in the Program's administration.

Second, these reformers took several steps to establish constituencies at the state and local levels which would advocate or at least accept a stricter categorical interpretation. They, for instance, encouraged the use of funds set aside for the state administration of Title I to establish special compensatory education units in each state department in order to circumvent the Chief State School Officers who generally were strong supporters of general aid. They actually invented the title of "State Title I Coordinator" and began bombarding these mythical figures with letters and bulletins and inviting them to regional meetings where Title I regulations and program materials were discussed, modified, and disseminated (Hughes and Hughes 1972). These figures are not so mythical today. In 1977, all states had categorical units headed by special directors of compensatory education.

The $26 billion spent on Title I has spawned a national-to-local professional hierarchy with careers dependent on and commitments more aligned with providing special services to disadvantaged children. With state and federal categorical programs assuming a larger percent of public school expenditures, most urban and large suburban districts have not only local categorical program directors, but also special program units operating at the district level. These staffs are versed in the technical skills required to cope with the bureaucratic minutia seemingly endemic to federal social programs. In California, the special program coordinators from the state's thirty-three largest school districts, to which more than eighty percent of the state's Title I funds are targeted, have formed an informal consortium which holds monthly meetings and provides a vehicle for frequent and rapid exchange of information about technical aspects of implementation. These state-wide consortiums are linked in a national network through regular regional meetings, yearly gatherings in Washington, and frequent newsletters and special bulletins under the auspices of the National Association of State and Federally Assisted Education Programs. These formal and informal organizations foster strong informal norms to watch-dog district decisions so that they are consonant with categorical program requirements.

Parents of Title I children and of several state compensatory education programs are also organized from the school to the federal level in district, state, and federal advisory councils. At the federal level, the Lawyers' Committee for Civil Rights under Law, National Advisory Council for Education of Disadvantaged Children and several Civil Rights groups have proven to be increasingly active and effective lobby groups.

Duane and Bridgeland (1979), in their study of Michigan's educational politics, noted (a) special and compensatory education lobbies were among the most powerful education lobbies in the state; and (b) directors of special education and compensatory education were among the most influential individuals in the state educational policy process. A Washington-based public interest law firm, the Lawyer's Committee for Civil Rights Under Law (LCCRUL) has played a substantial role in improving enforcement of Title I categorical requirements. Its activities have included the preparation of manuals for bringing suits against districts believed to be in violation of Title I statutes and comprehensive analyses of the Program's legal framework. Several of their recommendations for strengthening the program requirements are quite evident in the 1978 amendments. In fact, the final 1978 Title I amendments bear a striking resemblance to the draft statute prepared by Robert Silverstein formerly of LCCRUL.

The point to be made here is that the character of interest groups participating in implementation decision-making processes has slowly moved from a virtual monopoly of traditional professional interest groups (such as the National Education Association and the National Association of Chief State School Officers) with a strong general aid preference to a more diverse interest group situation. Numerous constituencies are now articulating an emphasis on enforcing the categorical goals for the Program. Further, from a longitudinal perspective, these incremental changes, when aggregated, have resulted in a substantive shift in the nature of the interest group agendas toward targeted aid as intended by the Congress and USOE. These enforcement-oriented interest groups found allies in the Congress such as Senator Mondale and Senator Kennedy. They were reinforced by aggressive OE Title I administrators such as former DHEW Assistant Secretary Timothy Wirth and former USOE Compensatory Education Director Richard Fairley.

Social movements.   Recently, political scientists have recognized that beyond relying on more readily observable, but perhaps somewhat myopic iron triangle explanations for public policy formation and implementation, some consideration should be given to the impact of broad-based social movements. Explaining longitudinal changes in Title I's implementation involves more than documenting how one or several ideologically consonant interest groups have co-opted other lobbying constituencies serving their own private interests. Increased monitoring and oversight of Title I operations need to be seen in the light of a broader public demand for accountability in government and business during the late 1960s and early 1970s. Malpractice suits, in unprecedented numbers, held physicians accountable for their diagnoses and treatments. Automobile manufacturers were made liable as never before for injuries resulting from improper design of their products. Few government agencies were immune from such accountability reforms as management by objectives, programmed budgeting, and PERT charts. Monitoring was just one remedy in the accountability movement's grand grab bag.

One spinoff effect of the desegregation and antipoverty movements over the last two decades has been to legitimate federal administrative and judicial intervention in the schools. Court-appointed monitors have taken control of entire districts when judges have deemed the response of local schools boards to be inadequate to longstanding desegregation mandates. Federally funded legal aid lawyers prepared a large number of lawsuits charging school districts and states with Title I violations.

Like Cyert and March, we have found vague, consensual goals are eventually more specifically operationalized in organizational routines or standard operating procedures. And we believe explanations for the direction of these changes, while influenced by numerous other factors, are best understood by integrating an interest group perspective with attention paid to the long-term effects of how relevant social movements affect policy reformulation and implementation.

4. Designing Longitudinal Implementation Studies

The Use and Analyses of Data

Recent meta-implementation studies have generated some useful guidelines for the use and analysis of data for a longitudinal implementation perspective. In examining the approaches of eleven "exemplary" implementation studies conducted over the last decade, Yin (1979) found that one salient methodological similarity of these studies was "to collect data from every possible source in every conceivable manner" (p. 19) including:

- unstructured discussions
- structured interviews
- documents and new reports
- participant observations
- field observation
- published reports written by one or more of the participants.

He concludes "one of the potential lessons is that two or more of these methods should be used in any given study of implementation" (p. 19).

The use of a confluence of sources can both increase the reliability of the findings and appear necessary in light of the gaps likely to exist and the biases that are inherent in any one source of information. Reliability is enhanced by the utilization of a confluence of data because once a proposition is confirmed by two or more sources, even with all their sources of error, the certainty of an interpretation is greatly improved (Webb, Campbell, Schwartz, and Sechrest 1971).

For instance, one of the more problematic yet pivotal considerations in implementation studies is the determination of congressional intent. Most researchers proceed with the implicit assumption that a careful reading of the statutes suffices for arriving at the legislative objectives. Our research has repeatedly demonstrated that a "triangulation" of evidence relying also on Senate and House hearings and their special reports in conjunction with the statutes provides a much more accurate portrayal of congressional intent than the statutes by themselves because the symbolic language of the statutes if often more fully articulated in these other documents.

Primary data sources for a longitudinal implementation study of this type should include:

- Legal Framework Documents

    (a) relevant statutes and subsequent amendments,
    (b) original regulations and subsequent modifications,
    (c) program guides.

- Technical Assistance Materials

    (a) program guides,
    (b) audit checklists,
    (c) other technical assistance packages and notices.

- audits and other compliance reports;

- House and Senate hearings and reports;

- position papers and correspondence from professional and advocacy interest groups;

- previous assessments of the Program's administration.

Secondary data sources could include:

- personal accounts of implementers (For Title I, these usually interweave the personal experiences of these individuals with a rich source of internal documents, conversations, interviews, and public documents that detail key sequences of events);

- short-run implementation studies by contracted research firms and internal compliance and enforcement reports;

- articles in professional journals and other publications.

Methodologically, then, longitudinal implementation research primarily involves a secondary and tertiary synthesis and reinterpretation of an extensive source of existing documents. When key pieces of information are missing or existing documentation is in conflict, interviews with appropriate staff members, congressional aides, or researchers involved in previous implementation studies can be helpful. Despite the biases and limitations of documentary evidence, we have found a good deal of truth in the Chinese proverb that "The palest ink is clearer than the best memory."

The substantive reliance on existing documentary evidence does require assessing the validity of the information in these documents since one can expect internal reports especially to contain as much a rhetorical as an informational intent. In weighing the validity of these secondary analyses, we consider three factors:

(1)   the position and agenda of the person or organization responsible for the writing and publication of the report;

(2)   the motivation for the report;

(3)   the factual accuracy of the information on which the interpretations are based.

Unless there is strong evidence to the contrary, we judge information contained in external reports by contracted researchers to be more valid than the agency reports. This does not suggest that analyses by external research organizations are without biases. Their analyses are limited by the data available to them, time constraints, personal and professional assumptions, and other factors. They, for example, generally lean toward a Washington-view of the world because their research services are typically contracted by federal agencies.

Besides these rather simple decision rules, the method in which the facts of the implementation experience are pieced together and how the evidence is merged from various sources remains largely an informal process which must be entrusted to the discretion of the investigator.

Methodological Considerations

Although empirical and theoretical arguments abound for assuming a longitudinal implementation perspective, little guidance exists for how to actually conduct such research. In our exploratory efforts to analyze the implementation of Title I over a thirteen-year period, three major methodological questions have continued to resurface which have generalizable import:

(1)   What explanatory and dependent factors should be traced across time? How is variation in these variables described?

(2) What types of evidence should be used?

(3) How is such evidence best analyzed?

Our response to these questions reflects as much the limitations of the present state of the art as they do shed light on partial answers to perplexing methodological issues.

Longitudinal implementation case studies which are most likely to contribute to theory building fit under the rubric of what Alexander George has called "controlled focused case studies." In such studies, seemingly idiosyncratic aspects of explanation for each case are formulated in terms of variables which can be compared across cases (i.e., across programs or time periods). In a longitudinal study, a "case" represents a block of years of implementation which can be compared to one or more other blocks of years.

We postulate at least three related dimensions describing implementation should be considered across time:

• policy outputs of implementing agencies;

• compliance with policy outputs by lower level subunits; and,

• actual impacts on intended beneficiaries.

Policy outputs of implementing agencies. A comparison of relevant policy documents, both for determining the internal consistency of these documents at a particular point in time, as well as for noting changes across time, provides one vehicle for assessing a program's implementation.

Such documentary analysis, of course, should include tracing changes in the initial enabling legislation and affiliated legal documents. However, statutes, sometimes allocating millions of dollars at the stroke of a single subsection, are often plagued with deliberately obfuscated language to broaden political support for the legislation. Winning coalitions are often held together by the adhesive of ambiguous language which successfully masks unresolved differences among competing interest groups and legislators. Statutes are as heavily laced with symbolic rhetoric as they are replete with allocative formulae and regulatory prescriptions (Edelman 1964). Therefore, in order to detect shifts in objectives and priorities, it is also necessary to closely analyze those documents which, in essence, operationalize the symbolic import characteristic of most statutes. These include regulations, mandatory and explanatory criteria, guidelines, technical assistance packages, audit checklists, application forms, evaluation mechanisms, and complaint resolution processes.

Some scheme for categorizing policy outputs is usually essential for comprehensive and manageable cross-period comparisons, given the typical proliferation of policy documents over time and the regulatory complexity characteristic of most federally sponsored social programs. (See Kirst and Jung (1980) for one method of categorizing policy outputs at one point in time for cross-time comparisons.) Such a categorization scheme would identify the major Program requirements and block them into some logical groupings. The Title I legal framework, for instance, contains fourteen major Program requirements which roughly can be divided into two categories: funds-allocation requirements and program-development requirements. Funds-allocation requirements are intended to ensure that Title I funds actually reach the intended schools and students and are spent on appropriate categories of expenditures. The program-development requirements encompass a potpourri of qualitative issues such as program evaluation, parent participation, and planning activities.

In order to maintain a manageable analytic scope, we have compared across time changes in two of the major Program requirements (or Program outputs): targeting and program design requirements. Title I schools are chosen on the basis of economic criteria so that limited Title I funds can be concentrated on those schools within a district with the highest concentration of children from low-income families. Once the schools in a district are identified by these economic criteria, children within each eligible school are selected for participation on the basis of lowest test scores or other methods for assessing educational deprivation. There are, then, two steps embedded in law to help ensure that funds are not spread too thinly: (1) economic criteria for limiting the number of eligible schools; and (2) educational criteria for restricting the number of children participating in Title I projects within these schools.

A focused comparison of the criteria used to operationalize these targeting requirements across time allows the analyst to determine whether auditors had adequate indicators for assessing if Title I funds were actually reaching the intended beneficiaries.

The program design regulation requires that a formal plan be developed by districts receiving Title I funds. This plan must set forth the school's objectives and specify the activities and services to accomplish the desired ends. A cross-time focused comparison of the criteria for these requirements provides partial insights into the detail of information federal officials could obtain from local districts on how they were spending Title I funds. These "snapshots" of policy outputs then can be compared across time along several dimensions:

- changes in the degree of local discretion;

- the legal force of the interpretation (a mandatory regulation vs. an advisory suggestion);

- the frequency and scope of the dissemination of these interpretations; and

- the specificity of the information required in application, accounting, and evaluation reports.

In addition to tracing any changes in the conceptualization of these requirements (usually in the statutes) and the operationalization (usually in the regulations, guidelines, and audit checklists), one needs to compare across time the monitoring and enforcement policies and procedures in place as well as other incentives for compliance with policy standards. Some descriptive scales for comparing variance could include:

- the types and frequency of sanctions for misspent funds;

- the types and frequency of monitoring reviews; and

- the types of procedures for adjudicating alleged violations of program regulations and for enforcing appropriate sanctions.

For both the requirements we have traced (targeting and program design) each of these dimensions has increased dramatically over the last thirteen years in terms of the procedures intended to enhance the congruence between the categorical intent of the legislation and actual local implementation activities (Goettel 1978; LCCRUL 1977; SRI 1977a; Stoner 1976).

Compliance by lower level subunits. For Title I, there are two major types of compliance documents. Primary compliance reports include comprehensive audits conducted by the Health, Education, and Welfare Audit Agency (HEWAA) and usually less rigorous Program Reviews conducted by USOE officials annually for each state since 1970. In addition, several external research agencies and special tasks forces have produced numerous "snapshot" compliance and enforcement reports covering one to five year periods. These reports have used a number of approaches including reanalyses of primary compliance documents, structured and unstructured interviews, field observations, and in-depth case studies of selected states, or some combination of these methodologies.

Even with this plethora of compliance documentation, several problematic methodological issues have surfaced in constructing cross-time comparisons of subunit compliance. First, federal efforts to monitor the Program have increased substantially over time. USOE did not begin conducting annual on-site visits to state and local districts until 1970, five years after the initiation of the Program. In 1967, only three states were audited by HEWAA. Now almost a third of the states are audited each year. Second, the process for selecting states for audits is hardly random. The principle selection factors are the date of the last audit, available manpower, requests or complaints from various sources, and other indications of problems. Third, the lack of mention of problems or noncompliance, especially in the early years, may be due to inadequate criteria for substantiating allegations of noncompliance, to a lack of interest in enforcing a requirement at a particular time, or to benevolent neglect in order to maintain a cooperative working relationship among federal, state, and local officials (SRI 1977a). Therefore, simple numerical comparisons of violations across time are likely to reveal more about the changes in the rigor of the monitoring efforts than improvements or slippages in state and local agencies' compliance. For instance, during the first five years of the Program, there were no quantitative criteria for determining whether a district receiving Title I funds was providing comparable services to Title I and non-Title I schools. Only after 1972 were "comparability" criteria integrated into the audit checklists, and it is exactly at this time that such violations began showing up in primary compliance documents.

In 1965, USOE had neither the history, resources nor mandate from Congress to closely monitor the expenditures of educational funds from federal coffers. Local control of schools, vested in over 16,000 independent school boards, remains a dominant, although increasingly myth-like value in the United States—a value which, prior to 1965, had run counter to federal employees observing elementary and secondary classroom activities and monitoring district-level operations. Before the passage of ESEA, USOE was known primarily as a check-writing and statistics-collecting operation. The original Title I statute merely required that states submit broadly worded assurances that they would approve local applications which complied with the ambiguous intent of the legislation. After a well-publicized wrangle with the Senate Education Subcommittee in 1967, USOE finally disseminated the first authorized set of guidelines in March of 1968, a full three years after the passage of the enabling legislation. The violations uncovered in the scattered HEWAA audit reports were not publicized until the publication of the Martin and McClure report in 1969 (Stoner 1976).

Quite a different scenario exists today. Although numerous problems persist, a magnum opus study of Title I's legal framework concluded that the Program's requirements are generally necessary, consistent, and flexible (LCCRUL 1977). In contrast to even five years ago, USOE has recovered nearly $1.5 million in misspent funds and is presently working to collect at least $2.2 million more as a result of audit findings over the last four years (OE collecting misspent 1980). Even though the funds actually collected by USOE for disallowable expenditures is a small percent of the dollar expenditure exceptions noted in DHEW Audit Agency reports, there is growing evidence that state and local education agencies now fear that they might be next and that a shift to federal aid with "no strings" attached is highly unlikely in the near future (LCCRUL 1977).

Impacts on intended beneficiaries. During the first seven years of Title I alone, over $50 million was spent on impact evaluations (McLaughlin 1975). Typically these studies have attempted to assess the Program's impact by reducing the goals of the Program to monthly or yearly growth rates on standardized reading, writing, and math tests. Much more has been learned about how not to go about conducting such impact studies and about the resistance of local education agencies to federal efforts at collecting the data for such assessments than about the actual impacts along these dimensions on Program recipients. In short, these types of impact studies have raised more questions than they have answered. And there is little to suggest that they have had much of an impact on Congressional attitudes about the Program. Measures of "impact" other than standardized reading scores merit consideration. Some attention should be given to the:

- influence of the Title I on the design and proliferation of state compensatory education programs;

- influence of Title I on the design of other more recent federal education program;

- the effects of ESEA and other federal categorical legislation on the involvement of parents in school and district advisory councils; and

- the affect of state "set asides" for Title I and other federal education initiatives on the growth and organization of state departments of education.

Our basic argument is that the concept of "impact" is often too narrowly defined and that indirect impacts of legislated social programs should receive further consideration. Our synthesis of the studies in the

Chapter 4

The Maturation of Redistributive Programs*

Paul Peterson, Barry Rabe, and Kenneth Wong

Cooperative federalism thrived during the 1950s and early 1960s in part because most federal programs were developmental. National and local administrators worked together on hospital construction, vocational education, and aid for federally impacted schools because federal and local governments had a common interest in seeing these programs prosper. But when the creators of the Great Society asked the federal system to carry out a host of redistributive programs in health care, education, housing, and other policy areas, they placed the cooperative intergovernmental system under considerable stress.

Although redistributive programs ultimately became almost as cooperative in their operation as developmental programs, a multiphase evolution in intergovernmental relationships was needed to achieve that cooperation. When redistributive legislation was first enacted and administrative requirements were promulgated, the programs were cast in the same vague language that had suited developmental programs. But the federal government soon discovered that these vagaries presupposed a commitment to reform, innovation, and redistribution at the local level as pervasive as the commitment existing in Washington.

When local officials turned out to be more recalcitrant than anticipated, the federal government initiated a second phase of legislative and administrative activity. This time regulations were more precise;

*Reprinted from Paul E. Peterson, Barry G. Rabe, and Kenneth K. Wong, "The Maturation of Redistributive Programs," *When Federalism Works,* Washington, D.C.: The Brookings Institution, 1986, pp. 131–159. Reprinted by permission of the publisher.

what had once been left to interpretation was now elaborated in exacting detail. Even congressional statutes showed a new precision as members of Congress and their increasingly numerous staff assistants wrote into law exactly what was desired and precisely how it was to be achieved (Lowi 1979). Regulations were followed by evaluations as the new tools of the social sciences were mobilized on behalf of institutional reform. In redistributive programs enacted after the mid-1970s, including the special education and health maintenance programs, this specificity was written in from the outset. Witnessing the resistance of state and local governments to vaguely expressed federal guidelines in earlier programs, Washington policymakers bypassed the first phase entirely, moving immediately toward a rigorously directive approach.

In the late 1970s, the federal system entered a third phase in which it began to work out a new cooperative federalism appropriate to the purposes of redistributive programs. These changes were less visible, less controversial, and less sweeping than the widely discussed cutbacks and simplifications of the Reagan era. But although the steps were incremental, ad hoc, and occurred in one program at a time, the overall effect was to diminish the difficulties of managing federal programs while keeping their purpose intact. Adjustments were made on the part of both local and federal participants. At the local level a new professional cadre more identified with program objectives was recruited to administer federal programs. As a result, local officials became more sensitive to federal expectations. At the federal level, policymakers began to doubt whether detailed regulations, tight audits, and complex evaluations were unmixed blessings. Appropriate changes and adjustments were made, expectations became more realistic, administrators began to identify with program goals in ways that transcended governmental boundaries, and citizen groups replaced contentious criticism with astute support to gain more federal resources. A commitment to a coordinated effort gradually emerged.

1. Transforming Compensatory Education

The federal compensatory education program, Title I of the Elementary and Secondary Education Act (ESEA), is perhaps the prototypical example of changing federal-local relations in redistributive programs. Between 1965, when legislation authorizing the program was enacted, and 1981, when Congress modified many of the law's statutory requirements, the program evolved through three distinct phases. Originally it was little more than a vague expression of a general federal commitment to help educate those in poverty. By the early 1970s the program had acquired a well-defined set of rules and guidelines that many state and local officials had difficulty understanding, to say nothing of implementing. Gradually, however, federal, state, and local policymakers worked out their differences so that by the late 1970s a stable set of expectations concerning program operations emerged.

Phase One: High Expectations and Vague Requirements

In the first phase of a redistributive program the central government is bold in its expectations, unclear in its objectives, imprecise in its stipulations, and inept in its administrative actions. A bold preamble is sketched, a vague program framework is developed, and the funding sluice gates are opened. Details regarding costs and implementation procedures are treated as secondary concerns, dust that will settle once the legislation has been enacted. If the program develops problems, rational analysis can presumably solve them. In the exuberance of the moment such programs are seen as points of departure for future federal action rather than definitive steps in the evolution of a social welfare state.

The compensatory education program followed just such a pattern. The legislation providing for compensatory education was shaped in part by the National Education Association, the Council of Chief State School Officers, the National School Board Association, the American Association of School Administrators, the National Association of State Boards of Education, and the National Congress of Parents and Teachers. Widely known as the "big six" in educational policy circles, these long established and influential organizations shared "an ideological preference for protecting local and state control of education and minimizing federal interference" (Kirst and Jung 1980). The sole lobby group promoting categorical restrictions on the program was the National Catholic Welfare Board, which was interested in making certain that some of the monies were used in non-public schools.

Federal direction of compensatory education funds was thus initially limited. Requirements for fiscal control and accounting procedures "as may be necessary to assure proper disbursement of, and accounting for, federal funds" and requirements for adopting "effective procedures" for program evaluation proved to be more exhortation than carefully crafted procedures with which local districts were expected to comply. Although the federal government also required that funds be denied to local school districts if the state found that "the combined fiscal effort . . . of that agency and the state (was) . . . less than (the) fiscal effort" of the previous year (Elementary and Secondary Education Act of 1965), state and local expenditures for education were increasing rapidly enough during the inflationary period that the provision proved neither restrictive nor meaningful. Consequently localities sometimes used part of the federal aid for local tax relief instead of using all of it to increase educational services. One econometric analysis discovered that in 1970, for every dollar in federal aid they received, localities reduced their own local expenditures on education an average of twenty-eight cents (Feldstein 1978).

Not only were federal restrictions minimal, but the administrative staff to enforce them was small and inexperienced. The job of administering compensatory education programs, observed Stephen Bailey and Edith Mosher in their authoritative chronicle, "fell to an agency with a long and pedestrian past." The professional staff of the Office of Education averaged more than fifty years of age, they suffered from "an almost pathological suspicion" of the Department of Health, Education, and Welfare, and they feared the change of federal control in a way that had a "crippling effect on initiative and leadership" (Bailey and Mosher 1968). Instead of being oriented toward compliance, federal administrators viewed themselves as professional educators; the idea of enforcing regulations was "simply incompatible with their view of public education" (Murphy 1971, p. 53). But even if federal and state officials had been more zealous in their commitment to the objectives of compensatory education, there were simply too many districts and classrooms for any single method of implementation to become dominant. As late as 1976 the Office of Education employed only one hundred persons with administrative responsibilities in compensatory education to supervise a program operating in 14,000 local school districts. Commenting on early program experiences, Milbrey McLaughlin observed, "The (Office of Education) does not 'run' Title I. The design and content of the more then 30,000 Title I projects across the country are determined by (local school systems). Consequently, the use of Title I dollars reflects multiple and diverse goals, which are not easily transformed into measurable, overarching objectives" (McLaughlin 1975). Perhaps the situation was best summed up, however, by Alice Rivlin: "No one really knew how to run a successful compensatory education program. There were hunches and theories, but few facts" (Rivlin 1971, p. 80).

If federal administrators had limited resources and experience, local administrators and teachers had only vague ideas of what a compensatory education program entailed. Indeed, it was this very vagueness that motivated some of the original supporters of the program. Testifying before the congressional committee considering the 1965 legislation, Robert Kennedy complained of having "seen enough districts where there has been a lack of imagination, lack of initiative, and lack of interest in the problems of some of the deprived children" (McLaughlin 1975, p. 2). If that was the state of affairs when the legislation passed, schools could obviously not be redirected overnight. Among the four school systems included in our study, Baltimore was especially slow in developing a special focus for its compensatory education program. As late as 1975, according to a Baltimore administrator, "federal auditors came in and said there was no comparability (local spending on compensatory schools equal to that on other local schools). We said, 'What's new?' There was no deliberate effort on our part to deceive the feds. There was some ignorance, some things we just didn't know, and some things we didn't want to do." Not only was there no comparability, but Baltimore, the most politicized of the four cities, was said to have allocated its funds according to politically defined criteria. One high-level administrator specifically acknowledged that in the early years of the program, political patronage influenced allocational decisions, an observation consistent with numerous other reports that schools run by politically well-connected principals received disproportionately high amounts of funding for compensatory education.

Inexperience, a small administrative staff, and ill-defined objectives combined to produce a diverse, inchoate program that failed to concentrate its fiscal resources on the population it was supposed to serve. Even several years after passage of the act it was easy to conclude that the program illustrated perfectly what a generation of analysts have come to criticize as a fundamental flaw of redistributive programs and of American federalism: "The federal system—with its dispersion of power and control—not only permits but encourages the evasion and dilution of federal reform, making it nearly impossible for the federal administrator to impose program priorities; those not diluted by congressional intervention can be ignored during state and local implementation" (Murphy 1971, p. 60).

Phase Two: Imposing and Enforcing Regulations

The second phase in the evolution of a new intergovernmental program attempts to correct the problems and abuses experienced in the first phase. As evidence accumulates that funds for redistributive programs are being diverted from the populations they are supposed to be serving, the federal government intensifies its oversight of local activities. New regulations are enacted to compel greater program unity, regulations that may be supported or even designed by organizations representing the program's intended recipients. Rather than continue to acquiesce in locally defined resource allocation, programs are adjusted to make the goals of federal policy clear. As local officials chafe under the new regulations, intergovernmental conflict and confusion increase.

The experience of the compensatory education program illustrated this pattern of change. Before the 1981 deregulations introduced by the Reagan administration, Congress amended the original legislation on four occasions—1968, 1970, 1974, and 1978. Each amendment resulted in new provisions that specified more clearly the congressional commitment to helping disadvantaged children from low-income families. The Office of Education developed its own increasingly elaborate set of regulations and guidelines, many of them stated in letters to specific school districts or in interpretations of specific decisions. Even if one looks only at the formal requirements, the number of federal regulations added is astonishing. In 1964 the program had eight requirements; by 1980 it had fifty-nine.

Several key regulations were promulgated to help define Title I. In general, local districts had to show that they were identifying as compensatory education schools those with the highest concentration of students in poverty, that they were contributing as many local resources to these schools as to any other school in the district, and that they were committing at least the same level of local resources as they had provided in previous years.

To help them achieve these objectives, the federal government established a number of specific guidelines. Under "maintenance of effort," districts' revenues from state and local sources could not be lower than those of the preceding year. "Comparability" ensured that locally funded services in every compensatory education school were at least at the average level of those provided to noncompensatory education schools in the same district. This concept was intended to prevent local districts from using federal funds merely to provide the poor with services already available in other schools. A "supplement-not-supplant" provision, added in 1970, specified that school districts were to use federal dollars "to supplement, and to the extent practical, increase the levels of funds that would, in the absence of such federal funds, be made available from non-federal sources" for programs and projects for the educationally disadvantaged (Amendments to the Elementary and Secondary Education Act of 1965). These funds were "in no case" to be used to supplant such funds from non-federal sources. This provision was clarified by the "excess cost" guideline, which stipu-

lated that compensatory education dollars pay only the costs of supplementary services that exceeded normal instructional expense. Another
provision required that all services provided to noncompensatory education students also be furnished to compensatory education children.
Each provision was intended to make certain that disadvantaged children directly benefited from federal dollars.[1]

Federal enforcement activities also became more rigorous as
auditors scrutinized state and local allocation practices and found many
inconsistent with the new guidelines. The increased enforcement effort
began in earnest during the early years of the Nixon administration.
One key federal bureaucrat recalled that before 1968 it had been politically risky to push for careful enforcement of federal regulations on
comparability and non-supplanting. But during the early Nixon years,
federal officials decided that the program was not working because
states and localities failed to follow regulations. Thus despite the
administration's dislike of excessive paperwork, the Office of Education
tightened federal controls. As one federal bureaucrat later admitted, "A
hell of a paperwork burden was imposed on the states and local districts for the sake of ensuring comparability."

These changes were enthusiastically supported by a wave of new
groups—among them the National Advisory Council for the Education
of Disadvantaged Children, the Lawyers Committee for Civil Rights
Under Law, the Legal Standards and Education Project of the National
Association for the Advancement of Colored People, and the National
Welfare Rights Organization. These organizations functioned as advocates for the low-income, low-achieving students compensatory education was designed to assist. Unlike the groups that had helped initiate
the legislation in 1965, these organizations argued repeatedly that
greater federal specificity was needed in allocating funds and overseeing their use. In the process they often provided reports or suggestions
that influenced congressional thinking and were sometimes simply
adopted in various amendments. The Children's Defense Fund and the
NAACP, for example, were instrumental in gaining congressional support for the comparability and nonsupplanting provisions. They com-
piled considerable evidence, much of it from previously unheralded
federal audits, that local districts were misusing federal money. Publication of these findings in a 1969 report, *Title I of ESEA: Is It Helping Poor
Children?* prompted a major intensification of federal oversight of the
program (Martin and McClure 1969).

During the 1970s such organizations became increasingly active
and effective. For example, the Lawyers Committee for Civil Rights
Under Law, a public interest law firm, was a constant thorn in the side

of local educators and their organizational representatives in Washington. The law firm not only published manuals advising citizens how to bring suit against districts believed to be in violation of federal guidelines, but "several of their recommendations for strengthening the program requirements (were) quite evident in the 1978 amendments" (Kirst and Jung 1982, p. 132).

At the same time, federal officials responsible for the compensatory education program became increasingly impatient as audit and other evaluation reports indicated considerable local divergence from federal requirements and expectations. Ultimately, some districts were charged with outright misuse of federal funds. Audits conducted in 1973, for instance, charged the Milwaukee school district with misuse of $5.9 million of compensatory education funds between 1968 and 1973 through violations of the supplement-not-supplant and comparability requirements. Federal dollars, the audits indicated, were used to pay for the salaries and related costs of many compensatory education teachers who had previously been paid from state and local sources. The audits also charged that some projects, such as an environmental education mobile laboratory and field trips to museums, served all students in certain grade levels (and not just the disadvantaged ones eligible for services). In 1980, after years of negotiations, Milwaukee returned $120,266 to the federal government (Wisconsin Department of Public Instruction 1982).

With its serious fiscal problems the Baltimore school district was even more resistant to federal restrictions on fund use. Baltimore officials mingled compensatory education dollars with the general school fund and often used the federal funding to supplant general school expenditures. A 1978 federal audit charged that the district had failed to fulfill its responsibilities to ensure that funds were spent in the Baltimore schools in conformity with federal regulations (U.S. Department of Health, Education, and Welfare 1980). From 1974 to 1978 the Baltimore school district allegedly misspent $14.6 million in federal funds, one-fourth of the total federal compensatory education allocation to the district during the period.[2] Most of the funds were allegedly used to cover general administrative costs and regular curricular activities that benefited all students. Although the leading state and local school officials contended that the allegations were inaccurate, many administrators and instructors with extensive experience in Baltimore's program agreed that the charges were generally legitimate. They concurred with audit findings that Baltimore had "operated the program inefficiently, used a deficient accounting system," and paid scant attention to many program guidelines.

The rigorous regulatory and enforcement efforts of the early 1970s did serve to concentrate compensatory education services on the low-income, educationally disadvantaged student, however. By 1976, the program had acquired sufficient definition that only three percent of the students who were neither poor nor educationally disadvantaged were participating in federally funded reading programs. The federal law, to be sure, did not give poor, disadvantaged students a right to compensatory services, so in fact only a third of the most eligible students actually were receiving them, a point often made by those calling for program expansion. But even though the program may have been smaller than advocates wished, poor, low-achieving students were eleven times more likely to be in the program than their better-off counterparts. Clearly, federal rules were shaping policy implementation at the local level.

Phase Three: Toward More Mature Program Operation

Repeated conflicts over program regulations generate a third stage in the administration of redistributive programs. Federal bureaucrats, facing complaints from local leaders and from their legislative representatives, once again modify guidelines and procedures. A new tolerance of local diversity, a new recognition that no single programmatic thrust is clearly preferable, and an appreciation of the limits as to what can be directed from the center steadily emerge. This appreciation of the limits of federal regulation does not mean that national oversight is eliminated or that federal grants are distributed with as little direction as existed in the first phase of the program. Federal expectations that the program will remain focused on those people with special needs are as evident as ever, but the expectations of this third phase are now shaped by a context in which federal professionals find local counterparts who seem as committed to the redistributive objectives as national policymakers. Intergovernmental disagreements can occur, new problems may arise, and new approaches may be advanced. But the issue is no longer one of securing local compliance with national objectives; the issue is instead how best to use limited resources to address common concerns.

The increasing maturity in the operation of the compensatory education program is particularly evident from the way in which the "pull-out" issue evolved. During the program's second phase, federal auditors often insisted on evidence that compensatory monies were being used exclusively for the benefit of educationally disadvantaged students, that is, that school systems were complying with supplement-not-supplant regulations. "Pull-out" programming satisfied the auditors' expectations because the disadvantaged students were "pulled" out of the classroom and given special instruction in reading and mathematics in small groups or tutorial sessions. The reading specialists and teacher aides who taught these special classes were paid for entirely with federal monies, and their presence in the school was clearly an additional school activity. Pull-out programming also became widespread because the practice helped legitimize the growing sub-professions in reading and learning disabilities, it justified recruiting teacher aides from the low-income community, and it reflected a respected, widely held view that socially disadvantaged students required special instructional techniques (Peterson 1986). The practice became subject to increasing criticism in the late 1970s, however. Critics pointed out that separating the educationally disadvantaged from other students could undermine their self-confidence by stigmatizing them as "dumb," that education in small groups conducted by teacher aides and less experienced reading specialists was not necessarily superior to that provided in the regular classroom, that shuffling children from one classroom to another disrupted the school day and reduced active learning time, and that the curricula of the regular classroom teacher and the compensatory educator were typically uncoordinated, thereby confusing students as to how and what they were expected to learn (Peterson 1986).

The pull-out concept gradually came into disfavor after a comprehensive review of the compensatory education program was conducted in 1976 (Kenoyer et al. 1981). According to one influential interpretation of the findings, compensatory education had positive, long-term effects on student achievement when program design did not involve pull-outs; it had no significant effects when the pull-out arrangement was used (Cooley 1981). By the 1980s, enthusiasm for the practice was on the wane, though the evidence as to its effectiveness or ineffectiveness remains open to further research and discussion (Archombault 1986).

In response to these criticisms, federal and state officials insisted that they had never required pull-out programs, that many educational strategies were consistent with federal guidelines, and that their only concern was to ensure that monies were used to serve the eligible population. After this, local officials felt greater freedom to explore such alternative strategies as the use of in-classroom aides, after-school programs, and reduced class sizes. But the controversy caused by pull-out programs continues. In 1986 one local official complained that the potential threat of a federal or state audit prevented the implementation of alternative educational strategies. "The greatest fear of (local educational) coordinators is a visit by the Inspector General's office.

Time and again programs . . . reviewed, approved, and monitored by (state educational) personnel are found to be illegal by the Inspector General's staff" (Rosica 1986). But this view was in the minority; as the evidence against use of the pull-out practice mounted, most observers felt that federal and state officials had relaxed their auditing requirements and a broader range of educational strategies was being explored (Jung and Kirst 1986).

The pull-out dispute was only one example of the administrative issues that required discussion and resolution, but by the late 1970s, regulatory provisions that had once been ill defined and poorly understood had become a way of life. Federal officials gradually began to concentrate on collecting only that information necessary to determine local compliance. Of the five criteria initially thought necessary to assess compliance with the supplement-not-supplant provision, for example, federal officials settled on two. They decided that knowing the number of staff and the expenditures per child would be sufficient to tell them whether local and state funds were being equitably spent. After these requirements became well established, evidence suggested that compliance was nearly universal, and the organizations that had represented compensatory education recipients so assertively in the early 1970s ceased to cite noncompliance as a problem. Federal audits conducted in the late 1970s also found a steady decline in the misuse of federal funds. The findings from these formal reviews were confirmed by more informal assessments in interviews with federal, state, and local officials.

As states developed a greater understanding of what was and was not permissible, they increasingly integrated the federal program into their overall efforts. Compensatory education no longer seemed peripheral to their mission. Florida, for example, revised state achievement testing during the 1970s to measure the performance of children receiving compensatory services and of all other children. The state also combined auditing for the program with auditing for overall school expenditures, enabling it to trace each educational dollar to individual schools and class levels. While the combined audit initially caused some confusion, especially for districts such as Dade County that had never examined the expenditure patterns of individual schools, it gradually became standardized and widely supported, in part because the new procedures enabled school principals to exercise greater latitude in allocating resources. Wisconsin developed a similar procedure for including audits of federal program compliance into a computerized comprehensive school audit.

Such intermingling of federal and state purposes also improved state and local relations. As states became increasingly adept at managing federal regulations, they sought more collaboration with local school systems. Florida increasingly solicited suggestions from local educators before deciding on state guidelines, and state officials set up regional meetings to review draft copies of proposed compensatory education applications before their formal submission.

All four states further embraced the federal program by enacting their own compensatory education programs. In 1981 Florida spent $34 million for its own program in addition to the $81 million it received from the federal government. Both programs were monitored by the same bureau and in both instances the state concentrated a disproportionate share of resources on students from kindergarten through grade three. Maryland also used federal funds in conjunction with those for its own program and other state categorical monies. Since the federal program served fewer than half of all eligible Maryland students, state funds were said to be concentrated on the rest. In 1981 Maryland added $5.5 million for program funding to $37 million of federal funding. Compensatory education was thus increasingly assumed as a state responsibility, both through Maryland's considerable role in federal program oversight and the emergence of its own comparable program.

California probably did the most to take advantage of the new federal flexibility. Like the others it combined the federal compensatory education program with its state program in an attempt to create a comprehensive policy. In the late 1970s it also developed a consolidated application form so that local districts could request money for a dozen different state and federal programs in one application. This form encouraged local principals and school personnel to develop a more integrated approach to the use of various categorical program monies. Meanwhile, reviews of compensatory education programs were combined with those of other programs to create a comprehensive review process. This development furthered the integration of the various categorical programs and encouraged communication among local educators, inasmuch as program reviews in any given district were normally performed by local educators from other districts.

California's innovations initially encountered considerable difficulties with the federal government. From Washington's perspective, the federal program in California had become so well integrated with state programs that it practically lost its identity and whether regulations on comparability and nonsupplanting were being followed had become difficult to determine. Arguing that its procedures ensured comparability and non-supplanting, the state reached an uneasy truce with the federal office for several years. The problem was resolved in the late 1970s when changes in the 1978 amendments to the federal law facilitated the coordination of federal and state compensatory programs. By 1981 several federal officials whom we interviewed were enthusiastic about the high quality of California's programs.

The increased cooperation among the central government and the four states and localities we observed seems to have reflected a national pattern. A major study by the National Institute of Education found a significant decrease nationwide in reported instances of supplanting. The decrease, according to the NIE, was largely a function of less assiduous efforts by federal officials to identify, report, and verify supplanting. The report even implied that higher-level education officials refused to accept as verifiable the reports of supplanting submitted by staff members (National Institute of Education 1977). But long-term employees of the Office of Education interpreted the decline as an indication that local officials had acquired an understanding of federal requirements and how to adapt to them. Certainly in the states we visited, efforts at greater compliance during the mid-1970s were described repeatedly. Perhaps both views can be accepted. Each component of the federal system was learning to be less confrontational and more cooperative: local school officials learned how to comply while federal administrators learned that more was to be gained from accommodation than from rigid rule enforcement. As one study reported, "State conflicts with federal programs did not exhibit the intensity we had expected from popular accounts." Instead, "administrative problems are overstated and inaccurately ascribed to federal programs as their singular source" (Moore et al. 1983). The results of econometric studies have agreed with these findings. Instead of using federal compensatory education monies as a substitute for local funds, states and localities were spending money over and above what they received from the federal government. One study (Chubb 1985) estimated the average additional expenditure to twenty-two cents for every dollar received; another study (Craig and Inman 1982) estimated it as twenty-eight cents.

This more cooperative spirit best explains the remarkable lack of local enthusiasm for the deregulation of compensatory education attempted by the Reagan administration in 1981. State and local officials complained that the new law and accompanying regulations were too vague. They preferred to keep in place the extra administrative work to which they had grown accustomed rather than risk being audited for noncompliance at some future date. Even Congress, in a bipartisan move, backed away from the deregulation of 1981, reinstituting in subsequent years a compensatory education program whose requirements remained much the same as those that had evolved during the preceding decades.

The long-term effects of the compensatory education program on educational attainment have not been precisely determined. The kind of evaluation required to assess conclusively the overall effectiveness of this large-scale, complex undertaking will probably never be conducted. (see "Methodological Note" in Peterson, Rabe, and Wong 1986, chapter 1). However, there are signs that differences in educational performance between minority and non-minority children have steadily narrowed since the early 1970s. A recent definitive review of the evidence concludes that eight of nine major studies "showed a consistent and unambiguous narrowing of the gap between black and non-minority students, leaving little doubt that this pattern is real and not an artifact of some aspects of the tests or groups tested." The review also notes that "differences between black and non-minority students . . . shrank more rapidly among elementary and junior-high students than among high-school students" (Congressional Budget Office, 1986).

The causes of these gains are difficult to ascertain conclusively. They may primarily be due to broad social changes, including the passage of new civil rights laws in the 1960s, that improved minority educational and employment opportunities and altered the expectations of teachers, parents, and students about the capacities of minorities to achieve. To the extent that the compensatory education program contributed to these general changes in perceptions and expectations, its most significant effects may have been intangible, indirect, and symbolic (Levin 1979). But a more direct, material contribution to minority educational gains cannot be ruled out. For one thing, gains in minority educational attainment have occurred despite the continued stagnation, and even deterioration, of minority well-being in other social spheres. The unemployment rate for young black males has escalated since the 1960s, black wages relative to those of whites have shown little improvement, and black families are even more likely to be headed by single parents than they were a generation ago when this problem first became a national issue (Wilson 1985). The one area of social life in which blacks have made clear, identifiable gains has been within the educational system. What is more, those gains have been greatest during the elementary years, the very years minorities attended the schools that were the focus of compensatory education policies.

2. Evolution of Other Redistributive Programs

The early years of the health maintenance and special education programs closely resembled phase two in the evolution of compensatory education. Federal regulations were more detailed and demanding than those for the developmentally oriented programs. But as rigorous as open enrollment, mainstreaming, and other provisions seemed on paper, their actual implementation was neither as sluggish nor as traumatic as early studies or the conventional wisdom of the period would suggest. By the early 1980s more than one hundred HMOs and virtually all local school districts in the nation agreed to certain federal regulatory provisions in exchange for federal funds and other program benefits. Not surprisingly, local administrators wished for fewer federal requirements, particularly less paperwork, and greater benefits, but there was no sense of despair and certainly no sense that federal efforts in health maintenance and special education had been inconsequential. Both programs provided sufficient incentives to overcome local reluctance to abide by federal regulations and sufficient latitude to avoid smothering the local professionals who provided the services.

The problems encountered by federal redistributive programs that have been highlighted in such vivid detail by critics of Great Society programs were most evident in the early phases of their operation. With a longer view, one that replaces quickly taken snapshots with less vivid but more comprehensive videotapes, federal programs look better. Points of conflict and confusion, so perplexing in early years, are resolved. Intergovernmental accommodation and cooperation increase. Even favorable effects of programs are more evident.

Federal programs, of course, do not necessarily differ in this respect from other organizational activity, public or private. Failure is always a possibility. "Even under the most salutary conditions, some enterprises in an emerging industry will fail," noted sociologist Paul Starr. "HMOs were no exception" (Starr 1982). Henry Ford, after all, took years to streamline automobile production and still more years to offer his customers a choice of color other than jet black.

Of course, making public sector programs operational is more difficult than undertaking comparable projects in the private sector. As Laurence E. Lynn, Jr., has noted, private sector managers are oriented toward "economic performance as measured by markets"; public sector managers are oriented "toward the public interest as determined in political forums." The latter emphasis does not lend itself to such precise measurement and goal setting. In fact, "the technology for achieving governmental purposes is often vague or nonexistent, thus compounding the difficulties of designing policies and programs" (Lynn 1981). As Hugh Heclo explained, "Knowing when a business has increased its market penetration from 40 percent to 42 percent is not like knowing when people have decent housing or proper health care" (Heclo 1977).

Consequently, public—including federal—programs can be expected to take an especially long time before they begin to operate effectively. This extended lead time is all the more reason to temper judgements until programs have been able to acquire a focus. Few recall that social security, to which Great Society programs were unfavorably compared, had had an unusual head start. It acquired administrative stability and political acumen gradually over several decades. And even at the beginning it had the luxury of setting up its program at a leisurely pace denied most of its successors. Social security began preparing its operations as early as 1935, well in advance of the first monthly payments in 1940. It was also relatively easy to administer because as an income transfer program to an age-specific population all the elements could be measured precisely. The new redistributive service delivery programs implemented by federal administrators of the Great Society were a good deal more complex and difficult to put in place.

As time passed it became increasingly possible to conclude that these programs also proved their worth. If that judgement is correct, it is only because policy professionals eventually acquired the expertise to manage complex intergovernmental programs.

Chapter 5

Interaction of State and Federal Programs*

Mary T. Moore, Margaret E. Goertz, and Terry W. Hartle

The proper organization of responsibility among federal, state, and local governments has become a central issue in public policy debates in the 1980s. Although the issue itself is timeless, finding a logical and appropriate division between federal and state functions and roles has proven largely exclusive to most administrations that have sought to do so. The Eisenhower administration found few activities to return to the states and even enacted two new major programs—the Federal Highway Act and the National Defense Education Act—that expanded the federal government's reach. The sixties witnessed an explosion in federal grant-in-aid programs to fulfill the goals of the Great Society. The Nixon administration reordered federalism modestly through two block grant proposals but by and large increased federal involvement and activities. In commenting on the Nixon and Ford administration efforts, the Advisory Commission on Intergovernmental Relations (1977: p. 42) noted the following:

> Although the New Federalism strategy contemplated a sorting out of functions by level government, by 1976 servicing responsibilities were more thoroughly marbleized than ever before as the federal government entered new functional fields.

*Reprinted from Mary Moore, Margaret Goertz, and Terry Hartle, "Interaction of Federal and State Programs," *Education and Urban Society,* vol. 15, no. 4, August 1983, pp. 453–478. Copyright 1983 by Sage Publications, Inc. Reprinted by permission of Sage Publications, Inc.

The marked expansion of federal education programs from the mid-1960s through the 1970s coupled with the gradual tightening and prescriptiveness of program requirements that characterized the last decade of federal aid to education has not caused concerns of federal dominance to abate from policymakers' rhetoric. Joseph Cronin (then the Illinois Superintendent of Schools) stated the following in an article:

> ... state and local taxes together still account for more than 90% of the dollar outlay for public schools in this nation. Yet the amount of federal regulation has increased in ways disproportionate to the amount of federal dollars received ... Slowly, inexorably, and incrementally, the federal government is taking over education. Especially since 1965, the country has moved almost every year toward a national system of education ... By 1980 the phenomenon of "federal takeover" may appear to be an understatement of the problem [1976: pp. 2–3].

As the 1980s unwind, the debate about the proper organization of responsibility among federal, state, and local governments in regard to education takes place on two related yet distinct levels. The first level questions federal intervention in education altogether. One faction posits education is the proper domain of state and local authorities, and therefore, federal involvement should be as minimal as possible; in other words, the familiar "marble cake" of American federalism should return to a layer cake (Grodzins 1960).[1] Opposing viewpoints hold that federal involvement and shared functions are critical to the pursuit of the national (as distinct from the state's parochial) purposes.

At a second level, the question focuses on the proper assignment of functions within various educational policy areas. Federal involvement is assumed here, but debate surrounds the issue of the appropriate balance between federal objectives and needs for accountability, on the one hand, and the recipients' need for flexibility and direction, on the other. Critics of the current federal role maintain that the education scales have tipped too far in the direction of the federal government, charging that federal requirements are administratively burdensome, uncoordinated and inflexible; supporters argue that careful controls are necessary to ensure that state and local governments faithfully pursue federal education goals and objectives.

To the extent that federalism issues in education ever are resolved, they are dealt with in conjunction with a myriad of other public policy concerns. Accordingly, the education federalism debate of the 1980s is associated with and influenced by questions of national budget deficits and economic stagnation. In addition to these concerns, public attitudes that reflect a yearning for simplicity and a reversal of government activism in general are present. The federalism debate in education cannot be totally isolated from these larger events nor from the broader course of federalism. Nevertheless, acknowledging the presence of these larger events and breaking the debate into discrete questions that are suitable for analysis can assist policymakers in making informed judgments that are less subject to the pressures of the times.

Are the states and local districts straitjacketed by federal programs and requirements? Are federal requirements overwhelming state and local administrative capacities and willingness to sustain new education endeavors? Conversely, are state and local governments the real shapers of federal education assistance programs and their accompanying requirements? Are state and local governments themselves able and willing to provide the services sponsored by federal programs?

In the summer of 1981 a study was undertaken to investigate these questions as they pertained to states.[2] The results of these empirical efforts form the basis of the findings reported in this chapter. The intent of the study was to examine how a broad combination of federal education programs affected states' administration of federal and related state education programs. The study was not an attempt to define what the federal role should be, but rather an effort to describe and analyze how states responded to, and were affected by, the combination of major federal education programs in operation in 1981–82. By pursuing this course, the study sought to expand policymakers' knowledge and understanding of how the current configuration of federal programs influenced the states.

In general, the results of the study do not confirm assessments of federal education programs as administratively burdensome and excessively restrictive at the state level. Neither were federal requirements found to be meaningless: they definitely affected states' administrative response to federal programs. State education agencies and states in general appear to have emerged from the last five years of federal assistance as stronger units of government. States assertively pursue their own agendas and tailor federal programs to the state context. But even though state education agencies and state governments are stronger, federal education programs provide a critical source of financial and political support for services and protection to special needs populations (the disadvantaged, handicapped, limited English speaking, and women). As a general rule, state priorities do not converge with federal priorities in these areas. Even when they do, many state programs today derive their strength from federal actions.

These findings do not translate into a conclusion that the design of federal education programs cannot be improved upon. However, they do suggest that improvements in federal education programs at the state level might be directed more usefully at resolving particular issues within programs instead of focusing on reports of administrative problems that appear to be outdated and possibly only relevant to an earlier era federal–state interactions.

1. Overview of Study

This study focused on two major dimensions of the intergovernmental system: state administration of a select set of major federal education programs and federal and state interaction surrounding special pupil programs. The federal programs and civil rights provisions examined included the following: Titles I, IV, V and VII of Elementary and Secondary Education Act (ESEA); the Education for All Handicapped Children Act (P.L. 94–142); the Vocation Education Act; Title VI of the Civil Rights Act of 1964; Title IX of the Education Amendments of 1972; and Section 504 of the Rehabilitation Act of 1973. The state programs studied included those analogous in purpose to these federal programs. This selection of programs provided a broad range of different federal approaches to the states and covered the major federal programs in existence in 1981–1982. The federal programs studied predated the revisions made by the 1981 Education Consolidation and Improvement Act (ECIA). That legislation had just been enacted when field work began making it impossible to assess its impact on the states.

After completing a thorough analysis of the legal and administrative requirements contained in these federal laws, in the spring of 1982 eight states were visited—California, Louisiana, Massachusetts, Missouri, New Mexico, New York, Virginia and Wyoming—to ascertain the administrative effects and program interactions associated with these programs. Those states were selected to represent a wide spectrum of political, economic, institutional, and programmatic environments relevant to administration of education policy. Table 1 describes the variation of these states on criteria identified as relevant to the issues addressed by the study.

The study relied on an examination of federal program requirements, documentary material from each state, and personal interviews with over three hundred individuals at the state and local levels. Within the states, interviews were conducted with state education agency officials and staff, legislators and their staff, interest group

Table 1 Study States' Variation Along Sampling Criteria

	First Tier						Second Tier
	State Support of General Education	Degree of State Fiscal Stress	Number & Magnitude of State Special Programs	Federal Aid as a % of Total Education Revenue	State Political Culture	Regional Location	State Policy Characteristics
California*	High	High	High	Low	Central	West	Pupil weighting; tax limitation (Prop. 13); Large state special needs programs
Louisiana*	High	Low	Medium	High	Local	South	Large rural population; large minority (Black) population; bilingual state
Massachusetts	Low	High	High	Medium	Local	Northeast	Pupil weighting; tax limitation (Prop. 2–1/2); large state special needs programs; few minorities
Missouri*	Low	High	Low	Medium	Local	Central	Urban/rural issues; low-profile SEA; private school bypass
New Mexico*	High	Low	Medium	High	Central	Southwest	Population growth; pupil weighting; non-participant in P.L. 94–142; large minority (Hispanic) population
New York*	Low	High	High	Low	Central	East	Pupil weighting; strong state role in education; large special needs population
Virginia	Low	Low	Low	Medium	Central	Southeast	Tradition of few public services; fiscal conservatism; modernization of state government; private school bypass
Wyoming*	Low	Low	Low	Low	Local	West	Very rural state; few minorities; strong local control state

*State also studied by SRI International's study—Cumulative Effects of Federal Education Policies in Schools and Districts.

representatives, local school administrators, teachers, and journalists who covered education. The wide spectrum of states and range of persons, coupled with the scope and intensity of the interviews, affirmed that the findings of the study could be generalized to apply to the fifty states.

2. Findings

Federal Requirements Imposed on the States

With respect to elementary and secondary education, the federal government has pursued two overarching objectives: the extension of civil rights protections, and the stimulation of particular programs and services to improve or expand educational opportunities available to all or subsets of the nation's children. Actions designed to extend civil rights protection largely have excluded any significant state role and instead have followed a path emphasizing regulatory relationships between the federal government and local service providers. In stimulating programs and services, (in contrast) the federal government has generally relied on financial assistance grants coupled with conditions on the use of funds. These grants typically involve considerable managerial oversight and reporting responsibilities for state education agencies (SEAs). Of course, exceptions to this general rule arise: P.L. 94–142 constitutes a blend of civil rights requirements embodied in a financial assistance program, and ESEA Title VII—the bilingual education grant program—makes only minor provision for the involvement of SEAs. Thus while many intervention strategies are available in addition to grants-in-aid and regulation for the pursuit of federal objectives (e.g., loans, loan guarantees, tax subsidies, government corporation, interest subsidies, insurance), federal actions in elementary and secondary education have rarely used these other techniques. This seemingly simple, bifurcated federal assistance and regulation role in elementary and secondary education is complicated by the fact that federal assistance grants and civil rights requirements differ significantly from each other. The six assistance grants examined in this study each embodied a separate strategy for state involvement that grew out of the unique history and purposes attached to the program. As a result, federal signals to the states in vocational education, for example, differ in important ways from those in compensatory education. No two assistance programs send absolutely identical signals to state officials, although some individual requirements like maintenance of effort can sound strikingly similar. Assistance programs vary in funding relationships they establish with states and locals (i.e., whether the federal government pays its own freight or leverages states and local revenues), the type of rules employed, and the management structure imposed (i.e., whether state is a funding recipient, an administrative agent, or bypassed altogether). Assistance programs differ noticeably in the way they are managed by federal officials. Some are tightly monitored through federal audit and compliance reviews; others are managed through inspections of state plans and data reported as a result of participation in the program. In contrast to this variety, civil rights requirements contain important distinctions for service delivery recipients[3] but send a fairly identical signal to the states: the states are not major instrumentalities of policy implementation. The bulk of federal efforts in the civil rights areas is directed at local agencies and service providers. Table 2 summarizes major structural differences characterizing the programs studied.

Looking up at the federal presence in education from the state perspective, one is struck by the uniqueness of each assistance grant program and the relative lack of federal bureaucratic impositions on states (as opposed to local agencies) in the field of civil rights. One is also taken by the history of federal disagreements and inconsistencies characteristic of specific programs; notably, ESEA Title I, Title VII, and vocational education. Title I and Vocational Education have received criticisms over the past five years for inconsistent administration. at the federal levels; Title VII and vocational education enjoy a history punctuated by shifting consensus about program objectives and the most appropriate means for accomplishing those objectives.

Surprisingly, discussions with state and local respondents did not trigger complaints about the number and variability of federal education programs operating in the states, although the officials who were interviewed did complain about the appropriateness of particular federal strategies. As will be noted later, state policymakers were eager to wade into the politically troublesome issues associated with civil rights enforcement (although this was less true of bilingual education). The relationship between federal legislative and administrative inconsistencies and state response was less obvious, an outcome attributable to the different strategies employed in the programs (e.g., bilingual education bypasses state administrators in most respects), the resolution of state problems over time (e.g., ESEA Title I has become less administratively controversial at the state level), and state forces that not only reflected but engulfed federal disagreements (e.g., vocational education is by and large a state-operated program).

Table 2 Legal Framework Choices by Statute

	TECHNICAL	FINANCIAL Grant Type		Type of Assistance FUNDING RELATIONSHIP			Regulation			Management Structure		
		Formula	Project	Full Federal	No Federal	Cost Shared	Program Rules	Nondis- crimination	Service Mandate	F-S-L	F-L	F-S
ESEA Title I Basic	X	X		X			X			X		
P.L. 94–142	X	X				X	X	X	X	X		
Vocational Education Act	X	X				X	X			X		
ESEA Title IV–B		X		X			X			X		
ESEA Title IV–C			X	X			X			X		
ESEA Title VII	X		X	X			X				X	
ESEA Title V		X		X			X					X
Title VI, CRA					X		X	X	X*		X	
Title IX, Education Amendments					X		X	X			X	
Section 504, RA					X		X	X	X		X	

Abbreviations:	ESEA	—	Elementary and Secondary Education Act
	P.L.	—	Public Law
	CRA	—	Civil Rights Act
	RA	—	Rehabilitation Act
	F	—	Federal
	S	—	State
	L	—	Local

*The *Lau* guidelines establish a service mandate for limited-English-proficient students.

Federal Education Programs:
Effects on the State Political and Institutional Environment

Federal programs can effect the state political environment and the institutions in two major ways. Some federal programs seek explicitly to improve the organizational capacities of state-level capacity to manage specific program mandates. Less direct federal influence may result from federal programs creating new constituencies or strengthening interest groups already there, thus causing a realignment of political power within a state.

The state political environment and the institutions are responsible for implementing them in two major ways. Some federal programs seek explicitly to improve the organizational capacities of state education agencies (e.g., ESEA Title V); others are less concerned about broad organizational improvements and aim at building state-level capacity to manage specific program mandates. Less direct federal influence may result from federal programs creating new constituencies or strengthening interest groups already there, thus causing a realignment of political power within a state.

The state political environment—while an important contextual factor in shaping state administrative responses to federal requirements—was not itself prominently influenced by the federal education programs studied. However, federal initiatives in some states played significant role in legitimizing state actions in equity areas. The state-level actors who shape state education policy beyond the state education agency were relatively untouched by federal programs per se. In spite of their newly assumed powers to reappropriate federal funds, most state legislators knew little about and paid minimal attention to federal education programs. A few governor's offices were not involved in federal education programs. Similarly, state boards of education were not major influences on federal programs.

In most states, interest groups for special populations targeted by federal programs appeared loosely organized, uncoordinated, and not consistently active in state level policy process. Some groups, however, (especially those supporting programs for the handicapped and occasionally groups supporting Hispanic programs) were capable of instituting pressure on state officials over specific issues of interest. Typically, however, interest group activity involving federal special needs programs or civil rights efforts was only sporadically in evidence in most state capitols.

On the other hand, federal influence on state education agencies was considerable. In combination with changing state education climates in the 1970s (i.e., increased state spending for education, state basic skills policies, and school finance reform), federal programs were quite influential in altering the size, staff, functions and support base of state education agencies. Compared to fifteen years earlier, these agencies had expanded significantly in size and complexity. Federal funds on the average supported 50% of the staff working in SEAs across the sample states. In general, current SEA staff are more diversified in background and skills. In contrast to an earlier emphasis on curricular expertise, SEA staff today spend most of their time in activities such as program monitoring, review, technical assistance, data collection and evaluation. As SEA functions and responsibility increased over the last fifteen years, there has been a shift toward greater SEA authority over school districts and the emergence of a more legalistic relationship between two levels.

The extent to which federal special needs policies are institutionalized in the states clearly varies from state to state and across federal programs, but program institutionalization at the state level appears limited for these programs that constitute the bulk of federal aid. There are several reasons for this. Uneven state initiatives for special needs students, limited state fiscal support of these efforts (except in special education), and sporadic interest group activity formed the basis of this judgement.

The strongest indicator of a state's commitment to a special needs program is the existence of a state mandate to serve special needs students. Table 3 identifies those states in the study with current service mandates for the major special needs groups. Handicapped students are protected by service mandates in all states. In three states these mandates preceded P.L. 94–142; in the remaining five, state laws "leveled up" to federal standards. This apparent strength of special education showed some signs of erosion, however. Respondents in all states predicted that if federal protections were removed, state laws would follow.

Groups other than the handicapped have had more spotty success at the state level. In four of the study states, advocates were able to build legislative coalitions that were strong enough to pass bilingual laws. Only three states in the sample had mandated remedial services, yet only two of these states (New York and California) maintained a large compensatory instruction program. With the exception of handicapped programs, state special needs funding levels were dwarfed by federal dollars within the state. Civil rights legislation in some form exists in all eight states but only two states (Massachusetts and New York) actively enforced these state policies.

Table 3 State Mandates of Services to Special Needs Populations

State	*Compensatory Education*	*Special Education*	*Bilingual Education*
California	Yes	Yes	Yes
Louisiana	Yes	Yes	Yes[1]
Massachusetts	No	Yes	Yes[2]
Missouri	No	Yes	No
New Mexico	No	Yes	No[3]
New York	Yes	Yes	No
Virginia	Yes	Yes	No
Wyoming	No	Yes	No

[1]A second-language program is mandated within any school in which 25% of the parents petition the Board of Education.

[2]In LEAS with twenty or more limited-English-speaking (LES) pupils per language group.

[3]However, the state constitution stipulates that the legislature is to provide training for teachers to become proficient in English and Spanish so that they may teach Spanish-speaking students.

Most respondents saw slim hope of passing state legislation analogous to federal special needs programs. While basic skills programs remain popular, fiscal pressures and a "different mood" in state legislatures were cited as impediments. As one chief state officer commented, "If we haven't had these programs here before, why should we expect to in the future?"

One observation merits noting. Because federal programs for special needs students have been in place for a number of years (with the exception of special education), advocates for these students have not needed to look to state governments for all of their support. If, as appears likely, federal education support continues to decrease, political activity related to special needs students at the state level presumably could increase. Based on an assessment of the state political and institutional environment, mounting such political efforts would be a tough uphill climb—particularly tough because of current fiscal limitations.

The Interaction of Federal and State Education Programs

As a whole, the study findings regarding federal and state program interactions portray a robust, diverse, and interdependent federal–state governance system. States do not passively administer federal education programs, nor are they reluctant to tackle educational agendas of their own—some of which reflect federal objectives, and others which do not. At the same time, federal program signals proved to be significant influences on states' actions with respect to management of federal programs and, in several instances, with respect to state programs. In contrast to a "senior partner and junior partner" depiction, federal growth and influence in education has been paralleled by the growth and influence of state government. This confirms a tendency noted by other scholars: The expansion of federal policymaking has expanded state responsibility and power as well.

State political traditions, political climate, and SEA priorities actively influenced the tradition of federal education programs and policies in the states studied. Because these state factors vary greatly across the states (particularly their contextual meanings), state administrative responses to the federal programs studied were quite diverse. For example, in one state, districts were free to adopt a variety of innovative designs in the ESEA Title I programs; in another, districts were restricted in their choice of instructional content and design. One state conducted considerable on-site compliance monitoring of P.L. 94–142; another state relied on off-site compliance review. These examples illustrate a few of the different ways states tailored federal programs to the state environment.

While state forces actively shaped federal programs and policies, federal program and policy signals also heavily influenced the course followed by the states. ESEA Title I and P.L. 94–142 programs retained considerable consistency from state to state in spite of individual state influences. Years of federal signals that have emphasized supplemental services and have targeted those services on educational disadvantagement, combined with the galvanizing force of federal audits, explain the marked congruency characteristic of Title I programs. Through its legal protections, service mandate, and requirement that state laws at a minimum follow federal law, P.L. 94–142 strongly influenced state administrative behavior. All of the states we visited altered their laws, regulations, or practices to comply with federal handicapped requirements. In spite of most states' discomfort with the new planning and set-aside requirements contained in the 1968 and 1976 vocational educational amendments, retaining federal dollars proved a powerful incentive for undertaking these functions in vocational education.

In addition to federal policy influence on state actions, there is a strong interplay between federal and state factors as they shape each state's administration of federal programs. The existence of state programs that address the educational needs of students as targeted by federal programs produces an even more dynamic situation in which federal and state programs influence each other's administrative direction. When state special needs programs were present, three patterns of administration emerged in the states studied: (1) isolation, when state programs were administratively and programmatically distinct from their federal counterparts; (2) coordination, when programs are similar in design or are planned to reinforce one another yet some distinctions (e.g., formula allocation) remain; and (3) integration, when the programs are administratively and fiscally indistinct.

Special education and the basic grants portion of the vocational education program resulted across the study states in integrated administration that treated state and federal programs as one. The federal 94–142 law's demand that state policy replicate federal policy largely ensured this outcome. In vocational education, the sixty-five years of discretion that states are allowed with respect to the basic grants program contributed to the integration of federal and state efforts. In contrast, the states studied administered the vocational education set-asides for special needs students and civil rights requirements in isolation from state education programs. Even in the two states that aggressively enforced state civil rights laws, federal and state efforts ran on separate tracks. State and federal bilingual education programs usually assumed a coordinated pattern of administration.

Administration of federal and state compensatory education programs varied across the states studied. Two states operated coordinated programs with three pursued courses of isolated, independent administration of federal and state programs. The less a program resembled the federal Title I program that emphasizes economic disadvantagement, and the more cautious a state was about not violating non-supplant requirements, the more likely it was that a state would isolate the administration of the two programs.

Aside from the direct administrative interactions occasioned by states' participation in federal education programs, a number of other problems are attributed to the current federal presence. Administrative problems frequently associated with federal programs—lack of coordination across programs, administrative burden, and a federal franchise in the states that countervails state policy—emerged in this study as complex issues that cannot simply be attributed to the operation of federal programs. While federal initiatives may be implicated to varying degrees in these problems, state programs' structures, administrative organization, and organizational incentives contributed substantially to these issues.

Because of the heavy federal subsidization of staff in federal programs, state official generally did not complain about the administrative burdens imposed by federal programs. Some officials did take exception to planning and reporting requirements in vocational education, but they acknowledged that these tasks were largely federally supported at the state level. In general, opinion at the state level did not indicate SEA administrative burden as a major source of dissatisfaction with federal involvement in education.

As just noted, vertical program coordination (between a federal and related state education program) was fairly evident across the states varied. Only the vocational education set-asides, civil rights activities, and some Title I programs were characterized by separate administration review procedures and by a more dramatic effort in California to coordinate a wide array of education programs as part of a policy emphasizing school-based improvements.

A state's effort to coordination programs, whether administratively or programmatically, are largely a function of the three broad factors that have been previously discussed—federal signals, state political traditions and climate, and SEA priorities. California's creation of a comprehensive philosophy to encompass all education programs that affect schools in an SEA priority that was facilitated by the state's political traditions and climate, which affirm strong state direction of education. The use of consolidated program application and review procedures appears to coincide with state and SEA policies to ensure that all districts and schools meet minimal program standards in a variety of areas. Federal fiscal requirements enforced through audit findings led some states to avoid vertical program coordination. Few state officials complained about coordination problems as an outgrowth of federal aid, however. Countervailing institutional pressures and other political priorities overshadowed these concerns at the same level.

Many observers have noted the significance of vertical networks in the implementation of federal programs (Derthick 1970; Hill 1979; Elmore and McLaughlin 1982). This study confirms that federal programs frequently are administered at the state level by fairly autonomous staff who form vertical networks, but it also suggests that these staff are cautious about maintaining fidelity to state priorities and political traditions. While federal program managers in the sample states were committed to federal goals and policies, they did not operate as a federal franchise that bypassed or undercut state policy. These managers had to be responsive to federal signals as well as state political and program priorities. In many states, federal program managers gained little capital by calling upon their federal program ties. As a result, they engaged in no overt attempts to redirect state policy decisions.

Finally, state conflicts with federal programs did not exhibit the intensity suggested by recent political rhetoric and by the various anecdotes that have come to the fore. Massive levels of tension between the states and the federal government did not materialize but some real conflicts were apparent, specifically in the areas of vocational education and special education. State conflicts in vocational education centered on the newer requirements regarding extensive planning, data collection, and set-asides for students with special needs. Special education conflicts focused on federal prescriptiveness, especially regarding due process procedures and the open-ended nature of requirements like related services. Both these areas of conflict represent federal requirements that are relatively new and that pressure states to alter existing program operations. In contrast, little state conflict was found with federal programs that gave states major discretion (ESEA Title IV) or that had existed for some time (ESEA Title I).

These findings may have resulted partially from new federal signals sent to the states through the Education Consolidation and Improvement Act (ECIA) of 1981 and through federal funding cuts in numerous federal education programs. Arguably, these changes may have altered officials' perceptions about conflict. But while state officials did convey a "wait and see" attitude toward these changes, they also reported that certain conflicts they had experienced with federal programs were reduced. In particular, they pointed to Title I provisions contained in the Education Amendments of 1978 that introduced flexibility for many states operating similar compensatory programs. Several SEA respondents feared that the ECIA 1981 revisions to Title I removed this flexibility.

The states handled their conflicts with federal policies and practices through the process of political bargaining, negotiation, and compromise. The more populous states exhibited a more assertive approach to influencing disagreeable federal requirements, yet all the states that were studied engaged in negotiations over state plans, audit exceptions, and criticism contained in program reviews. SEA officials in the sample states relied on state networks to inform them of discretionary leeway within programs and to raise common concerns about dealings with federal agencies. The flexibility added to the Education Amendments of 1978 with respect to the Title I program evolved from the pressure exerted by several states (most notably, California) to redefine the federal program's treatment of state programs. As a result, state Title I directors refer to the 1978 Education Amendments as the "Relief for California Act."

3. Conclusions and Policy Implications

The Status of the Intergovernmental System in Education

Based on these observations four major attributes mark the contemporary intergovernmental system of education:

- Both the states and federal government are strong actors in education.

- Federal and state policy priorities for the education of special needs students, while convergent.

- States have developed organizational capacities that surpass those of fifteen years ago, but these capacities remain partially dependent on federal dollars.

- While intergovernmental conflicts exist, they are neither massive nor common across all federal programs. Similarly, many state administrative problems are overstated and inaccurately ascribed to federal programs as their singular source.

These attributes are important for policymakers to ponder as they consider calls to maintain existing policies or proposals to develop new intergovernmental approaches in the field of education. Contrary to the dim assessments scholars made in 1965 about the states' abilities to manage federal programs, or the conventional zero-sum assumption that expanded federal actions have eviscerated state policymaking capacity, the states emerge today as vibrant entities in the intergovernmental system.

Yet in spite of this strengthened position, policymakers have little reason to expect that most states at this point will assume the equity agenda that defines much of the current federal roe in education. The lack of active political support for many of these programs and problematic fiscal conditions in many states suggests that building a strong base of political support for these purposes would take a great deal of effort. In addition, major reductions in federal support of SEA activities may leave the states not only unwilling but administratively unable to assume federal education programs.

Intergovernmental conflicts and administrative problems did exist across the states studied. However, the conflicts uncovered were most often derived from two programs; vocational education and special education. The usual administrative problems attributed to federal programs—lack of program coordination, administrative burden, and powerful federal franchise offices within state agencies—either became nonissues at the state level or proved to have more complications than just those stemming from federal program requirements. Readers should not infer that program coordination or unnecessary paperwork do not require policymakers' attention. The study concludes only that these issues are not perceived as major problems at the state level nor are they derived exclusively from federal sources.

Trade-Offs Among Federal Strategies

Decisions about existing and future federal activities in education require more than a current understanding of the intergovernmental system; they also require knowledge about the consequences of pursuing alternative strategies. Federal policymakers have a variety of strategic choices before them when designing and implementing a program or policy: whether to rely on regulation of financial assistance; how much decision-making latitude to allow states; whether to bypass states as administrative agencies; how to pursue oversight and enforcement of program requirements; and when to expect program results. All these choices require policymakers to weigh alternatives and assess expected benefits against the costs of pursuing particular strategies.

Based on this assessment of the state level impact of a range of federal program strategies, three broad propositions emerge:

- Federal actions can achieve a basic level of uniformity across the states, but they do so at the price of federal–state conflict. Time and the infusion of sizable amounts of federal money appear to mitigate this conflict.

  Strong federal requirements and oversight of state actions in response to those requirements (e.g., the ESEA Title I and P.L. 94–142 experiences) illustrate federal strategies that have resulted in relative program uniformity across the states. However, both strategies resulted in notable intergovernmental conflict. Time and a reliance on federal dollars to pay the costs of the program have allowed ESEA Title I to emerge today as relatively free for major conflict at the state level. The P.L. 94–142 strategy has not yet experienced the ameliorating benefits of time nor the infusion of federal dollars to cover most service costs. Consequently, the program continues to be a source of intergovernmental friction.

- Granting more decision-making discretion to the states results in wider program variations across the states. This strategy leads to little federal–state conflict because it subsidizes the support of state-selected initiatives. While a low level of conflict is often desirable, wide variations may be undesirable, if federal and state priorities do not converge.

  The basic grants portion of the vocational education program (as distinct from the special needs set-asides) and ESEA Titles IV and V varied markedly in their implementation across the states studies. These programs were uniformly popular and (with the recent exception of vocational education) have produced little conflict at the state level. But the new components of the vocational education program (the planning and reporting requirements and the set-asides) have caused considerable conflict. These components were instituted as a result of federal policymakers' dissatisfaction with the lack of state and local vocational efforts to address broader issues of appropriate occupational training and the inclusion of disadvantaged or handicapped youth in vocational programs. In short, federal and state priorities did not converge. Hence, policymakers shifted the program away from its original broad discretion engendering significant conflict in the process.

- Federal actions that bypass state-level administrative structures do not foster state efforts to address federal program objectives except those states where the political environment is receptive to such actions.

    ESEA Title VII and the civil rights programs—both embodying strategies that call for minimal state action—yielded similar state outcomes. The states in the study participated in these policy areas only when state factors (political climate and SEA priorities) spawned similar programs at the same level. The federal programs legitimized some of these state actions, but in the absence of a favorable political climate they resulted in inaction at the state level. Not surprisingly, federal strategies bypassing the states have led to minimal administrative conflict between the states and the federal government.

Implications for Proposals to Improve Federal Education Policy

The debate over the proper balance between federal accountability and state and local discretion has produced numerous prescriptions for improving federal policy. While the prescription of new directions for federal involvement exceeded the bounds of this inquiry, the research is relevant to four broad alternative policies recently advanced:

- consolidation of major programs into block grants;

- streamlining federal requirements;

- reformatting the design of current programs;

- formalizing federal differential treatment of the states.

Each of these broad categories embraces a range of more precise proposals to alter federal education programs.[4] Because the alternatives are so numerous and vary significantly in their precise formulation, this discussion of policy implications focuses only on the general assumptions and directions associated with each broad category.

Consolidation of Major Programs into Block Grants

Distinguishing block grants from categorical grants is more difficult than it appears. Hastings (1982: p. 330) notes the following:

> Block grant recipients must usually comply with some administrative, planning, and fiscal reporting requirements, as well as with various non-discrimination and environmental standards set by the federal government. On the other hand, many categorical grants allow recipients considerable discretion in program design and administration.

The block grants currently discussed with respect to future education policy typically involve clustering existing categorical programs together (ESEA Title I and ESEA Title VII, for instance) and increasing the discretion available to state or local authorities. The definition with which state and local authorities (SEAs, state legislators, state boards or governors) would wield this newly delegated authority would depend on the specific proposal under consideration.

The findings reported here indicate that increased state discretion will result in greater variation in the way programs are designed and implemented. In areas where federal objectives strive to promote more uniform treatment of special needs students, block grants are likely to prove counterproductive. The inclusion of new actors in federal program determinations will also constitute a significant departure from current program operations. State policymakers outside SEAs did not evidence widespread knowledge about existing federal programs in the states studied. Were they to become major decision makers in the future, they would be starting from a considerably different point than most SEA officials do.

Streamlining Federal Requirements

Proposals to streamline federal requirements run the gamut from deregulating federal programs[5] (and hence expanding state and local discretion) to clearing away unnecessary, ineffective, or costly requirements.[6] Given this breadth, it is difficult to capture adequately the major thrust of the streamlining approach. Nevertheless, most proposals fall within the general set of options normally associated with the ongoing bargaining and negotiation processes characteristic of the intergovernmental system.

The findings discussed in this article cannot address the issue of which federal requirements are unnecessary, ineffective, or costly relative to the benefits they provided, but they do have implications for other considerations involved in streamlining federal programs. As previously noted in considering the block grant approach, increasing the discretion of state officials (a frequent component of deregulation) is likely to decrease the uniformity of federal education programs across the states.

Not all streamlining proposals intent on increasing discretion would necessarily do so, however. State officials' initial responses to Chapters 1 and 2 of the Education Consolidation and Improvement Act are instructive. The officials interviewed in the course of this study believed they had lost valuable flexibility in the Chapter 1 (formerly Title I) program; moreover, they distrusted the program latitude allowed in the new Chapter 2 program. These responses raise two considerations for policymakers considering streamlining proposals. First, immediate removal of requirements by the federal government constitutes only one signal among many. State authorities wait to view the cumulative meaning of federal signals to weigh their significance. Streamlined programs may not attain the desired discretion for several years. Second, streamlining federal requirements can remove details that decrease the vagueness and ambiguity of federal signals. While several state respondents railed against federal prescriptiveness in vocational education and P.L. 94–142, they were equally disturbed by fuzzy, ambiguous, and incomplete signals. State officials seek definition and clarity (and thus more detail) almost as much as they do the removal of federal requirements.

Reformulating the Design of Federal Education Programs

The prescriptions falling within this category of reform proposals range even more widely than do those included in the streamlining category. They include proposals to alter the mix of federal compliance and assistance techniques (Elmore and McLaughlin 1981), ideas to restructure the incentives contained in federal programs (Hargrove 1981), and notions to incorporate school-level plans as alternative accountability mechanisms (Turnbull et al. 1981). While proposals vary, they share a common trait: the formulation of more effective policy instruments to achieve existing goals and objectives. The reformation approach is at heart a tinkering approach to federal education programs. Like streamlining, tinkering is a common technique in the federal–state bargaining and negotiation process.

The information collected as part of the research reported here cannot identify which incentives are more effective or which combination of compliance of assistance would generate desired improvements in services for special student populations. The findings do suggest, however, that federal enforcement mechanisms (fiscal audits in Title I and compliance reviews in P.L. 94–142) were quite influential in shaping state administrative behavior. It is important to note that these mechanisms did not operate alone; they were coupled with the long evolutionary program history of Title I, and in P.L. 94–142 they were linked to mandates. These observations underscore the importance of assessing the mix of signals attached to program goals. Individual signal alterations are likely to become meaningless or confusing.

For the intergovernmental system to function, one must expect tinkering and realignment of signals. Policymakers should be aware, however, that a shift in signals usually produces intergovernmental conflict because operating assumptions and routines must be altered. Relatedly, state response will not be automatic. Reformations of federal strategies, once decided upon, will take time to show their impact.

Differential Treatment of States

In many respects differential treatment could be categorized as a proposal to reformulate existing federal education policy designs. But because of the attention it has received, this discussion treats it as a distinct proposal category. Differential treatment has emerged since the 1960s as a means of tailoring federal policies to the different political, fiscal, economic, and cultural realities in which the states must implement federal education policies. Because federal policies are designed largely to catch the bad apples, all states are reduced to a lowest common denominator. Hence, federal policy fails to bring out the best in states. The ideas put forth to date as a means of achieving differential treatment include alternative customized monitoring and compliance strategies, financial incentives in the form of bonuses, waivers, and bypass arrangements for unresponsive state governments, and the adjustment of federal requirements for states that either exceed or fail to meet the mandated standards of performance (Murphy 1981).

As observers have noted, federal education policies already incorporate some different treatment mechanisms; (examples are Title I's incentive grants, P.L. 94–142's non-supplant waiver, bypass arrangements for states prohibiting aid to private school, and funds allocation criteria that attempt to adjust relative need (Murphy 1981). In addition, although government officials will disavow differential treatment publicly, federal political appointees and program managers informally inject levels of different treatment into their day-to-day functions.[7]

The major debate regarding future differential treatment designs

concerns their feasibility more than their desirability. Differential treatment proposals that base their operation on some determination of
how faithfully or successfully states are meeting national goals and
objectives typically run afoul of three interrelated issues: (1) gaining
political consensus to enact the proposal; (2) arriving at clear and
objective criteria for judging state performance; and (3) implementing
policies bureaucratically. As a result, differential treatment proposals
trigger a set of challenging questions. For example, how does one
know a state has achieved minimum standards? What are those standards? Who will judge state performance? In spite of these challenges,
some analysts have offered differential treatment schemes designed to
tailor federal interventions to the unique capacities and political conditions in the states.[8]

This chapter cannot resolve the questions that surround differential treatment proposals but the findings presented add perspective to
some dimensions of the debate. First, instances of informal differential
treatment in the administration of the federal education programs
studied were evident. Federal auditors investigating ESEA Title I visited some states significantly more than others. California officials
explained that they were audited for compliance more frequently
because of their high visibility and their parallel state programs. Consequently, federal policymakers already adjust their techniques to differences among the states.

Inquiries into state programs for special populations also raised
considerations about the extent to which federal policy could formalize
these informal administrative actions. Defining programs at the state
level is not easy. State programs (like their federal counterparts) are a
blend of legal provisions, goal statements, and administrative render-
ings. As a result, some legal provisions are never translated into action.
Local control traditions limit states from mounting administrative efforts
to monitor and oversee district compliance with state rules and requirements. These observations suggest that proposals to assess states' performance face serious technical difficulties in defining and assessing
minimal state performance.

Likewise, the political feasibility of differential treatment entails
casting a wide enough net through the proposed policy to interest sufficient numbers of Congressmen to vote for it; in other words, enough
states must believe they would benefit from the new policy. The priorities in the greater number of states studied did not fully converge with
federal priorities. While a changed federal strategy would almost certainly present the states with different cost-benefits trade-offs, the few
voluntarily adopted state programs with strong similarities to related

federal programs cast doubt on the political feasibility of most proposals for differential treatment unless minimal federal requirements in these programs are reduced considerably.

Final Considerations:
Federalism and the Tensions Associated with Expanded Government

These findings from an empirical investigation into federal–state interactions surrounding a broad array of federal education programs offer a relatively sanguine view of federal involvement in education— quite different from former Superintendent Cronin's prediction of "federal takeover" (1976: pp. 2–3). In 1982 the states did not appear to have lost their sphere of influence; in fact, in several respects they appear to have expanded it. States showed both the capacity for and commitment to tailoring federal programs to their respective environments and to pressing for modification in federal policies they found disagreeable and/or dysfunctional. From the federal perspective, federal policy choices clearly influence state behavior, and federal policymakers can rest assured that the states have grown accustomed to a federal presence in education. Intergovernment conflicts exist, but for the most part they are channeled and do not work to destabilize administrative operations.

Are these findings accurate portrayals of the federal–state relationship?[9] Empirical information is only as good as the sample it draws from, and the long range relevance of the time period is the study. The sample states used to derive these finding cover an extraordinarily broad spectrum of states in the nation. Moreover, the one failing of the sample—its failure to reflect the most depressed state economies in the spring of 1982—is in many respects a stabilizing force lending credibility to the study's long-term assessments regarding federal and state program interactions. Most analysts concur that state economies will gradually improve as the national economy rebounds.

The time frame surrounding the research may be more problematic. Data collection occurred in the spring of 1982—a transition period in which new federal block grant legislation (ECIA Chapter 2) was just being implemented, additional block grants were under discussion, and federal officials were promising deregulation in special education and other areas. Both federal and states officials were uncertain about which federal requirements would remain in force. These winds of change may have influenced state officials' views about federal actions. Clearly, the expected loss of federal funds in state agencies became a reality more than ever before. But while impending change may inspire nostalgia for retaining past procedures, it can also expose a deeper reality beyond the posturing and negotiating that forms much of the style and substance of intergovernmental relations. The spring of 1982 may have provided an opportunity to see federal–state issues more clearly. Only addition research can ascertain the answer.

If these findings are corroborated by other research, they raise a fundamental question about how to interpret the current (and possibly the past) debate about federalism. The absence of strong federal–state conflict and administrative problems stands in stark contrast with conventional wisdom and public attitudes. While those attitudes may be dated and not reflect the intergovernmental state of affairs that exists today, they also are likely to reflect a related yet significantly different dilemma: individual tensions associated with government expansion and prominence in daily life. These tensions may explain more about the current federalism debate than claims about administrative inefficiencies and federal dominance.

Chapter 6

Cumulative Effects of
Federal Education Policies at the Local Level*

*Michael S. Knapp, Marian S. Stearns,
Brenda J. Turnbull, Jane L. David,
and Susan M. Peterson*

This chapter presents findings and conclusions from a study that examined the cumulative effects of a number of federal categorical programs and related civil rights mandates on schools and school districts. The federal laws share the broad purpose of improving the educational opportunities for target groups of children and youth, although they vary in their more specific aims and provisions. The study was one of several supported by the School Finance Project, a research effort mandated by Congress in 1978[1] during a period of policy interest in school finance reform and equality of educational opportunity.

In particular, we investigated the influences of the following:

- Title I of the Elementary and Secondary Act (ESEA) of 1965, (now Chapter 1 of the Education Consolidation and Improvement Act of 1981);

- P.L. 94–142, The Education for All Handicapped Children Act of 1975;

- ESEA Title VII, the Bilingual Education Act of 1968;

---

*An earlier version of this chapter was published by Michael S. Knapp, et al., "Cumulative Effects at the Local Level," *Education and Urban Society,* vol. 15, no. 4, August 1983, pp. 479–499. Copyright by Sage Publications, Inc. Reprinted by permission of Sage Publications, Inc.

- The 1968 amendments to the Vocational Education Act (VEA), the set-aside provisions for the handicapped and disadvantaged; and

- Civil rights laws, in particular Title VI of the Civil Rights Act of 1964, Title IX of the Education Amendments of 1972, and Section 504 of the Rehabilitation Act of 1973.

Where parallel laws or programs existed at the state level, they, too, were included in the scope of research. Other laws that directly or indirectly target resources to special populations—the Indochina Refugee Children Assistance Act, the Indian Education Act, and the Emergency School Aid Assistance Act (ESAA)—were included, but played a less central role in the study. The Education Consolidation and Improvement Act of 1981—which subsumes and amends Title 1 (ESEA), and which combines ESAA and a host of smaller categorical programs into a block grant distributed to all districts—was not in effect at the time of the fieldwork. Local personnel were anticipating its implementation, however, and responses to it were reported where they were pertinent to the study's findings.

The study was designed to assess the collective impact of these laws on the following: students' access to instructional services within elementary and secondary schools; the organization and administration of schools and districts; and local decision making. It sought to understand—from the local perspective—what difference the full array of federal policies made to schools and to districts as these policies accumulated over time and as they interacted with each other and with local programs. Ultimately, the aim was to understand, in broad qualitative terms, the costs, benefits, and associated trade-offs of the federal programs and mandates as perceived by local educators.

It should be mentioned here what the study did not do. It did not assess the implementation of each of the programs studied; instead, it looked for the broader effects attributable to the sum total of many programs and mandates operating over time. Nor did it look at the effects of programs and mandates on student achievement outcomes. Interviewees sometimes cited test scores as evidence of program benefits, but this was not a systematic focus of the inquiry. In the context of current interest in improving the quality of schools, readers might also assume that the study addressed the question of whether the caliber of our nation's schools has improved. It did not. The concern embodied in the laws studied was that certain groups were deprived of educational opportunities; the study examined the effects—intended and unintended—of federal efforts to improve that situation.

1. Study Focus and Approach

Topics for Research

Educators, policymakers, and the research community have debated various issues about targeted categorical aid and service mandates since the inception of these policies. In recent years, concern has coalesced in six areas that imply or raise questions about federal policy effects at the local level:

- Instructional services for target students: Are the services considered appropriate? Are they reaching the intended targets?

- Fragmentation versus coordination of instruction: Is there a problem? How has it been addressed?

- Influences on the regular classroom and core instructional program: Do the services provided for target students influence the regular classroom or detract from the resources available for other students?

- Systematic approaches to instructional management: Do school and district staff assess needs, plan programs for individual students, or evaluate results more systematically? How elaborate are the procedures they use? How useful?

- Administrative burden: Have the requirements and administrative details of special programs hindered local professionals or detracted from instructional time?

- Local decision making: Has local discretion been reduced? Has power shifted within districts?

Numerous criticisms have been leveled at the structure of categorical programs and mandates, accompanied by calls for diverse reforms—elimination of federal education laws, consolidation or deregulation of programs, or the transformation of categorical programs into undifferentiated block grants.[2] The purpose of the study was to improve the base of information related to such proposals by exploring the asserted "negative" and "positive" influences of federal programs.

Conceptual Framework

In order to examine these topics, the study required both a definition of "cumulative effects," and an explanatory model that could do the following:

- Connect federal causes (policy actions at the "top" of the intergovernmental system") with local effects (school and district responses to policy action at the "base" of the system).

- Identify the areas of local activity that are most likely to be influenced by federal action.

- Display the various kinds of contextual factors that help to explain observed effects at the local level.

Cumulative Effects. The term "cumulative effects" was defined as the responses districts and schools have made to the array of federal and state targeted categorical programs and related mandates that affect them. These factors or responses are cumulative across three dimensions: time, levels of government, and programs. The cumulative impact over time is reflected in current practices, which are the result of an eighteen-year history of growth in government resources and regulation. The passage of time has also permitted people in districts and schools to develop routines that accommodate government initiatives in various ways. Across levels of government, federal programs and policies have inspired in varying degrees a complementary array of programs and policies at the state educational agency level; in turn, districts have reinterpreted this combined array to schools, often adding resources or restrictions in the process. Each level of government displays the cumulative effects of higher-level action, and these contribute to further cumulative effects at lower levels.

Effects accumulate across programs in additive and interactive ways. The presence of more than one categorical program may add to the resources of the school district, the services available to students, and the types of staff present in the school building; multiple programs may also add to paperwork or to the number of advisory meetings a principal must attend. In this sense, the cumulative effects of multiple programs and mandates are like those of individual programs but differ from them in degree. Interactive effects may take place as well. One program's purposes or requirements can conflict with another's and thus lead to local confusion and inaction. The lack of funds for one mandate can mean that the resources of another program are diverted to cover both; however, the presence of one program may also enhance the chance that another's goals will be achieved.

Explanatory Model. A schematic diagram of the conceptual model for the study is shown in Figure 1. The school, at the base of the intergovernmental system, serves students with and without special learning needs. The core instructional program is given to all students

Figure 1 Conceptual Model

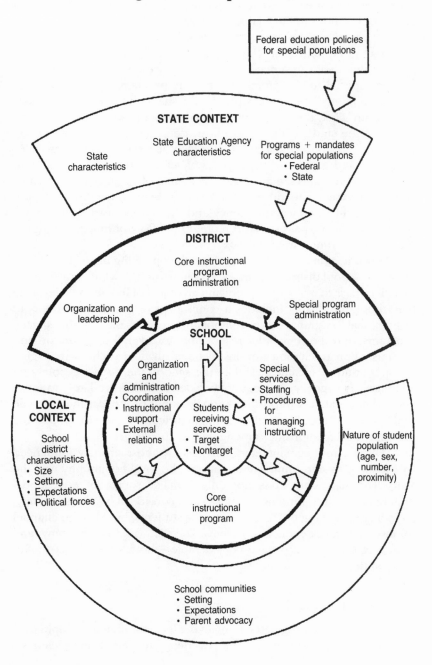

Federal education policies for special populations

STATE CONTEXT

State characteristics

State Education Agency characteristics

Programs + mandates for special populations
• Federal
• State

DISTRICT

Core instructional program administration

Organization and leadership

Special program administration

SCHOOL

Organization and administration
• Coordination
• Instructional support
• External relations

Special services
• Staffing
• Procedures for managing instruction

Students receiving services
• Target
• Nontarget

LOCAL CONTEXT

School district characteristics
• Size
• Setting
• Expectations
• Political forces

Nature of student population (age, sex, number, proximity)

Core instructional program

School communities
• Setting
• Expectations
• Parent advocacy

(except those with the most severe learning problems, whose core program is entirely specialized and separate). Special instructional services of various kinds are available to students with identified learning needs. Federal policies are most likely to influence the identification of the target group(s), the staffing and procedures of the specialized programs (and their presence in the first place), and the connection between specialized programs and the core program.

Two immediate contexts powerfully shape the school instructional program. First, the community served by the school determines the nature of the student body and places demands and expectations on the school. Second, the school district office sets policies, provides resources, and governs many aspects of school life. More distant contexts (regional, state) are an additional source of resources, constraints, and expectations. Federal policies reach the school, for the most part, through the state education agency and the school district; they interpret requirements, pass on (and redirect) the flow of funds, and monitor how these funds are used.

Since it is one level removed from the operating instructional program, the school district is both the medium through which government initiatives pass to reach the school and an object of federal policies. Like the school, the district includes a component responsible for the core instructional program, other components responsible for the special programs, and the remainder responsible for overall organization and administration (including non-instructional matters such as managing transportation or facilities). Unlike the school, the district is solely an administrative agency; consequently, federal policies are likely to influence administrative staff positions and the kinds of services they provide to the schools (e.g., materials, training, curricular supervision), and the organizational relationships among units in the district office.

District arrangements and activities are most strongly influenced by forces in its two immediate contexts: the local community and the state. The state context is not only a major source of educational requirements and funding (which vary considerably across states), including those targeted to special needs students, but also the channel for most federal categorical programs. The demography, economy, and setting of the state also have considerable—though less direct—influence on the school and district.

Methods and Sample

The study investigated cumulative effects through a multiple case design in a sample of twenty school districts across eight states.[3] Guided by the research topics described above, the data were collected primarily through focused, open-ended interviews with a variety of respondents at school and district levels. Data were systematically analyzed through a two-stage process: the first stage yielded case reports on each individual site and the second analyzed patterns across all sites.

The study selected districts and schools within them to maximize variation on the factors that were likely to influence the cumulative effects of targeted federal policies. States varied on the number and type of state categorical programs and related mandates aimed at special needs students, the relationship between the state education agency and school districts, and state wealth and demography. Within these states, districts were selected so that they varied in size and setting, concentration and diversity of special needs students, number and type of categorical programs, fiscal strength, leadership style, and orientation toward special populations. Within each district, two to five elementary schools were chosen and one or two high schools, depending on the size of the district. Altogether, the sample included fifty-six elementary and twenty-five high schools. Schools were not chosen to represent the full range of conditions within their respective districts, but rather the types of situations federal policies would be most likely to influence—that is, schools ranged from those with at least some students from one or more target groups to those with heavy, diverse concentrations of these students.

2. Findings in Review

This review of findings emphasizes general tendencies across sites. While numerous variations and exceptions occurred (and have been noted where especially important), there were many consistent patterns, despite the wide range of conditions across the study sample. The reader is referred to the full report (Knapp et al. 1983) for more detail on the exceptions to the general patterns reported below.

Instructional Services for Target Students

The study found that students who were intended to benefit from federal programs and mandates generally did receive special services in some degree tailored to their individual needs. The services were most often provided by staff who were specifically trained to handle the target students' learning needs and who could not (or would not) have been hired without federal funds and targeting requirements.

With few exceptions, teachers and administrators said these services were more appropriate than the instruction the students would
have received in the absence of any federal intervention. Where there
were negative comments about the special services, they reflected the
judgement of individual teachers or administrators that particular special staff were not competent, that program entry or exit requirements
were inflexible, or that the design of the instruction was inappropriate
(for example, bilingual education drew some philosophical criticism).

Students commonly spent time outside their regular classrooms in
order to receive special instruction. According to some educational
philosophies, this is undesirable at face level. However, many respondents suggested that classroom instruction often does not meet students'
needs. Missing "regular reading" to go to a pull-out class often means
missing little because the regular class is far beyond the target student's
achievement level. It was generally thought that participation in the regular classroom all day long is more likely to confuse and frustrate a student with special needs than to convey an instructional experience.

Most people interviewed insisted—and apparently believed—that
their schools were providing supplementary instruction for target students that is "over and above" the regular program. In a strictly logical
sense, this is untrue. A student who is pulled out for special instruction
always misses something, even if it is only recess. However, most classroom teachers indicated that the target students were receiving something extra and worthwhile in their pull-out classes.

The study also found that special services were targeted—that is,
they serve the students they were supposed to serve and not spread
around to all students. People in all districts and schools said that other
students could benefit from special resources also, but they usually
obeyed the requirements that define target categories of students.

Instructional Fragmentation Versus Coordination

Data collectors looked for evidence to determine if the
instructional programs offered to target students were or were not fragmented—that is, whether learning was impeded because students suffer interruptions of the school day (e.g., by attending pull-out classes)
or were taught by different methods. In many districts and schools this
had been a major problem. The great majority of these districts and
schools, however, had taken steps to address the problem. They had
limited interruptions of the classroom program (including local activities such as band practice) and had simplified school schedules so that
the comings and goings for each classroom were minimized. Indeed, in

their desire to reduce fragmentation they often limited the special instructional services that students could receive, even though the students may be entitled to more.

Schools and districts also addressed the problem of fragmentation by coordinating the content of the instruction offered under different programs. Classroom teachers were often given the responsibility of orchestrating special services (for example, by specifying what skills a particular child should work on each week). Specialist teachers are encouraged by their program directors to stay in close touch with classroom teachers. Partially as a result of these efforts, classroom teachers' sense of responsibility for target students seemed generally undiminished by the presence of specialists.

At an organizational level, the study examined the influence of federal policies on "administrative fragmentation," which is often asserted to contribute to problems of instructional coordination. It found that the presence of staff with different class loads and instructional approaches initially increased the potential for misunderstanding and conflict among school staff. However, in most cases these issues had been worked out over time. At the district level, federal policies had been partly responsible for administrative structures in which separate units or people oversee segments of the instructional program. Interdivision relationships were complicated by this fact, but the level of rivalry and friction was relatively low. There was little evidence of an adverse impact of district organizational arrangements on school functioning. Once again, at both school and district levels, there was evidence across all types of sites that local efforts to combat problems of administrative fragmentation had reduced these problems to a manageable level.

These efforts had not been successful everywhere. In some schools, no one had taken much initiative to coordinate services. "Turf" jealousies at the district level had sometimes impeded coordination. Where they occured, schoolwide morale problems had made the initial frictions between special and core staff difficult to resolve. However, instances of persistent fragmentation are exceptions to a more general rule: solving the problems associated with special services is largely a matter of local leadership, resolve, and time.

Effects on the Regular Classroom and the Core Instructional Program

Also investigated were the unintended effects of federal programs and mandates on the core instructional program of schools and districts: do nontarget students suffer interruption or impoverishment of their program, or was it enhanced? For the most part, few substantial effects of either sort were found. Although nontarget students may be distracted from their work by the comings and goings of classmates served in pull-out classes, teachers reported that the disruption was minimal once the scheduling routines had been worked out. Some classroom teachers lost instructional time due to matters related to special services (e.g., special education placement meetings), but this was not considered to be a major problem. A number of classroom teachers noted also that they gave more attention to nontarget students when the "difficult to teach" were out of the room. The presence of specialized staff and materials sometimes produced spillover benefits for nontarget students, but this seemed minimal due to widespread compliance with the federal targeting requirements.

There were hints, however, of more pervasive and longterm forms of beneficial spillover as well as more serious negative effects. In some sites new ideas and practices had been first introduced through federal programs. On the other hand, in districts where strong state enforcement of service mandates coincided with fiscal strains, some evidence suggests that the regular program budget had suffered. District officials in these states acknowledged that they were making some cutbacks in services for non-target students—such as a small increase in class sizes; in these cases, federal and state mandates had forced trade-offs among groups of students.

Systematic Approaches to Instructional Planning and Management

Many federal laws specify procedures for planning, needs assessment, and evaluation. These are intended to stimulate systematic thinking and accountability at the local level, with an ultimate result of more individually appropriate services for students. The study found that the use of systematic procedures had indeed increased over time. Programs for individual students in all target groups were developed with the aid of formalized procedures (such as tests, assessments, and meetings).

The overall management of special services at the district level was similarly marked by systematic planning, program evaluations, and needs assessments. Although not all districts implemented these procedures with equal zeal, all types of districts that were visited for the study used them to some degree. While it was not possible to judge whether students benefited from this state of affairs, many school and district staff (especially the managers of special programs) asserted that they did.

Respondents disagreed about the educational merit of systematic approaches or their usefulness in local program management. Proponents noted that systematic assessment and placement procedures got the "right" students into special services. Critics cited logistical problems (e.g., delays in handling referral for special services) as evidence. Nonetheless, there seemed to be a widespread feeling that systematic procedures of some sort represent good professional practice—a trend in the way people think about education that the federal role appears to have reinforced.

It seems unlikely that instructional management at either the student or district level would be approached as systematically in the absence of the federal role. People in schools and districts viewed many of these systematic procedures as devices for accountability to distant authorities in Washington and state capitals. Most of them accepted the need for such accountability as a condition for receiving outside funds.

Administrative Burden

Closely related to planning and management procedures is the issue of administrative burden—paperwork, extra meetings, and other administrative chores. Special attention was given to chores that took up the time of key core program staff (principals, classroom teachers, directors of curriculum). Although it is clear that special services have generated a great deal of administrative detail and some sense of burden, fewer complaints than had been expected were heard.

The people who deal with the administrative detail tend to be those whose salaries were paid out of special program funds—especially program managers in the district office, and teaching specialists or aides in the school. In all but the smallest districts, such people handled most of the administrative chores related to federal and state programs, thus minimizing the burden on classroom teachers and principals. Few of the core staff interviewed said that they resent the administrative burden related to special programs; they felt instead that the outside funds were adequate to cover the work. The instances of serious burden seemed restricted to particular roles and situations: locally paid counselors who take on special education management unwillingly; schools in which the principal has no "extra pair of hands" to help with the administrative detail; hard-pressed districts facing major, nonroutine challenges attributable to federal policies (e.g., desegregation).

The study found that most of the burden associated with any particular law seems to diminish drastically after the first year or two of the law's implementation. For example, teachers and administrators could remember their early struggles with individualized educational programs (IEPs) for the handicapped, but in only a few cases did they still find these plans burdensome. Familiarity had made the requirements seem less formidable, and district staff had routinized and streamlined the work that was involved.

Local Decision-Making

Despite the assertions of conventional wisdom that categorical programs and mandates "tie the hands" of local decision-makers, a more complicated picture emerged. It does not make sense to look at effects on something called local discretion because school districts contain varying interests and viewpoints—some of which are strengthened by federal requirements.

Local staff who take the role of advocate for target students gained power—often because service mandates and civil rights laws gave them legal backing and because their detailed knowledge of federal requirements strengthened their hand in local policy debates. District staff members had, in general, gained power over what goes on in schools because they have authority to oversee compliance with outside requirements. However, principals' discretion had increased, too, because their school programs had become more complicated; outside resources and special services increased the number of matters on which a principal could make decisions. In a similar way, the occasions for educators at all levels of the system to exercise discretion had multiplied as the complexity of the instructional program has grown.

Few, if any, community members who speak for target students had gained a foothold in district or school decision making. Parents of handicapped students have leverage because of the service mandate and due process requirements, and some of them use this leverage very effectively. Advisory councils, however, have very little access to decision making.

3. Conclusions and Policy Implications

Across these findings, three general conclusions emerge that have important implications for federal policy:

- Collectively, federal and state policies for special populations substantially improved and expanded the array of educational services for the intended target students.

- These policies increased the structural complexity of schools and districts, and thus appears to represent a necessary consequence of providing targeted services.

- Over time, local problem solving, federal and state policy adjustments, and gradual local accommodation generally reduced to a
  manageable level the costs associated with special services.

Each of these reflects a major cumulative effect of federal policy. The
reasons for these effects—including state and local actions and general
professional trends as well as federal actions—are discussed below.
Finally, we point out why the effects are important to policymakers.

Change in the Array of Local Educational Services

Federal programs and mandates for target students were
translated into educational services that, by and large, were perceived
as appropriate and targeted on the right students. In all type of districts
and schools, educators indicated that federal resources had permitted
them to offer more and better services to the wide range of students
that fall into one or another target group. They reported that federal
requirements had increased the concentration of resources on special
needs students and had helped reduce discrimination against such students. Moreover, the presence of multiple federal and state programs
had increased the total pool of resources to work with. While these
changes had not been equally extensive in every district and school,
the direction of the changes was consistent across the sample sites.

Together, the federal and state initiatives for special populations
present local educators with an accumulation of options that apply to
large numbers of students. In districts heavily impacted by poverty and
diverse needs, the expansion in educational services affects most students; in other districts, varying proportions benefit. In short, the
effects described above add up to a considerable expansion of instructional capabilities at the local level.

Many federal and state actions work together to bring about the
change discussed here. Although efforts were made to distinguish the
effects of specific program provisions, this effort was not fruitful. There
do not seem to be particular federal requirements that achieve their
aims more consistently than others. Instead, the important local effects
of federal policy appear to stem from the combination of many federal
and state policy tools, including funds, goal statements, program
requirements, and sanctions. These tools operate as follows:

- The funds available under categorical programs pay for a large share
  of the special staff and materials that serve target students. Funds
  also provide federal leverage for a more subtle reason. Local administrators and teachers, feeling that they have made a bargain with the

federal government, comply with rules because compliance is what Washington expects in exchange for its money.

- Federal statements of purpose have a profound effect on schools and districts. The mere existence of a federal law draws attention to an area of educational need and helps to mobilize the local supporters of the law's purpose, notably the local advocates for target groups.

- Federal requirements communicate what types of local practices are or are not acceptable. The specific practices developed to comply with requirements vary among states and districts because they reflect varying interpretations developed by administrators at those levels. However, there was ample evidence that most districts and schools would spread their resources more thinly and allocate more resources to "average" and gifted students, if it were not for the prohibitions conveyed by the federal requirements.

- The existence of sanctions strongly reinforces the effects of the other policy tools. The prospect of a visit from auditors—let alone an audit exception—exerts powerful leverage on local behavior.

Some readers may be surprised by the magnitude and consistency of the effects of federal policy found in this study. A decade or so of research on program implementation has created skepticism about whether federal programs can possibly have their intended effects at the local level. There appear to be three explanations for the apparent discrepancy between this study's findings and the implementation literature: the nature of the questions the study set out to answer; the nature of the programs studied; and the time frame for the research.

The research questions focused on broad effects, with relatively little attention to the details of local practice in each program. Had the study looked at the way each program provision was carried out (as implementation studies of single programs have done) there would have been far more variability at the state, district, and school levels. There certainly would have been variability in the answers to questions like, "How is the Title 1 target population defined?" or "What does an IEP look like?" However, the much broader changes attributable to federal programs—such as the existence of increased specialized instruction for target students—were consistent across the sample sites.

The second reason for the strong and consistent effects that were found has to do with the programs studied. Some important implementation studies have dealt with programs that accorded a great deal of discretion to local participants (e.g., Berman and McLaughlin 1978; Farrar et al. 1980; Pressman and Wildavsky 1973). The "Change Agent" study

(Berman and McLaughlin 1978), often cited as evidence that federal programs have weak and variable local effects, dealt with programs that involved very limited federal rules and monitoring. The programs and mandates considered in this study, however, have been designed and administered in a deliberate effort to bring about local compliance.

Third, unlike much of the implementation research, this study dealt with programs that are no longer new. The policies on which the study focused had all been in place for a number of years (eighteen in the case of Title I) by the time of the field visits. Over time, local variations have probably diminished.

The conclusion for policymakers is that federal actions can, indeed, make a substantial difference in local educational practice and can accomplish their intended purposes. Despite the vagaries of state and local handling of specific program provisions, the overall effects of federal involvement in the education of target students have been relatively clear and consistent. A sustained federal presence—enlisting state and local administrators as participants in the effort—and comprising funds, goal statements, requirements, and sanctions turns out to have more of an effect on school programs than many people would think.

Structural Complexity in Local Systems

A second broad conclusion is that federal policies have increased the structural complexity of schools and districts; these institutions developed more administrative apparatus to handle the staff, rules, and procedures that come with special programs. These changes take somewhat different forms at the school and the district level, but at both levels the increased complexity appears to represent a necessary local consequence of providing targeted services.

As a result of federal policies, schools house more differentiated and specialized staff, a wider array of materials, and more special settings in which students receive individual or small group services. Instructional programs for individual students have more separate components. The increase in program planning for individual students means that teachers' and aides' activities have become more formally structured and documented.

At the district level, the increases in complexity stem largely from the need to achieve and demonstrate compliance with multiple sets of requirements. Rules from the federal and state levels must be attended to, and they must be turned into local procedural guidelines. District staff have to monitor practices in the schools to make sure that the guidelines are understood and followed. They must follow a multitude of procedures to document program planning and funds allocation—applications, reports, special financial accounting systems, record keeping, needs assessments, evaluations, and so on. Other procedural requirements have been set up to make the district accountable to local audiences including the parents of handicapped students and the advisory councils that represent other target groups.

The structural complexity of the school and district reflects a fundamental trade-off. On the one hand, target students gain, educators get help with their most difficult teaching problems, and the responsiveness of the system to a diverse clientele increases. On the other hand, students' instructional programs lose some things, and an element of inefficiency is introduced into the system.

For students, the school-level changes mean that they can receive tailored services and individual attention from adults, often from specialists. Needs assessment and program planning result in a better match between student needs and program services. However, the students who participate in special services inevitably miss something in the core instructional program. They may lose some stability in instruction, and they are likely to experience the strain of following a complicated daily routine.

For the adults in the school, there are more ways to handle difficult learning (and disciplinary) problems, more occasions to communicate with parents, and more people to turn to for advice or support. Nonetheless, the time necessary to coordinate the components of the instructional program may be time taken away from working with students (this is more true of specialists than classroom teachers). Furthermore, the presence of specialists raises issue of staff relations that takes time to resolve.

For the staff at the district office, the new resources and associated requirements give them leverage over problems that formerly they were less able to solve. However, they pay a price in terms of staff time and the intricacy of administering an instructional program that is subdivided into many parts. The growth in numbers of administrative staff makes decision making more cumbersome. Their responsiveness to the school may also suffer somewhat in the process.

The costs associated with all the school and district administrative procedures are clearly substantial although impossible to tally precisely. When considered in isolation, these costs are an easy target for complaints and calls for reform. But the costs are difficult to eliminate. Efforts to reduce them may diminish the associated benefits as well.

Administrative inefficiency is probably an inevitable result of the variety of services offered and the increase in the districts' accountability.

As the student population includes more and more formerly unserved groups, increases in the variety of instruction and associated complications are unavoidable. And as local, state, and federal audiences require the presence of targeted services for special needs students, some explicit rules and procedures (though not necessarily those now in place) are necessary. District officials recognize that the rules and procedures not only generate more work; they also protect the officials by defining clearly what is expected of them and the schools.

When policymakers consider the disadvantages of the increased complexity in schools and districts, they should remember the problems that the complex arrangements were set up to solve. Without specialized, differentiated instructional services in schools, target students might languish in inappropriate regular instruction. Without formal mechanisms for coordinating these programs, fragmentation could predominate in the schools. And without rules and procedures for accountability, there would be no assurance that schools and districts were adequately attending to target students.

Settling in Over Time

Across most of the issue areas that were investigated in the study, respondents indicated that matters had improved over time. Services for target students had become more appropriate; instructional fragmentation had been reduced; administrative burdens were handled more efficiently; program managers had been stopped from building empires. Although problem-solving efforts had not been uniformly vigorous or successful across sites, at least some trend towards improvement was reported in every site. It seemed attributable to a combination of factors including active local responses to the problems associated with federal policies, policy adjustments at the federal and state levels, and gradual familiarization with federal initiatives.

People in most schools and school districts responded actively to the problems that accompanied categorical programs and mandates, taking steps to combat these problems. The problem solving included district policies (e.g., limiting the number of pull-outs for each student), school policies (e.g., rescheduling to facilitate staff interaction), and individual actions (e.g., conversations between teachers who share students). Local educators also responded to local problems by complaining about them to federal and state authorities, in hopes of changing the policies they held responsible for the problems. A more passive resistance also took place as problematic requirements are reinterpreted and streamlined.

In response to complaints and perceived deficiencies in the programs, federal and state governments made adjustments in policies. For example, the 1978 amendments to Title I allowed special staff to share in bus duty, cafeteria duty, and so on, thus easing the tensions among staff in many schools. Changes in several states' special education laws were credited in various sites with alleviating some difficulties.

The sustained presence of federal programs and mandates has meant that, apart from any efforts to mitigate problems, people became used to the laws, came to understand them better or fear them less, or simply forgot what a school was like without targeted instruction. (Many younger staff members have never known it any other way.) Simultaneously, the specialized staff became more experienced, less threatening, and probably more useful to their schools. Finally, perhaps through repetition alone, the key principles underlying program rules seemed to sink in and become part of local ways of doing things.

Another factor contributing to the generally positive perception of local cumulative effects may have been the shift in the terms of the policy debate in Washington. Many of the respondents, aware that major reductions in the federal role in education were being considered, made a point of saying that they would hate to see such reductions take place. These comments should not be interpreted as simple nostalgia for a federal role that seemed to be disappearing, in short, as a bias that distorts the true picture. Aware of the new policy debate, people who thought the local burdens of the federal role outweighed the benefits would have wanted to express that opinion on the assumption that it would be passed along to policymakers. Yet very few such comments were heard even from the people with no vested interest in the special programs (classroom teachers, principals, superintendents, and school board members). Instead, most people seemed to have weighed the pros and cons of the federal programs and to have concluded that the benefits warranted their speaking up in favor of the programs.

Still, the tendency for programs to settle in over time suggests one limitation of relying on local perceptions in this kind of research. Just as the perception of a very new program will probably exaggerate its defects, the perception of a long-standing program or set of programs may well exaggerate its benefits. Another limitation on local perceptions has to do with the frame of reference. While respondents could compare special programs with regular classroom instruction, their knowledge of the way these services work now made it difficult to imaging alternative service arrangements. For example, they were unsure what services might be provided with the same level of funds if federal regulations were different (since many state, district, and school decisions would shape these services).

There is an important countervailing trend to the generally positive picture of changes over time. In the sites where strong service mandates were combined with strained resources, the perception of the burdensome aspects of federal policy seems to be growing. Dwindling funds at the local, state, and federal levels create problems that are extremely hard to solve. A few of the study sites had begun to make small cuts in the services offered to nontarget students. When the overall pie is shrinking and target students are protected by service mandates, such cuts are inevitable. Fiscal trends at all levels of government suggest that this problem will become more widespread and severe, and that it warrants attention from policymakers.

The fact that programs tend to settle in more comfortably over time (barring new financial problems) should not be taken as an admonition to policymakers to leave the current federal role unchanged. Changes are obviously necessary as national problems and needs shift. However, knowing how local perceptions change over time can help in setting expectations for the effects of new initiatives. The short-term result of almost any policy change will be local resistance, confusion, and poorly organized services. Over a few years, things work better, and the true merits of a policy initiative can be assessed more realistically. (In the longer term, it may be that any initiative will come to be viewed as indispensable at the local level.)

Finally, policymakers should recognize and encourage the local problem solving and intergovernmental negotiation that develop around programs. The flexibility allowed for local decision making in designing, managing, and delivering services is what accounts in large part for the quality of the educational services provided under federal programs and mandates.

Chapter 7

Thinking About Program Quality

Allan R. Odden

The primary focus of most implementation analyses is determining whether programs get implemented. The previous chapters have argued that while there were substantial implementation problems in the initial years, by the close of the 1970s the large federal and state programs for special needs students—the economically disadvantaged, handicapped, limited-English-proficient, etc.—were implemented in compliance with rules and regulation. While it took fifteen years, by the dawn of the 1980s the programs basically were "in place."

A second step in implementation analysis, however, is to ask whether the programs had the desired effects, that is, whether the programs "worked." For most education programs, this issue relates primarily to whether student performance increased. This chapter first reviews data on the effectiveness of services provided to special needs students as a result of various federal and state categorical programs. The general finding is that, at best, programs have small, short term impacts.

The next section describes how programs for special populations actually "looked" in practice. Drawing upon several recent research studies that have gone beyond analysis of just impacts to describe actual program practices, this section synthesizes the nature of services provided to special populations. This section then compares descriptions of actual program practice to characteristics of services shown by research to be effective, and finds major discrepancies. This finding explains in part the programs' small impact on student achievement.

These findings raise the issue of how local programs and related state and federal policies could be altered to enhance program quality and impact. The third section identifies various concepts that could be used to structure how states, the federal government and local school districts could consider program quality issues in their redesign of future program structures for special student populations.

1. Research on Program Impacts

This section reviews research findings on the impacts of compensatory eduction programs, special education programs for handicapped students, and bilingual education programs. The focus will be on the impact programs had on student performance.

Compensatory Education Programs

The federal compensatory education program, Chapter 1 of the Educational Consolidation and Improvement Act of 1981 (formerly Title I of the 1965 Elementary and Secondary Education Act), reaches virtually every school district in the nation. It serves one out of nine students enrolled in elementary and secondary schools. It cost about $5.5 billion in 1990–91. Its goal is to improve academic achievement of poor students, i.e., to bring economically disadvantaged students at least to average performance levels.

The early 1980's national study of Chapter 1 concluded that the program was being implemented in compliance with the law, rules and regulations; that the dollars were distributed to eligible districts and schools and, within schools, to eligible students; and that the services met the Chapter 1 requirements on program scope and quality (Birman et al. 1987). While the authors of the federal study argued that rules and regulations could be changed to target Chapter 1 services more on students who were both poor and low achieving (Chapter 1 allocates dollars to districts and schools on the basis on the number of low income students, but within schools, services are provided to low achieving students whether or not they are poor), the study nevertheless showed that students being served were those allowed under extant rules and regulations.

Another report of that national study (Kennedy, Birman and Demaline 1986) showed that there had been modest success in accomplishing student achievement goals, but that larger impacts were needed. Kennedy, Birman, and Demaline synthesized over a decade of Chapter 1 (Title I) evaluation and impact data from numerous studies. Their general conclusion was that Chapter 1 produced a small, positive increase in student achievement but the impacts were not large enough to move students into the mainstream, and the impact eroded in a few years.

Their analysis indicated that since 1965, the average achievement level of poor and minority students, especially in reading, had improved relative to the general population; this finding was confirmed by reports of the National Assessment of Educational Progress (NAEP 1989). More particularly, Kennedy, Birman and Demaline (1986) found that low achieving poor students who received Chapter 1 services for reading and mathematics made achievement gains greater than similar students who did not receive such services. Further, they found that early elementary programs produced greater student achievement gains than later elementary or secondary school programs. But achievement gains that were made diminished over the summer, even when students participated in Title I summer programs (which generally were not academically rigorous).

Very low achieving students who received Chapter 1 services, moreover, did not appear to improve their relative rank in performance, i.e., they generally maintained their relative position, neither moving ahead nor falling behind. But on the bright side, evidence suggested that these students actually would have lost ground relative to their peers had they not received Chapter 1 services. Finally, when Chapter 1 services were discontinued, student achievement gains eroded over time.

In other words, students who received Chapter 1 services did a little better than similar students who did not receive the services, but the performance bump did not last very long and relative achievement rankings rarely changed. It is clear that low achieving poor students who received Chapter 1 services were not making sufficient achievement gains to move them substantially toward the achievement level of the average student—the hope of those who originally created Chapter 1 (Title I). These conclusions on the achievement impact of Chapter 1 are supported by two other major studies of the long-term impacts of federal compensatory education programs (Carter 1984 and Gabriel et al. 1985).

Special Education

A similar story describes the impact of special education services provided to handicapped students—the program has been implemented, but the impact is small. In an exhaustive review of a decade's experience with the implementation and impact of P.L. 94–142, the federal program providing services to children with handicapping conditions, Gartner and Lipsky (1987) concluded that "by and large [program implementation] has been accomplished." In the decade following enactment of P.L. 94–142, substantial numbers of additional students received special education services, substantially more funds supported the provision of special education services and, with few narrow exceptions, location was not a factor in the availability of services—special education services were available in all districts, in all states. These are remarkable findings given the systematic exclusion from public education services that many handicapped students had faced in the decades preceding the federal law.

Nevertheless, there are major questions about the effectiveness of this expansion of special education services. First, there is a lack of education program outcome data. Unlike the numerous studies and study syntheses of Chapter 1 student outcome data, there is no national data base on special education students' academic impacts, graduation rates, or post-secondary attainment (Gartner and Lipsky 1989). Thus, data on program impact are indirect. Indeed, as recently as 1988, the Office of Special Education said that improving program quality would be the major focus for the next decade, and that quality was student outcomes (Bellamy 1988).

While the basic premise of special education is that student achievement will increase by application of a specialized body of knowledge with intensive instruction provided in smaller classes, usually outside the regular classroom, Gartner and Lipsky (1989) argue that this premise has little research support. They cite a variety of research reviews that concluded that little or no student benefit derives from instruction in out-of-the-regular classroom settings. They specifically cite a review of programs for academically able handicapped students that find no consistent benefit for full-time, i.e., non-mainstreamed classroom, special education programs. Quite the contrary, the review found that full-time or part-time regular classroom services had a larger impact on student achievement as well as self-esteem and emotional adjustment (Madden and Slavin 1983). Further, Weiner (1985) found in a review of fifty studies that the mean academic performance of mainstreamed handicapped students with mild handicapping conditions was in the 80th percentile while that for students in pull-out classes was at the 50th percentile.

Dropout rates also are higher for special education students. Gartner and Lipsky (1989) show that dropout rates for handicapped students are about 10 percent above that of regular students, and is the highest—47 percent—for learning disabled students. This latter finding is especially troublesome because the increase in numbers of students served in special education programs is mainly in the mildly handicapped, i.e., learning disabled category, most of whom are low achieving students. Indeed, the dropout findings together with the achievement findings above show that for the mildly handicapped, who are primarily the learning disabled, the expansion of special education services, most of which are provided outside the regular classroom, could actually serve to their detriment.

In short, after fifteen years of implementing a major expansion of services for handicapped children, which primarily has provided more services to learning disabled and slower learning children, the evidence, although incomplete, suggests that the programs have had small if any long lasting positive impacts on these students' academic achievement.

Programs for Limited-English-Proficient Students

Similar findings of small, systemic achievement effects also characterize results of research on categorical programs providing extra services for limited-English-proficient students. While the controversies surrounding bilingual education center on both political support for bilingual education (however defined) as well as the specific efficacy of the bilingual-transition program in which limited-English-proficient students are initially instructed in their native language, even the reviews that are sympathetic to such programs and find a clear programmatic impact, find—at best—a small overall impact. Since the debate has been less the general effectiveness of services for limited-English-proficient students and more the effectiveness of bilingual-transition programs, conclusions have to be viewed with caution. Nevertheless, the general conclusion is that systemic achievement impacts are inconsistent and small (Baker and DeKanter 1983; Willig 1985). While more focused analyses show that the effects are higher for "good" transitional-bilingual programs that have "solidified" in local practice, the overall finding for programs labeled bilingual is not high. Thus, the story for the impact of categorical services for limited-English-proficient students is similar to that for special education and compensatory education—the general achievement effect across most studies and most programs is at best modest.

In short, if one major goal of categorical programs that provide additional educational services for students with special needs—including low achieving poor students, handicapped, learning disabled, and limited-English-proficient students—was to increase substantially their academic achievement, that goal has not been reached. Programs have been implemented in compliance with existing law, rules and regulations, but the impact on students is far short of what it was hoped to be.

2. Research on Program Characteristics

Why are student achievement effects so small? There are no definitive answers, but one hypothesis is that the characteristics of additional services typically provided tends not to reflect the characteristics of services shown by research to be effective with the types of students served in most categorical programs. This section first summarizes research on program characteristics typical of most compensatory, special education, and bilingual education programs and then compares these characteristics to research based effective program characteristics.

Compensatory Education

Two recent national studies provide information on the characteristics of Chapter 1 programs and services (Rowan and Guthrie 1989; Birman et al. 1987). Information was gathered on program structure, curriculum focus, instructional strategies and coordination with the regular program. In terms of program structure, the studies found that a variety of structures were used, including both in-class and pull out programs. The general finding was that compensatory education services were usually but decreasingly provided in pull-out structures where students received instruction in resource rooms outside of the regular classroom. These studies also found that no one structure—pull-out or in-class—was better or worse than another, a finding which counters the conventional assumption that pull-out structures are inherently flawed. This finding has been confirmed by two extensive program and literature reviews that identified effective programs that used both in-class (Slavin and Madden 1989) and pull-out structures (Madden and Slavin 1989).

In terms of curriculum, Rowan and Guthrie (1989) found that Chapter 1 programs emphasized remedial instruction in reading and mathematics focusing on basic skills and knowledge. Few programs provided opportunities for instruction in higher level cognitive processes. Thus, Chapter 1 services in the main ignored thinking and problem-solving skills, focusing instead on basic skills in reading and mathematics.

Rowan and Guthrie (1989) and Birman et al. (1987) found several typical characteristics of instructional strategies. First, Chapter 1 instruction was provided to small groups of students, usually between six and eight pupils. Second, the instruction most often was provided by a trained teacher but increasingly was being provided by instructional aides.

Third, the additional Chapter 1 instruction, typically in reading and mathematics, was provided for an average of thirty and forty minutes per day, for four to five days a week. But the instruction tended to be substituted for instruction in other subjects, such as social studies and science. Thus, Chapter 1 students tended to receive more instruction in basic reading skills but less for reading comprehension in other subject areas such as social studies and science. Very little net extra instruction was provided; the studies found that Chapter 1 students received a total of ten extra minutes of instruction, which was a combination of less instruction in comprehension and more instruction in basic skills. There were, moreover, few systemic attempts to really increase instructional time through summer programs with an academic focus, before- or after-school programs, or extended day kindergarten programs.

Fourth, during the extra instruction time that was provided, instruction tended to last only 50–60% of the extra time for reading and 35–40% of the extra time for mathematics; much extra time was consumed by non-instructional activities. Further, while provided in a lecture format, the instruction did not necessarily reflect the direct teaching strategies documented in the effective teaching research (Brophy and Good 1986; Rosenshine and Stevens 1986). Thus, Chapter 1 students tended to receive a modest amount of additional instruction, it was focused on basic skills in reading and mathematics, it was provided to small groups, and it was presented in a lecture but not research-based, direct teaching format.

Finally, the studies found wide variation in the degree to which the extra instruction was coordinated with instruction for the regular curriculum program. While some programs coordinated the two programs, most did not. As noted above, moreover, Chapter 1 instruction usually replaced other components of the regular instruction program—not mathematics and reading, but often social studies or science. And last, few Chapter 1 schools with high poverty rates were found to have two important characteristics of effective schools—a safe, orderly learning climate and active parent involvement.

In comparing these program characteristics to research-based characteristics of effective programs for low-achieving students, there is a mismatch between the two that makes the small achievement effects of Chapter 1 somewhat understandable. While, contrary to conventional wisdom, neither a pull-out nor an in-class format was found to be a critical program characteristic, many of the other characteristics of the program were, on the contrary, found actually to counter research on what is effective. There are four major areas of discrepancy, though.

First, the focus on basic skills essentially reduces emphasis on higher level cognitive skills yet research suggests that low achieving students are those students most likely to benefit from specific instruction in thinking and problem solving. Few Chapter 1 programs include a focus on developing higher level thinking skills. The underlying assumption tends to be basic skills first, thinking skills second. Yet, new research from cognitive psychology (Resnick 1987; Peterson 1989; Stein et al. 1989) suggests that basic skills are learned best in problem-solving situations, that students who work through problems not only learn problem-solving strategies but also acquire more basic skills, and that lower achieving (as compared to higher achieving) students increase their performance more on higher level cognitive processes when exposed to instruction that emphasizes problem solving techniques.

Second, group size is small (six to eight students), but it is not small enough to make a significant difference. Research on class size and student achievement primarily supports only individual or very small group tutoring at the elementary level. Only when classes are tutorial in size (one to three students) do significant achievement gains result (Odden 1990; Slavin 1989).

Third, additional instructional time is not increased enough to make a substantial difference in achievement. Research shows that increased academic learning time (the amount of time allocated to instruction during which the student is engaged in learning tasks at high rates of success) improves student academic achievement (Denham and Lieberman 1980); increased academic learning time is produced by both more allocated time and use of effective teaching strategies. Typical Chapter 1 instruction tended to increase neither of these variables. More instruction is provided in basic skills and less in comprehension, suggesting a decrease in reading comprehension instruction which would translate into a decline in reading comprehension achievement. Also, only an extra ten minutes of instruction is provided overall, which is an insufficient increase in allocated time. In addition, the pedagogy itself tends not to include direct instruction strategies identified by the effective teaching research that improves achievement in basic reading and mathematics skills (Brophy and Good 1986; and Rosenshine and Stevens 1986), such as active teaching, high expectations, monitoring student progress with specific feedback, and high success rates of student learning.

Lastly, program content is not aligned with the core curriculum, and a student's overall instructional program is not coordinated among teachers. Stein et al. (1989) show that curriculum content is an important factor in student performance; students learn more in a content area when they are exposed to more instruction in it. But Chapter 1 students tend to be exposed to two uncoordinated and therefore different curriculum programs and to receive less instruction in other courses such as science and social studies. Furthermore, when students return to the classroom from Chapter 1 mathematics and reading services, they may have missed parts of history and science lessons and have to try and catch-up with the class—a task difficult for any student. Even when the general content might be the same, the curriculum programs and emphases can differ. Thus, rather than concentrating instruction on the regular school curriculum, in most schools, Chapter 1 provides a separate curriculum mainly in basic reading and mathematics skills.

In sum, Chapter 1 services tend to be inconsistent with research-based effective strategies and the core curriculum. Thus, the small and inconsequential impacts are at least partially understandable. One promising approach to increasing Chapter 1's effects on student achievement would be to incorporate more research-based effective strategies into Chapter 1 services provided. These strategies are discussed in the next section.

Special Education

Special education services, especially those provided to students labeled mentally retarded or learning disabled, suffer from the same disjuncture between typical characteristics and research-based effective characteristics as do compensatory education services. First, 74 percent of special education students are provided services in pull-out or separate classroom program structures, yet research suggests that this is not the best nor even a healthy program structure for mentally handicapped students (Gartner and Lipsky 1987; Leinhardt and Pallay 1982; Madden and Slavin 1983). Indeed, the same research shows that students receiving services in special education resource rooms rarely perform better than similar students who are mainstreamed and receive no additional service.

Second, Gartner and Lipsky (1987) show that special education services are characterized by a focus on basic skills with little emphasis on higher level cognitive processes. This, again, reflects a misunderstanding of how students learn basic skills as well as thinking skills. Indeed, low achieving students, with characteristics similar to students typically labeled learning disabled, who are taught various problem-solving strategies and are engaged in problem-solving situations for which they need the basic skills to reach solutions, not only become better problem-solvers but also become more proficient at basic skills (Peterson 1989).

Third, students receiving special education services at best have the same instructional time as regular students, i.e., they have no increase in academic learning time. Allington and McGill-Franzen (1989), for example, found that instruction for students experiencing reading failure differed dramatically, depending on whether they received extra services through special education or Chapter 1 programs. Mainstreamed handicapped students received services in pull-out resource rooms that replaced regular classroom instruction; as a result they actually received thirty-five minutes less classroom instruction in reading during the day. Although special education students received more instruction in special resource rooms than did Chapter 1 students, it was not large enough to offset their loss of regular classroom instruction.

Fourth, Gartner and Lipsky (1987) found little evidence of effective teaching instructional practices in special education classrooms; there was little direct instruction with active learner response and feedback and a low frequency of contingent teacher attention to students. Allington and McGill-Franzen (1989) further found that the resource room instruction itself consisted of less research-based direct instruction and more seat work than either the regular classroom or instruction in modal Chapter 1 programs.

In general, the typical program structure for special education services for mildly handicapped and learning disabled students is a structure (pull-out in a resource room) associated with lower student academic and social impacts; students rarely receive additional instruction and often receive less instruction because their special services supplant rather than supplement instruction in the regular program, and the instructional strategies themselves do not reflect research-based effective strategies. Again, these findings may at least partially explain the small academic achievement impact of most special education services.

Programs for Limited-English-Proficient Students

There are several problems in many classes labeled as providing "bilingual" education services. First, few of these classes across the country are taught by certified bilingual education teachers, i.e., teachers who are fluent in the student's second language. That means that in too many classrooms, even though there is an attempt to instruct students in their native language (until the student learns English), the attempt is incomplete. Often the teacher provides regular instruction in English, and a bilingual teacher's aide instructs the limited-English-proficient student in his/her native language. In these instances, limited-English-proficient students are provided instruction by a person who works hard but is not a trained teacher. It is no wonder that achieve-

ment impacts are small. Indeed, while research shows that the bilin-
gual-transitional instructional strategy works (Krashen and Biber 1988),
there simply are too few certified bilingual teachers to make the strategy work on an overall system basis.

Second, even if a teacher is bilingual, the teacher rarely uses
research based effective strategies, just as for compensatory and special
education. Yet, research shows that the same pedagogical strategies that
are effective for low income and minority students, also are effective
strategies when used in a bilingual education structure (Tikunoff 1983).

Third, many evaluated bilingual education programs have been
characterized by "instability" of operations, i.e., the programs had not
settled into a smoothly functioning set of activities. They had frequent
reorganizations and high teacher turnover. These programs, thus, did
not provide a consistent set of services, making them both difficult to
evaluate but also inadequate generally as a program. Indeed, it could
be argued that a "program" per se did not exist. Clearly, a program
that changes frequently will not compare well with research-based
effective practices.

Finally, many bilingual education programs "transition" students
too soon from native language instructed classes to regular English-
taught classes. Most state regulations require the transition when students essentially learn just conversational English. But research concludes that students need to learn the language imbedded in a content
area in order to function successfully in a regular classroom, and that
an intermediate placement in a "sheltered-English" class is a much
more effective practice (Krashen and Biber 1988; Cummins 1989).

Thus, common practices in most classes labeled as "bilingual education" also fall short of what research suggests as effective for limited-
English-proficient students. Many bilingual education classes also suffer
from constant change and such program instability is an overarching
detriment to many programs. Again, the mismatch between research-
based effective practices and typical practices probably explains in part
the modest to small impact of bilingual education program services.

3. Strategies for Improving Program Quality

Clearly, there is a need to improve the quality of services
provided in most categorical programs. The above sections show quite
starkly that while the education system has been relatively successful in
developing new programs that meet the attendant rules, regulations
and legal requirements, the programs need to work more effectively. In

special education, student performance rarely improves with the extra services, in bilingual education student performance increases overall but only a small amount, and in compensatory education, student achievement improves but not very much and not for very long.

How then can program quality be improved? What role can government policy play in program quality improvement?

This section begins to answer these two questions. It first identifies research on programs and strategies that produce significant improvements in student performance for students eligible for compensatory, special education and bilingual education programs. It then identifies alternative ways to structure government use of these research-based strategies to help stimulate changes in local practice that will produce larger student achievement impacts.

Despite the ineffectiveness of typical services provided in compensatory, special and bilingual education programs, there is a rapidly growing literature that identifies programmatic structures, curriculum and instructional strategies that produce substantial increases in student performance for low achieving, poor, learning disabled or mildly handicapped, and limited-English proficient students (see, for example, Slavin and Madden 1989b and Slavin, Karweit, and Madden 1989a). Eight strategies are identified below. Some are broad and programmatic in nature; others deal with actual classroom practice. Interestingly, the strategies work successfully for all categories of students. Two additional strategies, one specifically for handicapped students and one for limited-English-proficient students, are also identified.

1. *Early childhood education for three and four year olds.* Nearly all studies show that early childhood education programs have long-term impacts and, even when future benefits are discounted to present values, have significant net benefit-cost ratios (Barnett 1985; Grubb 1989). Early childhood education programs for poor children improve student academic performance in the basic skills in elementary through high school, decrease failure rates and below grade level performance, decrease discipline problems, and improve high school graduation rates (Karweit 1987). At the Education Summit in 1989, President George Bush and the nation's governors agreed that expanding the federal Head Start Program should be a priority Federal initiative.

2. *Extended day kindergarten programs.* Kindergarten was a full-day program until World War II when teacher shortages cut it to a half-day. Research syntheses suggest that students from poverty backgrounds who receive a full-day kindergarten program perform from 0.5 to over 1.0 standard deviations better on basic skill

activities in the early elementary grades (Puleo 1988; Slavin, Karweit, and Madden 1989) than those who do not. Both expanded early childhood education and extended day kindergarten for students from poverty backgrounds produces a substantial boost in successfully learning the basic skills in early elementary grades.

3. *Extensive use of pedagogical strategies based on the effective teaching research.* Rosenshine and Stevens (1986) and Brophy and Good (1986) identify a wide array of instructional strategies shown by research over the past two decades to improve acquisition of basic skills and knowledge, especially for poor and minority students who comprise the bulk of students receiving compensatory, special education, and many bilingual education services. These strategies are effective for low achieving students, including learning disabled, mildly handicapped, and even limited-English proficient students.

4. *Continuous progress programs in reading and mathematics.* Slavin and Madden (1989b) show that programs in which students are periodically regrouped, with cross-grade ability grouping in reading in grades 1–3, within-grade ability grouping in mathematics, and heterogeneous class groupings for all other subjects (Slavin 1987) improve disadvantaged student performance by at least 0.5 standard deviations.

5. *Curriculum programs with the goal of developing students' complex thinking skills.* These would include an approach to language arts that emphasized reading comprehension (Resnick 1987), a process approach to writing (Graves 1983), a natural language approach to children with limited-English-proficiency and sheltered-English programs in academic subjects before full transition to English only instruction, (Krashen and Biber 1988; Cummins 1989), and a problem solving/manipulative based approach to mathematics (Schoenfeld 1987). Categorical program services need to be designed to help students learn this curriculum, not a different or watered-down curriculum.

6. *Cooperative learning across all of the above curriculum topics.* Slavin (1989) has shown that cooperative learning, especially in the upper elementary grades, has a broad range of large impacts (over 0.5 standard deviations) on both student academic performance, student attitudes towards other students, and skills in working in group situations. Furthermore, cooperative learning "works" for improving student achievement for low income, ethnic minority students and language minority students (Kagan 1986).

7. *Peer or volunteer tutoring.* Several peer and volunteer tutoring programs in schools with high concentrations of poor and ethnic

and language minorities have been shown by controlled research studies to produce significant (0.5 to 1.0 standard deviations) gains in achievement of students tutored (Slavin and Madden 1989a). Other research typically shows that tutors also improve their academic performance. Peer tutoring is also a highly cost-effective program (Levin, Leitner and Meister 1987).

8. *Computer assisted instruction.* A number of computer assisted instruction programs, most of which have emphasized basic skill acquisition, have produced 0.5 or more standard deviations of achievement gains, including the type developed by the Curriculum Computer Corporation for the Los Angeles Unified School District (Slavin and Madden 1989b). Further, new computer-based instructional programs (Pogrow 1990) not only develop higher level cognitive strategies for Chapter 1 students but also produce large impacts on basic skill acquisition as well.

For special education programs, the primary additional strategy is to provide as much of the extra educational in the regular classroom as possible (Lipsky and Gartner 1989). This strategy is bolstered by the above curriculum and pedagogical suggestions, as well as by providing a "consulting teacher" who would work with regular classroom teachers to develop the special skills needed for their mainstreamed students (Huefner 1988).

For non-English-proficient students, content area instruction in their native language until they can transfer to sheltered-English subject matter classes is commonly accepted in research circles as effective (Krashen and Biber 1988). While other language-sensitive instructional strategies also can work, major modifications other than just immersion into regular classroom instruction need to be made for non- and limited-English-proficient students.

In short, there are several research-based strategies that schools, districts, states and the federal government can deploy or stimulate to be deployed that are likely to produce significant academic achievement gains for students in typical compensatory, special and bilingual education programs. Research not only shows these strategies to be individually effective (Slavin, Karweit, and Madden 1989) but also effective when implemented all together in one school (Madden et al. 1989).

New Governmental Roles

Knowing a battery of strategies that works is the first step. Incorporating these strategies into new governmental roles is a more difficult step. This part outlines ways of restructuring governmental roles to improve program quality.

To begin, it is helpful to identify major mechanisms that federal and state governments can use to influence local behavior, and from those, to identify which might be most effective in getting improved local practices deployed. First, higher level governments can provide general aid grants, hoping that the reason local governments (school districts) have not provided the needed extra services is a resource shortage. But general aid grants are inefficient mechanisms to focus local attention on new issues; new resources also allow local leaders to focus on issues high on their own policy agendas which may not be those issues important to the federal and state government. Second, higher level governments can provide categorical grants. That has been the strategy of federal and state compensatory, special and bilingual education programs but, as this chapter has argued, it has not been sufficient to insure program quality. Third, governments can develop rules and regulations to focus and solidify local program operations. Again, this and the preceding chapters show that current regulations have helped get programs implemented, but they have not been successful in insuring program quality; those items that can be easily regulated—dollar allocations, student identification, and program structure—tend not to be the important variables that make programs effective in improving student performance. Fourth, governments can fund research to discover new knowledge and finance knowledge dissemination strategies. While much of the research identifying effective practices for special needs students has been funded by federal and state governments, more knowledge is needed. The knowledge which is available has not affected local practice very much. Still, research on effective practices should be expanded. Fifth, higher level governments can provide technical assistance to help build state and local capacity to improve program quality. Finally, higher level governments can provide leadership by articulating new system missions, developing goals and objectives, and expanding visions. Both of these latter strategies could be useful in improving program quality.

While these strategies are those available to the federal government, state governments can tap these as well as three additional mechanisms. States certify teachers, accredit schools and make curriculum and testing policy—areas much closer to the curriculum and instruction issues that are likely to improve programmatic impacts.

Elmore (1988) suggests that further emphases on rules and regulations are unlikely to produce the desired impacts. He argues that the current system has accomplished about as much as possible with regulations on inputs; the assumption that a certain standard of input, such as a range of resources from acceptable to exemplary, would provide an adequate level of effective service, simply has not worked, as noted above. He then discusses the possibility of regulating process variables to focus local attention on curriculum and instruction practice that have been shown by research to be effective, but suggests that regulations would have difficulty being sensitive to local contexts and would likely bureaucratize and rigidify rather than stimulate professional practice. While output regulations would signal a vote of confidence in local capacity, Elmore concludes that the technology is insufficient to measure outcomes, that it would be difficult to determine who should set standards even if they could be measured, and that there is little likelihood of a federal interest in imposing national performance standards. On the latter point, he is probably overly pessimistic about measuring important student outcomes since the National Assessment of Educational Progress already produces such data (NAEP 1989) and each year NAEP improves as a student assessment program. And Elmore wrote his chapter before the October 1989 Education Summit at which President George Bush and the nation's governors pledged to develop and implement national education student performance standards.

As alternatives, Elmore (1988) suggests using the "bully pulpit" to highlight good as well as bad practice, providing performance awards to reward successful local practice, allocating discretionary dollars to stimulate local creativity in developing new practices (similar to Title III innovation grants originally in the Elementary and Secondary Education Act), and targeting funds to underwrite new program development in areas where it has been most difficult to raise student performance, such as in the core low income areas in large cities. All of these strategies are likely to be fruitful in helping to change local practice towards using the research-based effective strategies noted above.

Odden (1988) suggests coordinating compensatory education program services with the regular education programs, and reformulating the regular program to include current knowledge of effective curriculum and instruction practices. The fact is that the bulk of instruction that special needs students receive is in the regular program. Thus, the regular curriculum program needs to be high quality, and the impact of extra services will be strengthened if designed to help students learn the core curriculum program.

In a similar vein, Kirst (1988) proposes a strategic change in the orientation of Chapter 1 to focus federal regulations more on aligning local compensatory education services with a regular classroom curriculum program that would include many of the research-based elements outlined above. The federal oversight role, thus, would shift from emphasizing fiscal compliance to technical assistance, research, and using the bully pulpit to facilitate program integration. Kirst contends that the federal role needs to catch up with research-based curriculum and instruction approaches, without obliterating the special services that Chapter 1 provides low achieving, poor students, that P.L. 94–142 provides handicapped students and that bilingual programs provide to limited-English-proficient students.

Kirst (1988) outlines the policy implications of making this strategic change in the federal role in Chapter 1; the strategies also can be applied to special education and bilingual education programs. First, federal leadership would need to orchestrate a large-scale media campaign to alter state and local orientations towards these programs. The new federal bully pulpit role would then be reinforced with widespread technical assistance and network building that provides consultants with expertise in curriculum and instruction to states and local school districts, to develop better methods of providing technical assistance, to establish locally based networks, coordinate field services, and produce curriculum handbooks for local use.

State categorical program review strategies would need to emphasize the new linkages of categorical program services with the academic content of regular classes and the core curriculum program. It could include model ways to incorporate categorical programs into school-wide improvement plans and major efforts to retrain classroom teachers to improve their instructional techniques in teaching disadvantaged students. Such a new strategy would not change categorical program fund allocations. It would simply seek to fuse the linkages between categorical services and regular curriculum and instruction services, and to insure that regular services included research-based effective practices.

Kirst calls for reconsidering the basic program considerations currently undergirding Chapter 1; this reconsideration could apply as well to special education services, especially those for learning disabled and mildly handicapped students, as well as limited-English-proficient students. Recognizing that it will not be easy to blend a core curriculum approach, teacher inservice training, and school improvement with extant financial accountability and targeting requirements for any current categorical program, Kirst suggests renewing the search for differential treatment of states and localities, depending on whether they use the type of research-based strategies outlined previously and by Odden (1988). The states that succeeded could be allowed by the Education Department to merge their categorical program strategies more closely with the core curriculum. Districts with very high concentrations of special needs students could have different and less restrictive criteria for using categorical funds to reinforce the core curriculum in order to enhance the total school program.

4. Conclusion

The general messages of this chapter are straightforward. The quality of current categorical program services is inadequate; curriculum and instructional strategies do not systematically reflect knowledge about effective practices. In part as a result, program impacts are small and short lived. Yet there is a large body of research-based curriculum and instructional approaches that "work." Federal, state and local policies need to be modified to stimulate local school and classroom implementation of research proven effective practices. Knowing what practices need to be used and focusing change strategies on getting those practices into classroom behavior is a complex undertaking which is the focus of the following chapter.

Chapter 8

The Rand Change Agent Study:
Ten Years Later

Milbrey Wallin McLaughlin

From 1973 through 1978, the Rand Corporation carried out, under the sponsorship of the United States Office of Education, a national study of four federally funded programs intended to introduce and support innovative practices in the public schools, each with substantively different objectives. Title III of the 1965 Elementary and Secondary Education Act (ESEA) provided support for local innovative projects. Title VII of ESEA supported district bilingual education efforts. Programs financed by the 1968 Vocational Education Act encouraged practitioners to develop new approaches to career education. The Right-to-Read program funded local efforts to "eliminate illiteracy." Despite programmatic differences, these programs shared a general, common purpose—the stimulation and spread of educational innovations—and a common policy instrument—the provision of temporary funds or seed money to support new practices.[1]

Rand's four year, two phase study examined a sample of 293 local projects funded by these four federal programs in eighteen states. Reported under the general title *Federal Programs Supporting Educational Change*, the findings of the so-called Change Agent study marked a significant shift in the ways policymakers, practitioners and researchers thought about affecting and understanding planned change in education (Berman and McLaughlin 1974; 1975 a,b,c,d; 1977a,b; 1978).

The projects included in the Change Agent Study were the products of federal policies conceived in the late 1960s and local plans developed in the early to mid-1970s. They represented the first significant federal-level attempts to stimulate change in local educational practices and were based on relatively unexamined assumptions about change in public schools and the role of government (or policy) in affecting it. Policymakers formulating these early federal education initiatives assumed a relatively direct relationship between federal policy "inputs", local responses, and program "outputs." Policy of that period generally ignored the contents of what economists called the "black box" of local practices, beliefs, and traditions. The common idea behind these substantively distinct federal programs was that more money or better ideas—enhanced "inputs"—would enable local educators to improve school practice. A cynical, retrospective description of that era of federal education policy might dub it the "missing input model of education policy."

In the approximately fifteen years since the programs examined by Rand were initiated in districts around the country, and in the ten years since the final volume of the Change Agent study was published, practice has changed, policy has matured, the social and political context of schools has changed, and more research on planned change and educational reform has accumulated. This chapter first reviews the major findings of the Rand Change Agent study and then addresses the following questions:

- Which of the findings have endured? Ten years later, which conclusions continue to be accurate descriptions of the local change process and the role of policy?

- Which of the findings have not held up? Ten years later, which findings should be rethought or revised?

- What are the implications of this "revisionist" analysis for policies aimed at improving educational practice and for researching aimed at understanding the relationship between policy and practice? Where are we now?

1. Rand Findings in Review

The final volume of the Rand study (Berman and McLaughlin 1978) included a summary of study findings. Rand found that federal change agent policies had a major role in prompting local school districts to undertake projects that generally were congruous with federal categorical guidelines. Local initiatives were by and large consistent with what policymakers had in mind in framing broad program objectives. However, Rand analysts found that "adoption" was only the beginning of the story: Adoption of a project consistent with federal goals did not ensure successful implementation. Further, Rand found that even successful implementation did not predict long-run continuation of projects initiated with federal funds. The Change Agent study concluded that "the net return to the general investment was the adoption of many innovations, the successful implementation of few, and the long-run continuation of still fewer..." (Berman and McLaughlin 1978).

While federal seed money was essential to local efforts, Rand found that money did not always buy the things that mattered most to successful implementation and continuation of local change agent projects. The consequences of the various federal policies examined by Rand depended primarily on *local factors*, not federal guidelines or funding levels.

Rand examined how characteristics of projects and school districts affected the outcomes of innovations and reached the following five conclusions:

1. The *educational methods* used by a project determined its implementation and continuation only to a limited extent. Projects with essentially the same strategies could be and were implemented differently in different sites. In other words, what a project *was* mattered less than *how* it was carried out.

2. *Project resources* did not predict outcome. More expensive projects were no more likely than were less costly efforts to be successful. Money mattered in terms of enabling practitioners to get a project underway, but resources alone did not secure successful implementation or project acceptance.

3. *Project scope* was an important consideration. Ambitious efforts were more likely to stimulate teacher change and involvement than were modest, narrow projects. However, projects aiming at significant, system-wide change proved difficult to implement all at once. Planned change efforts, it seemed, needed to be sufficient in scope to challenge teachers and kindle interest, but not so ambitious as to require too much too soon from the implementing system.

4. The *active commitment of district and site leadership* was essential to project success and long-run stability. Without the active support of the superintendent, district central office staff, and principals in project schools, individuals responsible for implementation typically did not put forth the effort necessary for successful implementation and, once federal support was withdrawn, resources necessary for continuation were unavailable. Further, this commitment, Rand found, needed to be present at the outset to undergird implementation efforts.

5. Locally selected *implementation strategies* about how to put a project into practice dominated the outcome of federally supported change agent projects.

The study found both a set of ineffective and effective local implementation strategies. The following strategies generally were seen to be *ineffective* because they were incompatible with aspects of district realities or with the dominant motivations, needs or interests of teachers responsible for implementation:

- Reliance on outside consultants

- Packaged management approaches

- One-shot, pre-implementation training

- Pay for training

- Formal, summative evaluation

- Comprehensive, system-wide projects.

In general, these strategies were ineffective because they failed to provide the ongoing and sometimes unpredictable support teachers needed, excluded teachers from project development and (intentionally or not) signaled a mechanistic role for teachers.

In contrast, Rand found that *effective* strategies promoted *mutual adaptation,* or the adaptation of a project and institutional setting to each other. Effective implementation strategies supported that process of adaptation by provision of timely feedback, identification and correction of "errors", and building broad-based commitment to the project. The following strategies generally were effective, especially when applied in concert:

- Concrete, teacher-specific and extended training

- Classroom assistance from local staff

- Teacher observation of similar projects in other classrooms, schools or districts

- Regular project meetings that focused on practical issues

- Teacher participation in project decisions

- Local development of project materials

- Principals' participation in training.

Local implementation choices were determined by institutional context to a significant degree. They reflected local expertise, capacity, and sophistication in project implementation as well as local motivation and management style. Change Agent policies, Rand concluded, operated through and within this local context.

2. Which Findings Hold True Today?

A general finding of the Change Agent study that has become almost a truism is that *it is exceedingly difficult for policy to change practice,* especially across levels of government. Contrary to the one-to-one relationship assumed to exist between policy and practice, the Change Agent study demonstrated that the nature, amount, and pace of change at the local level was a product of local factors that were largely beyond the control of higher-level policy makers. To further complicate matters, these local factors changed over time and so created substantively and strategically different settings for policy. The specific findings of the Rand Change Agent Study that hold today are corollaries of this general observation about the relationship between macro-level policies and micro-level behavior.

Implementation Dominates Outcome

The dominance of local responses (in contrast to policy inputs) has been underscored in subsequent research and has generated what has been called the "implementation perspective" in policy research. Although the policies under study differ from those that were the focus of the Change Agent study, Rand's conclusion still holds that local choices about how to put a policy into practice have more significance for policy outcomes than do such policy features such as technology, program design, funding levels, or governance requirements. Change continues to be a problem of the smallest unit.

Policy Can't Mandate What Matters

What matters most to policy outcomes are local capacity and will. The local expertise, organizational routines, and resources available to support planned change efforts generate fundamental differences in the ability of practitioners to plan, execute or sustain an innovative effort. The presence of the will or motivation to embrace policy objectives or strategies is essential to generate the effort and energy necessary to a successful project. Local capacity and will not only are generally beyond the reach of policy, they also change over time. Local events such as teachers' strikes, fiscal retrenchment, desegregation orders, or enrollment decline can negatively affect both capacity and will as they engender competing pressures and define constraints upon local action.[2]

Local Variability is the Rule; Uniformity is the Exception

While classrooms, schools, and school districts share common features—curriculum structures, grade structures, and student placement policies as examples—they also differ in fundamental and consequential ways. A high school English course in a wealthy suburban classroom differs substantially from a course offered under the same title in an inner city school. The problems confronting California school administrators differ markedly from those faced by colleagues in Kansas. Dade County's site-based decision-making project will bear only scant resemblance to a "restructuring" activity in Santa Fe or shared decision-making in Los Angeles.

Traditionally, variability has been an anathema to policymakers and cast as the plague of efforts to reform schools because it signaled uneven local responses to policy objectives. Variability also has been interpreted as warning of trouble in the system. Today, however, there is recognition that variability may be a good thing—that it signals a healthy system, one that is shaping and integrating policy in ways best suited to local resources, traditions, and clientele. However, good or bad, it is as true now as it was when Rand studied Change Agent projects, that local practices do and will vary in significant ways among sites and over time.

3. Findings Requiring Revision

The Change Agent study examined the local responses to the various federal programs supporting educational change within a particular moment of educational policymaking. The programs we studied were based on programmatic assumptions and realities that have themselves changed in response to experiences such as those described by the Change Agent study. A number of the conclusions or interpretations drawn from the study require revision in light of that changed reality and understanding.

Commitment

First, the study overemphasized the importance of initial motivation. One interpretation of the Change Agent study was that policy could achieve its goals only when local implementors supported it and were inspired to carry it out. This analysis was based primarily in the distinction we saw in the field between projects undertaken for opportunistic reasons—available dollars—and those initiated out of perceived programmatic need or promise. In part, this conclusion has continued veracity. It is true that initiation and implementation of a planned change effort receive important energy from the motivation of advocates—individuals who believe in the effort and are willing to commit energy and effort to its success.

But experience also has shown that we did not see or did not recognize instances in which *belief follows practice*. Individuals required to change routines or take up new practices can become "believers." This omission may have been a function of the programs we were studying—innovative efforts that were, for the most part, "voluntary" from the perspective of the implementing system. The local Right to Read, Title III, Career Education and Bilingual Education programs supported by federal funds were elective and the consequence of local competition for limited federal funds. Thus, the Rand program sample did not provide instances of programs or strategies imposed upon the local system, such as desegregation efforts, or system-wide entitlement programs such as Title I (compensatory education). Nor did we look to see what happened to skeptical or unwilling individual participants over time.

Had we done either, we would have seen that belief or commitment can follow mandated or "coerced" involvement at both the individual and the system level. Findings from an investigation of local responses to the policy changes associated with the transition of federally funded compensatory education programs from Title I of ESEA to Chapter 1 of ECIA highlight both the importance of local will and the fact that individuals or institutions originally opposed to an idea can change their minds (McLaughlin et al. 1985).

Title I mandated local evaluation of compensatory projects supported through the program; additionally, it required parent involvement in the planning and governance of the local Title I program. Both mandates initially were greeted with objection by local educators and defined significant characteristics of the Title I program. Chapter 1, in an effort to redefine the federal role and reduce federal regulation of local practices, dropped these requirements. Once the regulatory thumb of federal mandate and oversight was released, parent involvement essentially came to an end in all but a few districts which had reason to value it. Local evaluation of federally supported compensatory education programs, in contrast, continued even after locals no longer "had to" evaluate their efforts. In a few districts, evaluation continued because local managers were fearful that federal auditors would return and demand evaluation. However, most districts that continued a strong evaluation effort did so because they found it useful. Originally resisted as an intrusion on local autonomy, a waste of time and money, evaluation required by Title I gradually became viewed as important once districts gained competence in carrying out and using evaluation.

The observation that belief can follow practice is important from the perspective of policies aimed at social change. The Change Agent study's conclusions reinforced the conservative tendencies of the system and implied that policy attempting to change people or practices in ways they were not motivated to change were apt to be futile. Subsequent and different experience has shown that conclusion to be overstated and directs attention to the fit between policy strategies and the incentives or motivation of the implementing agent.

External Technical Assistance

Second, our conclusions were too skeptical about the role of external agents and their ability to promote positive change in local practices. The Change Agent study concluded that outside consultants, external developers or technical assistants were too removed and insufficiently responsive to particular local conditions to provide effective support for planned change efforts.

Here, too, we were a captive of our sample. By and large, the packaged programs and the outside consultants we observed as part of the Change Agent study were ineffective because they did not acknowledge features of the local setting that demanded modification or special attention. But the study's negative conclusions about the role of external agents failed to consider what might be. As the Network's DESSI[3] study and other, subsequent research has shown, externally developed programs and external consultants can be extraordinarily effective in stimulating and supporting local efforts to improve practice. In these instances, the external agents acted to enable local efforts to respond to or modify external practices or advice to suit the local setting (Crandall and Associates 1982).

In this sense, the Change Agent study's finding about the importance of "mutual adaptation" and the DESSI study's conclusion about the positive outcomes associated with fidelity of replication and outside technical assistance are not incompatible as they might appear on their face. Rather, these two studies were based on programs and experiences that were different in at least one critical respect. Rand looked at

programs and advisors that generally ignored local factors in an effort
to encourage standardized practices. DESSI looked at programs that
had incorporated the lessons about the counterproductive aspects of
such uniformity. "Replication" no longer meant exact reproduction.

This modification of the Change Agent study's conclusion about
the role of external agents, like the one above, rewrites a discouraging-
ly conservative position regarding the possibilities of change. One
implication of the original Rand conclusion is a "tribal" or "village"
model of change which relies on local resources and capacity. Social
learning of the type assumed by many change agent strategies of dissemination and development consequently would be unlikely to occur.
However, we have seen that the broader policy system can learn from
its investments and that experience can be telescoped and effectively
shared. We understand now that it is not so much the "externalness" of
outside practices and experts that inhibits their effectiveness, but how
they interact with the local setting.

Factors Affecting Teacher Behavior

Third, while the Change Agent study correctly stressed the
significance of the actions and choices of teachers, or what Weatherley
and Lipsky (1977) called "street-level bureaucrats," and while the
study's conclusions underscored the embeddedness of local implementors in a larger system, our conception of the structures most relevant
to teachers was too narrow. Our research and analysis took the policy
system for granted. That is, we assumed that the structure most relevant to teachers was the policy structure—the federal, state, and local
policies—that eventuated in classroom practice. Had we made those
assumptions problematic, rather than taken them as givens, we would
have seen that while we as policy analysts were chiefly concerned with
the policy system, it was not always relevant to many teachers on a
day-to-day basis.

This misunderstanding is important because many of the study's
conclusions about local responses to change agent programs were
based in the assumption that teachers responded to specific policy
objectives or strategies. In fact, for many teachers, these policy goals
and activities were simply part of a broader environment that pressed
in upon their classrooms. Thus, to ask about the role or consequences
of a particular program or strategy for practice risked misspecification
because it gave policy a focus or significance it did not have in the
daily matter of classroom life. We didn't look beyond the policy structure to consider that the "embedded structure" of greatest import to

teachers might have nothing or little to do with policy—it might have to do with professional networks, with school departments or other school-level associations, or with colleagues however organized.

Ironically, although the Rand study was among the first to map backward from the perspective of local implementors and to analyze planned change efforts associated with macro-level policies, it still was a top-down study because the driving questions reflected macro-level concerns not micro-level realities. Because the Rand study did not understand that fully, its analysis fell short as a description of planned change at the local level and as advice to policymakers and practitioners about how to enhance local practice.

4. Implications for Policy

This reanalysis of the Change Agent study raises a number of implications for policy aimed at improving educational practices.

Maintain a System Orientation

One is that special projects, or reforms aimed at discrete elements of the education policy system, are likely to disappoint. The dominance of local implementation, the local factors that make variability the rule, the fluid and often unpredictable character of the local institutional environment, all underscore the *systemic* nature of the problems change agent policies address. Special projects focussed on single issues or single inputs, typically (by necessity) ignore the systemic and interconnected conditions that influence classroom practice.

Special projects also are incompatible with the realities confronting teachers and administrators on a day-to-day basis. Educators must respond to multiple, simultaneous pressures and demands. The single-focus assumptions implicit in special projects are inconsistent with schools and classrooms. Further, the demands of special projects can actually diminish overall operations because "the innovation becomes the focus rather than the more holistic, organic, classroom and school life . . . innovations becomes ends in themselves, and paradoxically, turn out to be diversions from the more basic goals of improvement" (Fullan et al. 1989).

Finally, special projects are often unproductive because they promote a view of the problems before the education policy system and practitioners as bounded and short-term. The episodic intervention embodied in programs such as the federal change agent programs

Rand studied ignore the fact that reform is steady work (Elmore and McLaughlin 1988). Many special projects implicitly or explicitly set out to "fix" the problem they address—poor reading outcomes, high dropout rates, or limited English proficiency, for example. But the problems addressed by current state-driven reforms or change agent programs are not acute; they are chronic. "Reform" needs to be systemic and on-going; special projects frame the problems of reform artificially and superficially and so are limited in their ability to significantly change educational practices.

Address Content and Process

A second implication for policy and practice relates to the enterprise policy hopes to affect. The problems addressed by education change agent policies or strategies for reform lie at the intersection of teacher, students and subject matter. Content matters as much as process. Many of the so-called innovations or reforms undertaken during the 1970s were correctly chided as simply rearranging the deck chairs, pursuing the appearance of constructive change without meaningful substance—"content-free process". If pre-1970 reforms such as the "new math" or Sputnik-motivated science curriculums fell short because specialists ignored process and the importance of local implementation, many of the post-1970 reforms failed because they passed over the "stuff" of schooling in attempts to install new strategies of decision-making, classroom management or staff development to the neglect of content. Policy intending to promote more effective educational practice must address both and acknowledge the need for the quite different kind of expertise associated with the management of organizational change and with improved content.

Use Natural Networks of Teachers

A third implication for policy has to do with frame of reference and the need to look beyond the formal policy structure as channels for promoting improvement and stimulating change. For example, if teachers lie at the heart of successful efforts to enhance classroom practices, then the professional networks that engage teachers comprise promising vehicles for change. The apparent success of teacher groups such as the Bay Area Writing Project, the Puget Sound Consortium, or the Urban Math Collaborative suggest that change strategies rooted in the natural networks of teachers—in their professional associations—may be more effective than strategies that adhere solely to a delivery structure outlined by the policy system. Reforms or policies that engage the natural networks of teachers can support change efforts in a more sustained fashion. Further, since teachers rather than policy are responsible for integrating new practices with traditional routines, it is possible to acknowledge the systemic nature of change. Reforms acknowledging the naturally occurring relationships of practitioners also open policy to the involvement of new institutional actors and promising organizational connections overlooked in policy tied to the formal delivery system.

Focus on Improving Classroom Practice

A fourth implication also has to do with the frame assumed by policy (and by policy research). Many reform policies focus on removing or buffering *constraints* to effective practice—inadequate materials, lack of appropriate teacher preparation, insufficient teacher voice in curriculum decisions, to cite a few recent concerns. However, an important lesson of the past decade or so is that removing constraints or obstacles does not by itself ensure more effective practice. A teacher with reduced class size or new materials, for example, does not necessarily do a better job in the classroom.

Other and often different factors are required to *enable* practice.[4] And, the factors that have been seen to enable practice—productive collegial relations, organizational structures that promote open communication and feedback, leadership that "manages" opportunities for professional growth and nurtures norms of individual development as examples—are not amenable to direct policy "fixes" because they do not operate singly or consistently across settings.

A focus on enabling practice—within the presence of existing constraints—highlights the conditional, mutually reinforcing and contextual nature of factors that support effective teaching. For example, shared mission and school-wide goals that encourage teachers to do their best requires leadership at the school site to manage the necessary resources and processes. However, in order for shared mission and supportive leadership to enhance classroom practices, institutional structures need to be in place that provide regular feedback about teachers' performance, that permit teachers to be heard in the area of curriculum decision-making, and that promote collegial interaction (Fullan et al. 1989). All of these "enablers", in turn, are enhanced by the presence of multiple opportunities for teachers' professional growth. By itself, any one of these factors can promote better practice, but only in the short term. Sustained support for effective classroom practice assumes the co-occurrence of these and other enabling factors at the school site.

This perspective—which moves from understanding policy implementation to enabling effective practice— underscores essential contribution of teachers' perspectives as informant and guide to policy. We have learned that we can't mandate what matters to effective practice; the challenge lies in understanding how policy can enable and facilitate it. These are the questions that, ten years later, a Change Agent study should be asking.

Chapter 9

Getting the Job Done:
Alternative Policy Instruments*

Lorraine M. McDonnell and Richard F. Elmore

Policies work by bringing the resources of government—money, rules, and authority—into the service of political objective; and by using those resources to influence the actions of individuals and institutions. The first generation of policy implementation research focused primarily on whether results were consistent with intentions. The second generation focused on variations in the response of individuals and institutions, and on the conditions of successful implementation. The next generation, we believe, should build on the lessons of the first two by focusing on the instruments common to different policies and on the conditions under which these instruments are most likely to produce their intended effects.

Over the past decade, implementation research has developed as a major strand of policy analysis. Numerous studies with an implementation focus have documented the importance of local context in understanding the variable effects of policy (McLaughlin 1987). This research tradition has played a significant role in moving institutional analysts beyond an almost sole concentration on policy enactment and in infusing evaluation research with a more sophisticated notion of the process that shapes policy outcomes. Yet implementation research has come under increasing criticism for its lack of parsimonious theory

*Reprinted from Lorraine McDonnell and Richard Elmore, "Getting the Job Done: Alternative Policy Instruments," *Educational Evaluation and Policy Analysis*, vol. 9, no. 2, Summer 1987, pp. 133–152. Copyright 1987 by American Educational Research Association. Reprinted by permission of the publisher.

(Ingram, in press), its neglect of longer term policy effects, and its primary focus on discrete federal programs.

Our interest in assessing the effects of recent education reforms across multiple states and local districts required us to address these "next generation" research issues. The education reform movement presents a unique opportunity to analyze a large number of different policies, focused on similar substantive areas and enacted within a few years of each other. However, past research provides only limited guidance because it has tended to study relatively narrow categorical programs, rather than ones targeted at all students and aimed at the core of schooling. In addition, little effort has been made to specify in any systematic way the relationship among the policy problems being addressed, the basic design features of a policy, the implementing organization and the political and organizational context in which policy targets must respond.

To address these shortcomings, we selected a framework that centers on the notion of alternative policy instruments, or the mechanisms that translate substantive policy goals (e.g., improved student achievement, higher quality entering teachers) into concrete actions. This focus builds on a promising, new direction in policy implementation research that concentrates on such mechanisms, conceptualizing them as the "technological core" of policy and categorizing them into several groups of "implements" (Elmore 1985; Bardach 1980). The categories typically analyzed include regulations, rights, grants, loans, and technical assistance. Although we expand on the notion by identifying a broader range of instruments, our basic formulation of two instruments, mandates and inducements, is also similar to ones in the economics literature (e.g., Stigler 1971; McKean 1980; Gramlich 1977; Barro 1978).

We define four generic classes of instruments:

mandates are rules governing the action of individuals and agencies, and are intended to produce compliance;

inducements transfer money to individuals or agencies in return for certain actions;

capacity-building is the transfer of money for the purpose of investment in material, intellectual, or human resources; and

system-changing transfers official authority among individuals and agencies in order to alter the system by which public goods and services are delivered.

(Each of these instruments is discussed in a subsequent section.)

Our long-term purpose in pursuing this approach to policy analysis is to be able to answer the question: Under what conditions are different instruments most likely to produce their intended effects? In
order to do that, we need to move the notion of alternative policy
instruments beyond just a simple taxonomy. We need to specify why
policymakers choose different instruments, how these instruments
actually operate in the policy arena, how they differ from one another
in their expected effects, the costs and benefits they impose, their basic
operating assumptions, and the likely consequences of their use.

This article represents the initial step in that process. The first
section provides a rationale for our focus on policy instruments. The
next one defines the four classes of policy instruments, while the third
describes how each characteristically works and with what consequences. The fourth section identifies the factors that shape the choice
of one instrument over another. The concluding section outlines a
research agenda for developing an analytical framework based on the
concept of alternative policy instruments and as a way of assessing
educational reform policies.

Why Focus on Policy Instruments?

Our focus on policy instruments stems from two interests, one
conceptual and the other practical. As indicated above, the conceptual
reason is a desire to help forge a next generation of implementation
research. In our judgement, the most promising approach is to work
toward a more parsimonious model of the determinants of implementation outcomes and ultimate policy effects, while retaining those variables that have produced the greatest explanatory pay-off—namely,
ones embedded in the local political and organizational context. Policy
implementation research now faces a dilemma. The most insightful
studies have tended to focus on one aspect of the process such as
organizational context or practitioner response to new programs. This
research has produced a greater sensitivity to the sources of variation
in implementation outcomes, but has not produced a complete explanation (and may even have led some analysts and policymakers to
assume that implementation outcomes are largely idiosyncratic). On
the other hand, empirical studies and analytical work that have
attempted to be more comprehensive have usually resulted in long lists
of conditions for effective implementation, lacking a clear specification
of how independent variables interact with one another to affect implementation results (e.g., Mazmanian and Sabatier 1983).

Our solution to this tension is to move back from specific programs and focus on their underlying mechanisms as a way of generating hypotheses about the links among policy, implementation patterns, and ultimate effects. A conceptual framework focused on policy instruments not only holds the potential for moving beyond static descriptions of the implementation process, but it also embeds key variables such as local response patterns in a larger, theoretically richer context.

Although little conceptual or empirical work has yet been done using this approach, other policy analysts are also beginning to view it as a useful one. For example, one author has suggested that a fruitful way to maneuver the field of implementation research out of its current "rut" is not to continue to focus on individual programs or groups of programs, but instead "on the generic tools of government action, on the 'techniques' of social intervention that come to be used, in varying combinations, in particular public programs" (Salamon 1981, p. 256). Our research is an attempt to do that by analyzing what is meant by the successful application of a given instrument, and by identifying the conditions necessary for different policy instruments to work as intended.

The second, more practical, reason arises from a concern that past research has done little to expand knowledge about the choice of instruments available to motivate policy action. Policymakers often lack information about the full range of instruments available to them. Many times the imposition of new mandates seems the most feasible option because it appears relatively inexpensive and presumably sends a clear signal about what policymakers expect from those being regulated. Inducements like grants-in-aid are most often used when policy must move through the intergovernmental system or when consensus about the change that needs to occur is low (Ingram 1977). Although they may sometimes use these two instruments together or in combination with other approaches, policymakers rarely have sufficient information about how much strategies can most effectively be integrated with one another or what other instruments are available.

Officials also lack systematic knowledge about the relative effectiveness of alternative instruments in addressing different types of problems, their underlying dynamics, comparative costs, attendant problems, and how well they fit into the existing policy environment. This deficiency is a particular problem in policy areas like education because of the wide range of problems that must be addressed and the numerous local settings in which policy must operate. As a result, the link between policy and action is not as strong as it might be and policymakers may turn to mandates by default, because they lack information about the full range of policy instruments, their feasibility, and likely effects. Consequently, one purpose of this research is to help expand the policy community's range of choice in the instruments it uses to solve different policy problems.

The task of conceptualizing a range of policy instruments and hypothesizing why policymakers select different instruments can be approached in two ways. Traditional social scientists would focus on the formal properties of different policy instruments. They would attempt to identify the assumptions underlying each and would assess their relative costs and benefits, often through the use of fairly abstract, mathematical models (e.g., Shepsle and Wiengast 1984). Such an approach is systematic, but often provides little practical information for the policy community. On the other hand, a politician might formulate his choice of policy largely in terms of which key constituents would lose or gain with different alternatives, how much each alternative is likely to cost, and who would bear that cost. This approach is more representative of what actually happens in the "real world," but it is also more ad hoc and idiosyncratic to individual politicians. Consequently, it contributes little to the building of generalizable models of policy implementation.

However, as Behn (1981) suggests, these two approaches are not dichotomous, but rather represent two ends of the same continuum. At one end lies a set of theoretical constructs; at the other, more instrumental concepts. But they are linked. The politician does consider what kinds of assumptions or conditions are necessary for different policies to operate effectively, and the analyst typically incorporates some elements of institutional context into his models. Because our analysis of alternative policy instruments is designed both to advance theory and produce useful information for policymakers, we have attempted to draw on the strengths of both approaches, and to negotiate the boundary between what formal constructs tell us can be done and what policymakers actually do. Consequently, we lay out the formal properties of four types of policy instruments, and we examine how they typically operate and what political and organizational factors shape policymakers' choices among them.

Range of Policy Instruments

When legislators or executives make policy, they seldom see themselves deliberately choosing among different ways of accomplishing some purpose. More often than not, they advocate particular solutions or adjudicate conflicts among political interests who advocate positions. Problems make their way onto the policy agenda by political advocacy. Responses to those problems are dictated by the stock of available solutions, by the advocacy of certain solutions, and by the resources (money, knowledge, political support, and organizational capacity) available to frame solutions (Kingdon 1984).

As policy analysts, we take a different, but complementary, perspective from the one taken by actors in the fray. We are concerned about the *range* of options available for addressing a particular problem, about the underlying theoretical premises of those options, about the "fit" between problems, objectives, and options, and about special implementation problems associated with certain classes of options. These concerns can be captured, we think, by a relatively parsimonious set of categories, which we have labelled mandates, inducements, capacity-building, and system-changing. Table 1 presents these categories and their constituent elements.

These categories of policy instruments are constructed from two main sources: (a) existing theories about the effects of governmental action; and (b) observed patterns in the choices of policymakers. Our discussion of mandates, for example, draws on theories of regulation, which address the conditions under which the targets of regulation can be expected to comply given various levels of enforcement, sanctions, and costs and benefits of compliance. (See, e.g., Bardach and Kagan 1982; Mitnick 1980; Stigler 1971). Our discussion of inducements draws on theories of public finance that deal with intergovernmental transfers. These theories address the conditions under which government agencies can be induced to perform certain actions by conditional grants of funds from other governmental agencies. (See, e.g., Gramlich 1977; Ingram 1977.) These are areas in which the basic theoretical issues are relatively well-specified; hence the problem is one of mobilizing existing theory around a somewhat different set of questions.

In the other two areas, capacity-building and system-changing, it seems to us that a strong *prima facie* case can be made for distinguishable categories of policy instruments, based on observed patterns of policymaking, even though their theoretical basis is less well-developed. As we shall see, capacity-building, like inducement, involves the conditional transfer of funds from one governmental agency to another, but introduces the additional element of investment in uncertain future benefits. In this sense, capacity-building draws on theories of regulation and intergovernmental transfers, but raises the question of how those mechanisms work in situations where the expected outcomes are distant and ambiguous. System-changing entails transfers of authority, rather than money, with the aim of altering the institutional structures

Table 1   Policy Instruments Defined

	Primary Elements	Expected Effects	Costs	Benefits	Examples
Mandates	Rules	Compliance	*Initiators* Enforcement *Targets* Compliance Avoidance	Specific benefits to individuals Diffuse benefits to society	Environmental regulation Non-discrimination requirements Speed limits
Inducements	Money (procurement)	Production of value; short-term returns	*Initiators* Production Oversight Displacement *Producers* Overhead Matching Avoidance	*Initiators/Producers* Increased budget authority *Clients* Value received	Grants-in-aid to government In-Kind grants to individuals
Capacity-building	Money (investment)	Enhancement of skill, competence, long-term returns	Short-term costs to initiating government	Short-term, specific benefits to receiving agency Long-term, diffuse benefits to society	Basic research Preservation
System-changing	Authority	Composition of public delivery system; incentives	Loss of authority by established deliverers	Gain in authority by new deliverers	Vouchers Deinstitutionalization New providers (HMOs, Community Mental Health Agencies)

by which policies are implemented.[1] To some degree, system-changing instruments owe their theoretical underpinnings to the critique of public bureaucracy growing out of political economy (Moe 1984; Niskanen 1971; Tullock 1965). But that literature has spoken only indirectly to the problems of policy analysis.

Capacity-building and system-changing, it seemed to us, were sufficiently different from mandates and inducements, in their composition, expected effects, and implementation problems, to require separate treatment. The notion of investment in future benefits underlying capacity-building captures a common problem reported in earlier implementation research—that mandates and inducements often fail for lack of knowledge, skill, and competence rather than the will to comply. Capacity-building also captures those policies that focus mainly on longer term developmental objectives rather than short-term compliance or production. The notion of transfers of authority underlying system-changing captures a common problem confronted by policymakers—how to match purposes with existing or potential institutions. Selecting or creating an implementing agency is often as important a choice for policymakers as transferring money or specifying rules. Yet the choice of agency is often not treated by policymakers as a distinguishable problem.

Our theoretical aims in constructing these categories are both positive and normative. We expect that by specifying policy instruments in this way, we lay bare certain recurring problems that policymakers face and give them a predictive structure. In this sense, our aims are positive. We also expect that specifying policy instruments contributes to policymakers' understanding of the instrumental relationship between objectives and policy choices. In this sense, our aims are normative.

Mandates are rules governing the actions of individuals and agencies. The expected effect of mandates is compliance, or behavior consistent with what the rules prescribe. In their pure form, mandates entail no transfer of money as an inducement to comply. They require enforcement, and enforcement is costly to the enforcing agency. They also entail the imposition of costs on the objects of enforcement—individuals and implementing agencies. These costs typically take two forms: Compliance costs are the costs borne by individuals and agencies as a consequence of behaving consistently with mandates; avoidance costs are costs borne as a result of circumventing mandates, bargaining with enforcement agencies about the terms of compliance, or using political influence and litigation to change mandates (McKean 1980). The benefits of mandates sometimes accrue primarily to specific individuals or groups, as, for example, when handicapped or disadvantaged students benefit from federal or state-mandated programs in local school. Often mandates are intended to benefit a broader community or society as a whole, as, for example, when polluters are required to install abatement equipment to reduce bad air or water.[2]

Inducements are transfers of money to individuals or agencies in return for the production of goods or services. Inducements are a form of procurement, in the sense that an agency is empowered to transfer money or authority to an individual or another agency in return for something of value (Bardach 1980). The expected effect of inducements is the production of value. The thing of value may be a program addressed to a particular clientele (compensatory education for disadvantaged students, work incentives for welfare mothers) or it might be a tangible project (and interstate highway).

Because inducements are conditional grants for money, they are frequently accompanied by rules (often called regulations) designed to assure that money is used consistently with policymakers' intent. These rules create oversight costs to the implementing agency. They entail costs to implementing agencies, in the form of unreimbursed administrative expenses, matching requirements, and avoidance costs designed to mitigate the effect of undesirable conditions on the transfer of money or authority. The benefits of inducements accrue both to implementing agencies, in the form of increased budget and authority, and to individual beneficiaries, through the value that is produced by the implementing agency. Often however, the interests of implementing agencies and those of the intended beneficiaries are not completely consistent, so that a certain amount of money transferred through inducements is lost to the production of valued benefits and siphoned off into activities that have value mainly to the implementing agency (see Gramlich 1977).

The main differences between mandates and inducements, however, are threefold: First, mandates use coercion to affect performance, while inducements transfer money as a condition of performance. Second, mandates exact compliance as an outcome, while inducements are designed to elicit the production of value as an outcome. Third, as we shall see in more detail later, mandates assume that the required action is something all individuals and agencies should be expected to do, regardless of their differing capacities, while inducements assume that individuals and agencies vary in their ability to produce things of value and that the transfer of money is one way to elicit performance.

Capacity-building is the transfer of money to individuals or agencies for the purpose of investment in future benefits—material, intellectual, or human resources. As with all investments in material or human capital, capacity-building carries with it the expectation of future returns. But these returns are often uncertain, intangible, immeasurable, and distant. Sometimes capacity-building involves intermediate products or services, such as the federal government's investment in science and mathematics curriculum development, which produced both materials and future capacity to teach, or federal investment in high energy particle accelerators, which produced both pork barrel benefits for local constituencies and future capacity to carry out basic research. In other instances, capacity-building involves only distant returns, such as those entailed in the preservation of wilderness, or unrestricted income support for children (as in children's allowances in Canada and European countries).

The costs of capacity-building accrue to the government making the investment and to society in general. The benefits of capacity-building accrue in the short term to the specific individuals and the institutions that are their recipients, but the ultimate beneficiaries are future members of society, whose interests cannot be clearly determined in the present. Hence, policymakers use immediate measures as proxies for their longer-term effects. Is the particle accelerator actually built and is it used for basic research? Are adequate numbers of science and mathematics teachers entering the teaching force and are they staying long enough to provide instruction to students? Society's willingness to invest in intangible, immeasurable, and distant benefits may affect its future ability to respond to mandates and inducements. It is difficult, for example, to envision a policy of inducements designed to improve the quality of science instruction working in the absence of a generally literate and well-educated teacher force. In this sense, capacity-building may be instrumental to mandates and inducements.

The main difference between capacity-building, on the one hand, and mandates and inducements, on the other, lies in the proximity and tangibility of their effects. Capacity-building has distant and ambiguous effects, mandates and inducements have proximate, and tangible effects.

System-changing is the transfer of official authority among individuals and agencies. The expected effect of system-broadening or -narrowing is a change in the institutional structure is by which public goods and services are delivered and often a change in the incentives which determine the nature and effects of those goods and services. System-broadening, as a policy instrument, is best understood by imagining a constant budget for a given public service—education or health care, for example—and then imagining some dramatic change in policy toward the provision of that service—allowing private schools to receive general public aid, for example, or nationalizing the provisions of health care. The key shift in these new arrangements is in the *authority* to provide a publicly-supported or subsidized product or service. In the case of schools, the shift was from a public quasi-monopoly to a public-private competitive market (system-broadening). In the case of health care, the shift was from a predominantly private market in which in-kind transfers to individuals serve public purposes to a public monopoly (system-narrowing).

System-changing policies may be based on the expectation that transferring authority will increase efficiency, as with the preferential treatment of Health Maintenance Organizations (HMOs) in federal health care policy. Or they may be based on the expectation that transferring authority will alter the distribution of political power, as when the federal government created local community action agencies in cities, during the 1960s War on Poverty, to strengthen the political influence of poor and minority citizens against local governments.

One effect of system-changing policies may be to alter the distribution of public funds to providers or consumers of public goods and services, and in this sense they may resemble inducements. But the fundamental property of system-changing policies is the distribution of authority, not money. Changes in the distribution of money, in other words, follow changes in the distribution of authority in system-changing policies.

System-changing policies may result in the creation of whole new classes of agencies, as with HMOs and federal health care policy, or community mental health centers and federal mental health policy. Alternatively, they may result in the dissolution of significant parts of public delivery systems, as with the closing of state juvenile detention facilities with deinstitutionalization. These changes may dramatically alter the distribution of money among agencies and individuals, without necessarily altering the total amount spent in a given sector or the mandates and inducements under which agencies and individuals operate. On the other hand, system-changing may be accompanied by changes in mandates and inducements that are designed to enhance their effects.

In summary, policymakers face a discrete number of potentially powerful choices when they respond to a policy problem. They can set rules, they can conditionally transfer money, they can invest in future capacity, and they can grant or withdraw authority to individuals and agencies. Each of these options is expected to carry a particular effect—compliance, production, capacity, or authority. And each carries a package of benefits and costs to different actors.

How Instruments Work

Different policy instruments carry different assumptions about problems and solutions. Once specified, these assumptions tell us a good deal about the fit between problem and policy and about the basic conditions for successful implementation (Table 2).

Mandates assume (a) that the required action is something all individuals and agencies should be expected to do, regardless of their differing capacities, and (b) that the required actions would not occur, or would not occur with the frequency or consistency specified by the policy, in the absence of explicit prescription. Rules, in other words, are introduced to create uniformity of behavior or, at least, to reduce variations in behavior to some tolerable level.

Problems that prompt mandates are typically ones in which coercion is required to change behavior, and in which the expectation is that the behavior prescribed by policy is correct in its own right. Occupational health and safety regulations, speed limits, nondiscrimination requirements, compulsory school attendance laws, student graduation standards, and entry standards for teachers are all examples where governments have decided to use coercion as the chief means of creating uniformity or reducing variation in behavior.

Because mandates assume an essentially coercive or adversarial relationship between enforcers and the objects of enforcements, they place the major responsibility for assuring compliance on the initiating government. The level of enforcement which the initiating government is willing to pay for is a key determinant of the level of compliance it can expect. Since the investment of additional resources in enforcement typically entails diminishing marginal returns in compliance, implementation of mandates usually consists of trying to achieve the highest level of compliance possible within the resource constraints imposed on the implementing agency. Mandates seldom, if ever, result in uniform compliance, since the last unit of compliance usually involves prohibitively high enforcement costs (Stigler 1971; Viscusi and Zeckhauser 1979). Hence, it is usually in the interests of some individuals or agencies to resist compliance, or to spend money on avoiding compliance, if by doing so they can reap positive benefits.

Mandates typically set minimum standards for compliance, and in doing so introduce disincentives to exceed those standards. If, for example, the median reading achievement level for high school seniors in a given state is at the eighth grade level, a 12th-grade reading achievement graduation standard would create compliance problems for many high school seniors, as well as a significant number of school

Table 2   Policy Instruments—Assumptions and Consequences

	Assumptions	*Consequences*
Mandates	Actions required regardless of capacity; good in its own right	Coercion required
	Action would not occur with desired frequency or consistency without rule	Create uniformity, reduce variation
		Policy contains information necessary for compliance
		Adversarial relations between initiators, targets
		Minimum standards
Inducements	Valued good would not be produced with desired frequency or consistency in absence of additional money	Capacity exists; money needed to mobilize it
		As tolerable range of variation narrows, oversight costs increase
	Individuals, agencies vary in capacity to produce; money elicits performance	Most likely to work when capacity exists
Capacity-building	Knowledge, skill competence required to produce future value; or	Capacity does not exist; investment needed to mobilize it
	Capacity good in its own right or instrumental to other purposes	Tangible present benefits serve as proxies for future, intangible benefits
System-changing	Existing institutions, existing incentives cannot produce desired results	Institutional factors incite action; provokes defensive response
	Changing distribution of authority changes what is produced	New institutions raise new problems of mandates, inducements, capacities

districts. The standard would also create enforcement problems for the state education agency. On the other hand, setting the standard at, or slightly above, the median score allows the state to assert standards, while at the same time minimizing its own enforcement problems and the costs it imposes on local districts. This standard, however, contains little incentive for improved performance on the part of low-achieving students and districts.

Standards, even when they are clear, are limited in the degree to which they can significantly change behavior. Reducing the speed limit on interstate highways from 70 miles per hour to 55 miles per hour significantly reduced the median speed of automobiles, highway fatalities, and fuel consumption. It also created large problems of enforcement and noncompliance. The important feature of the speed limit law was that the law itself contained all the information necessary for individuals to comply. By contrast, high school graduation standards based on academic achievement do not contain the information necessary for compliance. In order to comply, individuals must not only read and understand the standards, they must engage in other activities—teaching and learning—that require skill, motivation, and resources. So graduation standards might fail either because individuals and school systems deliberately fail to comply, or more likely, because of some failure of capacity on the part of individuals or schools.

Inducements assume (a) that, in the absence of additional money, one would not expect certain valued things to be produced, or to be produced with the frequency or consistency prescribed by policy; and (b) that individuals and agencies vary in their ability to produce things of value and the transfer of money is one way to elicit performance.

Problems that prompt inducements are ones in which the absence of money directed at the appropriate purposes is the key determinant of the problem. Inducements assume that the capacity exists to produce whatever is required or can be readily acquired if the right monetary incentives are provided. Inducement problems are, at some fundamental level, production or procurement problems; the object is to get individuals and agencies to produce something of value with the money that is transferred.

Individuals and agencies vary, of course, in their capacity to produce things of value. Individuals vary in their food consumption practices, even though we prescribe limited uses for food stamps. School districts vary in their ability to teach English to non-English speaking students, even though we transfer money in a more or less equitable way to enhance bilingual instruction.

A central issue in the implementation of inducements, then, is how much variation policymakers are willing to tolerate in the production of things of value, and how narrowly they are willing to prescribe how money is to be used and what is produced. As the range of tolerable variation narrows, and the restrictions or inducements increase, the problems associated with the implementation of inducements begin to look more and more like those associated with mandates. The key difference, as noted above, though, is that mandates expect compliance without compensation, while inducements use conditional compensation as a lever to elicit the required behavior.

In addition to differences in capacity, individuals and agencies vary in their preferences and priorities. District A may see bilingual education as a major priority, it may have a vocal political constituency that favors bilingual education, and it may invest a large share of its own resources in bilingual education in addition to any inducements it receives from the state or federal government. District B, on the other hand, may regard bilingual education as a distraction from its locally-initiated academic excellence program, bilingual education may have no constituency, and it may use state or federal inducements to fund the bare minimum of required activities. Both districts have bilingual programs, yet the effect of the inducement varies considerably.

Inducements are most likely to be effective when the capacities exist to produce the things that policymakers value and when preferences and priorities support the production of those things. Large variations in capacity or preferences and priorities will produce similar variations in the results produced by inducements. The degree to which inducements come to resemble mandates in their enforcement problems depends on the degree of variability in capacities, preferences, and priorities policymakers are willing to tolerate.

Capacity-building assumes (a) that, in the absence of immediate investment, future material, intellectual, or human benefits will not be realized by society; and (b) that these longer term benefits are either worth having in their own right, or are instrumental to other purposes that policymakers regard as important.

The kind of problems that prompt capacity-building responses are fundamental failures of performance by some set of individuals or institutions. Issues of capacity enter the political agenda when, for example, policymakers realize that the country will lose its competitive edge in high-energy physics if the federal government does not invest large sums of money on a new particle accelerator, or that more than one million of the nation's 2.4 million teachers will leave their jobs in the next six to eight years.

The intangible and uncertain results of capacity-building create major problems for policymakers. Investments in basic knowledge— social science research, language instruction, particle physics—are difficult to justify in themselves, because they are made at the expense of other uses of public funds that have more immediate, tangible pay-offs.

Because of the intangibility and uncertainty of the results of capacity-building measures, there is a tendency in policy discussions either to emphasize their present utility or to discount future benefits because of their intangibility. Investments in particle physics research are "really" useful in this view because of their short-term utility for military weapons development, or they are not useful at all because of their dubious value in producing immediate returns. Investments in curriculum development are "really" useful because they produce tangible materials, or they are not useful at all because they fail to produce immediate effects on school curriculum. Capacity-building is seldom, if ever, successful as an inducement because there are basic contradictions between mobilizing material, intellectual, and human resources for future purposes and the immediate production of value.

The tendency to mistake capacity-building for inducement often leads policymakers to confuse the immediate production of results and the creation of capacity for future production. A federal program to produce greater competence in mathematics and science, as a response to competition from abroad, can only produce limited results in the short-term because it is calling on the limited capacity of existing elementary and the secondary schools to teach mathematics and science. By the time investments in capacity reach maturity, in the form of more highly qualified, better trained teachers, policymakers may or may not still be worried about the nation's competitive edge. The only way to assure a short-term response, in other words, is to call upon existing capacity.

System-changing instruments assume (a) that existing institutions, working under existing incentives, cannot produce results that policymakers want; and (b) that altering the distribution of authority among institutions, by broadening or narrowing the type of institutions that participate in the production of things of public value, will significantly change the nature of what is produced or the efficiency with which it is produced.

The kind of problems that prompt system-changing responses are either unresponsiveness of existing institutions to respond to important changes in their environment. When state hospitals and private psychiatric clinics seemed unable to respond to growing need for mental health treatment, federal and state policy shifted to funding community-based treatment. When juvenile detention institutions failed to respond to growing demands for less punitive, more rehabilitative care of juvenile offenders, federal and state policymakers moved to reduce or eliminate the authority of detention facilities and transfer that authority to less punitive organizations. When federal policymakers saw increasing problems with health care costs containment, they expanded eligibility for subsidized health care to a new set of institutions, health care maintenance organizations (HMOs) and introduced strong financial incentives to form such organizations. The perennial issue of education vouchers is an example of an unsuccessful attempt to capitalize on discontent with existing public schools to broaden the array of publicly-subsidized providers of education and to alter the relationship between those institutions and their clients.

Granting authority to new institutions or redistributing authority among existing institutions sets the initial conditions for a response to the failure of existing institutions, but it also introduces a new set of problems for policymakers. Existing institutions can blunt or co-opt system-broadening policies, as when school practitioners worked to reduce the level of parent influence in the educational voucher experiment in Alum Rock, California. System-broadening policies can fail for lack of capacity in the institutions to which authority is transferred, as in the case of deinstitutionalization of the mentally ill, where community residential treatment did not develop fast enough to respond to the outflow of patients from state mental hospitals. Introducing public service providers raises the issues of how closely they should be controlled, whether they should be allowed to choose their own clients, and what performance expectations they should meet. System-changing policies, then, have a tendency to devolve or degrade into incremental modifications of existing institutions and into more traditional mandates and inducements.

Choosing a Policy Instrument

The four generic classes of policy instruments we have defined could all be used to address the same policy goal. Yet policymakers typically choose to rely on one of these instruments, or to supplement their primary reliance on one with some combination of instruments. What leads policymakers to select one instrument over another?

We have identified two factors that we hypothesize shape this choice: how a policy problem is defined, and the resources and constraints policymakers face.[3] Problem definition for policymakers occurs within an essentially political context in which decisions are tempered by a variety of feasibility considerations (May 1986). We assume that these factors constitute the resources and constraints that enter into policymakers' calculations throughout the process of matching policy problems and instruments. However, for the sake of conceptual clarity, we consider each of these factors separately, beginning with problem definition.

The Definition of a Policy Problem

Past research has examined the role of problem definition in policy analysis (Dery 1984; Wildavsky 1979) and in agenda-setting (Kingdon 1984). In hypothesizing about its role in instrument selection, we assume that problem definition functions much the same way there as it does in agenda-setting, and further assume that it consists of several components.

The first embodies a basic set of facts that most people can agree upon (e.g., that student test scores have declined, that traffic fatalities have increased). Marshalling such facts to define a policy problem often depends on the existence of relevant indicators—statistics that describe the state of the policy system and provide a benchmark for comparing current conditions with those of earlier times or different places (Kingdon 1984; for a comprehensive discussion of policy indicators, see MacRae 1985).

Once a problem has been identified, the search for causes and potential solutions contains both analytical and normative aspects. For example, research indicates that achievement is linked to the number and types of courses students take, and indicator data showed that students were taking fewer courses during the 1970s. However, while such research-based information might help define the nature of a problem and its probable causes, it is not the only source.

Policymakers hold values about the preferred state of the social system and which mechanisms should be used to achieve that condition. This more normative dimension generates two types of policymaker judgments. The first are casual statements about assumed relationships among key components of the policy system. For example, some policymakers observing test score declines may attribute them primarily to incompetent teachers, while others may assume that they are due to "watered-down" texts, lazy students, or unconscientious parents. These differences stem from differing casual theories about how social systems actually operate.

A second aspect can be classified as a set of intentional beliefs about how the system *ought* to work. This intentional aspect is analogous to MacRae and Wilde's notion that a social problem can be defined as the contrast between an observed state of affairs and a valued expectation (1979, p. 23). So, for example, implicit in a concern about student test score decline is an expectation that students of a given age ought to perform at a particular achievement level.

This intentional component also manifests itself in the relationship between how policymakers define the level of changed behavior they hope to effect and the instruments they choose. For example, given the way different instruments operate, we would expect that if policymakers perceive a policy problem as the need to move behavior *beyond* an expected minimum, they will be more likely to choose inducements. On the other hand, if they view the purpose as moving behavior to a specified minimum, they will be more likely to select a mandate approach.

Intentional preferences manifest themselves not just in judgments about the way a particular policy system ought to look, but also in how that desired state might be best achieved. Included in this category are those values typically associated with policymaker ideology or political philosophy—for example, whether market mechanisms are preferable to nonmarket ones, or what governmental levels should perform different functions. Regardless of what indicator data may suggest about a particular policy problem, policymakers prefer policy instruments consistent with their own values. So, for example, we would argue that those believing in a strong governmental role are likely to look to mandates; those who believe in the preeminence of market mechanisms are likely to prefer inducements or system changing instruments.[4]

The notion of policy problem definition, then, includes both analytical and normative components. Through the use of such mechanisms as indicator systems, policymakers process information about the scope and nature of a problem. Such analytical sources can also help them in identifying the probable causes of various problems by providing data about relationships among key factors in a given policy system. However, policymakers also interpret this information using their own pre-existing values about how the system actually works and how it ought to work. This is the normative component of problem definition with both its casual and intentional aspects. We make these distinctions within the more general concept of problem definition because we believe that these separate factors may have an independent effect on the choice of policy instruments.

Resources and Constraints

The way a policymaker defines a problem may, in many cases, indicate a clear choice of instrument. However, few policymakers act alone, or operate in an environment without constraints that limit their range of choice. Consequently, the selection of a policy instrument depends on the constraints a policymaker faces and the resources available either to diminish the force of those constraints or to enhance the effectiveness of a given instrument. In simplest terms, identifying resources and constraints is how policymakers assess what is feasible, given how they define a policy problem.

Resources and constraints are rarely mutually exclusive categories. Most resources and constraints are mirror opposites of each other. For example, money and information are resources; the lack of them may constitute a constraint. Resources are also not completely exogenous to the individual policymaker. A skillful politician may create resources to further his policy agenda where they did not previously exist. Conversely, less skilled politicians may create constraints where none existed, or deplete available resources too hastily. We believe that six types of resources and constraints are particularly significant in the choice of a policy instrument. They are: institutional context, governmental capacity, fiscal resources, political support or opposition, information, and past policy choices.

Institutional context. Institutional context is a multi-dimensional factor. It includes a set of enduring characteristics—the allocation of formal and informal authority among policy actors, and the structure and function of existing agencies. These characteristics persist regardless of which individuals occupy a particular office or role position. We assume that in a state where the political culture supports strong local control norms, state policymakers are less likely to enact mandates than in a state where the notion of strong central government is widely accepted. Similarly, the structure and function of state agencies may strongly determine what instruments are chosen. We know, for example, that state education agencies whose primary function has been the enforcement of federal program mandates experience great difficulty in implementing capacity-building policies: they often lack the appropriate personnel and their organizational structure must be radically changed (McDonnell and McLaughlin 1980). Institutional context is manifested not just in the implementation of a policy, but also in its enactment. Which branch of government initiates a policy or which legislative committee (Shepsle and Weingast 1984) has jurisdiction over it may shape the choice of policy instrument.

Most of the time institutional context acts as a constraint on policymakers, particularly if they are considering a major departure from past practice. They may lack sufficient authority because it is shared with other actors at their governmental level or across levels in the intergovernmental system. Or they may find that the transaction costs of existing bureaucracies adapting to new roles and responsibilities are prohibitive. Hence, institutional context often serves as a strong bias towards the status quo in choice of policy instruments.

Governmental capacity. Governmental capacity defines both the ability of the initiating level to implement a policy and the ability of the target to meet the policy's requirements. It includes the numbers and types of personnel available, their level of expertise, and relevance to the demands of a particular policy instrument. Instruments require varying levels of capacity, with mandates demanding the greatest amount and capacity-building (by definition), the least. Research on regulatory policy has typically portrayed the likelihood of compliance as based on a calculation that weighs the costs of compliance and non-compliance (i.e., the severity of sanctions and the likelihood of enforcement). However, this assumes that targets have the ability to comply if they decide the costs of non-compliance are sufficiently high. Yet an equally important factor in determining compliance may be the capacity of implementing agencies and the ability of those subject to a mandate to meet its requirements.

Capacity-level is one dimension; the other is the distribution of that capacity across targets. One critical characteristic of the intergovernmental system is the amount of variability across state and local settings. These differences in personnel resources and skill levels often preclude the use of mandates because they assume a near-uniform response. Rather, variability in capacity levels may lead policymakers to the other three types of instruments because they permit greater latitude in the response of targets.

Fiscal resources.   Past research suggests that organizational and fiscal slack is a necessary (though not sufficient) condition for policy innovation (Cyert and March 1963; Nelson 1978). Organizations and governmental agencies which have more resources than they need to perform required functions can devote the excess to experimenting with new approaches.

Without the existence of slack resources, the opportunity costs of enacting new policies become a major constraint on policymakers' options. If, for some reason, additional funds are available, then the choice of policy instruments can be made on other grounds. If, however, the alternatives are either to trade-off resources with other policies or to raise revenues through increased taxation, policymakers are likely to look to those instruments that appear to cost less.

We assume that mandates impose the least cost on those initiating a policy because most of the burden of compliance (and hence, the cost) is likely to be borne by the policy target. System-changing instruments also appear to cost less than the other two instruments. Most system-changing policies now in place in education either have only limited participation (e.g., alternative routes of teacher certification) or reallocate existing expenditures from one target to another (e.g., allowing high school students to attend post-secondary institutions removes state aid from one educational level and gives it to another).

When used to address the same policy problem as a mandate or system-changing instrument, inducements and capacity-building instruments, on average, are likely to impose a higher cost on those initiating the policy. However, policymakers, faced with other constraints such as the nature of the institutional context or limited political support, may decide an inducement is the only viable instrument, despite limited fiscal resources. The proliferation of small categorical programs within the federal government during the 1960s and 1970s typifies this situation. Finding it necessary to respond to growing demands from various interest groups and lacking sufficient authority to impose new mandates, Congress used limited federal resources to create a variety of small-grant, inducement programs. Much of these programs' ineffectiveness can be attributed to their inadequate funding, and the lack of realization that if requisite fiscal resource levels are not considered in choosing a policy instrument, serious inefficiencies may result.

Political support and opposition. Given that policymakers can seldom act autonomously, they need to anticipate other actors' preferences in order to build the political coalition necessary for their favored instrument's selection. Other policymakers, organized interests, and constituents may have *a priori* preferences for certain instruments over others; these preferences constitute a potential resource or constraint. In addition, however, policymakers have the potential to manipulate elite and public opinion in favor of their choice. They can use the size of their electoral plurality as a mechanism for commanding policy support. Policymakers might also be able to argue that their preferred instrument is consistent with the political ideology of various actors, or that benefits such as visibility or future electoral support will accrue as a result of supporting a particular instrument.

Conversely, the strength of opposing interests is a constraint—particularly if they are well-organized, have an alternative definition of the policy problem, and prefer a different instrument. In the face of strong opposition, a policymaker may find that an inducement (such as a small grant program) may be the only option for addressing a policy problem as he or she has defined it. The alternative would be to do nothing or to accept the opposition's approach.

Generally an inducement will require the lowest level of political support. Mandates usually require higher support levels to enact because the burden they impose on targets is perceived as widespread and fairly uniform. (Inducements, on the other hand, can take the form of pork barrel legislation where perceived costs and benefits can be differentiated according to local preferences, and then traded-off against each other.) Capacity-building instruments tend to be visible only to direct participants, and hence do not provide a broad enough base on which to build a strong political coalition. System-changing instruments are often controversial because they represent a radical departure from current policy, and focus the political debate on deeply-held beliefs about the utility of market mechanisms. Consequently, they require a very strong political support coalition.

Information. We hypothesized that the information, likely to shape the choice of policy instruments, is of three types:

- about what is preferred by other policy makers, organized interests, and constituents—*political intelligence;*

- about the target, its capacity to implement and probable response to various instruments—*strategic information;* and

- about the technical requirements of various instruments and which are likely to work under different conditions—*analytical information.*

Clearly, the match between policy problem and instrument will be best when all three types of information (and particularly the latter two) are available and reliable. The availability of such information is particularly important for a policy area like education because control is so fragmented among policy actors and governmental levels (Weiss and Gruber 1984). Weiss and Gruber imply that it may be important for a policymaker to expend greater effort in obtaining information about the likely response of targets to mandates. With inducements, however, targets may have a greater incentive to produce useful knowledge about their own competence (Weiss and Gruber 1984, p. 230). Schultze (1977) also makes a similar point, arguing that inducements lessen the need for the most difficult-to-collect information (viz., about individual production functions and demand curves), and substitute the more efficient information-processing and feedback mechanism of the market.

Although the information needed for inducement strategies may be easier to obtain, the costs of not having such information are still high. As Bardach notes, the lack of adequate information about the effects of inducements often results in inefficient reward schedules that generate incentives which turn out "to be too weak or too strong, or just plain perverse" (1980, p. 7). Analytical information about the effects of inducements is limited because most research in this area has either focused on intergovernmental grants (for a review of this literature, see Gramlich 1977) or tax policy (for a review of this literature, see

Bosworth 1984). However, when the intended effect of an inducement is to motivate actions other than changes in economic behavior (e.g., better teaching), much less is known about which inducements are most effective or how they should be combined with other policy instruments. In many policy areas, we also lack the ability to measure performance reliability and then to connect rewards to performance. For example, research to identify the elements of a fair and accurate evaluation system for awarding teacher-directed inducements is still in the early stages (Wise, Darling-Hammond, McLaughlin, and Bernstein 1984).

Similar gaps in information also exist for capacity-building and system-changing instruments. This lack may constitute one reason why policymakers turn to mandates so frequently. Although the costs of obtaining adequate information on mandates may be high, the underlying theory and technology are available. Because that capacity is less highly developed for the other policy instruments, the risks involved with choosing them may be significantly higher, at least on the informational dimension.

Past policy choices. The cumulative effects of past policy choices shape the selection of policy instruments in several ways. First, past policies may significantly influence what the public wants from government and how it expects those goals to be accomplished. These expectations, in turn, affect the standards by which a policymaker's performance is judged by the electorate, and the range of acceptable alternatives available. For example, if past administrations have traditionally relied on inducements to accomplish their goals in a particular policy area, it may be very difficult for subsequent administrations to use a different instrument, even if their definition of the policy problem would lead them to do so.[5]

Second, the cumulative effects of past policies may circumscribe the use of fiscal resources. The budgetary commitments made by past administrations can seriously limit the alternatives available to their successors. Given this constraint and confronted with a serious problem, policymakers may turn to those instruments which impose less cost at the initiating level and more on policy targets.

This budgetary effect of past policies is especially significant since it works, in effect, as a secular constraint, independent of any particular policymaker or administration. In fact, it may be that as this type of constraint grows over time, it will lead more policymakers to consider system-changing instruments that reallocate existing resources and authority, with necessarily requiring additional amounts.

As this discussion of past policy choices and its relationship to fiscal resource levels indicates, the resources and constraints we have identified are not always mutually exclusive of one another. Their relative significance in the choice of a given instrument may also vary considerably from one context to another. As a first step, however, we feel confident in conceptualizing resources and constraints as those factors that modify policymakers' initial preferences for certain policy instruments, based on their feasibility in an essentially political world.

Conclusions and a Future Research Agenda

A major challenge for the next generation of policy research will be to apply the lessons of past implementation studies in building a more powerful conceptual framework and at the same time, in producing more useful information for policymakers. By focusing on alternative policy instruments, we are attempting to do just that. Because we view the instruments through which substantive goals are translated into action as lying at the core of any policy, we feel this approach will allow us to develop a parsimonious framework that specifies the key relationships among problem definition, instrument choice, organizational context, implementation, and effects. We believe that our four classes of policy instruments capture the major dimensions along which some mechanisms differ—namely, the instrumentality motivating policy action (rules, money, and authority), expected effects, primary costs and benefits, and the time frame for accomplishing policy objectives.

We came to the topic of alternative policy instruments because of our interest in the reform policies that states and localities have enacted over the past few years to improve the quality of public education. As we observed policymakers search for alternatives to mandates, we realized that a conceptual exercise, defining the range of policy instruments and examining the political and organizational conditions needed for each to work as intended, could also generate practical applications. In this sense, our approach to the next generation of policy research is also aimed at producing useful information about the broader range of policy instruments.

We view this paper as a first step in a long process of refining our categories of instruments and empirically testing hypotheses about their interaction with different policy problems and contexts. The next step will consist of empirical research that attempts to classify a diverse set of policies, operating in different institutional contexts, according to our four instrument types. We want to make certain that the policy instruments we have defined actually exist in that form in the policy arena. For example, do a set of policies fit our definition of mandates and have more in common with each other than with other policies that could be classified as inducements, capacity-building, or system-changing instruments? One empirical test of our framework will be the degree to which the variation across classes of instruments is greater than the variation within any one type (e.g., among different kinds of mandates).

Our initial approach to this research is a multi-year examination of state-initiated education reforms in six states. While working in the same time frame and addressing similar problems, states have chosen to emphasize very different instruments and to use them in diverse combinations. Consequently, this focus provides a unique opportunity to explore the concept of alternative policy instruments. If this initial research is productive, we hope that other education policies, as well as ones in other policy areas, can be examined using the same framework.

A number of other questions will be addressed as part of the research on state education reforms. For example:

> What factors are most significant in shaping policymakers' choice of instruments?

> Are certain instruments typically used by different policy actors (e.g., legislatures vs. state boards of education) or for different types of implementing agencies (e.g., state bureaucracies vs. local school sites)?

> Are different leadership strategies used to advance different policy instruments?

> Do different policy instruments interact with policy targets (e.g., school districts, teachers, students) in the ways we have hypothesized?

> Is the organizational and political context in which policies are implemented more important in explaining implementation patterns and policy effects for some instruments than for others?

Another component of the empirical research will be aimed at developing finer distinctions within and across categories of instruments based on how they actually operate. In conceptualizing classes of instruments, we have discussed them singly in order to make the distinctions among them clearer. However, we know that in selecting from a menu of options, policymakers often choose a combination of strategies for achieving a particular policy goal. At this point, we would hypothesize that for any given policy problem, policymakers will select a dominant policy instrument, but that others may be used to supplement or follow the primary one. For example, a voucher scheme changes which institutions have the authority to receive public funds for providing educational services, but it is also accompanied by financial inducements to motivate private institutions to participate. Similarly, a career ladder is essentially an inducement to encourage better performance from teachers, but it might also be supplemented by capacity-building policies such as ones to train principals to evaluate teachers more effectively. This line of research will not only identify the different ways that instruments can be used in combination with one another, but also which factors influence whether such combinations occur.[6]

Despite the number of unanswered questions and the size of the future research agenda, we feel that a focus on policy instruments is a productive approach. Because it seeks to develop a predictive framework that links the major components of the policy stream, it holds the potential for producing a theoretically richer generation of policy research. In essence, this approach to policy research asks: Does the notion of policy instruments, as we have defined it, help explain why policies take the form they do, and does it help predict their ultimate effects?

However, another set of questions are equally important if we are to provide useful information to policymakers. These ask whether the notion of policy instruments provides policymakers with additional insight about the range of alternatives available to them, and whether it gives them a useful perspective for better understanding the links among policy, practice, and effects. In some sense, these latter questions require only that our framework function well as a descriptive device without being strongly predictive. Yet the ability to provide the policy community with new insight, beyond that gained from other theories or analytical frameworks, may be the strongest test of whether our four classes of policy instruments constitute a valid depiction of public policy and its effects.

Chapter 10

Learning from Experience:
Lessons from Policy Implementation*

Milbrey Wallin McLaughlin

"Implementation" joined the working vocabulary of policy analysts in the early 1970s when ambitious, sweeping federal reform efforts cast "implementation problems" in bold relief. The Great Society's comprehensive intergovernmental initiatives meant that implementation was no longer primarily a management problem, confined to relations between a boss and a subordinate, or to processes within a single institution. Implementation of the Great Society's social policies stretched across levels of government—from Washington to state capitals to local communities—and across agents of government—from legislative to executive to administrative units. As federal, state, and local officials developed responses to these new social policies, implementation issues were revealed in all their complexity, intractability, and inevitability.

Discovery of the implementation problem came as something of a surprise to planners and analysts. In the mid-1960s and early 1970s, prevailing theories of governmental action and organizational behavior assumed away implementation issues or overlooked them altogether. Economists, who were among the chief architects of the Great Society, emphasized markets, incentives, and production functions. Sociologists were caught up in theories of scientific management and subscribed to Weberian notions of hierarchical authority and bureaucratic control.

*Reprinted from Milbrey McLaughlin, "Learning from Experience: Lessons from Policy Implementation," *Educational Evaluation and Policy Analysis,* vol. 9, no. 2, Summer 1987, pp. 171–178. Copyright 1987 by the American Educational Research Association. Reprinted by permission of the publisher.

Thus while economists interpreted disappointing program outcomes as market failures and sought solutions in incentives, sociologists and organization theorists saw signs of inadequate organizational control, and counseled new penalties and increased oversight.

Experience ultimately showed these to be weak solutions that misrepresented the reasons why federally supported reform initiatives often disappointed. "Rational man" was one of the first casualties once analysts turned their attention to issues of policy implementation. Implementors, we discovered, did not always do as told (as proponents of scientific management would have it) nor did they always act to maximize policy objectives (as many economists would have it). Instead those responsible for implementation at various levels of policy system responded in what often seemed quite idiosyncratic, frustratingly unpredictable, if not downright resistant ways. The result was not only program outcomes that fall short of expectations but also enormous variability in what constituted a "program" in communities across the nation.

This initial surprise about the myth of the rational man and the immutability of implementation issues was heralded by Pressman and Wildavsky in 1973 (1984). They were first in the first generation of implementation analysts who showed that implementation dominates outcomes—that the consequences of even the best planned, best supported, and most promising policy initiatives depend finally on what happens as individuals throughout the policy system interpret and act on them (Bardach 1977; Berman and McLaughlin 1978; Elmore 1977; Van Meter and Van Horn 1975, for example). This first generation of implementation analysis showed how local factors such as size, intra-organizational relations, commitment, capacity, and institutional complexity molded responses to policy.

Making matters more complicated, these analyses also established the broad and important local variation in the actual problems addressed by policy. Bilingual education issues in Puerto Rican New York City are substantively different than are problems of educating Mexican-origin youngsters in Los Angeles. Parent involvement in urban districts poses a different problem than does parent participation in rural school settings. Issues of teacher certification are strategically and substantively of a different stripe in New York and in Mississippi. Problems addressed by policy vary not only in definition, then, but also in seriousness and tractability.

These early analyses established what has been called the "implementation perspective" and laid the groundwork for a second generation of implementation analyses. Whereas first generation analysts discovered the problem and sketched its parameters, the second generation began to unpack it and to zero in on relations between policy and practice. This essay takes up a number of central lessons that emerge from these up-close examinations of the implementation process.

Lessons from the Field

Perhaps the overarching, obvious conclusion running through empirical research on policy implementation is that it is incredibly hard to make something happen, most especially across layers of government and institutions. It's incredibly hard not just because social problems tend to be thorny. It's hard to make something happen primarily because policymakers can't mandate what matters. We have learned that policy success depends critically on two broad factors: local capacity and will. Capacity, admittedly a difficult issue, is something that policy can address. Training can be offered. Dollars can be provided. Consultants can be engaged to furnish missing expertise. But will, or the attitudes, motivation, and beliefs that underlie an implementor's response to a policy's goals or strategies, is less amenable to policy intervention.

In part, questions of motivation and commitment (or will) reflect an implementor's assessment of the value of a policy or the appropriateness of a strategy. Organizational compliance with affirmative action policies, which had vague goals and few resources, for example, is explained almost entirely in terms of the values of key individuals (Milward et al. 1983). Similarly, the success of the Tennessee Valley Authority (TVA) initiative is attributed primarily to consensus at state and federal levels about program goals (Rawson 1980). In contrast, mandated parent involvement strategies associated with federal programs such as the former Title I of the Elementary and Secondary Education Act of 1965 were implemented unevenly at best. Most districts did not move beyond *pro forma* response because teachers and administrators saw little merit in parent participation (McLaughlin and Shields 1986). However, these feelings about a policy initiative are not entirely resistant to policy. Encouraging evidence is accumulating to show that belief sometimes follows action (Fullan 1986). For example, teachers required by their principals to interact with low-income parents on matters of homework often changed their minds about the contribution these parents could make to their children's schooling (Epstein 1984).

But motivation or will also is influenced by factors largely beyond the reach of policy. Environmental stability, competing centers of authority, contending priorities or pressures and other aspects of social-political milieu can influence implementor willingness profoundly (see

Yin 1981). For example, the planning model central to California's School Improvement Program was ignored in one of the state's largest districts because a teachers' strike co-opted the necessary resources and attention. In short, policy at best can enable outcomes, but in final analysis it cannot mandate what matters.

This emphasis on individual motivation and internal institutional conditions implies that external policy features have limited influence on outcome, particularly at lower levels of the institution. Yet another lesson learned is that successful implementation generally requires a combination of pressure and support from policy (Elmore and McLaughlin 1982; Fullan 1986; McLaughlin and Pfeifer, 1988; Montjoy and O'Toole 1979; Zald and Jacobs 1978). Pressure by itself may be sufficient when policy objectives contain their own implementation directions—a 55 mph speed limit, for example. Pressure alone may be sufficient when policy implementation requires no additional resources or normative change. But pressure alone cannot effect those changes in attitudes, beliefs, and routine practices typically assumed by reform policies. Opportunities for co-optation, symbolic response, or non-compliance are multiple in the loosely structured, multi-layered world of schools and education policy, for example. Further, even an army of auditors would be unable to force compliance with the *spirit* of the law—which is what matters in the long run. District officials may be compelled to establish a parent involvement mechanism consistent with mandated practices, for example, but mandates cannot require them to welcome parents and facilitate their participation.

Support, alone, also is a limited strategy for significant change because of the competing priorities and demands that operate with the implementing system. In particular, vague mandates and weak guidelines provide opportunity for dominant coalitions or competing issues to shape program choices. For example, some districts diverted federal support for innovative projects to subsidize other less flexible objectives or program requirements (special education mandates for individualized services, for example) (Kimbrough and Hill 1981).

Experience shows that some balance of pressure and support is essential. Pressure is required in most settings to focus attention on a reform objective; support is needed to enable implementation. Pressure from policy can be important even in settings that subscribe voluntarily to reform objectives simply because most institutions and individuals are allergic to change. And in settings where there is uneven consensus about the merit of a policy or where policy aims at weak beneficiaries, pressure can provide necessary legitimacy for program officials. Administrators of Title I (now Chapter 1), the largest federally supported compensatory education program, for example, comment that even in communities with a high minority population, federal regulations provided necessary protection and legitimacy for compensatory program efforts. In the press of competing demands, they expect that these targeted federal funds would have been diverted to general uses in the absence of federal requirements.

A related lesson from detailed studies of the implementation process is that change ultimately is a problem of the smallest unit. At each point in the policy process, a policy is transformed as individuals interpret and respond to it. What actually is delivered or provided under the aegis of a policy depends finally on the individual at the end of the line, or the "street level bureaucrat" (Weatherly and Lipsky 1977).

This perspective shifts the focus of analysis away from institutions and institutional goals to individuals and individual incentives, beliefs and capacity. Organizations don't innovate or implement change, individuals do. Individuals responsible for carrying out a policy act not only from institutional incentives, but also from professional and personal motivation (see, e.g., Sabatier and Mazmanian 1980). Initial interpretations of individuals' failure to carry out policy directives fully or faithfully tended to be cynical. Teachers, for example, often were diagnosed as "resistant to change," or just simply lazy when they ignored or subverted curricular innovations. Second generation analysts, however, recognized that teachers' responses to planned change efforts may instead represent best efforts to do their job and to provide the best they can for the youngsters in their classrooms. Their failure to implement, as planners hoped, may signal their assessment that new practices are not as good as the ones they replace or their certainty about outcomes for children. Motivated professionals, we have seen, generally make every effort to do their job well. Yet many early analyses assumed implicitly that the "right" policy was that contained in policy directives. However, one ironic consequence of this street-level policymaking and professionals' priority for client service is that reformers often may not get what they want, but get what they need as policy is put into practice (Johnson and O'Connor 1979).

We've learned additional lessons about the importance of environment for both individuals and their institutions. Because implementation takes places in a fluid setting, implementation problems are never "solved". Rather they evolve through a multi-staged, iterative process. Every implementation action simultaneously changes policy problems, policy resources, and policy objectives (Majone and Wildavsky 1977). New issues, new requirements, new considerations emerge as the process unfolds. For example, the first challenges of implementation generally are to learn the rules of the game. What is supposed to be done? What are the legal requirements determining program activities? Clear goals, well-specified statutes, and effective authority are important *external* policy variables at this initial stage (Elmore and McLaughlin 1982; Sabatier and Mazmanian 1980). Generally, it is only after these compliance concerns have been understood that implementors can move on to address issues of program development or the *quality* of implementation. At this stage in the implementation process, external factors recede in importance as internal factors such as commitment, motivation, and competence dominate.

This evolutionary process is not always linear or predictable. Supports previously available may disappear as budgets are redrawn or new requirements are imposed on the implementing unit. For example, the use of federal "risk capital" available under Chapter 2 changed from support of untried teacher ideas to purchase of equipment as state and local education budgets tightened. Administrative attention to and support for a school-based improvement effort may be deflected by new state-level curriculum requirements, leaving project staff effectively stranded. Shifts in individual interest, motivation, and involvement are inevitable products of the multiple goals that influence individual choices and incentives—bureaucratic, political, and service goals. Although the rational man and policy planners tend to frame expectations in terms of services goals only, fluctuating bureaucratic necessities or political demands can eclipse these delivery considerations. Plans for a strengthened teacher evaluation program, for example, may be shelved until decisions are made concerning school closings, regardless of a superintendent's commitment to the program goals (McLaughlin and Pfeifer, 1988).

And because the implementation process itself creates a new reality and changes the system, often unanticipated problems or counter-cyclical consequences emerge. For example, analysts presently are concerned about the implications for equity attendant in many current reforms aimed at increasing excellence. Tightened graduation requirements, for instance, are driving out vocational courses for the less able students.

Finally, we have learned that there are few "slam bang" policy effects. This is because policy effects necessarily are indirect, operating through and within the existing setting. Thus policy is transformed and adapted to conditions of the implementing unit. Consequently, local manifestations of state or federal policies will differ in fundamental respects and "effective implementation" may have different meanings in different settings.

But we have also begun to understand that this kind of incremental, creeping, locally defined change is often for the best. Again, local response may provide what reformers need, not what they want. Slam-bang effects threaten the core operations of an implementing system, disrupting routines and established practices (Meyer and Rowan 1977). The consequences of such disruption may be the policy outcomes planners hoped for. But more possibly, the destabilization attending a slam-bang effect may leave the implementing system less effective than it was at the outset, or yield only ephemeral gains. The marginal, incremental responses natural to managers and practitioners in fact may ensure that the changes associated with a reform effort take more time than expected but that once in place, they are stable. Likewise, externally induced practices inconsistent with local routines, traditions, or resources are likely to be rejected in time, despite early apparent "compliance." "Muddling through" then can be seen not only as an adaptive response to demands for change but also as the more beneficial response in the long term.

Taken together, these lessons describe a model of implementation that moves from early notions of implementation as transmission or as a problem of incentives or authority to conceptions of implementation as bargaining and transformation (Ingram 1977; Majone and Wildavsky 1977; Ripley and Franklin 1982, for example). This perspective on the implementation process highlights *individuals* rather than institutions and frames central implementation issues in terms of individual actors' incentives, beliefs, and capacity. Implementors at all levels of the system effectively negotiate their response, fitting their action to the multiple demands, priorities, and values operating in their environment and the effective authority of the policy itself. Further, this bargaining or negotiation is a continuous process, proceeding over time as policy resources, problems, and objectives evolve and are played against a dynamic institutional setting. This means that the nature of the bargain will change over time within settings and will most likely differ across units of the policy system.

Implications for Evaluation and Analysis

Viewing implementation as a process of bargaining or negotiation makes it evident that the very reasons it is hard for policy to affect practice also make it difficult for analysts to learn about those effects. Policy effects are complex, sometimes hidden or invisible, often unanticipated or nominalistic. And even when they are apparent, they may be transitory. Learning from experience, then, requires moving away from a positivistic model to a model of social learning and policy analysis that stresses reflection and assistance to ongoing decision-making. A number of broad guidelines for analysts and evaluators follow from this perspective.

One is that the relevant frame of analysis is the implementing system, not a discrete program or project. There are a number of reasons why this broader view is essential. The supports, incentives, and constraints that influence implementor capacity and implementor motivation reside in the broader system. To bound examination of implementor behavior with a project focus means that individual choices and actions may be misunderstood. For example, what may appear as teacher disinterest or incompetence from the perspective of a special remedial project may actually reflect teacher isolation and lack of adequate information about participating students. Also, program effects may be interpreted differently within a system context. For instance, an art magnet program may appear successful when assessed in isolation. But how successful can it be judged to be when, in the broader institutional context, it becomes apparent that its success comes at the cost of art resources for the rest of the district?

Taking the implementing system as the analytical frame also is essential in order to sort out the effects of policy *qua* policy from policy as transformed through various individual interpretations and choices. For example, did a program fall short because program policy provided insufficient training or because implementors made ineffective training choices? Conversely, is program success related to policy strategies or to particular local capacity deployed in the service of policy objectives? To assess the activities and outcomes of a special program in isolation from its institutional context ignores the fundamental character of the implementation process.

Analysis also must reflect the multi-staged, developmental character of the implementation process. "Outcomes" will differ depending on the point in the process under study. In the early stages of implementation, summative measures usually are inappropriate. More appropriate questions for analysis involve the extent to which necessary resources are available to support implementation, whether there is evidence of good-faith efforts to learn new routines, or indication of commitment and support within the implementing system for policy strategies and goals. Analysis or evaluation of the implementation process requires development of multiple, intermediate measures that can gauge the vitality of the process and the extent to which implementation efforts are on track. The analyst, thus, must be familiar not only with the broad stages of an implementation process, but also with the substantive aspects of a policy problem. What, in particular, are the problems presented by a specific policy at various points in the process? What is evidence, then, of successful implementation? What are danger signs?

Related lessons for evaluation and analysis stem from the dynamic character of the institutional settings in which implementation takes place. As Cronbach quipped, "generalizations decay" (1982). Today's program consequences often are eroded by tomorrow's realities—staff moving on to new positions, different program clientele, changed resource availability, competing demands for time and attention. Summative statements are inherently conditional and time-bound. Thus it is crucial to understand the contextual factors associated with various program activities and outcomes. "Why" and "how" are as critical as "what" and "how much" to program analysis.

In addition, this local variability, the plague of macro-level planners, offers important opportunities to learn. Variability is not only inevitable in social policy settings, it is desirable. Local responses generate a vast natural experiment—combinations and permutations of practice that highlight niches for intervention and promising solutions—and should be exploited by analysts.

A bargaining model of implementation further complicates the task for analysts because it gives prominence to the diverse information needs of various actors in the process over time. Different actors require different kinds of information about the consequences of a particular policy for their institutional setting—information cast in terms of their particular incentives, goals, and constraints. Beyond these diverse information requirements, this perspective also suggests that the relationship between knowledge and practice or between knowledge and policy is acute, not chronic.[2] Knowledge generated by analysis and evaluation comes into play when it is needed. For example, developmental psychologists were surprised at their sudden "policy relevance" in the mid-1960s as early childhood education programs were drafted in Washington. A few of the policy system's needs such as legislative budget cycles are predictable. But many important demands for information and analysis are unanticipated consequences of fluctuations in the policy system—a budget crisis, a teachers' strike, a legal challenge. Nonetheless, these acute information needs require chronic information collection and analysis—an ongoing strategy of monitoring and assessing progress and activities associated with a policy at different levels of the policy system.

Finally, these various requirements for useful analysis generate what is perhaps the most vexing problem of all and frame a major challenge for the third generation of implementation analysts: linking macro and micro levels of analysis. Different levels of the policy system support different communities of discourse, different uses for information, and different models for analysis (see Lerner 1986). Macro analyses operate at the level of the system. They stress regularities of process and organizational structures as stable outlines of the policy process and frame individual action in terms of position in a relational network. Micro analyses, conversely, operate at the individual level. They interpret organizational action as the problematic and often unpredictable outcome of autonomous actors, motivated by self-interest. Macro-level analyses generally provide insufficient guidance to policymakers or practitioners interested in understanding program outcomes (positive or negative), evaluating alternatives, assessing internal work requirements, or developing models of how policies operate in practice. For example, a county board's decision to enlarge a drug treatment program based on an extremely positive summative evaluation resulted in program failure. By enlarging the program, the factors that underlay its success (but were overlooked in the evaluation) were eliminated: its dedicated staff, small size, and personal contact with patients (Edwards 1980, p. 9). Conversely, micro-level analyses ignore systemic attainments and unanticipated consequences for the institutional setting as a whole so it cannot speak to the expected organizational consequences or system-wide effects of a policy. Micro-level analyses, thus, provide limited guidance to policymakers faced with system-wide decisions.

The problem for analysts comprises linking the nominalistic world of the street level bureaucratic to the systemic patterns that comprise the world of policymakers—combined intentionality or collective action and predictable institutional effects. The quality of individual-level responses determines the quality of policy implementation; the nature and level of changes evident in the organization or in the aggregate status of target groups determine the extent to which policy has addressed macro-level problems. The complementarity is evident, but how far up and down the system can one usefully apply a single mode of analysis? Can a framework that reveals the individual-level factors that shape policy outcomes also inform the structural and allocative decisions confronting policymakers?

The conceptual and instrumental challenge to third generation implementation analysts lies in integrating these two communities of discourse in models that accommodate these multi-level, multi-actor complexities. Second generation analysts caution that a single model likely will fail to incorporate micro- and macro-level realities. However, two decades' examination of the relation between policy and practice suggests that a productive approach might model the very implementation process that generates that difficulty. Strategies for analysis and evaluation might become self-consciously multi-staged, developmental, and iterative, keying questions and methodologies to the point in the process under study, to the needs of key decision-makers, and establishing a regularized system of feedback to actors at all levels of the system. Policy analysis and evaluation thus becomes both as contingent and as regularized as the process it seeks to understand and inform.

Chapter 11

Research on Education Reform: Lessons on the Implementation of Policy*

Susan Fuhrman, William Clune, and Richard Elmore

Education reform was the major state policy activity of the 1980s. Beginning in the early years of the decade and continuing with new momentum following the publication of *A Nation at Risk* and other reform reports, states increased their standards for student performance, revised their systems of teacher certification, improved teacher compensation, and enhanced accountability mechanisms. Virtually every state made new policy in these areas; some, such as Indiana, embarked on comprehensive reform as recently as 1987. The reforms were accompanied by substantial increases in state aid, on the average about 21 percent in real terms between 1983 and 1987 (Odden 1987).

The reforms pose numerous distributional and allocational issues. For the most part, state dollars that accompanied reform packages were funnelled through equalized school aid formulas but special incentive programs, pilot efforts, and categoricals raise questions about the distributional equity of state aid. Early evidence indicates that the new policies are contributing to a reallocation of resources at the school level to support more course taking in academic subjects by all students. We explore these tentative findings below in the section concerning reforms of student standards.

However, the main focus of this chapter is on a reallocation of a

---

different sort—namely, new definitions of roles and relationships by state and local policymakers. The reforms are not just about academic excellence and teacher quality, they are also about the distribution of political authority among units of government. At stake in the reform movement, along with school curriculum and the nature of the teacher workforce, are issues about leadership and initiative in education policymaking (Clune 1987).

As we examine changing patterns of state and local relationships evident in the shaping and implementing of the reforms, we are acquiring a new understanding of the policy process. The paths taken by these reforms are not entirely consistent with histories of other educational changes. They differ from what we would expect from past research on policy enactment and implementation.

In this chapter, we report findings about the reform process and initial effects in Arizona, California, Florida, Georgia, Minnesota, and Pennsylvania where we interviewed state and local policymakers and educators in twenty-four districts and fifty-nine schools. These interviews, which took place between April 1986 and June 1987, constitute the first phase of a five-year study of the reforms. We compare our findings about the reform process and local implementation to what we expected from past research in policy implementation and suggest a new model for the implementation of state reform that accounts for the trends in this current reform movement.

A few cautionary words are necessary as a preface to the discussion. We do not suggest that these six states are representative of the entire nation. Rather, they represent a range on particular characteristics we expected to affect the translation of policy into practice: the scope and volume of reform and the instruments used to address policy problems. California and Florida were among the first states to enact comprehensive reform packages; Georgia followed two years later. These states addressed dozens of reform issues in one massive piece of legislation. Pennsylvania and Arizona took more incremental approaches, considering one or two reform issues at a time. Minnesota undertook few state-level policy innovations; one policy it did adopt was a unique choice plan, quite unlike other current state reforms.

The states also vary in the policy instruments or strategies used to deal with reform issues. For example, Georgia and Pennsylvania rely heavily on mandates to local districts. California's program was marked by the use of incentives or financial inducements to districts to participate in programs; over time, Florida shifted from mandates to an approach more dependent on incentives.

Our study is also limited because we visited only four districts in each of the states, on the average. Finally, what we report is based entirely on perceptions of policymakers and practitioners. Much of the objective evidence of reform impact, such as course enrollment statistics and dropout rates over time, were either not gathered systematically by states and districts in the study or would not yet reflect the effects of reforms that are just being phased in.

1. Lessons from Past Research

When we began our research, we realized that the state reforms of the 1980s might take different paths from the education policies that had received the attention of policy researchers in the past. We knew that past research would provide only partial guidance for understanding this new set of policies. Most research on education policy formation and implementation had concerned federal policy. Although states had long been active in several policy areas, such as finance and school district consolidation, the federal government provided much of the programmatic leadership in education prior to the current wave of state reform. Also, previous research centered on individual programs, many of which were for special need students and were more peripheral than central to core elements of schooling. They were discrete and amenable to study. By contrast, the current reforms deal with central issues of who shall teach, what shall be taught, and in what manner. Furthermore, the state reforms of the 1980s typically came bundled together; they were packages that delivered tens of new policy initiatives at once in the most comprehensive states and several in the states that acted more incrementally. However, we expected that lessons from past research would provide a solid foundation for understanding the nature and course of the state reform movement.

Drawing on earlier studies,[1] we made the following predictions about the new state reforms:

1. State political culture and context would lead to wide variation in the choice of policy instruments and implementation strategies; states would take pieces of the national reform agenda that best fit their own goals and capacity.

2. Participants in the policymaking process would be those with the most stake in the outcome—that is, interests would participate in proportion to their stake in the policies being shaped.

3. There would be wide variation in local response; some local districts would resist reforms or refuse to comply; some would comply literally to the reforms; and most would adapt, taking from

reforms the elements that best suited local goals and shaping them to local context.

4. Implementation success would be enhanced to the extent that reforms delivered clear, coherent signals to local districts.

5. Local actors would more readily adopt policies that match their technical expertise.

6. The effects of reform would be lagged; there would be little impact in the short term as people adjusted and began to translate policy into practice and much more actual change in the long term over years of phase-in and application.

7. The reforms would be mixtures of the symbolic and the actual; some reforms would result in real changes in school practice, others might give the appearance of change but would mean little in the course of a student's school career.

8. The implementation process at the local level would be smoother to the extent that local actors were involved in shaping the state-level reforms; ownership would be important.

9. The amount of state policy activity and the increase in state aid would translate roughly into an enhanced education policy-making role for the state. Increased state regulation in areas such as curriculum would mean diminished local control.

The model suggested by these lessons depicts a reform process that is heavily dependent on context at both state and local levels, that relies for success on the active engagement of those most interested in reform outcome, and that predicts little in the way of real change without such participation. We expected few significant impacts within the first few years; rather, we expected to see some evidence of resistance, and many changes that were more important on paper than in reality. We anticipated that even though some districts would resist, the model response would be mutual adaptation (McLaughlin 1976), whereby the district and the state each adjusted its goals to find an accommodation satisfactory to both. Even if part of the reforms were without real bite or substance, we thought they embodied enough new state regulation to translate into a widespread perception that the state role was increasing to the detriment of local autonomy.

Our actual findings suggest a much more complex picture. In the following sections, we detail these findings in four areas: the politics of reform, the state role, student standards, and policies related to teaching. We then return to the original model and draw new lessons that provide a richer understanding of the reform process.

2. The Politics of Reform

As indicated, the reforms enacted by the six study states varied in their scope, in the policy instruments used, and in their comprehensiveness. Arizona enacted two major education reforms: a pilot career ladder and new graduation requirements. The career ladder was passed in 1985. It proponents wanted a statewide plan but resorted to a pilot to save money and avoid facing the state's constitutional spending limit. Initially five, and later fifteen, districts received competitive grants to implement a plan that, by state law, must include student achievement and classroom performance as promotion criteria. In 1983, the state board increased graduation requirements from sixteen to twenty credits. The changes included a rather large (2.5 units) and specific social studies requirement. Other recent reforms, enacted in serial fashion—one or two a year—include the imposition of teacher testing, changes in the criteria for approval of teacher education programs, yearly student assessment, and the establishment of competencies for grade to grade promotion.

California's 1983 SB813 was an $800 million dollar reform package that was extraordinarily complex. It included the imposition of statewide graduation requirements; provision for state board definition of competency standards; incentives for a longer school day; continuing education requirements for teacher certification; a mentor teacher program of annual stipends for teachers who help new teachers or develop curriculum; increased beginning salaries; an alternative certification route for high school teachers; reforms in personnel management that made it easier to dismiss and transfer teachers; expanded authority for expulsion and suspension of problem students amid dozens of other provisions. The comprehensive legislative education reform had become a familiar feature in the California education policy landscape; other notable "big fixes" were the introduction of compensatory education in 1964, early childhood education in the late 1960s, school finance reform and school improvement in the 1970s.

The Florida legislature passed comprehensive education legislation in 1983 after at least a decade of fashioning and enacting a new, major piece of education legislation each session. The reforms included mandated statewide standards for high school graduation and a mandated seventh period of instruction; a minimum gradepoint average; the Florida Quality Instruction Incentive Program (merit schools); the Meritorious Instructional Personnel Program (the master teacher plan); and improvements in math, science, and computer education. Funding, derived primarily through a unitary corporate tax, amounted to $73.8

million in 1983–84 and $130.5 million in 1984–85. In the last several years, the legislature tinkered with or fine-tuned a number of the original provisions: The mandated extended day became an incentive, the minimum gradepoint requirement was delayed, and a career ladder program was enacted in place of the master teacher program. The career ladder, which called for locally designed systems expired as funding was not provided during the 1988 session.

In 1985, the Georgia legislature enacted the Quality Basic Education Act (QBE). The legislation gave statutory confirmation to a variety of previously adopted regulations, including graduation requirements, student testing, teacher testing, and beginning teacher evaluation. It extended testing to veteran teachers, provided for a statewide basic curriculum, instituted a school readiness test, required statewide norm-referenced testing, established incentives for structural changes such as the creation of middle schools and the consolidation of school districts, and completely overhauled the school financing system. QBE was the third attempt at major education reform undertaken by Georgia governors and legislatures since the 1970s but the first to be funded. Georgia's astonishing economic growth provided the $2 billion necessary to fund QBE without a tax increase.

Minnesota's reform program was quite unlike those in the other study states. Pride in the high achievement of its students and schools and widespread trust in school personnel combined to restrict the inclination of state policymakers to regulate schooling. Consequently, Minnesota did not institute major statewide increases in student standards. It embarked on several other reform initiatives including a $3.2 million a year incentive and training program in technology, yearly local student assessment, and district-run programs of competency testing and remediation. The reform that has attracted the most attention is the Post-secondary Enrollment Options Act, which permits any eleventh or twelfth grade student to attend a post-secondary school free of tuition. The state education aid allotment follows the student and goes to the post-secondary school in an amount proportionate to the student's percentage of full-time status. The program's proponents saw it not only as a way to increase student opportunities but also as a means to shake up the educational bureaucracy by introducing competition. Other choice programs including statewide open enrollment were enacted in the 1988 session.

In Pennsylvania, the major reforms were embedded in the 1984 revisions of two chapters of state code. Chapter 5 was changed so as to increase high school graduation requirements from thirteen credits in grades ten to twelve to twenty-one in grades nine to twelve. Additional years of math and science were required. Chapter 49 requires tests for new teachers in four areas; district-conducted induction programs; and continuing professional development credits (CPD) for certification renewal. Subsequent legislation exempted teachers with a master's degree from the CPD requirements and permitted districts to design programs to meet those requirements in lieu of university courses. Another important reform was the establishment of TELLS, a program to test and remediate students in math and reading in grades three, five, and eight. With the exception of TELLS, unique in its categorical nature, the reforms were funded by yearly increases of 8 percent and then 6 percent in the basic state aid formula.

Despite the important differences between the states, some key aspects of the reform process were similar across the states. First, legislators and governors played critical roles in reform in each of the states (McDonnell and Fuhrman 1986). The academic excellence reforms, like the school finance reforms of the 1970s, did not initiate in the education community; in fact educators and representatives of state-level education associations in many of our states complained that the reforms were "done to" them and defined them as part of the problem rather than the solution. Although some chief state school officers were important reform proponents, the impetus came from outside state departments and state boards of education.

In five of the states, legislative chairmen and leaders shaped and shepherded packages, some of which were designed by gubernatorial task forces. Where governors were not actively involved in designing reforms, their support was important in securing funding. In California, SB 813 was legislative reform although it swept along with it a number of the student standards and curricular policies of Superintendent of Public Instruction Honig. The package was constructed by the Senate education chair, who cosponsored it along with the House education chair. The governor's assistance was important in securing the support of Republican legislators, although the price for his activity was less funding than Democratic sponsors wanted. Florida's 1983 reform united three themes, each initiated by one of the major reform actors: the master teacher and merit pay ideas of the governor; the Senate-initiated increased high school graduation requirements and longer school day mandate; and improvements in math, science, and computer education that stemmed from the House Speaker's task force. Georgia's reform resulted from a gubernatorial task force, the Education Review Commission, whose recommendations were translated into legislation that was unanimously endorsed by the legislature, under the guidance of its leaders. In Arizona, the major reform component, the teacher career ladder, was entirely a product of the legislature; interestingly, it was implemented by the staff of the Senate Education Committee rather than the State Department of Education. The governor in Arizona was not an initiator, but his support for increased teacher salaries and increased spending provided important pressure. Finally, Minnesota's Post-Secondary Options Program is seen as a joint product of the governor and legislature.

Pennsylvania was the only study state in which the reforms came primarily through state board regulation. However, Governor Thornburgh's agenda, as carried by his Secretary of Education Wilburn, determined the substance of the reforms. The board had been considering expressing high school graduation requirements as competencies instead of courses; with Wilburn's movement from the Department of Administration to Education specific course requirements were adopted. The legislature traditionally defers to the State Board of Education in making substantive education policy, preferring the flexibility afforded when policy is embedded in regulation rather than statute. Legislative comfort with state board control was considerably enhanced by the addition of the legislative education chairs to state board membership in the early 1980s. However, the legislature can be a court of appeals for interests dissatisfied by board action and pending legislation can exert strong leverage on the board. In the case of the current reforms, legislation embodying the revised graduation requirements was dropped only when the board adopted a virtually identical package. The legislature's influence on the reforms in the area of teaching policy was even stronger. After the board revised the portion of code dealing with certification, Chapter 49, unhappy teacher associations successfully petitioned the legislature to exempt teachers with master's degrees from the requirement for continuing professional development credits as a condition of maintaining certification and to permit local districts' discretion in designing continuing education programs. State board regulations were then made to conform to legislative directive.

Educational associations joined state departments and boards of education in playing a secondary rather than a leading role in the reforms. Business interests predominated in most of the states, in comparison to past years when businesspeople showed little interest in education policy except to stop tax increases. Business groups were prominent in Minnesota's PSOE reform, Florida's Master Teacher and Merit Schools Programs and in the process leading up to Georgia's QBE. Even where they continued to oppose increased spending, as in Arizona, business leaders were key in certain aspects of reform. Business leaders serving on the state board led the effort to increase graduation requirements.

In contrast, education interests were not active players in the reform process, despite the centrality of reforms dealing with curriculum and teacher certification to their professional interests. Teacher associations accommodated to reform rather than shaping it. Their influence prior to reform passage was limited, in part because of the ascent of other groups, especially business. Although not strong supporters of reform, they also did not wage all-out opposition for the most part. They were able to veto or block parts of reforms they particularly disliked, but they determined that the probability of pay off from virulent resistance was low. In addition, the reforms did carry increased education funding, often for the first time after several years of recession. This factor and the strong backing for the reforms from policymaker and business elites led the associations to suppress their antagonism. In some states their strategy was to voice opposition privately to policymakers but to take no position or a mildly supportive stance in public (McDonnell and Pascal 1988).

Finally, even though there were important differences from state to state, the reforms everywhere were the products of coalition politics. They were born of many motives and were amalgams of many ideas. Most had components that appealed to fairly diverse interests so that enough support for passage could be aggregated. In spite of public enthusiasm for education reform and the national fever of reform activity, designing winning coalitions was a challenging task. The reforms had to pass without the active support of education interests, over their opposition in some cases, and they often involved substantial new sums of money.

Although most reform rhetoric referred to improving the United States' competitive position and striving for academic excellence, some reform leaders had more particularistic motives. For example, California Senate Republicans were primarily interested in curbing the power of organized teachers. A number of Pennsylvania legislative leaders were concerned with increasing state aid to local school districts; the reforms offered a political opportunity to do something they might have pursued in any case.

Similarly, the same reforms were supported for varied reasons. For example, while some state policymakers in Pennsylvania imbued new student standards with significant promise of enhancing student performance throughout the state, others saw the same standards as explicit statements to "laggard districts," to the 20 percent of districts who did not already meet the new minimum requirements; still others expected their impact to be primarily symbolic, sending a signal to students and districts that academics was important. In like manner, Arizona's career ladder garnered the support of the governor because it meant higher teacher salaries; eventually the teachers' association came to support it for the same reason. Legislative sponsors had a variety of other goals: to improve the quality of teaching and teacher morale, to provide a more collegial atmosphere in schools, to improve the quality of teacher evaluations, and to strengthen public support for schools.

Much like their counterparts in Arizona, Georgia policymakers came at the Quality Basic Education Act from different perspectives. Most were primarily concerned with improving Georgia's economic competitiveness and ability to attract industry. However, some also saw reform as a not so subtle pressure for school district consolidation, on the theory that school districts unable to meet new standards would seek merger and seize upon the component of the legislation that provided incentives for consolidation. Others intended the reform as a strong signal to elected local school superintendents who were not trusted to seek quality education. Still others saw QBE as an opportunity for reform of school finance and the introduction of a more equalized funding system.

Not only did the reforms satisfy a variety of different goals, the reform packages also combined several different, and sometimes disparate, approaches to improving schools. In addition to new standards, they carried significantly increased funding, which for some of the sponsors was the key to fixing the system. To these actors, the standards were either exchanges for the money, part of a "big bargain"; ways to pacify other interests, such as the business supporters who agreed to increased spending and taxation only because of accountability guarantees; or window dressing. For example, key legislative actors in California saw SB 813 as a way to increase funding for schools in return for some relatively innocuous reforms. They grafted together Honig's student standards provisions, the Senate education chair's teacher development proposals that he had been generating over several years, and the relatively punitive teacher evaluation and credentialing requirements supported by opponents of the major teacher association. Mentor teachers were seen as a reasonable alternative to merit pay, since teachers were being paid more for additional work, rather than judgement about their quality. Student standards were seen as affecting few districts, but as giving a clear signal about the importance of student performance. The so-called personnel management provisions were seen as having relatively little effect, but as delivering a clear signal to teachers' organizations that they were not as powerful as they thought.

To summarize, the education reforms of the early 1980s were

strongly reflective of state political context. Nonetheless, in each state studied, legislators and governors, with the powerful support of business groups, played leading roles. Education interests were at most supporting players, accommodating to rather than shaping reform. The reforms are often discussed as if they are seamless, speaking with one voice about improved schooling through higher standards. However, the reform packages were complex bundles of many approaches and were supported by policymakers with diverse motives.

3. The State Role

Common wisdom about the reform movement characterizes it as a landmark in state control of education. Several factors lend support to this theory. First is a tendency to equate the amount of state policymaking activity with influence over local district behavior. It is certainly true that the reforms represented a significant increase in state activity by sheer volume alone. For example, legislatures considered over 1,000 pieces of legislation dealing with teacher certification and compensation during the 1980s, an unprecedented amount. Virtually every state enacted policies to reform teacher education, licensing, and compensation in this period (Darling-Hammond and Berry 1988).

The reforms signaled a surge in state activity at a time that the federal government was retiring from policy initiation and reducing education spending (Kirst 1987). Many observers link increased state leadership directly to federal retreat, arguing that the states were filling a vacuum (Clark and Astuto 1986). Similarly, some commentators interpret state ascendance as a reaction to an abdication of local responsibility. They cite visible failures of large, urban school districts, high dropout rates, and disappointing test scores as evidence of the need for state action.

As the reforms build on two decades of significant increases in state education spending, they can be interpreted as natural impulses to ensure accountability for the ever larger state aid dollar. The state share of spending on elementary and secondary education went from almost 40 percent in 1970 to 48 percent in 1983. The 1985–86 state share is estimated at over 50 percent (Center for Education Statistics 1987).

Another factor cited by those who believe that the reforms signal the end of local control concerns the nature of the reform policies. Several specific reforms appear to be very directive of local behavior. For example, many states that had left compensation issues entirely to local discretion and negotiation entered into the field of setting teacher salaries for the first time (Darling-Hammond and Berry 1988). The student standards policies incorporated a number of elements that could be expected to drive school curricula: increased and more specific course requirements, new exit exams and other statewide assessments, state-developed competencies for each subject, new curriculum guides. In some states, new sophisticated monitoring techniques could permit state policymakers to track the progress of individual students, as well as schools and districts.

Finally, what most appears to alarm spokespersons for local interests is that they were left out of the reform policymaking process. Leaders of state-level local associations in the study states say they were represented on task forces and commissions, but that they do not feel they were able to have any real input or role in shaping the result. They claim reactive victories, successes in blunting what they saw as some of the more onerous aspects of reform. For example, the Pennsylvania School Boards Association pressed to have new funding distributed through the Equalized Subsidy for Basic Education (ESBE) formula, rather than in categorical programs. ESBE represented a well-compromised and politically supported distributional scheme; it also delivered general aid, without restrictions on use by local districts.

Local concern about exclusion from the reform process and the top-down nature of the new policies suggested a rocky road for the reforms as they reached the schools. Some analysts of reform legislation predicted widespread resistance; on the other hand, some predicted total loss of local independence (Doyle and Finn 1984). The choice posed for local districts was sometimes depicted in tones almost as solemn as those used when Americans first faced the same dilemma: disobedience or loss of self-governance.

However, our research has revealed a much more complex picture about state-local relations that is portrayed by forecasts of the death of local control or assumptions about massive local resistance. There was, in fact, not much resistance to many of the reforms in most places.[2] The ease of compliance has a number of roots. First, examination reveals that many of the new standards were already met by local districts prior to state legislation. In fact, new state high school graduation requirements were met or surpassed by most districts in most states (CPRE 1988); the reforms simply legitimated local practice. For example, in Pennsylvania, a state department study revealed that 75 percent of districts already exceeded new state requirements; in Georgia the new requirements were already in force for all students in the state who pursued an academic diploma prior to the Quality Basic Education Act.

Compliance was also made easier by the widespread public support for the intention of the reforms and the fact that most of the new policies called for changes that school personnel were comfortable with and knew how to achieve. They knew how to add courses in math and science and how to incorporate new testing into their programs. Many, if not most, of the reforms were well within the technical expertise of school personnel, and in fact, required them merely to do more of what they were inclined and educated to do.[3]

One of our most interesting and important discoveries is that many local districts are going far beyond compliance; they are responding very actively to state reforms. In over half of our local districts, administrators saw opportunities in the state reforms to accomplish their own objectives, particularly as the state reforms provided significant funding increases. Local districts are actively orchestrating various state policies around local priorities, strategically interacting with the state to achieve local goals. For example, one major urban district coordinates almost all state teacher policies, including its mentor teacher program and alternate route, to meet the prime objective of hiring a large number of new teachers. Another district in the same state uses the mentor teacher program for curricular and staff development activities that are current district priorities. Mentor positions are advertised to attract applicants interested in working in these specific areas. In a like manner, a Florida district has expanded the state merit schools program, adding criteria for success and supplementing state funding with local dollars in order to reward all schools reaching their own goals.

In the states we studied, state student standards policies have provided opportunity for and lent momentum to a significant movement already evident in many local school districts of varying size: centralized curriculum regulation and alignment of curriculum, tests, texts, teacher evaluation, and other mechanisms. Districts throughout the nation are standardizing their curricula for a variety of reasons. Pressure from minority parents can lead to a desire to make curriculum more uniform across a district; so can concerns about high mobility from school to school. Technological advances, such as computer programs that map standardized tests against major texts in key subject areas, support the movement. However, it is clear that the state reforms furnished an influential lever. For example, administrators in one Pennsylvania district stated that the new definition of a planned course located in the Chapter 5 revision was "a good excuse" to address curriculum revision. New state testing affected the curriculum to some extent in every district we visited. In approximately half of them, state testing was cited as an important impetus for district-level curriculum standardization. Student standards have also been used as levers for more resources, such as adding more central district personnel in curriculum and assessment and more teachers where the standards meant that a longer school day was needed.

Another phenomenon we observed was the tendency of some local districts to get out ahead of the new state reforms in a way that distinguishes them from their peers. For example, several districts in our study raised high school graduation requirements beyond new state increases in deliberate attempts to stay ahead of other districts. This includes districts that did not already exceed the new state criteria and those that did. One California district that had a requirement of 120 units raised its requirements to 160 units when SB 813 was passed. This placed it thirty units ahead of SB 813's 130-unit requirement and five units ahead of the state board's model requirements. A Pennsylvania district that had nineteen credits to the state's thirteen raised to twenty-two when the state went to twenty-one. Two districts that we visited, one in Georgia and one in Florida, were developing career ladder plans in anticipation of state programs. The Georgia district was designing a student-achievement-based teacher evaluation scheme, expecting that the state would use such criteria and preferring to fashion its own system than to respond to a mandate. The Florida system included career ladder development in a landmark professionalization effort jointly undertaken with the teachers' union.

Many local district personnel were actively engaged in networks that influence state policy before it is formalized. Several of the new state programs were modeled after practices already underway in local districts. Florida's Meritorious Schools Policy is very similar in spirit and requirements to policy previously enacted by a county well-known for its school improvement program. Florida's effort to develop subject-area tests draws on the experience of a major district that is now under contract to the state to develop subject matter standardized tests for statewide use. Sometimes, state policymakers learned about local initiatives through customary information networks; for examples, legislators frequently turn to the superintendents in their legislative districts for information about practice and potential policy impact. In addition, reform commissions often included leading local actors. The superintendents of two Georgia districts we visited were members of the Education Review Commission and, as much as possible, shaped QBE to the needs and capacities of their districts.

Increasing sophistication among local actors means that they increasingly engage in strategic interaction with state actors both in responding to and affecting the content of state policy. Although it is too soon to draw a balance sheet on state-local roles in the wake of reform, it is clear that it would be a vast oversimplification to chalk up the movement as a massive increase in state power.

4. Student Standards

Student standards were the most popular type of policy intervention in the recent waves of state reform. State graduation requirements were increased in forty-three states; other types of student standards, such as longer school days, minimum gradepoint averages and new exit tests, were also popular. The increases in standards were well supported by theory. High standards represent high expectations, and high expectations are an important component of effective schools (Purkey and Smith 1983; Cohen 1983). Standards are also supported by the concept of "opportunity to learn"—that is, students learn more if they are exposed to more content (Wolf 1977; Good et al. 1978; Brophy and Good 1986; Raizen and Jones 1985). However, from the start vigorous questions were raised about the potentially negative effects of increased standards on dropping out and student success (Cusick 1984; McDill, Natriello, and Pallas 1985).

Early in our research we learned that the graduation requirement reforms were not as large as they looked on paper. As pointed out above, most local districts already met the new state requirements. They were more sensitive to increased university and college admission requirements. Even when local requirements fell below the new level, college bound students were already taking at least, if not more than the new requirements. However, even those districts that exceeded state requirements generally had to add courses to meet the specific subjects highlighted in the new reforms. Most districts in our study had to add an extra course in math and science, and sometimes in social studies, language, and fine arts. The remainder of districts added additional sections of existing courses (Clune 1988). For example, a major urban district had to split a generalized "science" offering into separate classes for physical and biological science. Another urban district across the country added an environmental science course as a new third-year science course that was not chemistry or physics.

School-level respondents told us that the state reforms were leading to more students taking courses in academic subject areas. In fact, because more students, including the non-college bound, are taking more math, science, and social studies, enrollments have declined in vocational education, business education, and, in some cases, art and music. The high school curriculum has become more concentrated around core subjects, with students taking fewer electives and having less time for career preparation, particularly where the day is short. However, even though the new courses added are in major academic areas, most have not been academic. They have generally been basic or remedial, with titles like "Math Applications," and intended for the non-college bound. The college bound third- or fourth-year courses in these subjects were already in place prior to the reforms.

Increases in student standards present both benefits and hazards for at-risk students. Higher standards represent higher expectations, expose marginal students to more academic content, and marshal resources for previously underserved students. However, increases in standards may also be related to increased pressure on many students and a reduction of choice for students with special needs and goals, such as those who need remediation or who want vocational education in high school. Practitioners report that higher course requirements, and related reforms like minimum grade point averages, make graduation a more difficult goal for at-risk students while limiting the time available for remediation and retaking failed courses. Such effects depend strongly on the responses of individual schools, on whether schools have a five-period or a seven-period day, for example, and on how students are counseled. School responses and the course-taking patterns of different types of students will be important to document over 1987–88 and 1988–89 as juniors and seniors in many states first become subject to new requirements.

The addition of new courses did impose some expenses on districts, but none reported major costs. Some districts had trouble finding teachers, particularly in math and science, and initiated programs to recertify teachers, such as business education teachers. Others had facilities problems, including insufficient laboratory space. However, the implementation problems were minor. The real questions about student standards policies concern the nature of courses students are taking, whether in fact they provide a more academic curriculum as reformers hoped, and how different students are affected.

In summary, the new student standards posed few problems for school districts. Course requirements led to modest adjustments without much dislocation. Important questions about how individual schools are responding to the needs of individual students remain unanswered, but school personnel believe that the reforms accomplished a major purpose: creating a more academic secondary school experience for all students.

5. Teacher Policies

State efforts in the area of teacher policy were much less coherent than the student standards reforms. States seem to be going in several different directions at once. The six states we studied stiffened requirements for entry into the profession with tests, course, and grade average requirements. At the same time, they provided for alternative routes that required no specific course preparations. Some tried career ladders intended to make teaching more of a profession by differentiating responsibilities and creating a career structure. However, many teachers found the evaluation instruments and criteria demeaning and unprofessional. There is still little agreement on what a teacher ought to be able to do, the nature of teaching and the roles of teachers. Some policies view teachers as professionals relying on an abundant knowledge base, while others view teachers as workers needing extensive direction (Darling-Hammond and Berry 1988).

Initial analysis of the implementation of state teacher policies indicates that the conflicting assumptions embodied in different approaches are reflected in implementation problems in the field. Particular difficulties are associated with career ladder plans. Such plans are very sensitive to the validity of evaluation. Teachers in Florida complained bitterly about the master teacher program, a 1983 reform that has been scrapped in the wake of severe first-year substantive and administrative difficulties. A number of the issues contributing to the program's demise concerned the evaluation procedures: Tests were available in some subject matter areas and not others, so that some teachers could advance without testing; the observation instrument was designed for beginning, not experienced teachers; non-classroom personnel were subject to evaluation as classroom teachers; trained teacher evaluators became very savvy about doing well on their own evaluations, causing others to resent them; some principal-evaluators were suspected of stealing good teachers they evaluated in other schools; and part of the process called for teachers to be evaluated by their own supervisors, leading to dissension.

The Arizona career ladder suffered from fewer administrative problems and aroused less concern about evaluation procedures than Florida's plan. However, Arizona teachers and evaluators complained about enormous paperwork demands and the vast amounts of time required to prepare and evaluate portfolios.

The difficulties in Florida led to a decision in 1986 to create a career ladder program that would permit local districts to design their own approaches. Although state funding for the new career ladder was not provided, the concept of local design seems important for differentiated staffing and reward plans. The issues of eligibility, criteria for promotion, and how and by whom teachers should be evaluated are immensely difficult. Some of the problems are related to a weak knowledge base; for example, educators are just beginning to develop assessment instruments that appraise important aspects of teaching, such as teachers' ability to reflect on practice (Peterson and Comeaux 1988). Many problems are political. Differential reward schemes involve constructing consensus on key values, like what constitutes "good" teaching, and matching desires to recognize success to available resources. Such issues have proven at least somewhat troublesome in every district we visited where a state career ladder exists. It may be the case that these questions need to be resolved locally, with each district creating solutions to suit its needs. Although we have no experience in our study states with locally designed career ladders, the mentor teacher program in California, where districts set their own definitions of exemplary teaching; appears to have better support than schemes in which states determine advancement criteria. The mentor program is not free of implementation troubles and perceptions of its success and utility vary, with many respondents seeing it as an insignificant and peripheral program. However, the widespread dissension surrounding state career ladder plans is absent.

District response to state teacher initiatives is heavily dependent on local needs, even more so than in the case of the student standards policies. In particular, those districts that were hiring new teachers in significant numbers or had concerns about retaining teachers were most enthusiastic about policies they could use for recruitment and training of novices. Diverse policies were put to such use by districts in several states. For example, the induction program in Pennsylvania was relevant only in the one district that needed to hire several hundred teachers a year and was experiencing shortages; that district volunteered to pilot the induction program in 1986–87 and was eager to expand it to a full program in 1987–88. The district also used the state's alternative route, an old program that has been recently revived and expanded, to fill shortages. The Arizona district that found the state career ladder most appealing made new teachers as well as more experienced teachers eligible in order to increase retention in the beginning years. Similarly, respondents in the California district with the great need for and problem finding new teachers were the most positive about the state's various teacher programs including the mentor teacher, teacher trainee, and minimum salary provisions.

In the districts we visited, teachers' associations and unions participated in the implementation of teacher policies. For example, they were active members of committees designing induction programs in Pennsylvania, developing career ladder pilots in Arizona, and selecting mentor teachers in California. However, with a few exceptions, they saw these policies as fairly insignificant compared to their key concerns about salary and working conditions. They accommodated them rather than seizing leadership. Although the reasons for the stance of unions varied considerably, ranging from their limited influence in some states to the rather narrow scope of the reform policies in others, it seems clear that union accommodation and acceptance was vital to the local implementation process. Local unions could easily have blocked reforms had they decided to; they did not (McDonnell and Pascal 1988).

In summary, teacher policies in the six states were encountering significantly more difficulties in implementation than other types of reforms. Some, like the Florida Master Teacher Program, were poorly designed and administered. The issues posed by differential reward schemes are so difficult that they may require negotiation and resolution at each site, suggesting the need for local discretion. However, our findings indicate that state teacher policies were put to enthusiastic use by districts that had a critical need for new teachers and that local teachers' associations participated in implementation, even in the cases of policies they opposed at the state level.

6. A New Implementation Model

Our findings about reforms in these six states suggest several new ways of thinking about policy implementation. We found that certain factors were less important to implementation success that we predicted based on past research; other elements were more important than we predicted. Finally, some developments were simply different than we expected.

Among the factors less critical than our original model posited is ownership stemming from participation in the reform process. Our findings suggest strongly that policymaker and educator support for reform, which is key to successful implementation, does not depend on participation in reform initiation and design. State departments and boards were generally not reform leaders, yet they have actively engaged in reform activities such as designing tests, establishing course competencies, and assisting and monitoring districts. In fact, although they may have felt their role usurped by legislators and governors, they were by no means left without portfolio. In many cases reform legislation gave them more to do by mandating that they respond to broad legislative directives.

In none of the six states did associations representing local actors inaugurate or mold the substance of the reforms to any significant extent, yet in every state there was substantial compliance and frequent examples of districts that seized the reforms and embellished upon them. Similarly, teachers' unions barely controlled their opposition to reforms at the state level but participated in their local implementation. Even though the unions were not enthused about the potential of the reforms to affect teachers' lives or district ability to recruit and retain good teachers, they ultimately helped make the reforms happen.

A second factor that was less critical than expected in the implementation process is the clarity of the policy. Student standards mandates were notably more straightforward and understood and more easily implemented than teacher policies that predictably ran into trouble, but they were not entirely unambiguous or without multiple meanings. We found widespread compliance with reforms of student standards and testing policies, even though those reforms did not give unclouded, unadulterated signals. School personnel easily absorbed the new standards, and even sought to exceed them, knowing that the standards were often carrying messages other than or in addition to academic rigor and knowing that they were sometimes proxies for distrust of local districts, concealed goads toward consolidation, or sops to business supporters. The fact that reform packages combined several different programs, some leading in different directions, also did not appear to cause local districts problems.

Two factors turned out to be more important to successful implementation than we predicted and account in large measure for the extensive compliance and lack of resistance encountered. First, compliance depends heavily on the extent to which relevant technical knowledge exists and school personnel feel competent to make the change. Although the student standard reforms often caused disruptions—more sections, more teachers in shortage areas such as math and science, more facilities—and were not "easy" in that sense, they were policies with which educators felt comfortable. Creating more academically oriented high schools was a task for which their training and school experience had prepared them and toward which they were favorably disposed. In contrast, the weaker knowledge base supporting career ladder and teacher evaluation policies contributed to implementation problems.

District context was also more influential than we predicted. The importance of local context, the extent to which policies coincide with local goals and capacity, has long been appreciated by researchers. However, our findings suggest a much less passive role for districts than past implementation research posits. We have tended in the past to view districts as reactive—first to federal and then to state policy—determining which pieces of policies from other governmental levels districts to accept and modifying such policies to suit their needs. But many of the districts we have observed are busily making their own policies, engaging in networks with and borrowing from other local districts. Such districts do not merely adapt to state policy, they orchestrate and amplify policies around local priorities, whether or not any of the other conditions that would make those policies easy to implement exist. Active districts do not wait for state policies to happen, they make them happen. To the extent that district activity is related to the political, social, and economic milieu, district context appears not only important but paramount.

Finally, we discovered that certain of our predictions about the effects of reform and governance in the wake of reform simply did not come true. For example, we did not find long delays in translating reform policies into practice or widespread resistance. Past research led us to expect long lags in implementation and little short-term impact. However, the student standards reforms, for example, were swiftly translated into new courses and sections and new state-tested competencies were incorporated into curriculum. What remains a question is whether this immediate response is the precursor to further change, or whether it represents the extent of reaction in itself. If modifications in the high school curriculum amount to the addition of basic or general courses in academic subjects rather than a more fundamental overhaul of content or course sequence, then reform in this area will have had an immediate but fairly modest impact.[4]

Of particular interest is our finding that the reforms do not signal the end of local control. States are certainly making more policy in more areas of education than ever before, but so are local districts. States are increasing standards and testing; so are local districts. Locals are ahead of states in standardizing curriculum; both states and locals are actively experimenting with teacher evaluation and reward systems. What we have found is not a zero-sum game but a net increase in governance. Every policymaker is making more policy. A key question for the future, and one we have posed for ourselves in our continuing study in the six states, is the extent to which all this policymaking impinges on teacher or student discretion or autonomy. What does the surge in policymaking mean for classroom practice?

Our findings about local response to reform significantly extend our understanding of the implementation process. We anticipated that the range of local behavior would be captured by three concepts: resistance to policy change, formal compliance, and adaptation. Instead we have observed performance that may constitute a new point on the continuum of response by implementing agencies, behavior that we have begun to call "strategic interaction." Strategic interactors seize policy opportunity, coordinate and expand state policies to meet their needs, and anticipate and actively shape state policy. Because we deliberately visited a number of districts that were judged to have a high capacity to respond to reforms, our sample may overrepresent strategic interaction behavior. However, conversations with policymakers throughout the nation and accounts by journalists and researchers of innovations in districts like Rochester, New York; Dade County, Florida; and Hammond, Indiana, lead us to believe that such local activity is increasingly apparent.

When we contrast what we are finding in our study of state reform with what implementation research predicted, we find a more complex model of the process. Although policy formulation and implementation are strongly shaped by context and are therefore extremely variable, other maxims now seem to hold less force. Ownership is possible without participation in the shaping of policy; and short-term reactions can be expected, especially where technical capacity exists. Traditional modes of describing local response to policy interventions—resistance, compliance, adaptation—fail to account for the active appropriation of policy we are witnessing. The nature, extent, and reasons for the strategic interaction behavior we have described are among the issues we intend to explore in our continuing research.

Chapter 12

Implementation of the California Mathematics and Science Curriculum Frameworks

David D. Marsh and Allan R. Odden

Policymakers and analysts have a legitimate and intense interest in how state and federal policies can enhance the technical core of schooling—the curriculum and instructional program of the school—and its impact on students. Policy concerns about improving the technical core have gone through several stages since 1983. Initially, the concern was to do more of the traditional curriculum. When *A Nation At Risk* recommended that the American educational system could help citizens be more competitive in the international economy, it proposed higher standards and more years of traditional "academic solids" like mathematics, science, and English.

Subsequently, concern about the technical core shifted toward a curriculum that emphasized concepts rather than isolated facts, thinking and the creation of meaning rather than passive knowing, and problem-solving and expression so that knowledge could be used to address meaningful problems. There has been a corresponding shift in instructional strategies away from just direct instruction on a narrow view of issues to a complex set of instructional strategies that promotes inquiry, active learning, group cooperation and social cohesion in a heterogenous classroom.

Elsewhere, we have discussed the frequent finding that educational reforms were implemented quickly and with less resistance than would be predicted by a genre of policy implementation research (Odden and Marsh 1989). The finding has been confirmed by other scholars such as Murphy (1990a), Fuhrman, Clune and Elmore (1989) in a major multi-state study of reform implementaton, and by Firestone (1989).

Yet the early reforms are not like the current curriculum reforms, and the differences are sizeable. Whereas early reforms sought to stretch the existing system, recent curriculum reforms seek to revise the system and fundamentally change the classroom. The policy issues in this context are new and exciting, especially given the rather recent pro-active stance of state departments of education as curriculum reform leaders. The policy issues include whether the new approaches to curriculum can be implemented across districts and whole schools rather than just in isolated classrooms, whether this form of curriculum positively impacts on students, and whether state policies can meaningfully enhance implementation of this type of curriculum practice.

1. A Focus on Mathematics and Science Education

There has been considerable interest in dramatically improving the teaching of mathematics and science in elementary schools. Impetus for such reforms comes from several related sources. Numerous reports demonstrate the strong link between mathematics and science and the job future of U.S. students (Johnston 1987). Yet, by several standards, students have serious deficiencies in mathematics and science. When compared with students from other industrialized nations, our students fare very poorly in mathematics computation and mathematics reasoning (McKnight et al. 1987) and science (Jacobsen 1986). Similarly, the National Assessment of Education Progress (NAEP) in mathematics " . . . clearly shows that although most students are reasonably proficient in computational skills the majority do not understand many basic concepts and are unable to apply the skills they have learned in even simple problem-solving situations" (Romberg 1988, p. 5). The situation is equally serious in science where NAEP documents declines in science achievement (Hueftle et al. 1983) and lack of improvement in higher order reasoning about science (Applebee, Langer and Mullis 1989).

Impetus for reform also derives from related concerns about equity of educational opportunity for students. Five out of six new entrants to the work force between now and the year 2010 will be either minorities, immigrants or women—a disturbing problem when considered in light of a school system that Resnick and Resnick (1977) have characterized as a dual track system of "high literacy" and "low literacy" schools. Unfortunately, the "low literacy" schools tend disproportionally to serve ethnic minority students. Sex gender differences in mathematics and science performance also contribute to the nature of the problem facing our schools and society.

A host of national reform reports have provided extensive proposals for public school mathematics and science education reform. Building on early reports (especially *A Nation at Risk* and *Educating Americans for the 21st Century*), extensive mathematics education reforms have been proposed including: *What is Still Fundamental and What is Not?* (Conference Board of the Mathematical Sciences 1983a), *New Goals of Mathematical Sciences Education* (Conference Board for the Mathematical Sciences 1983b), and *School Mathematics: Options for the 1990s* (Romberg 1984). Similarly, excellent science reform proposals include: *What Science Is Most Worth Knowing?* (National Council on Science and Technology Education 1987) and *Educating Our Citizens: The Search for Excellence* (Center for National Policy 1983). The National Center for Improving Science Education provides an extensive analysis of these proposals and their contribution of current thinking about directions which should be taken (The NETWORK 1987).

While important conceptual work remains to be done, these reports provide considerable consensus about the goals, content, and instructional strategies that should be incorporated into contemporary elementary school mathematics and science programs. For example, in mathematics education, the National Council of Teachers of Mathematics has provided a major synthesis of desired curriculum changes (NCTM 1987; Romberg 1988) and in science education, the Council on Science and Technology has provided a similar set of proposals which can be found in the Phase I report of Project 2061 (National Council on Science and Technology Education 1987).

In addition to being comprehensive, these curriculum proposals have considerable research support. An excellent review of the teaching and learning of mathematics is provided by Romberg and Carpenter (1986) and a similar review of research on the teaching of natural sciences is provided by White and Tisher (1986). A more specific review of exemplary science programs for elementary schools points both to the "good news" and the "bad news" about elementary science programs (Bredderman 1973). The good news is that when inquiry-oriented, activities-based elementary science programs are compared with traditional programs, students in the inquiry/activities programs are significantly better at: 1) carrying out the process of science; 2) having more positive attitudes about taking more science; and 3) retaining more science content. The bad news is that many teachers, even those who participated in the NDEA Institutes of the 1960s, were unable to sustain classroom implementation of the inquiry-oriented programs. Only 20 to 25 percent of the teachers had successful implementation of these programs (Bredderman 1973).

From a policy perspective, previous, post-Sputnik, National Science Foundation (NSF) supported efforts to improve science education were based on an effective curriculum orientation that simply was not implemented despite considerable federal government policy initiative. The national curriculum projects developed sophisticated but inflexible curriculum packages that often fit neither district curriculum priorities nor other aspects of the policy context such as testing or textbook adoption in the district or state. Moreover, teachers attending the summer institutes needed help in implementing the programs back at their schools. This help was frequently inadequate, or even nonexistent. Further, the implementation process ignored the organizational and systemic nature of the reform. Principals, district curriculum leaders and others failed to understand and support the reform sufficiently—and the problem was both of will and capacity to do so. Sarason (1982) and Atkin and House (1981) provide an extensive analysis of the failure of these early curriculum reforms at the local school and district level.

Currently, state-stimulated reforms in mathematics and science offer considerable promise for improving on these old curriculum implementation problems. Recently, Smith (1988), Dean of the Stanford University School of Education, argued extensively for the need to:

> Focus change on a state by state basis. The state is the only place where the key policy levers all exist. States exercise or could exercise control over the pre-service training system, licensing, the curriculum framework, textbook adoptions and student testing. Each of these different aspects of the system will have to be harnessed together to provide the kind of major effort that is needed (p. 3).

In this context, Smith made several more specific recommendations about the critical ingredients of state curriculum frameworks. He argued that the state framework should provide much of the reform details that will have to be undertaken locally. He believed that the framework should:

1. Represent the very best shot of thoughtful and experienced teachers, scientists, psychologists and curriculum specialists in the state;

2. Have content that is challenging, coherent and contains a logical and substantial core of knowledge and skills upon which to build; and

3. Provide guidance that is sufficiently complete and precise to build a solid structure on which to base an instructional and testing pro-

gram, yet open enough to allow substantial creativity and ownership by teachers at the local school and system level.

For states that want a head start, he recommended two existing state
science frameworks, including the California framework.

Like Smith, we see California's leadership in state-initiated curriculum reforms, specifically its curriculum frameworks, as being especially promising as a means to inform researchers, policymakers and
practitioners about how the content, implementation and outcomes of
today's curriculum reforms can best be carried out. We and others have
conducted considerable research about state-initiated reforms that had
a narrower focus (Anderson et al. 1987), about the implementation of
state-initiated high school reform (Odden and Marsh 1987; Odden and
Marsh 1988; Odden and Marsh 1989; Marsh and Odden, 1990) and
about state-initiated curriculum reform in middle schools (Marsh,
Brown, Crocker and Lewis 1989).

But the research/policy community has an inadequate research
base about how state-initiated reform can work when the reform
requires such a dramatic change in classroom practice as do California's
current mathematics and science curriculum reforms. What is needed is
a focused, indepth look at the role that progressive state policy initiatives can play in the reform of elementary mathematics and science programs. This research is especially needed regarding districts and schools
that serve diverse student populations and have been active in implementing quality programs. While the recent Educational Commission of
the States study of the impact of state science initiatives suggests that
states can be successful in changing district practice, it still does not
answer the question of how to get real changes in classroom practice
and equitable impact on students (Armstrong et al. 1988).

2. The Mathematics and Science Curriculum
Implementation Study

This study explored the generic issue of whether state policies
can enhance local curriculum reform. More specifically, the study was
designed to determine: 1) how school districts and schools could successfully implement the California mathematics and science curriculum
frameworks; 2) the extent to which such programs were actually used
in classrooms; 3) the factors that explained successful implementation,
including the role state policy levers played in the implementation process; and 4) the impact of the reform in classrooms. To accomplish

these purposes, a coordinated set of intensive case studies were undertaken using a statewide sample.

Methodology

Sample.   The study used a purposive sample featuring fourteen elementary schools that had been especially active in implementing California's mathematics and science frameworks over the last several years. While the schools included the diversity of students found in the state, they were located in small-to-large size suburban districts and one big city district. The sample did not include either the largest or the very smallest districts because of the need to find patterns of implementation that could be useful to the typical California school district. Schools that had always had excellent programs were also excluded because of the need to study the improvement process itself.

Instrumentation.   The study was based on indepth case studies featuring a methodology developed by Miles and Huberman (1984) and applied to the study of state-initiated reform by Odden and Marsh (1987, 1988). The case studies were designed to provide comparable information about: 1) the district and school mathematics and science program —what it was, how it was developed and the roles which state policy levers played in shaping it; 2) the implementation process for the mathematics and science programs including information about specified key factors, the way these factors fit together at each site, and site-specific circumstances that influenced the implementation process; and 3) the results of the implementation process including classroom practices, outcomes for students and changes in school organization or practice.

The case study methodology was selected to provide comparable qualitative information about predesignated factors drawn from previous research about mathematics/science programs or change process dynamics. At the same time, we anticipated factors that appeared to be important to reforms characterized as Wave III by Murphy (1990a), or as second-order reforms by Cuban (1984a). The structure of the case study data collection also allowed the research team to obtain information about site-specific unique factors and a global picture of how these factors fit together at a site.

In addition to the case study, several other instruments were used. A teacher questionnaire was used to determine the teacher's background (pre-service preparation and staff development experience in mathematics or science) as well as their orientation to the teaching of mathematics or science. To explore the extent and nature of classroom practice in mathematics and science, eight teachers at each school were randomly selected (using stratified sampling), interviewed and observed. The teachers were asked to describe their mathematics (or science) curriculum and instructional practice over the current month and their plans for that subject area for the next semester. The teacher then was observed to provide a classroom practice context for understanding the interview. Information from the interview and the observation was used by the data collector to complete a rating form derived from the content of the state curriculum framework in that subject area.

Data Collection.   Data collection required approximately eleven days of effort per site and was conducted in two rounds where each round had a substantive focus and required qualitative and quantitative information collection. At each site, the data collection led to completion of a case study of approximately eighty single-spaced pages.

Cross-site data analysis.   The cross-site analysis took place in several stages, including: 1) development of cross-site detailed descriptions; 2) development of high inference summary ratings for each variable; and 3) exploration of major relationships across policy initiatives, implementation process, program content and outcomes.

3. Study Findings

Study findings are organized around three topics. The first is a set of site-specific factors critical to the implementation process. Five factors are discussed because they captured the essence of the implementation process and offer the most policy-relevant insights about how it could be facilitated.

The second topic is the role of state policy initiatives in enhancing/retarding the implementation process. These policy initiatives include the obvious ones such as the state curriculum frameworks and the textbook adoption process, but also includes several other policies that had considerable impact on the implementation process.

Finally, the impact of the programs on classrooms, teachers and students is discussed, even though this impact is only partially understood at this time. Impact is discussed in terms of tentative findings as well as emerging dilemmas for policymakers as they work to enhance the adoption and implementation of important new curriculum initiatives.

Critical Factors in the Implementation Process

While many implementation factors were examined in the larger study, the following discussion is focused on five especially important ones: 1) vision; 2) the coordination and staging of the implementation; 3) assistance; 4) pressure/latitude/monitoring of the implementation process; and 5) teacher effort to implement the change.

Vision. The role of vision was critically important to the success of the implementation process; but vision worked in new and surprising ways. Two general findings document the unique role of vision in these settings. First, both the mathematics and the science curriculum frameworks represented a major change for the schools and districts involved. In Huberman and Miles' (1984) terms, the "scope of change" was extensive, or "ambitious" in McLaughlin's (chapter 8) terms, as seen by both district and site leaders. More specifically, the new frameworks were seen as requiring:

1. Fundamental change at the classroom level.

2. Substantial change across many classrooms.

3. Change across the spectrum of classroom dimensions (including goals, content, materials, instructional strategies, learning strategies, grouping, space, time, evaluation of students).

4. For most teachers, a change in their conceptual "paradigm" about their curriculum and instruction.

5. Change nested in a new concept of schooling.

6. Restructuring of school leadership to support the classroom changes.

7. Change in the policy environment (district/state) to support the classroom changes.

The second general finding is the rapid and strong district adoption of the state-developed curriculum frameworks. By the end of the two-year adoption phase, all districts and respective schools had made a decision to adopt all aspects of each state curriculum framework. This pattern of early and rapid adoption fits with other recent findings of educational reform (Fuhrman, Clune, and Elmore, chapter 13; Murphy 1990b; Firestone 1989; Odden and Marsh 1988). What is surprising in the current study is the early and rapid adoption of the vision when the "innovation" is such a complex one as described above.

We found several critical reasons for quick adoption of the complex vision. First, the curriculum frameworks were seen as representing a "quality program", i.e., more than just a state mandate. In most of the districts, the curriculum frameworks were seen as representing the "best" of what was known about curriculum and instruction in these subject areas. Second, using the distinction provided by Peterson, Rabe, and Wong (1986), the curriculum frameworks met a developmental need of districts and thus, as predicted, would be adopted more readily than if the policy initiatives were redistributive in orientation. Finally, the vision was adopted readily because the district leaders met the criteria of "active use" synthesized by Firestone (1989) in that these leaders (the dominant coalition described by Firestone) had a high propensity to action and interpreted the policy as meeting their interests.

Within this general set of findings about vision are some specific insights particular to the complex changes represented by the curriculum frameworks. Scholars of the local change process typically describe the process as including several phases: initiation and adoption, implementation, and institutionalization. To make sense of the vision found in these districts and schools, we found an additional phase to the local change process: an antecedent phase that is more than just antecedent conditions in the traditional sense. While the phase itself will be discussed later in the chapter, the vision developed in the antecedent phase played a critical role in the initiation and adoption phases as well.

In the antecedent phase, all schools were using "program pieces" such as, for example, *Math Their Way*, a popular and effective manipulatives based mathematics programs for primary grade students. These pieces were "plump" in that they: 1) were closely congruent to the new goals found in the mathematics and science curriculum frameworks; 2) included many dimensions of classroom practice such as integrating teaching strategies, instructional materials, and new content; and 3) allowed teachers to develop conceptual clarity about the vision (see McLaughlin and Marsh 1978). The vision during the antecedent phase was held primarily by teachers, principals and curriculum-focused district staff but usually not by district line administrators.

For the adoption phase, the typical metaphor would be "generic skeleton for the whole" rather than "plump pieces" as found in the antecedent phase. The skeletal/generic vision during the adoption phase was held by the district leaders and the formal district textbook adoption committee, and typically was synonymous with the framework itself and the particular textbook adopted by that district. Some districts also included a generic set of curriculum principles for that subject as part of the vision; but very few districts had an extensive and robust vision that was collectively held by the dominant coalition.

Implementation Coordination.   During the antecedent phase, the locus of coordination was at the site rather than the district level. The focus was on the use of program pieces, and in nine of the fourteen cases, involved participation in regional networks of program users who were linked to national curriculum projects.

During the adoption phase, the locus of coordination shifted to the district level, and focused on: 1) reviewing the current district curriculum in either mathematics or science against the curriculum design found in the new state curriculum guides; and 2) selecting a new set of text-books/instructional materials (from the state-approved list). Coordination during this phase was the most formal of the three phases: it included the broadest range of role groups, had the most formal organizational structure, and provided participants with training on the procedures to be followed as well as on the substantive issues involved. McMahon (1990) described these district coordination structures as follows:

> Every district had at least one district cross-role team whose member-ship was usually composed of someone from the central office, the principal or vice-principal, and teachers. Most members received some kind of formal, upfront training which resulted in being able to share their expertise and/or train others regarding the mathematics program implementation. The most frequent demands of the district cross-role teams were selecting textbooks, providing training and inservices, and gaining an understanding of the adoption/alignment/ implementation of the mathematics framework. (p. 161)

A similar pattern held for the science curriculum framework.

Analysis of the coordination structures during the adoption phase showed several patterns. First, using Firestone's concept of a "dominant coalition" (Firestone 1989), the dominant coalition in this case was not primarily the superintendent and board members, but included two groups: 1) teachers and site administrators included on the district coordination structure primarily because of their substantive expertise and their previous experience in this curriculum area (usually developed in the antecedent phase); and 2) district staff who bridged the technical/bureaucratic boundary, i.e., who both understood the curriculum framework and had considerable influence with the superintendent and the board. Second, using McLaughlin and Marsh's (1978) concept of "vertical coordination" this district coordination structure clearly linked the school district vertically rather than horizontally.

Third, using McLaughlin's (chapter 10) concepts of will and capacity, the district coordination structure during the adoption cycle served to consolidate the district will, or vision, rather than create it totally anew. District capacity for understanding and implementing the new curriculum frameworks often was built during the antecedent phase and was brought to the district coordination structure by teachers, site administrators and district leaders who really understood the curriculum. In an important sense, district capacity was developed by key district leaders prior to the adoption phase. Thus, the adoption and implementation phases were opportunities to expand rather than initiate this capacity.

In the district adoption process, one also can see the confluence of two cultures: the professional and the bureaucratic. As described above, the professional culture derived primarily from teachers, site administrators and some district leaders who understood the curriculum as well as the district coordination structure. These people brought considerable knowledge built over at least several years—knowledge often based on successful use of "plump" program pieces in their own classrooms, involvement in regional networks, and extensive inservice education. These people often had experience in providing help to others but had been blocked in getting other teachers to use the new programs. Their goal in district level participation was to build structures/policies that would foster wider implementation.

Members of the professional culture developed a new appreciation for the bureaucratic culture during the adoption phase. They recognized their need for what the bureaucratic culture offered: authority to demand attention and a signal that the new curriculum frameworks were important. The bureaucratic culture also was important because board approval of the new curriculum direction and the selected textbooks were required.

During the implementation phase, coordination structures shifted back primarily to the school level. This shift appeared to happen for several reasons. The multiplicity of curriculum frameworks (districts were engaged in implementing science and mathematics change with language arts and history change set for the next year) represented a complex set of changes that overwhelmed the district capacity for coordination in several respects. District curriculum leaders also had competing demands for their attention. The formal district staff was typically a very small group who had a new major curriculum framework to address each year. Despite their knowledge that implementation takes considerable time and energy, they felt they had to shift their attention to the adoption phase for other frameworks, and to other curriculum and instructional responsibilities. Moreover, there was a tradition that the district textbook adoption committees focused primarily on the adoption rather than implementation issues. Finally, since the professional talent was primarily at the site level and since sites differed in many ways, it was understandable that implementation was structured at the site level.

In short, district leaders simply did not have the resources to coordinate implementation from the "top" and sites had to mount implementation activities to keep the curriculum change process moving. As discussed more below, the capacity developed during the antecedent stage was critical in sites being able to address this implementation challenge.

Assistance.   Four major trends characterized the assistance sites received to implement the curriculum frameworks. First, formal district capacity for providing assistance was clearly overwhelmed. Formal capacity included provision of district leadership, sufficient resources, and a comprehensive plan for coordinated implementation support services. Compared to the extensive adoption phase, the formal capacity during the implementation phase can be characterized as haphazard and opportunistic.

Second, despite this lack of formal implementation capacity, site staff found extremely creative ways to transform the skeleton vision into a living "operational curriculum." This transformation happened in several ways:

1. *Continued Use of Program Pieces.* Continued use and integration of "plump" program pieces begun during the antecedent phase. The typical school in the study had four to seven plump pieces such as *Math their Way, Family Math, Equals* (from the Lawrence Hall of Science) etc. These pieces were not dropped but instead were integrated into the new curriculum program as a specific way to operationalize the new curriculum framework.

2. *Use of New Textbooks.* Use of new instructional materials drew primarily on the new textbooks. Most districts adopted not the most innovative of the possible textbooks, but instead, typically selected texts that balanced the need to follow the new curriculum framework with what the district thought was feasible to implement, given the many constraints found in the district. Consequently, the Open Court series (judged to be the best aligned with most demanding view of the curriculum framework in mathematics) was adopted in only two districts, and specifically not adopted for that reason in many of the others.

3. *Use of New or Existing Instructional Materials.* Many sites obtained considerable new instructional materials or adapted existing materials (often from the plump programs) to use in the new curriculum. As was found in the *Study of Schooling* (Klein, Tye, and Wright 1979), the availability of these materials strongly influenced teachers' willingness to try the new program.

4. *Use of District Curriculum Guides and Model Curriculum.* Most districts created summer institutes where lead teachers created curriculum units or examples which were shared with other

teachers. These proved to be extremely helpful to teachers. Only one district created an extensive curriculum guide, however. Practicality was the dominant theme in the curriculum units; usable examples were a very persuasive means to help teachers implement the new curriculum.

These curriculum strategies did much to help teachers see how to transform the skeleton of the district adopted curriculum into a classroom reality.

Third, at the same time, extensive staff development was provided to teachers. The formal district staff development workshops often focused on upfront awareness training regarding aspects of the framework or on related instructional strategies such as cooperative learning. At many of the sites, the amount of additional inservices, workshops and assistance was often extensive. In her analysis of the implementation process at these sites, McMahon (1990) reports:

> Half of the districts provided extensive ongoing assistance for the mathematics program during the implementation phase (p. 162) . . . Ongoing assistance was less for science than it was for mathematics. Districts typically provided workshops but not as many as during the initial implementation phase. Teachers typically stated that science had gone to the "bottom of the stack" as district interest had turned to other subject matter areas. Half of the districts made little use of institutes and consultants during the initial awareness, content and skill training in science. More resources had been used in mathematics (p. 165).

Finally, the creation of new assistance-related leadership roles was a typical strategy used at the sites. Most sites used mentor teachers to provide extensive help to other teachers through demonstration lessons and informal assistance. The mentor teaching program is a state-funded but locally-directed program that lets selected lead teachers help other teachers. Districts in the study redeployed these mentors to help with curriculum framework implementation. Some of the sites also organized teachers into learning teams facilitated by a lead teacher. In four districts, and especially in science, an especially active and energetic mentor teacher (or other site leader) became the district leader for continuing the implementation of that curriculum framework.

Monitoring/Latitude/Pressure. In mathematics, administrative support was "high" in nearly every district and appeared in the form of workshop, meetings and funds allocation for implementing the programs. Administrators typically took an active part in planning and arranging training for teachers. Monitoring the mathematics program took the form of daily or weekly walk-throughs or having teachers incorporate goals into their monthly or yearly plans. Pressure to implement the mathematics program came from the "bottom-up" as well as from the "top-down." In the "bottom-up" districts, pressure usually came from a core group of teachers, often those involved in the antecedent stage, who were skilled in mathematics education and who wanted to see the program in place. In some districts where there was "top-down" pressure, teachers complained of administrators who wanted to make too many changes too quickly. The extent of latitude varied throughout the districts, but the smaller ones had the most latitude. In these districts, the teachers were left essentially on their own to implement the mathematics program in their classrooms.

In science, the pattern was somewhat different. There was less administrative support for science than there was for mathematics. Some districts had no ongoing assistance or program facilitators, and support for science had become symbolic. In other districts support was rated "high" and was evidenced by administrators who played a large part in obtaining funds and resources to keep their science programs in place. Administrative involvement was also less for science than it was for mathematics. Administrative involvement appeared in the form of visibility at workshops and presenting training sessions or modeling lessons for teacher.

Pressure to implement the science program was about equally distributed from "high" to "low." Districts rated "low" in pressure usually had little ongoing assistance or monitoring and staff development. Half of the districts were rated "high" in latitude and "low" in fidelity which resulted in many of the science programs being "watered down."

Teacher Effort. For mathematics, teachers at nearly all sites were rated "high" in teacher effort. Most teachers had received a sufficient amount of information about the mathematics framework and had experienced enough administrative support to "buy into" the program. Extent of teacher effort varied more for science than it did for mathematics. In some districts, few teachers seemed to care about science and were feeling overwhelmed with other subjects.

Role of State Policy Initiatives

We found that many state policy initiatives were related to use of the state curriculum frameworks. These initiatives included:

1. *The Curriculum Frameworks Themselves.* The frameworks were written by a committee of school, district, university and state

Department of Education staff and consisted of several documents outlining the overall philosophy of the curriculum, the key themes and content to be addressed and an overview of the instructional process needed to give vitality to the curriculum.

2. *The Seven Year Textbook Adoption Cycle.* This cycle is designed to help districts carry out three phases of curriculum adoption and implementation. The first two phases are designed to take a total of two years. Phase I consists of a comparison of district curriculum to the new curriculum guide (a mandate) and an assessment of current strengths and weaknesses. Phase II consists of comprehensive planning and the selection/adoption of instructional materials.

In the words of the memo from the State Department of Education, during Phase III, "all schools in the district begin implementing the revised curriculum. Schools with additional program resources use their (School Improvement Program councils) and other committees to initiate their regular planning process in the development of curriculum and instructional improvement strategies." (Smith 1987).

3. *The Approved List of Textbooks and Instructional Materials.* The state curriculum frameworks served as the intellectual guide for the state committee process of selecting approved textbooks and instructional materials. For both mathematics and science, this state-level selection process was controversial in nature resulting in modifications of the approved textbooks/materials themselves. For example, in science, the treatment of evolution and human sexuality was revised. In mathematics, textbook companies were forced to revise their materials to include more inquiry oriented lessons and examples.

4. *The State Testing Program (CAP) Including the Public Report Card For Each School.* The California Assessment Program (CAP) uses matrix sampling to test students at grades 3, 6, 8, and 12, in order to portray school- and district-level achievement trends. For the third and sixth grades, the test includes mathematics, but not science, at the present time. Moreover, the 8th and 12th grade tests have recently been revised to be aligned more closely with the new curriculum frameworks. The elementary school level testing had not undergone this revision; consequently, the new curriculum directions reflected in the curriculum frameworks was not aligned very well with the elementary school CAP program. Given the public nature of the reporting of scores, schools raised considerable concern about this problem which is in the process of being addressed.

5. *School Improvement Program.* A comprehensive reform process which provides a planning process and funding directly to local

schools. Almost all of the elementary schools in the state have had this program for over ten years. A recent feature of the SIP program is the Program Quality Review (PQR) that includes a self-study and subsequent external review by peers from the geographic region. These reviews are based on Quality Indicators drawn directly from the state curriculum frameworks. The Quality Indicators portray what a classroom should look like if it is in keeping with the curriculum directions found in the state curriculum frameworks.

6. *Mentor Teachers.* A state-funded program that allows district-level selection of up to 5% of teachers who are paid a stipend to assist other teachers or to develop innovative curriculum within broad state guidelines. Various districts have deployed their mentors in dramatically different ways: some emphasizing individual mentor-defined projects while others using mentors more "strategically" to help all teachers implement district priority programs, such as new curriculum frameworks.

7. *Various funding for staff development.* In some cases, the state has funded recognized curriculum leadership centers such as the Lawrence Hall of Science (on the UC Berkeley campus) to offer curriculum programs and staff development to a network of schools in that region of the state. In other cases, the staff development funding goes directly to the district and/or school.

Several observations are relevant about the state policy initiatives and their influence on the local adoption/implementation process. First, at the state level the policies were designed to "fit" together and coordinate the policy arena in which local implementation takes place. Moreover, the state had the resources and clout to alter the nature of instructional materials available to local schools. Without this clout, the policy arena might not have been as supportive of local program change.

Second, for several reasons, the curriculum frameworks had considerable influence on the local adoption process. There were several reasons for this extensive influence:

1. They fit with national views of "good" science and mathematics as reflected in national reform reports and were supported by a strong tradition of visible research. In many of the districts, a few leaders knew of this national pattern, partly through the regional networks which were so important during the antecedent phase.

2. They fit with local priorities. Like Firestone (1989) and others, district leaders in our study reported that they were already working in the directions proposed by the curriculum frameworks.

3. The frameworks were credible for other reasons. For example, recognized teacher, district and county leaders in that subject area helped write the frameworks. Moreover, the frameworks (mathematics more than science) were seen as user-friendly, i.e, accessible, understandable, and feasible.

4. The frameworks were generic enough to allow for flexible adaption by districts yet focused enough on essential and new concepts to represent a powerful new view of curriculum in that subject area.

5. The state had a tradition of activist activity in education and conducted quality dissemination of the frameworks through state and regional conferences.

At the same time, the comprehensive planning/implementation process proposed in the seven year curriculum cycle was not as effective. During adoption, districts conducted much simpler and cruder comparisons of current curriculum with the new state curriculum frameworks than was proposed: the adopted curriculum was a skeleton rather than a comprehensive design. During implementation, planning was informal, fragmented and opportunistic rather than extensive and formal as proposed in the state memo. In short, the state curriculum frameworks overloaded local capacity, especially in the area of comprehensive planning, but also in many other ways.

Third, some state policies not directly linked to the curriculum frameworks were critically important to the success of the implementation process. Mentor teachers were a crucial resource for staff development and curriculum development and revision; at the same time, they allowed the informal lead teachers of the antecedent phase to achieve more formal authority, access to resources, and attention. Another critical state policy initiative was the PQR process of the SIP program. This process provided the obvious pressure directly on local sites but also served an important educative function as to what the curriculum framework would look like in practice. This education came not from district bureaucrats, but instead, from professional colleagues.

Finally, the state policy initiatives influenced all phases of the local change process, and at the appropriate organizational level (site vs. district). During the antecedent phase, staff development in the regional networks and the use of SIP funds to implement the plump program pieces were critical to developing site and district capacity for implementing the curriculum frameworks. Other state policy initiatives, especially the curriculum cycle, the frameworks themselves, and the textbook adoption process strongly influenced the creation of new district visions of mathematics and science and the coalescing of the dominant coalition to promote it in the adoption phase. Many of the state policy initiatives helped during the implementation phase, but in a rather haphazard and uncoordinated way.

The frameworks themselves helped in many ways. They served as an opportunity for a new content vision, provided an outline that could be expanded, gave access to the best of "good practice," confirmed that certain ideas and people were "on the right track," consolidated and integrated previous plump pieces, and became a source of momentum, a flywheel that continued the momentum which otherwise would have been dissipated. Perhaps most importantly, the frameworks served an educative function: they helped local practitioners focus on what to learn.

Impact of the Implementation Effort

For several reasons, the study could not provide an extensive analysis of the impact of these policy initiatives on classroom practice. It was too early in the implementation process to collect definitive impact data and an extensive collection of such data was beyond the scope of our available resources. However, it was possible to document several significant trends.

First, both the new mathematics and science curricula theme were implemented in classrooms. Our study involved classroom observation and indepth interviewing of randomly-selected teachers at all sites. In most cases, teachers were using most of the appropriate curriculum themes found in the state frameworks.

This study could not, however, assess the "depth" of implementation, nor the degree to which the paradigm shifts embodied in the new curriculum frameworks were fully understood by teachers and fully implemented in the classroom. Indeed, Cohen (1990) observed over a full year several teachers implementing the new California mathematics curriculum and concluded that authentic and full implementation in the classroom had not occurred, even though teachers were covering the new topics and trying to use the new teaching strategies. The deep and fundamental changes included in the frameworks, while received positively by teachers, require such basic new understandings and expertise that it will be difficult to get them fully implemented.

Second, mathematics curriculum implementation clearly exceeded science curriculum implementation. Moreover, in seven sites, there was clear indication that use of the new science program had receded or been discontinued. This lack of institutionalization happened for several reasons. At the district level, one important pattern was the less active nature of district involvement in the implementation process itself. Compared to district involvement in the mathematics framework, the implementation process for the science framework had less district support, less monitoring and pressure and more latitude given to local sites. In short, the science curriculum was more frequently discontinued because it was ignored as the district moved on to mathematics. As a result, science enjoyed less support and assistance from the time of early implementation.

In turn, this district pattern also can be seen as portraying less district will and less capacity for implementing the science framework. Since the CAP test did not assess the science learning in students but did assess other curricular areas, district leaders understandably focused on these other areas. This shift in focus was accentuated by the inadequate staffing and resources at the district level for curriculum and instructional leadership in general; when demand exceeded supply, mathematics demand held over science demand. Moreover, the capacity for science leadership was always weaker than it was for mathematics.

At the site level, signals from the district that other curricular areas were important was a reality driven home by the more compelling insight that elementary teachers were facing a new curricular reform every year. The year after the mathematics framework was implemented, teachers were to undertake a major revamping of the English/language arts curriculum towards a whole language approach to reading/writing/literature. Teachers were understandably focused on that more central and critical reform—a reform made doubly significant given the large number of Limited-English-Proficient students in the California schools these days. Further, the new history curriculum framework also had been released so teachers knew yet another curriculum area was stated for major overhaul in the short term.

Moreover, the science curriculum involved use of numerous instructional materials that either were lost over time or were designed to be used only once. Districts typically couldn't afford to replace these materials, which were the heart of an inquiry-oriented science program.

Policy Implication

This study provides five lessons about policy implementation of the more recent reform initiatives. First, an antecedent phase was very important for building local capacity for implementing the complex new reforms. This antecedent phase preceded the formal adoption phase and allowed for the development of "plump pieces" of the new programs, development of lead teachers who were very competent in the new program, and a network linking teacher leaders to regional technical assistance networks. For reform that requires extensive change at the classroom level, some capacity development must precede formal adoption.

The second lesson centers on teacher professionalism. Beyond willingness to experiment and develop a common technical language, teacher professionalism in this reform process focused primarily on developing expertise in the new innovation. Development of teacher expertise often came from other teachers within regional networks of assistance. As McLaughlin (chapter 8) has pointed out, these professional networks were very powerful and were the source of reform-focused assistance.

Conversely, teacher professionalism as "control" was not a critical factor in the reform process. It was not the parity arrangements of the School Improvement Process that led to teacher professionalism; instead, it was professionalism based on expertise that was critical.

The third lesson relates to the nature of the implementation process in terms of its being "top-down" versus "bottom-up" in nature. In implementing recent waves of reform, a new pattern of "top-down" and "bottom-up" linkage was seen. During the antecedent phase, efforts were primarily "bottom-up" in that teachers and schools, rather than district leadership, were often the initiators of the linkages to regional networks of assistance and program development. During the formal adoption phase, the reform was coordinated at the district level (the "top-down" dimension) but often utilized the vast talents of the lead teachers (the "bottom-up" dimension). During this phase, these lead teachers represented technical expertise rather than merely the "workers" who know the classroom and its realities best.

However, during implementation, the process again became primarily site-based rather than district led. With multiple major reforms being undertaken, the district leadership was overwhelmed in several ways: a) the leadership had to coordinate the adoption of programs in other curricular areas, and b) it lacked the expertise, resources, and time to facilitate the details of the implementation process. Consequently, intensive, ad hoc, site-based efforts were the key to successful implementation of these reforms.

The fourth lesson is that policy initiatives were very important to each phase of reform implementation. During the antecedent phase, the regional networks were often state-funded efforts. These networks included the program development and staff development efforts, such as were provided by the Lawrence Hall of Science on the UC Berkeley campus, as well as regional awareness conferences funded by the State Department of Education.

During the adoption phase, the state curriculum frameworks were extremely important in setting the vision for the reform and educating local leaders about this vision. District leaders were required to compare their current district curriculum with the new framework as well as undertake an extensive process for selecting appropriate instructional materials from a list of state-approved alternatives. Since the state was providing the funding for the purchase of these materials, it was able to command the attention of district leaders to this process. The local process of defining curriculum directions and selecting related instructional materials was also influenced by several state-initiated accountability mechanisms such as the state testing program and the accountability report card required of all districts.

Moreover, during the adoption as well as the implementation phases, the state mentor teacher program often provided the specification and formalization of teacher leadership roles. Mentors were also given the incentives and rewards that increased the attractiveness of this role. Many other state initiatives provided resources and a planning process for focusing local assistance efforts on these important reforms.

The final lesson is that implementing these far-reaching and fundamentally new notions of school curriculum will be complex. They require paradigm shifts in understanding mathematics and science, shifts that basically require a brand-new view of mathematics and science. The good news is that teachers and local educators are responsive to these new views. But full, deep, and complete implementation of them is likely to take at least several years of concerted effort.

Chapter 13

Ideas and Values in Implementation Analysis: The Case of Teacher Policy

Lorraine M. McDonnell

Policies and their outcomes are influenced not only by the immediate context in which they are implemented, but also by the larger ideas that shape the perspectives of political authorities. Most implementation studies, however, focus narrowly on issues of policy and practice. The research task is to determine whether a policy has been put into practice consistent with its legislative intent and, where implementation outcomes differ from initial expectations, to identify the factors that explain those differences. Rarely, do analysts ask whether more basic and enduring ideas about the goals of public policy or the dynamics of social change have animated a policy and shaped its implementation. Yet, the inability of conventional implementation studies to account fully for the gap between policy intentions and outcomes suggests the need for a more penetrating look at this aspect of the policy process. The value of examining the role of ideas in future implementation studies is further strengthened by recent efforts to broaden the explanatory approach of research on other aspects of politics and policy (for example, see Reich 1988; Kingdon 1988).

This chapter, argues that just as ideas have become a key factor in explaining why policies are enacted at certain times and in particular forms, they may also increase our understanding of policy implementation. This argument is illustrated by examining two sets of ideas or values that underlie recent state policies to improve public school teaching, and their influence on the design and implementation of those policies. In the first section, recent political science and policy analysis literature exploring the relationship between ideas and public policy is

241

summarized. The second section outlines the role of two key values
that undergird much teacher policy: professionalism and democratic
control. The third section explores how the natural tension between
these two values helps explain why teacher policies have encountered
so many problems in their implementation. The final section suggests
how greater awareness of the power of these two ideas and their more
effective accommodation in policy design can improve future teacher
policies. It also concludes that models of policy implementation—particularly, those designed to explain policies representing major shifts in
how educational problems are addressed—need to pay greater attention to ideas as explanatory factors.

1. The Role of Ideas in Politics and Public Policy

To argue that ideas and values influence the conduct of politics
and its policy outputs is not new to political or historical analysis. One
need only think of the role of major philosophical ideas such as those
of the eighteenth century Enlightenment on the design of U.S. political
institutions, or the endless debates about the relationship between ideology and politics that occurred in the aftermath of World War II.

The Self-Interest Model

In the 1970s, however, something of a paradigm shift occurred in
political science, economics, and policy analysis. The major explanatory term in models of voting, policymaking, and bureaucratic behavior
became self-interest as defined by neoclassical microeconomics. In
their simplest form, such models assume that in politics, as in the marketplace, people act in pursuit of their own self-interest rather than
from any form of altruism or sense of public interest. Consequently,
"politicians act solely in order to attain the income, prestige, and
power which come from being in office . . ." (Downs 1957, p. 28); congressmen and presidents make those policy decisions most likely to
maximize the probability of their re-election (Mayhew 1974; Fiorina
1974); and bureaucrats act so as to maximize their budgets and protect
their turf, rather than to promote the aims of the principals who
employ them (Niskanen 1971; Moe 1984). Since much political behavior is motivated by self-interest, these models have gained considerable
prominence in recent years. But in politics, the concept of self-interest
is seldom as simple or constant as it is in the marketplace, and the
inability of these models to illuminate the social goals or values that

shape individuals' definitions of their interests limit the models' applicability outside of economics. Economic models, for instance, take actors' preferences as given, avoiding empirically "messy" issues such as enumerating the ideas or theories that shape those preferences, analyzing the link between ideas and different definitions of self-interest, or depicting actors' beliefs about how to achieve goals through political institutions and processes.

Emergence of Ideas as Relevant

While the economic model's parsimony is attractive, discomfort with the limitations of self-interest or rational choice approaches has grown over the past several years. Some of it has been normative, coming from those who believe "we need a social norm that it is appropriate for people to try to do the right thing in public behavior and inappropriate simply to advance their personal interests" (Kelman 1988, p. 52). For others the concern has been empirical, as evidence has accumulated that "at least in some cases policy development is caused more by changes in beliefs and values than by changes in economic and political interests" (Majone 1989, p. 148). Examples of major policies that could not have been predicted from a simple self-interest-based model include: the 1964 Civil Rights Act, environmental protection legislation, airline deregulation, and the 1986 tax reform. In all these cases, the legislation did not reflect the triumph of powerful, well-established interests or the ascendency of other well-organized groups. Rather, they arose from either an emerging belief that such changes were good for the society as a whole (Reich 1988), or the prevalence of new ideas about how the economy or political system could be made more effective (e.g., see Derthick and Quirk 1985).

Still other social scientists have argued that even in those cases where people pursue their own self-interest single-mindedly, they need ideas about how "the world works" in order to act (Kingdon 1988; Weatherford 1989). These ideas are analogous to theories about how political and economic systems actually operate and how different interests might be effectively pursued through those systems. They, in effect, specify the relationship between different types of governmental intervention (or purposeful non-intervention) and desired outcomes. So, for example, manufacturers who want government to help make them more competitive against foreign imports may have different theories about how their interests can be most usefully advanced (e.g., through import tariffs or quotas, exemption from environmental regulations to lower their costs, or tax subsidies). Finally, in some instances, ideas may be intended as no more than tools of persuasion in political debate. Yet, over time, these ideas can take on a life of their own, independent of the interests that originally promoted them. For example, the notion of parental choice was first used by proponents of tuition tax credits and private school vouchers, but it has now taken on a much broader meaning in the current school restructuring movement.

Interests and Ideas

As a result of these prescriptive and empirical concerns, a consensus is emerging among analysts that models of policymaking need to encompass both interests and the ideas that shape and support them. As Kingdon (1988) notes, the concept of "ideas" includes two distinct dimensions: 1) goals—conceptions of what is desirable for individuals, specific groups, and the society as a whole; and 2) theories about how the world works—cause-effect notions that help people decipher how social phenomena work and strategies for achieving their goals (i.e., means rather than ends).

Although "ideas" as a theoretical concept is gaining acceptance in models of policymaking, it has not yet been incorporated into the analytical frameworks that guide policy implementation research. Yet it is likely to be as important a factor in explaining implementation outcomes as for policy enactment. For example, if one were to use a policy instruments framework (see McDonnell and Elmore, chapter 9), the analytical task would be to understand the relationship among problem definition, instrument choice, organizational context, implementation, and effects. Central to that effort is identifying how policymakers defined the problem(s) they saw a particular policy instrument addressing. Ideas are often a key component of problem definition, particularly for major new policies such as the ones comprising the educational reform movement of the past several years. If we fail to take into consideration policymakers' prior views about the relationship between politics and public education, about how the educational system ought to work, and their assumptions about why its current status deviates from that ideal, we will have incompletely specified their definition of the policy problem they attempted to solve. This failure will, in turn, mean that assessments of the match between policymaker expectations and implementation outcomes will necessarily be incomplete. This example is just one illustration of how the role of ideas needs to be incorporated into implementation frameworks. Considerably more conceptual work is needed, however, before we will fully understand how ideas interact with other factors to shape policy enactment and implementation.

Nevertheless, as the analysis of recent state teacher policies discussed in the remainder of this chapter demonstrates, going beyond the basic contours of a policy to examine the ideas and values that undergird it can provide a much fuller understanding of implementation outcomes and the design factors that contribute to effective policy.

2. Popular Control and Professionalism: Competing Ideas in Teacher Policy

Policies to change how teachers are trained, licensed, and compensated comprise a major part of the educational reform agenda advanced by state governments over the past several years. These state policies have also been the most difficult to implement, and state officials face the prospect that many will need substantial modification. Yet this area continues as a target of increased policy activity and the focus of far-reaching proposals for change (e.g., the Carnegie Forum on Education and the Economy 1986). What is not entirely clear is why these policies have generated so many problems. Some would argue that implementation problems are inevitable, given the competing interests that intersect around teacher policy—e.g., teacher unions vs. school management, state legislators vs. local school boards, schools of education vs. those advocating alternative certification, and so on. Others see the problems as stemming from policy design factors such as whether state government or local school districts have the major responsibility for designing and implementing a new program. However, it became clear in examining state teacher policies that even when critical factors such as the nature of the policy instrument, resource-levels, and the amount of local discretion allowed by a policy were taken into consideration, the explanation for why various teacher policies followed a similar course across very different interest group configurations and organizational contexts was incomplete. Something more fundamental lies behind these proximate explanations.

Ideas and Teacher Policy

An examination of the ideas shaping the design of recent teacher policies led to a focus on democratic control and professionalism. Both of these values have been espoused by different groups pressing for teaching reforms. Sometimes the interests embodied within each have been consistent, but often they suggest contradictory policy goals and strategies. Consequently, understanding the extent and manner in which these differences have been reconciled in the design of teacher policies helps provide a fuller explanation of implementation outcomes and intermediate effects.

Democratic control. Democratic or popular control rests on the belief that the legitimacy of all governmental institutions derives from the consent of the electorate and therefore, must answer to them and their representatives. It presumes that the public will regularly hold legislators and executives accountable for the performance of public institutions such as schools (Dahl 1982; Gruber 1987). Democratic control further posits that a larger public interest transcends the interests and values of any single class of persons, and that its pursuit is best ensured if individual behavior is held accountable to the larger body politic. Consequently, it argues not just that public employees' behavior should be constrained, but that the constraint be externally-imposed.

This external constraint is typically operationalized through a variety of mechanisms that include elections, various forms of political action such as lobbying, the exercise of judicial authority, and the imposition of performance standards on public sector institutions and their employees. All are predicated on the assumption that sufficient information will be publicly available about the quality of institutional performance for elected officials and citizens to make informed decisions.

Professionalism. Professionalism, on the other hand, embodies a different set of tenets. It assumes that members of an occupation possess a specialized body of knowledge, and that, because their work poses complex and nonroutine problems, their behavior in applying that expert knowledge should be regulated by a code of ethics internal to the profession and by the voluntary groups representing them (Barber 1965). For instance, professional knowledge requires judgment in its application to individual clients' needs, so that it cannot be reduced to rules or prescriptions for practice; thus professionals as a group require autonomy from administrative control in determining tasks and functions (Boreham 1983). In other words, professional values argue that teachers should be held accountable through standards and procedures collectively specified and enforced by their peers, not by externally-defined and enforced criteria. Professional values are assumed to be consistent with the community's interest, but the norms of professional autonomy and self-governance deny the community's claim to hold them accountable for that consistency at regular intervals.

Differences Between Democratic Control and Professionalism

The differing assumptions underlying democratic control and professionalism are sharpest on two dimensions: interest and authority.

(Table 1 summarizes these and other major differences between democratic control and professionalism.) The primary interest or concern of professionals, particularly those working in service organizations such as schools, is presumed to be the welfare of clients (Blau and Scott 1962). Democratic control, on the other hand, assumes a range of interests that extend far beyond those of individual clients such as students. It argues that elected representatives should serve the public welfare broadly defined. Although theories of representation differ on how such interests are best served, they all assume that elected officials will aggregate and balance their own conception of the public interest, the diverse interests of their local constituents, those of their political party, the broader state or national interest, as well as the expert judgments and preferences of various professional groups (Pitkin 1967). Democratic control further requires that institutions implementing policy and delivering public services reflect the public interest as it has been articulated through the political process.

Table 1 Two Different Ideas about how Public Education Should Be Governed

	POPULAR CONTROL	*PROFESSIONAL CONTROL*
Practitioners	Electorate and its epresentatives	Professional norms and through those to clients and the public
Interests Served	Constituents Political parties Organized groups Public interest as defined by political ideology Personal	Client welfare as defined by professional norms and standards Personal
Basis of Authority	Consent of the governed	Expert knowledge and judgement
Implementing Mechanisms	Elections Executive and legislative policymaking Courts Public bureaucracies	Training and licensing Professional associations Teacher involvement in school budgetary, personnel, and curriculum decisions

Professionalism and democratic control also differ in their sources of authority or legitimacy. Those acting on the basis of professionalism derive their authority from their ability to apply expert knowledge and judgment in the service of clients. Those acting under the rubric of popular control derive their authority from electoral mandates or the tenet that in a democracy, the legitimacy of all government derives from the consent of the governed.

Balancing Democratic Control and Professionalism in Public Education

In the extreme, the issues distinguishing professionalism and democratic control come down to a fundamental question of whether education is best controlled by lay decisions expressing majoritarian preferences or by professional decisions based on guild-like knowledge and expertise. Yet subscribing to either of these values in their pure form makes policy design and implementation very difficult. The dilemma of democratic control is that politicians are neither experts nor responsible to the individual clients of public services: their constituencies are far broader and represent diverse interests. The dilemma of professional control is that in responding to an authority outside the direct reach of either clients or the public at large, practitioners may misperceive the interests of both groups. The debate is a longstanding one. As Cremin (1965) notes:

> There is a tension here, of course, that has been at the heart of the popular education single system from the very beginning. On the one hand, there is the prerogative of the public to set policy, determine direction, and fix support: we speak of public control, not merely public sponsorship or public influence. On the other hand, there is the prerogative of the teaching profession to govern its own work, set standards, and determine the nature of teaching practice: the teacher is committed to teaching truth as he sees it and to following truth wherever it leads (90–91).

As this discussion indicates, both popular control and professionalism are strongly-held values with deep historical and philosophical roots. Both presume a causal process. Democratic control assumes that good outcomes will result for all participants (in this case, students and the larger community) if policymakers hold teachers accountable to standards that reflect community expectations and meet basic due process criteria, and if they are held accountable to the public through regular popular elections. Professionalism assumes that autonomy and self-governance will attract competent people, keep incompetents out, encourage better teaching tailored to the unique needs of students, and thus result in improved learning. Yet even if it could be validly measured, the relationship between educational practices that maximize either of these values and actual student learning is an indirect one, at best.

It is also clear that either value can be used to rationalize practices that are detrimental to the interests of an individual, a group, or to the larger public interest. For example, the majoritarian popular control of schools has been used as a powerful argument against school desegregation (Hochschild 1984). Similarly, professional expertise has sometimes been used as a shield by practitioners to avoid grappling with policy changes supported by the broader public (Gruber 1987; Elmore and McLaughlin 1988). Furthermore, both democratic "knowledge" of what is best for local schools and communities and professional knowledge of what is best for individual students cannot be applied with certainty in all cases. Both values must also contend with a third party who is relatively powerless in the educational accountability equation—the student, who is obliged by law to attend school and whose interests may not be served by either political accountability mechanisms or professional accountability standards.

Consequently, the major dilemma for policymakers is how to balance these two values in the best interests of students. How should policies governing the training, certification, evaluation, and compensation of teachers be designed, in light of the public's democratic claim and the profession's expert claim to know what is best for students? The task is not easy, and raises a host of normative and practical issues. For example, those advocating greater professionalism for teachers cite the educational research literature, arguing that students will learn more effectively if individual schools are granted more autonomy to diagnose and solve problems, and if teachers and principals have greater flexibility to exercise their professional judgment (e.g., Goodlad 1983; Carnegie Forum 1986). Yet individual schools cannot be held directly accountable through the electoral process, and other forms of accountability (e.g., creating a quasi-market mechanism through greater parental choice) may resolve part of the dilemma, but at the same time, present a different set of limitations and trade-offs. But the essential mechanism of democratic control—elections to select who governs states and school districts—is an indirect and often uncertain vehicle for making local schools more responsive to the immediate needs of the students they serve, and efforts to increase top-down accountability can become an unwieldy and costly process.

Practical issues to resolve. Even if the normative issue of how much weight should be accorded each of these values can be resolved, a host of practical issues arise. For example, how do policymakers monitor teacher performance without creating perverse or unintended consequences (e.g., encouraging a single model of teaching that may be inappropriate for some teachers and students; lowering teacher morale; incurring high costs to ensure that the monitoring process is fair and reliable)? How can they balance the uniformity needed to guarantee equal access to good teaching for all students with the flexibility required to meet the diverse needs of local communities and individual students? How can policymakers encourage teachers to exercise their professional judgment without generating a kind of paternalism that ignores the wishes of the electorate (Thompson 1987), or shields self-interest from checks and balances?

3. Teacher Policy in Five States[1]

These questions are precisely the ones that state legislators have had to grapple with over the past few years. Research staff from the Center for Policy Research in Education examined the enactment of recent teacher policies in five states—Arizona, California, Florida, Georgia, and Pennsylvania—as part of a larger study of educational reform.[2] At first glance, dissimilarities in political culture, size, fiscal capacity, and educational organization among the five states would suggest that their choice of teacher policies and their experience in implementing those policies would be significantly different. Certainly, as Table 2 indicates, there are differences in the number and types of policies that these states selected. Two chose to focus on only the compensation aspects of teacher policy, while the others concentrated on multiple areas, including teacher training, certification, compensation, and professional development. Despite their varied emphases, however, four of the five states decided to stress teacher compensation and to rely on inducements to accomplish their purposes. In their level of activity and choice of policy strategies between 1983 and 1986, these five states represent a range that is quite typical of state governments generally.

How Policies Balanced Democratic Control and Professionalism

Regardless of which policy instruments they selected, state policymakers in all five states attempted to balance democratic control and professionalism in their design of teacher policies. Both values entered into policymakers' definition of the problems they saw themselves addressing and in their expectations of what a particular policy

Table 2   **Major Teacher Policies in Five States**
                              (1983–86)

STATE	POLICY
Arizona	Demonstration Career Ladder
California	Mentor teacher program
	Minimum starting salary
	Alternative training for program non-credentialed beginning teachers
	Stronger management prerogatives over teacher retention
	Requirement for continuing professional development
Florida	Merit pay and master teacher program (now replaced by a school incentive program)
Georgia	Stiffer recertification requirements
	Market-sensitive minimum salary
Pennsylvania	Increased requirements for teacher certification, induction, and continuing professional development

ought to accomplish. Rarely, however, were the two values accorded equal weight. Their relative status at any given time depended on a variety of political, organizational, and teacher labor market issues.

On balance, across the five states, state-level *attention to democratic control* in public school teaching was greater than the emphasis on professional values. This concern was most often expressed by performance standards that were defined through the political process, with limited input from teachers or the organizations that represent them (McDonnell and Pascal 1988). Implicit in this emphasis was the belief that teacher quality had diminished and no longer met the electorate's performance expectations for a public institution. This perception was further validated by data showing that new teaching entrants were scoring lower on tests of academic ability than peers choosing to join other professions, and that the more academically able left teaching earlier and in greater proportions than their colleagues (Schlechty and Vance 1981; Weaver 1983; Darling-Hammond 1984). As a result, rather than allowing the teaching profession to rejuvenate itself from within, state officials enacted policies requiring teachers to conform to performance criteria designed by public agencies and private test developers. They assumed that such an approach represented standards the electorate would view as legitimate, and that these actions would convince the public that policymakers were taking active responsibility for the state's schools.

At the same time, *strengthening teaching as a profession* was also a goal of state policy agendas. Policymakers recognized the need to make teaching a more attractive occupation, and enacted mechanisms such as career ladders and mentor teacher programs as ways to further those goals. In requiring that local districts involve teachers in the design and operation of these programs, they also acknowledged the legitimacy of professional self-determination. However, even with policies such as the career ladder in Arizona that permit considerable local discretion in program design and implementation, policymakers still pushed for a form of accountability (linking student achievement with assessments of teacher performance) that was at odds with professional judgments about good teaching practice.

Policy Design and Local Capacity

A concentration on policies that originated and were managed some distance from individual schools and classrooms, at the expense of professional self-governance, also meant that the expectations inherent in some exceeded state and local capacity. This was particularly true of the evaluation procedures for the career ladder in Arizona, the master teacher program in Florida, and certification testing in Georgia. These assumed not only that teachers had the capacity to respond in ways consistent with the policies' intent, but also that those monitoring their performance could measure it reliably without either incurring undue costs or distorting classroom practice. States are now seeking to redress this problem by, for example, decentralizing data collection as is the case for Florida's merit school program or investing in more research and development as Georgia has agreed to do to improve its teacher testing program. Still, the inability to measure teacher performance reliably and to collect relevant data cost-efficiently remains one of the most serious problems associated with a broad range of teacher policies. In fact, the greatest obstacle to states in their struggle to balance democratic control and professionalism may very well be their inability to resolve the questions of who should evaluate teachers and how they should be evaluated.

At the other end of the continuum are policies such as the mentor teacher program in California that make few demands on local district capacity and embody a minimal concern with public accountability. This approach is likely to make a program easier to implement and to encourage greater professionalism, but the trade-off may be that the goals of the larger political system are side-lined. In establishing the mentor program, state policymakers saw themselves addressing a generic problem of needing to provide teachers with greater status and more support. However, the problem being addressed was never well-defined; notions of professionalism were vague; and few accountability mechanisms were included. The result was a program that generated benefits largely limited to the mentors themselves, unless a district was willing to shape it to meet a critical local need. The absence of state direction gave districts the flexibility to do this, but it also meant that if districts chose not to do so, the program's impact was quite limited.

Florida: A Case Study in Competing Ideas and Interests

Although its teacher policies were more problematic than most states, Florida's experience illustrates how those espousing policies based on democratic control and those advocating greater professionalism have competed in the policy arena, and how state legislators' inability to balance these interests and their underlying ideas has led to ineffective implementation.

Recent teacher policy in Florida has been among the most problematic in the country, and represents a continuing tension between democratic control and professionalism. As part of its 1983 reform legislation, the state enacted a master teacher program that provided an annual award of $3000 to the state's most highly qualified teachers. Selection decisions were to be based on a high score on a subject matter test or the possession of a master's degree, and superior achievement on a performance evaluation. The program was designed and implemented from the state-level. Awards were subject to annual appropriations and annual evaluations, thus creating uncertainty among teacher candidates and an additional assessment burden. In the first year (1984–85), $9.5 million was appropriated for the program and three percent of the state's teachers qualified (about ten percent of those who applied). Funding for the second year was less than for the first, and payments to teachers remained uncertain, because in the summer of 1986, the AFT-affiliate filed suit challenging legislative appropriations for the program's second year.

The choice of such a mechanism is largely explained by the sources of political support for education reform in Florida and by how major actors defined the policy problem. The impetus for the master teacher program came from the Governor, several key legislators, and members of the business community. Not only did the state's teacher organizations oppose the program, but they were generally excluded from the policy development and enactment process. Policymakers saw themselves addressing the problem of low teacher salaries in Florida, but doing so in the context of the strict external accountability that the business community was demanding in return for supporting increased fiscal resources to education. As one legislator explained:

> First and foremost were teacher salaries. Too many people were not going into teaching because of the salaries. Florida is the lowest tax state, forty-eighth or forty-ninth, so it is hard to get extra money. Business was resisting, they thought they were just throwing money down a rathole. They didn't want to raise revenues and dump it in education without any guarantee of results. I agreed with them—money is dumped in and never gets to teachers. Also, unions are protective of teachers—they protect the ones that are not so good. You could not get the money to the teachers who deserved it.

The master teacher program encountered serious problems in its implementation. The performance measurement system that was selected had been designed to test beginning teachers, not veteran ones. There were serious logistical problems during the first year; large numbers of applications were lost; tests were scored incorrectly; and test administrations were scheduled without notifying teacher applicants. In 1985, a move was made to abolish the program, but it continued for two more years, largely because of the Governor's strong support. The program was repealed, effective July 1 1987.

During this same period, however, those interested in strengthening teaching as a profession sought alternatives to the master teacher program. In 1984, the legislature enacted the Merit Schools program which was viewed as a partial replacement. The program is voluntary for school districts and is locally-designed within state guidelines. It awards additional funds to schools (to be shared among school personnel) based on students' test scores and a variety of other criteria.

At the same time, a working group comprised of education and business representatives proposed a career ladder for the state. Individual districts would design their own program within broad state guidelines, and the local career ladder would have to be implemented within the scope of local collective bargaining. Although the program was enacted, no funds were appropriated for it. The enabling legislation remained in force through fiscal year 1988–89, after which it automatically expired because the legislature failed to appropriate the $90 million statutorily required to trigger the program. State policymakers attribute the legislature's unwillingness to appropriate funds for the career ladder to a backlash from the master teacher program and a lack of support for the program from teachers. However, the president of the state's AFT affiliate has vowed to work to restore the career ladder program (Mathis 1988), and is considering ways that it might be implemented even without state funding (Olson 1987).

Over the past few years, the balance between popular control and professionalism in Florida teacher policy has been skewed in favor of popular control. Political support patterns, the traditional centralizing tendency of state government, and the relative influence of the business community largely explain the emphasis on statewide performance standards and a differential compensation system. Policymakers understood the importance of higher salaries for attracting and retaining competent teachers, but in not including teachers in the policy design process, they negated professional assumptions about participation in work-related decisions and governance.

State policymakers also jeopardized the success of the master teacher program by assuming that state government had the technical and administrative capacity to monitor teachers' performance reliably—a key condition for effective democratic control. Given the state of teacher evaluation research and its inability to identify a set of teacher behaviors that are uniformly linked to effective student learning across grade levels, subject areas, and types of students, such capacity was extremely limited (Darling-Hammond and Berry 1988). It was further constrained by a short implementation time-frame that led to the state's reliance on a performance evaluation system designed to assess beginning teachers for minimal competencies. As would be predicted, experienced teachers were able to redirect their actions consistent with the evaluation instrument and to perform well on it. Consequently, the master teacher program ended up serving neither the goals of democratic control nor professionalism well.

4. Towards a More Effective Accommodation of Professionalism and Democratic Control in Teacher Policy

Understanding the role of ideas in policy enactment and implementation holds only academic interest if we cannot use that knowledge to improve the design of future policy. This final section suggests how new teacher policies can be more effectively crafted if state officials recognize and consciously seek to accommodate both values.

The teacher policies, enacted between 1983 and 1986, are now characterized as the "first wave" of educational reform. As their short-comings have become more evident, reform advocates have proposed a second generation of policies that emphasizes teacher professional-ism—high entry standards established and implemented by the profes-sion itself; greater teacher collegiality and autonomy within individual schools; and a differentiated staffing structure giving some teachers expanded leadership responsibilities. At the same time, however, demands for greater external accountability are also growing. The other category of education policy that has gained increased visibility over the past few years is the effort to provide policymakers and the public with more statistical information about how schools are performing, and then to reward, punish, and assist schools based on that information. Thus, the need to accommodate both democratic control and professionalism continues for the second generation of reform proposals.

The experience of state governments in designing and implement-ing teacher policies over the past few years is instructive in identifying strategies for striking a more effective balance between democratic con-trol and professionalism in future policy design. Three are suggested here.

Move in the Areas of Greatest Agreement

The first, and clearest, strategy for balancing the two values is to concentrate future policy in the areas where those espousing greater democratic control and those advocating increased professionalism show the greatest agreement. The findings from this study and a vari-ety of other sources strongly suggest that a widespread consensus exists in favor of stiffer entry standards for teachers (e.g., Gallup and Elam 1988). Although it is less strong and well-specified, a consensus is also growing around greater differentiation of teaching tasks and responsibilities in combination with some form of performance-based compensation—though not necessarily of the kind currently operating. Because teacher opinion data show considerably less consensus about the form that increased teacher participation in school decision-making should take (Metropolitan Life 1987) and because the political and administrative feasibility of these options is largely unknown at this point, such policies should probably be accorded less immediate prior-ity, and continue as diverse, small-scale experiments.

Consider a Broader Range of Policy Instruments

A second step that policymakers can take is to consider a broader range of strategies in designing future teacher policies. The "first wave" policies were based on a rather narrow range of policy instruments. Mandates were used to ensure that minimum standards were met (e.g., testing for initial certification). When states viewed the policy problem as the need to stimulate teacher performance beyond some specified minimum, they used a variety of inducements (e.g., additional compensation, differentiated responsibilities and status).

However, if teacher policy is to strike a more effective balance between democratic control and professionalism, policymakers also need to consider expanding the range of strategies beyond policies based just on mandates and inducements. One finding from this analysis of recent teacher policies is particularly clear: insufficient capacity is a primary reason why these policies have not worked as intended. State agencies, local districts, schools, and individual teachers currently lack the tools to ensure professional-level entry standards, to evaluate practicing teachers fairly and validly, or to reorganize teachers' responsibilities in more meaningful ways. If professionalism is to be strengthened without sacrificing democratic control norms, states will have to fund a variety of capacity-building instruments that have been largely ignored in recent years. These include: investment in better measures of teacher performance (for both new and experienced teachers) and equally important, greater attention to professional development—so teachers can engage in constructive peer review and work collaboratively with fellow professionals.

Address the Bureaucracy Problem

Whether future teacher policies favor professionalism, democratic control norms, or are able to balance the two, they will be implemented through some type of bureaucracy. Given that some large states have over 100,000 teachers and that even moderate-sized school districts employ several thousand teachers each, no teacher policy can be implemented except through an organization with a systematic division of labor, uniform rules of procedure, and some element of hierarchy. Even if policymakers were to delegate complete control of teaching to the profession itself, the sheer size and complexity of the enterprise would require that professional control be implemented through some type of bureaucratic organization.

Somewhat ironically, those advocating greater professionalism (Friedson 1973; Wise 1979) and those seeking to promote democratic control (Yates 1982; Yin and Yates 1975; Gruber 1987) have traditionally viewed bureaucracy as a potential threat to fulfilling their objectives, and each tends to blame the other value for the growth of bureaucracy.

This is particularly true of those advocating greater teacher professionalism. In their view, the governance of teaching through public policy is
synonymous with bureaucratic control.

Such a distinction confuses means and ends. Democratic control
and professionalism are both legitimate values (or ends) that American
society esteems and that teacher policy should seek to promote.
Bureaucracy, on the other hand, is the means that must be used in a
complex world to implement policies advancing either or both of those
goals. Therefore, the challenge for future teacher policy is not to eliminate bureaucracy, but to shape its structure and activities so that it is
accountable both to the teaching profession and to the public. This
admonition is easier spoken than accomplished. One of the most difficult, continuing responsibilities of democratic government is to hold its
institutions accountable to those they serve. This task will never be
fully accomplished. But in the case of teacher policy, an acknowledge-
ment that democratic control and professionalism are both legitimate
goals that can be accommodated through careful policy design and
implementation is a critical first step.

5. Conclusions

Not all policies embody fundamental ideas about the purpose of
public institutions such as schools, or cause-and-effect theories about
social change. Some are no more than attempts to balance quite limited
and transparent interests. Where broad-based consensus exists about
ends and means, policies attempt to meet governmental responsibilities
in the most efficient manner. However, when new policies represent
decided shifts in governmental strategies for addressing major social
problems, then implementation researchers may need to look beyond
the immediate aims expressed in those policies to the more enduring
ideas and values that underlie and shape them. Incorporating this factor
into the frameworks that guide implementation studies will take considerable time and thought—after all, the models we use today are the
result of almost twenty years of iterative theoretical and empirical work.
Yet, as the case of teacher policy has begun to demonstrate, the pay-off
from such effort can be a richer and more valid depiction of the links
among ideas, interests, policies, and their effects.

Chapter 14

School Restructuring:
Implementing Middle School Reform

David D. Marsh and Patricia S. Crocker

Since 1983, states have been active in directing educational reform. In general, the reforms have been implemented in "waves" leading to increasingly sophisticated proposed changes in classroom practice. Early reform waves emphasized higher graduation requirements and a return to a traditional academic high school. Recent research has established that such "early wave" changes have been implemented in many schools and that the changes are substantive rather than merely symbolic (Fuhrman, Clune, and Elmore 1988; Odden and Marsh 1990).

Both proponents and critics of these reforms, however, quickly note that the "early waves" of reform are insufficient. Schools need to adopt vibrant programs featuring powerful modes of inquiry and communication, a better integration of a core curriculum, more real-world relevance and application of courses of study, and examination of ethical issues in social and scientific matters. These later reform waves (Murphy, 1990b) will require much more fundamental changes in curriculum and instructional practice. They also raise a more fundamental research question: Is it possible to create this new wave of innovative curriculum and school restructuring by state-initiated reform efforts?

This chapter examines an example of the more recent wave of reform: an approach to middle school reform that includes school restructuring, comprehensive curriculum reform and a sensitive approach to young adolescents. This reform was studied in California where a state task force synthesized elements of middle school reform into a report known as *Caught in the Middle* (Superintendent's Middle

School Task Force 1987). This report served as a voluntary guideline and reference for an active, state middle school reform effort. The report syntheses elements of a middle school around five clusters of components. These clusters include: a) curriculum and instruction, b) student potential, c) organization and structure, d) teaching and administration, and e) leadership and partnership.

Two policy implementation issues are examined in this context, including: 1) the extent to which this new type of reform has actually been implemented; and 2) the ways that various state policy initiatives have enhanced or retarded this form of change. Two types of state policy initiatives are examined in depth: 1) the type that enhances local capacity for designing and implementing reform, of which the California School Improvement Program (SIP) is a good example; and 2) the type that represents state-initiated comprehensive reform, of which *Caught in the Middle* is a good example. These strategies are studied in the context of the evolving nature of policy implementation research.

1. State Education Reforms

The nation focused intensely on the issue of quality education during the decade of the 1980s. Prompted in part by concern for U.S. competition in international markets, most states enacted comprehensive educational reform legislation. Topics in the early waves of this state activity included teacher training and certification, finance, length of school days and year, graduation standards, testing programs, and curriculum. Most prior policy implementation research had analyzed federal government initiatives that encouraged schools to adopt programs for special needs populations. State education reform initiatives, even in the early waves of reform, were complex and comprehensive reforms dealing with the regular curriculum and instruction programs. These state efforts were aimed at all students and signaled an aggressive state stance (Kirst 1984; McDonnell and Fuhrman 1986).

Both the speed of enactment and comprehensiveness of these reforms raised questions about the likelihood of faithful implementation. Previous federal program implementation research found long periods of bargaining and mutual adaption before the federal programs were fully implemented. But while the multitude of education reform issues was great, especially in states like California, these new state policy initiatives had some advantages over earlier federal programs. States were regarded by locals as insiders and had both an interest in and access to the key components of the educational system. Reform legislation like California's SB 813, was a developmental rather than redistributive policy approach, focused on improving the core curriculum and instruction program impacting all teachers and all students (Odden and Marsh 1988). Further, the early 1980s education reforms did not require new staffing patterns, new intake processes, or new relationships with parents as did programs for disadvantaged or special education students. Rather, education reforms often represented a return to the more academic, traditional schooling, a pattern which most teachers support based on their past training and experience.

State Reform Implementation Research

Three major studies have examined the implementation of the early 1980s, "Wave I" flurry of state policy activity and made initial recommendations based on their findings. Anderson et al. (1987) studied ten states including California. They found that state efforts were most successful when state pressure to improve education linked curriculum and testing programs and were balanced with high levels of technical assistance. Ongoing political support accompanied by increased funding was particularly helpful when used by locals to plan and train for program implementation. State departments of education which developed collegial relationships with districts and whose efforts were integrated within departmental structures were more likely to increase local capacity for change.

These findings were similar to those found in the six state study conducted by Fuhrman, Clune, and Elmore (1988, chapter 11). This research found rapid and cooperative support of local districts in responding to state reform activity. Local response appeared to depend much less than expected on the up-front participation by local educators in policy initiation and design. Rather, implementation depended more on the knowledge and capacity of local educators to make necessary changes. Much of this state reform activity supported ongoing local change efforts and was consistent with the "regular" educational process.

Rapid and effective implementation of California's SB 813 also was affirmed in a comprehensive series of case studies conducted by Policy Analysis for California Education (PACE) (Odden and Marsh 1987). These studies also substantiated the link between state reform and existing efforts to improve local schools. California's state education reform initiatives effectively provided direction, materials, technical assistance, and monitored and reinforced success.

The Evolving Character of State-Initiated Educational Reform

In assessing the impact of state educational reform since 1983, it is clear that the agenda was impressive in both diffusion and breadth (Kirst 1988). Visions of reform were evolving and expanding while implementation was taking place. In an attempt to delineate the character and complexity of reform efforts, Odden and Marsh (1987) suggested a series of phases or waves of reforms:

> *Wave I:* Higher standards, increased high school graduation requirements, more traditional academic courses.
>
> *Wave II:* A return to the "traditional" good high school, better courses, new model curriculum standards, better textbooks, curriculum alignment, beginnings of new teacher roles, educational program quality indicators, reduction in dropouts.
>
> *Wave III:* More radical curriculum change, curriculum integration across content areas, greater emphasis on writing and communication, higher order thinking skills, problem-solving skills, broader uses of technology, interpersonal small group skills.
>
> *Wave IV:* Teacher professionalism, teacher decision making, national standards board, career ladders, policy trust agreements to augment traditional collective bargaining, restructured schools, more parental choice, system incentives, merit schools.

The California PACE Study (Odden and Marsh 1987) confirmed the rapid implementation of Wave I and Wave II reforms in secondary school settings. These schools, however, were just beginning to engage in the more complex and demanding issues characteristic of Wave III. The study found that the quality and extent of assistance necessary to change teacher practice and to support a more demanding curriculum were not in place, suggesting that new patterns of district and site cooperation and a variety of new implementation strategies were needed to accomplish Wave III and Wave IV reforms. Marsh and Bowman (1988, 1989) showed that a top-down, i.e., state initiated, strategy could provide a design for a new, local curriculum focus. However, the implementation design required a mixture of strategies to succeed. Changing teacher practice to implement a "new" curriculum for an increasingly diverse student population required a sustained and complementary effort on the part of all players who had a stake in the educational process.

Wave IV involves a restructuring of school organization and resources to support fundamental changes in curriculum and instruction. The restructuring typically involves shared decision-making, site-based management, major curriculum reform and a renewed sense of teacher professionalism. But rather than seeing these reforms in isolation, Wave IV involves linking these reforms to changes in the schooling experience for students.

In trying to assess the impact of state policy on restructuring schools, it was important to distinguish between two major sets of California policy initiatives. State school improvement initiatives, begun prior to 1983, were school based and focused on technical assistance, program planning, and local capacity building (Berman et al. 1984; Odden and Odden 1984). California's SIP was an example of this policy strategy (see Marsh and Bowman 1989). By contract, state education reform policies, most of which were developed since 1983, focused on curriculum, instruction, standards and school organization. California's middle school reform was an example of this policy strategy. While both school improvement and educational reform policies operated simultaneously, the connection between them and their interaction at the local level was as yet unclear. One of the problems which this study sought to address was the linkage between the two policy initiatives at the local level, using California as an example.

California's SIP seemed to be a promising vehicle for helping to implement the school restructuring included in *Caught in the Middle.* SIP was redesigned in the 1980s to provide a state-stimulated catalyst for local school improvement through the use of several strategies including a local governance board known as the School Site Council (SSC), and a schoolwide planning process that included a self-study using Quality Criteria and a Program Quality Review (PQR) Process developed by the state. While the SIP was conceptualized and operated for many years as a bottom-up improvement strategy, the new SIP approach included program features, such as the Program Quality Review, that linked SIP and its influential PQR to the state vision of middle schools and a curriculum that stressed higher order thinking skills, cooperative learning, problem solving, and analysis. An important issue was the role of SIP in these Wave III and Wave IV reforms.

2. The Middle School Study

The generic policy issues studied were the extent that state-initiated Wave III (curriculum change) and Wave IV (school restructuring) reforms that included major curriculum change were implemented and the extent that a "bottom-up" school improvement process helped local implementation. The study's purpose specifically was twofold: 1) to examine the extent that components of *Caught in the Middle* had actually been implemented; and 2) the role SIP or similar "bottom-up" mechanisms played in enhancing local implementation.

Methodology

The focus of the study was on the extent to which "lighthouse" middle schools in California implemented the key elements of *Caught in the Middle* and the role which SIP or similar mechanisms played in enhancing local implementation. All schools studied had had state SIP funding for at least six years. Additional information about the methodology is available in Marsh, Brown, Crocker and Lewis (1988).

Sample. A purposive sample of eight schools that had been recognized for their accomplishments in implementing the middle school concept was selected. The number of schools was limited to eight so that intensive data collection could be undertaken at each site; intensive data collection was needed to analyze the extent if implementation of the major *Caught in the Middle* reforms as well as details of the local implementation process.

Instrumentation. Two broad perspectives were used for studying each site. The first was the way that the middle school program had been designed and implemented. From this perspective, the SIP program may or may not have played a major role. The second perspective was a focus on the SIP program per se and how this program had been implemented. Consequently, it was an open question as to whether SIP had played a significant role in building the middle school program. An extensive case study outline was developed that incorporated the two perspectives; the outline guided the data collection.

Data collection. Training for the study covered the conceptual framework for the study, review of the case study outline, and practice with the data collection strategies. Each data collector spent approximately five days at each site and another five days preparing the case study write-up which typically averaged forty single-spaced typewritten pages.

Data analysis. After reading each case study, the team developed cross-site comparisons using low inference and high inference summaries following techniques developed by Miles and Huberman (1984). These analysis techniques had been applied to the study of state policy implementation in a recent study of high school reform in California (Odden and Marsh 1987).

3. Local Implementation of Middle School Reform

Study findings are summarized under three headings: 1) the extent of implementation of elements from *Caught in the Middle*; 2) the nature of SIP at the site; and 3) factors related to successful implementation of *Caught in the Middle*. Additional information about the findings is available in Marsh, Brown, Crocker, and Lewis (1988, 1989) and Crocker (1989).

Extent of Implementation of Elements from Caught in the Middle

This reform contains five clusters of components. Under the heading of curriculum and instruction were six components: 1) a core curriculum, 2) essential content knowledge, 3) thinking and communication skills for all students, 4) character development, 5) learning how to learn, and 6) appropriate use of a variety of new instructional practices, especially cooperative learning.

Under the student potential cluster, *Caught in the Middle* argued that middle schools should address the developmental needs of early adolescents, to help students reach their potential during this complex time of life. These components include 1) an academic counseling program, in addition to several new orientations for the whole school, such as greater attention to 2) equal access for all students, 3) more attention to the at-risk student, and 4) more attention to the physical, emotional, and developmental needs of students.

To reshape the curriculum and instructional program and provide the support for all students described above, the report also called for changes in school organization and structure including: 1) shifts in the culture of the school, 2) revision of the extra-curricular offerings of the school, 3) new student accountability, 4) better assistance to help students transition into and from the middle school, 5) new structures, 6) better scheduling arrangements that support the school's instructional program, and 7) more sophisticated approaches to assessment.

Table 1 shows the extent of initiation and implementation for each of the eight sites in the study. Most schools initiated all program elements found in *Caught in the Middle*. But, most schools made the most progress in implementing the curriculum and instructional features of the middle school concept, especially concerning character development and learning to learn. Schools typically made only moderate progress in implementing a core curriculum, a focus on thinking and communication skills, and use of active learning strategies. For every school in the sample, the implementation pattern was not a uniformly average new program across the school. Instead, in every case, the implementation pattern was several lighthouse program pieces within the school which were not extended to the entire school. Each school had very advanced and sophisticated program elements in each of the areas of core curriculum, student knowledge, critical thought and innovative/active instruction for some aspect of the schools. But these lighthouse efforts were not the norm for all parts of the school.

While schools adopted many of the features designed to enhance student potential, implementation of the student potential elements was less extensive. But, equal access, attention to student diversity and at-risk programs were extensively implemented, especially in light of the two schools where these issues were not highly relevant to the needs of the student body. Attention to the physical/emotional needs of the student body was extensively implemented in the schools where this was part of the vision, but three schools had given this only recent attention, and for them implementation was less advanced. Finally, the marginal implementation of academic counseling programs was a surprising finding.

All schools in the study gave extensive attention to improving school culture in their school vision. This was typically an early effort in the sequence of school restructuring and focused on creating a safe school environment, student accountability, rewards and incentives for student accomplishment in areas other than (or in addition to) athletics, affective support for students, and stronger school spirit. These school culture aspects reflected a sense of order and purpose and "student centeredness" found in *Caught in the Middle*. The report also emphasizes commitment to high academic standards and high standards of personal and social behavior. While most schools reflected the standards dimension, only two had strong emphases on the "jointly developed and enforced" dimension reflected in *Caught in the Middle*. Deeper organizational changes involving school structure, student transition between elementary/middle/high schools, school scheduling and student assessment were desired by the schools but were often not implemented very extensively.

Understandably, pre-service preparation for teachers or administrators was not a major feature of the vision articulated at these middle schools. However, at some sites, a few teachers had obtained some pre-service teacher education that was linked to the middle school reform effort. Since middle school reform is fairly recent and most teachers at the school were quite experienced, most middle schools did not have staff who obtained their *middle school* expertise through pre-service education. Similarly, site administrators did not obtain their middle school leadership perspectives/training through initial administrator training.

Table 1 Number of Schools with High, Moderate, or Low Initiation and Implementation of Program Elements

PROGRAM ELEMENT As Described in Caught in the Middle	EXTENT OF INITIATION (N = Number of Schools)			EXTENT OF IMPLEMENTATION (N = Number of Schools)		
	HIGH	MODERATE	LOW	HIGH	MODERATE	LOW
CURRICULUM & INSTRUCTION						
Core Curriculum	6	2		3	5	
Essential Knowledge	7	1		2	6	
Thinking/Communication	7	1		2	6	
Character Development	8			5	3	
Learning to Learn	5	3		4	1	3
New Instructional Practice	7	1		2	5	1
STUDENT POTENTIAL						
Academic Counseling	5	3		1	5	2
Equal Access	8			5	2	1
Student Diversity Focus	6	2		3	4	1
At-risk Focus	6	2		5	3	
Physical/Emotional Development	5	3		4	3	1
ORGANIZATION & STRUCTURE						
School Culture	8			6	2	
Extended Curriculum	6	2		4	2	2
Student Accountability	7	1		5	3	
Transition Across Schools	5	3		3	4	1
School Structure	6	2		4	4	
School Scheduling	5	3		4	4	
Student Assesment	4	4		3	4	1
TEACHING & ADMINISTRATION						
Professional Preparation	3	5		3	4	1
Staff Development	6	2		4	3	1
LEADERSHIP & PARTNERSHIP						
Parent/Community Involvement	5	3		3	4	1
State-of-the-Art Focus	6	1	1	4	2	2

The key role of staff development in the creation of these middle schools will be discussed later in the chapter. While one program element specified in *Caught in the Middle* is staff development, staff development was extensive in the schools studied, yet it engaged some faculty much more than others. Consequently, at most schools, the overall amount of staff development was rated by the researchers moderate as often as it was rated extensive. This schoolwide average, however, masked several important trends in staff development, discussed later, that were central to implementation of most parts of the total reform.

Most schools identified a desire to have greater parent/community involvement. Yet, in practice this partnership was extensively implemented at only three schools. Four other schools achieved moderate levels for implementing this element. While schools had very pleasant working relationships with parents and community in most cases, the partnership did not include formal cooperation in the education of students. Parents were often politically active in supporting the school. Parent concern about the quality of education of middle school aged students was a major reason four of the eight middle schools were formed.

Schools also wanted to be a part of a network of middle schools. Four of the eight schools had become extensively associated with such a network. The role of this networking was important to the development of these schools, as explained below.

The Nature of SIP at the Site

The California School Improvement Program is a state-funded local process designed to serve as a catalyst for locally defined change. The SIP program provided state funding for a systematically designed local process of school improvement that included: 1) a planning year leading to a school-wide multi-year plan for local reform, 2) a School Site Council consisting of parents, teachers and administrations which governed the school reform effort, 3) staff development and other implementation support strategies conducted at the local site, 4) continual monitoring of the program by the local School Site Council and on-going revision of the goals and strategies of the local change effort, and 5) program reviews of the local effort by trained review teams consisting of state monitors and/or peers from nearby districts, and a yearly review of revised plans by the State Department of Education.

Following 1986, SIP was revised so that it no longer was exclusively a "bottom-up" program. Specifically, the Program Quality Review (PQR), which required the local school to conduct a Self Study using an external set of standards against which to compare local school practice, was redesigned. The new standards were based on the new state curriculum frameworks (see chapter 12) and the *Caught in the Middle* restructuring vision. Following the Self Study, an external review is conducted by colleagues in the geographic region.

All middle schools in this study had participated in the SIP program for at least eight years. In the early years, SIP was a vehicle for school-wide planning, attention to poor performing students and creating special programs, usually outside the regular classroom. Schoolwide restructuring, nevertheless, was new to the schools and difficult to carry out. The schools adopted the middle school concept between 1982 and 1986, and were among the first in the district to do so. Half the schools chose the middle school concept primarily because they were drawn to the ideas. For the others, the decision to become a "middle school" was a combination of district/community pressure (such as declining enrollment) and attraction to the middle school concept.

Between 1985 and 1987, the restructuring of these sites into middle schools was primarily a school-based and not a district-led effort. However, after 1987, the year in which *Caught in the Middle* was published, most of the districts began active efforts to develop middle schools and give district leadership to this effort. Further, after 1987, SIP began to support site development of the middle school concept by formalizing the school restructuring directions, legitimizing new school leaders, and providing developmental resources such as new instructional materials and more staff development. The expanded staff development took two forms: 1) funding staff development, especially for selected teachers who became highly proficient in their teaching content area; and 2) providing legal authority, time and resources to extend staff development to all teachers at the school.

In addition, SIP provided a mechanism for schoolwide planning and coordination, but often was not the dominant force for developing the middle school vision. Instead, SIP was the "flypaper" that caught good ideas and incorporated them into schoolwide formal plans. All schools reported that SIP was "critical to the initiation and implementation of the middle school concept" through the roles described above.

The Self Study portion of the PQR was surprisingly non-controversial in engaging teachers about desired directions for curriculum, instruction and school restructuring and was highly effective. The Self Study process was greatly aided by: 1) previous experience of lead teachers; 2) perception among school staff of the fear of losing SIP funds should the Self Study not be successful; 3) strong management processes by administrators and teachers at the school, 4) the process assistance given by district state/federal office staff, 5) previous experience with the SIP program as a schoolwide planning and reform process, and 6) *Caught In the Middle* as a document that synthesized and made more explicit desirable middle school features. The Self Study worked especially well in English/Language Arts.

The Self Study was less effective when only one teacher taught full-time in the content area or when schoolwide programs were needed. It also was less effective when linkage to the district curriculum and textbook adoption was weak, or when constrained by a lack of restructured organizational features at the school.

The PQR had a positive impact on the school including; 1) providing a vision of curriculum; 2) generating excitement and support for the curriculum vision and confirming that the progressive actions taken by the school to date were important and 3) encouraging staff to become more involved in staff development and professional growth. The PQR also reinforced the concept of lead teachers as competent professionals able and ready to help other teachers, the concept that teachers' collegiality could be based on competence rather than merely friendly interaction, a common technical language and the development of competence in relation to this technical language, and risk-taking of lead teachers as being helpful to obtain improvements in curriculum.

Factors Related to Successful Implementation of Caught in the Middle

Successful implementation at the school level was aided by two major sets of factors: schoolwide change processes and implementation of a specific program elements. For success in the schoolwide process, all schools in the sample had strong, principal leadership who had a middle school vision that often was developed through networking with other "lighthouse" middle schools, through reading the professional literature, or by attending conferences featuring exemplary middle school practice. Each school typically had an external network that provided ideas to the principal and key staff. Within the school, the principal typically pushed groups of key teachers to implement program components, then formed schoolwide discussions of the middle school concept. The principal typically used the SIP program to consolidate plans and provide resources for the implementation process. Again, the SIP plan itself served more as "flypaper" to catch good ideas at the school, rather than as the primary generator of bold, new middle school proposals.

In this leadership role, the principal exhibited many of the change process factors described by Huberman and Miles (1984), including strong sense of vision which was communicated across the school as well as ongoing leadership and commitment to change. Huberman and Miles give emphasis to the importance of a "perception of organizational fit" by school leaders rather than the entire school staff. Principals in this study reported that they perceived the middle school concept to have a strong organizational fit at their school even though this perception was not widely shared across the school.

In most cases, the principal did not pursue implementation of the individual middle school program elements. Instead, the principal formed small committees that worked implementing the program elements. In many cases, these teams were only somewhat related to the actions of the School Site Council, i.e., the teams did not report directly to nor were they coordinated by the School Site Council.

It is important to note that the site middle school vision was created at the school site rather than at the district office and sent down to the school. The schools studied typically were only loosely coupled with district offices and were able to overcome district neutrality, or in two cases, district resistance to strong site leadership.

Implementation of individual program elements. "Lead teachers" played the critical roles in implementing the individual middle school program elements. Lead teachers were created, developed and nurtured into these roles, not born into leadership roles. At each school, there were at least two lead teachers who had become highly competent in innovative program directions within their content area. This competence typically was developed through attendance at regional workshops such as the California Writing Project. These workshops emphasized in-depth discussion and practice of new approaches to, in this example, writing. The workshops included weeks and months of staff development rather than hours of workshop practice. Lead teachers often were able to develop networks with other effective teachers (lead teachers at other schools) and to practice providing help to other teachers as a function of their own professional growth.

Lead teachers then typically took the time and energy to try out these new approaches in their own classroom. At the schools studied, this professional growth phase usually lasted from one to three years. At the same time, these teachers were providing informal staff development for friends and colleagues at this school. This staff development represented a new phase of activity in staff development at the school.

This second phase of activity typically was bottom-up and featured aspects of dissemination theory described by House (1974) and McLaughlin (chapter 8) that included the importance of face-to-face contacts and social networks for disseminating effective program ideas. The good news is that the teachers were able to get a small cadre of colleagues to learn new instructional approaches. This activity was greatly enhanced by the SIP program that provided resources, including release time for teachers, to meet and work on effective instructional practice. At three schools, this bottom-up strategy led to reforming entire curriculum areas. In all schools, this bottom-up strategy helped establish effective core programs in at least one subject matter area and for at least one grade level.

This bottom-up strategy, however, had limitations. The strategy was based on enthusiasm and recognition of professional competence and assistance from lead teacher colleagues. Such a strategy, however, was not able to overcome organizational constraints to widespread implementation nor totally resolve the problem of blending this professional culture style of improvement with curriculum reform that the districts had been nurturing in response to the new California curriculum frameworks. In short, improving the professional culture of teaching significantly enhanced teacher expertise and it was most successful when it was joined with the bureaucratic culture of the district that coordinated new curriculum scope and sequence and textbook selection activities.

In the last year or two, lead teachers from these "lighthouse" middle schools were increasingly being asked to provide district staff development to teachers at other schools. In many cases, the lead teachers had become mentor teachers, thus having their role formalized in this assistance effort. Similarly, the lead teachers were being placed on textbook committees so that their knowledge of new curriculum and instructional strategies within a content area could be tapped in district review of state-initiated curriculum reforms and the selection of important textbook materials.

The role of the SIP. As discussed above, SIP made an important set of contributions to the successful middle school implementation. First, SIP enhanced both the schoolwide vision and its implementation by providing; 1) the "flypaper" that helped consolidate the vision created by the school principal and several key teachers; 2) the resources that allowed these people to develop and enhance their external networks; 3) the cross role team which helped consolidate plans and the planning process for the school vision; and 4) help in forming committees that developed schoolwide plans and implementation and monitoring processes.

Second, SIP simulated program-specific implementation. It was the important resource that developed lead teachers. Lead teachers used SIP funds to attend workshops and summer institutes over a several year period. After this time period, SIP funds then provided release time, instructional materials and staff development resources that allowed lead teachers and other staff development personnel to assist teams of teachers at the school to learn about innovative instructional practices and then use them in their classroom. It is unlikely that many schools would have been successful in getting teams of teachers to undertake the new curriculum or instructional activities had SIP not provided the flexible funding both to develop lead teachers and then let them provide schoolwide staff development.

Finally, the PQR played the role of consolidating schoolwide middle school directions. It provided a positive way for the school to examine itself in light of new curriculum and middle school restructuring directions proposed by the state. The self study served as an educative and reinforcement device for these directions. It also provided a sense of satisfaction for teachers who had been highly innovative in implementing new program directions and was the impetus for other, more reserved teachers to begin a process of becoming lead teachers.

State policy levers. Besides the PQR, the state curriculum frameworks, the Mentor Teacher Programs and the new CAP exams affected local implementation. The state curriculum frameworks more directly were an important source of information and a set of pressure on the district, but especially on the school, for curriculum reform. The state's mentor teacher program was an important device that allowed site lead teachers to assume a more formal technical assistance role, that was sanctioned by district authority. The revised CAP examination, especially for eighth graders, importantly reinforced the new curriculum directions proposed. Many schools talked about the importance of revising their curriculum so that students would do well on the eighth grade CAP.

Information networks. School-based change processes would not have been nearly as effective without regional networks, often stimulated by the State Department of Education, that provided resources and ideas to lead teachers at the school. These networks were discussed in two ways: middle school-related networks that stimulated the schoolwide vision, and program element-specific networks that nurtured the development of lead teachers.

It is clear that the document *Caught in the Middle* was an important state-initiated device that helped consolidate the schoolwide vision. Regional conferences and networks of schools continued to use this document as a reference in discussions and assistance to specific schools. Similarly, the California Writing and California Math projects as well as other regional networks with universities and county offices were an important feature in developing program-specific elements of the middle school concept. The schools studied had extensive networks outside the school district which were critical in explaining the success of the school in implementing *Caught in the Middle* program features.

The Program Quality Review process was well managed at each of the sites, especially those that had a review in Spring 1988. The

Quality Criteria had a positive educative function; they helped the staff understand new curriculum and middle school directions. The PQR was designed by the state to fit with other state-initiated reform efforts in the district. However, in practice, the Program Quality Review process was very loosely coupled with the district's curriculum and instructional goals and visions. Instead, the PQR fit more easily with the district state/federal office in organizational and functional terms. The study identified many reasons for this pattern.

4. Discussion and Policy Implications

This section discusses implications from three sets of findings: 1) extent of implementation of this Wave III and Wave IV reform and its implications for policy implementation; 2) the role which "bottom-up" mechanisms such as California's can play in school restructuring; and 3) factors that enhance the implementation process.

Extent of Middle School Reform

These schools had made only modest progress in implementing the twenty-two components of *Caught in the Middle*. Further, implementation was "uneven" across each school; some parts of the school fully implemented positions of *Caught in the Middle* while other parts did not. All schools had difficulty making deep organizational structure changes, such as implementing a core curriculum for all grades. The district and sites in this study supported the rapid and enthusiastic response of local educators to state policy initiatives found in earlier studies (Anderson et al. 1987; Fuhrman, Clune, and Elmore 1988, chapter 11; Odden and Marsh 1987, 1989). Schools in this study demonstrated both the will and capacity to accomplish Wave I and Wave II reforms, and were vigorously working as Wave III and IV reforms. Districts and sites in this study all participated in at least several of the following; state programs, all designed to foster curriculum reform and/or middle school restructuring; California Leadership Academy, Administrative Training Centers, Mentor Teacher Program, TECC Centers, Cash for CAP, and Distinguished Schools.

In short, current state policy initiatives, however powerful and exciting to local district and school leaders, could not create a fully-implemented schoolwide and organizationally "deep" school restructuring reform despite attention to these reforms for approximately five years. Moreover, these conclusions apply to lighthouse schools with highly energetic and capable leaders. Fullan (1988) and others have emphasized the complexity involved in this recent wave of reform. This study is further evidence that the road to *meaningful* reform is still a difficult one even for the best of schools.

The Role of Bottom-Up Mechanisms in School Reform

Senate Bill 813, the middle school reform and state curriculum efforts did not, however, exist in a vacuum. California's history of policy initiatives in the late 1960s and 1970s created a plethora of categorical programs that remain. One was SIP which was examined specifically in the relationship to middle school restructuring. In examining how new education reforms and old categorical programs impacted the school, it was apparent that the policy to school flow was multidimensional. Rather than an integrated state policy package moving in a singular fashion to the district and then to the school, policy levers from the state impacted the local educational agency in a shotgun fashion. Once these policy inputs arrived at the district, they were also filtered through existing organizational structures that separated general curriculum and instructional from categorical programs administered by the state/federal project office.

One impediment to efficiency of SIP for middle school reform was the history of established links between the district state/federal projects office and the school site. These links represented not only technical assistance but established SIP as part of a categorical culture, a culture which continued to influence school site SIPs. Berman et al. (1984) noted earlier that only substantial changes in SIP would assist its potential to develop local capacity and implement broadly based curriculum reforms. Marsh and Bowman (1988 1989) further suggested the SIP, while contributing to staff development, could have a greater impact if linked to the district and site organizational structure which supported the regular school program. Without these structural links, SIP remained only loosely coupled to ongoing curriculum reforms. While the revised PQR experienced by four sites in this study did assist in broadening the focus of the evaluation process, it was not well integrated with the structure and process of ongoing curriculum and instructional leadership and so left the PQR action plans unintegrated with other district and site improvement activities.

These findings suggest that state policy makers need to examine existing categorical policies and programs and assess their potential value in assisting students to meet success in the core of the general education curriculum. Particular attention should be given to strengthening the links between general fund programs and categorical programs in delivering the regular academic program to all students. In addition, consideration should be given to placing administrative responsibility for categorical programs within the regular curriculum and instruction delivery system, thus integrating both services and resources necessary to support schoolwide change.

A related set of issues concern the viability of SIP or other "bottom-up" mechanisms, per se, in enhancing complex reform such as the middle school reform studied here. Berman et al. (1984), extended by Marsh (1987), found that School Site Councils were able to catalyze reform primarily in elementary schools. Marsh and Bowman (1988 1989) complement this analysis with findings about the limited utility of SIP in secondary schools when compared to more direct school reform strategies.

Recent attention to the role of school-site management and restructured schools has led to new research that has extended concern about the viability of process-oriented site-base coordination mechanisms to play a sufficient role in complex school reform. Malen and Ogawa (1988) questioned whether site-based management mechanisms really created the new management norms and practices as envisioned. They found, instead, that site-based management mechanisms maintained traditional patterns of administrative leadership. Moreover, David (1989a) reported that many school restructuring activities changed decision-making and created new roles at schools but had not fully addressed the curriculum/instructional patterns at schools nor changed the accountability/incentive structures.

This study suggests that "bottom-up" mechanisms, like the SIP program, can play a critical role in complex reform. However, the "bottom-up" mechanisms was more a responsive/supportive strategy than the proactive or main vehicle for such reform. Other "bottom-up" strategies such as are found in the Coalition of Essential Schools (Sizer 1984) emphasize school restructuring that directly supports complex curriculum change, and emphasizes collaboration typically around "houses" rather an entire large school. This approach to site-based restructuring, especially when linked to the policy initiatives found in the Relearning project coordinated by the Educational Commission of the States, hold considerable promise.

Important Implementation Factors

Translating state reform goals into practice at the local level required the cooperation, knowledge, and skills of local educators.

This study supported the importance of a set of factors in implementing policies and programs. Earlier studies (Crandall, Eiseman, and Louis 1985; Fullan 1982; Huberman and Miles 1984; Odden and Marsh 1987) identified seven critical variables. While this study confirmed the presence of all of these factors in the sample schools, it did show some variations both within sites and across sites. In two sites, district pressure and support for educational reform was either limited or unproductive. Adverse labor relations, distrust of district personnel, and ineffective administrators all contributed to the problem. Despite these factors, both of these sites engaged in significant improvement activities although it was more fragmented and isolated than the activities in other schools, which were surrounded by more skillful district leadership and a more collegial culture.

All of the schools in the study had strong school principal leadership. While variations existed in management style, all principals had a vision of an excellent middle school, possessed effective working relationships with the staff, and knew how to mobilize resources, both human and financial, to move the school forward. Joining these strong principals were key teacher leaders. Lead teachers had been involved in several professional development networks for many years before the site began its middle school restructuring. These staff members often developed into "lead" teachers at the site and became critical links in changing the curriculum and pedagogy within their departments. Even with these staff members who had the will to change, developing the capacity to change was an intensive, time-consuming process.

While these "lead" teachers were not a substitute for leadership and support from the principal, they provided much of the impetus for and ongoing training needed for instructional change. These committed and trained teachers had both the opportunity and the acceptance to change whole departments within a site. Since the schools in this study were all at the secondary level, the role of "lead" teachers in turning around departments and programs might be more critical than in self-contained elementary settings where change occurs teacher by teacher.

The role of "lead" teachers in changing instructional programs and practices at the secondary level needs further exploration. Such exploration could add to the body of knowledge regarding local capacity and teacher professional expertise, issues reemphasized by McLaughlin (1987, chapter 8). This study supports the importance of "lead" teachers' activities being linked to existing organizational structures that support educational change. Lead teachers acting alone had little systemwide impact. Lead teachers were most effective when they had access to existing systems that created new curriculum programs, selected new textbooks, adopted new assessment tools, and provided staff development.

These findings not only support the need for statewide resources to build local capacity, but suggest that the speed of state curriculum cycles may be too ambitious given the time necessary to change teacher practice, even in these exemplary settings. It certainly suggests that such changes may be difficult, if not impossible, in other districts that lack the human and organizational supports found in these schools. Such findings indicate that states could further assist local districts by differentiating the pressure and support provided so that they were more tailored to local conditions. Adaptation to local conditions may be especially necessary in poor performing schools where the breadth and depth of state initiatives seems overwhelming if not impossible. Special external assistance teams might be necessary to begin the reform process in these settings.

Chapter 15

Legislative Oversight of Education Policy Implementation

Priscilla Wohlstetter

Programs that are created by legislation can be thought of as contracts for services between the legislative and executive branches of government. Agencies that accept monies from legislatures to implement programs, in effect, are agreeing to the terms of an "implementation contract" and confirming they are capable of providing the services. During program implementation, the legislature monitors the contract in an attempt to control the agency so that its actions will produce the intended results. As true of any contractor, legislators are interested in how their money is being spent—How have policies been translated into practice? Is implementation consistent with legislative intent? What effects have the policies produced? Legislators collect answers to these questions by conducting oversight of program implementation.

Oversight, as defined by Congress, is the "review and study" by legislatures of the "application, administration, and execution of laws" (Section 136, Legislative Reorganization Act of 1946, as amended 1970). Oversight relies on a wide variety of techniques and occurs in a number of settings, not only legislative committee hearings labeled oversight (Ogul 1976). Other means range from appropriations and reauthorization hearings to informal meetings between legislators and agency officials. Staff outside legislatures, such as auditor generals and program evaluation units, also may be involved in oversight.

Prior research on the oversight process, mostly at the federal level, has found that institutional and political factors can either encourage or inhibit legislative oversight activity. The institutional environment defines committee structures and the capacity of legislatures for oversight. Oversight is less likely, for example, when committee staff is inadequate, when committee leadership is uncommitted to oversight, or when committee power is centralized (Kaiser 1977; Ogul 1976; Bibby 1968; Scher 1963). At the state level, part-time legislatures and part-time legislators also constrain oversight activity (Rosenthal 1981).

The political context likewise has been found to affect when and under what conditions legislative bodies conduct oversight. For example, oversight is more likely when committee leadership believes that the interests of important constituents cannot be satisfied by routine intercessions between congressmen and agencies (Ogul 1976, Bibby 1968; Scher 1963), or when committee or congressional relationships with the executive branch are characterized by a lack of confidence (Aberback 1979; Ogul 1976; Scher 1963), a tendency that also has been observed in studies of state legislatures (Hamm and Robertson 1981).

The study presented in this chapter found that legislators conducted oversight in ways that minimized time commitments and maximized political benefits. Institutional factors identified by others as influencing oversight failed to distinguish between states with effective oversight strategies and those without. Prior research found that institutional factors affect the use of formal oversight strategies. But by examining both informal and formal strategies, the present study found that characteristics of legislatures were less important than the political context in determining who the monitoring parties would be and in shaping the purposes served by oversight.

In this chapter, two questions are examined, largely from a political science perspective:

- How are legislatures overseeing state education reforms enacted during the mid-1980s?

- What are the motivations for oversight of education reforms?

The main theme of this chapter is that oversight is best understood as an integral part of legislative-administrative politics rather than as a critical accountability mechanism. State legislatures were interested in oversight as a means of promoting the success of program implementation primarily to help members better serve constituents and gain influence in the legislature. This finding poses a challenge to top-down implementation analysts who view oversight more as a rational tool for achieving democratic accountability (Mazmanian and Sabatier 1983; Sabatier 1986).

This chapter is based on a study of ways in which legislatures in six states (Arizona, California, Florida, Georgia, Minnesota, and Pennsylvania) oversaw education reforms and controlled and influenced their implementation.[1] The sample was selected to highlight various approaches to education reform, to maximize regional diversity, and to illustrate different stages of implementation.

In line with national trends, education reforms in the sample states focused on raising academic standards for students and improving how teachers were trained, recruited and compensated. Reforms increased course requirements for graduation (Arizona, California, Florida, Georgia, Pennsylvania); expanded student testing programs (Arizona, California, Georgia, Pennsylvania); and lengthened the school day (California, Florida). Minnesota's major reform allowed eleventh and twelfth graders the choice of attending high school or a postsecondary institution such as a community college or vocational center. Reforms directed at improving teacher quality stiffened teacher certification requirements (Georgia, Pennsylvania) or moved toward performance-based compensation systems (Arizona, California, Florida).

The research, which was conducted in the spring of 1987, included fifty-seven elite interviews with legislators, committee staff, and legislative agency staff with responsibility for overseeing education reforms enacted in the previous four years. Interviews focused on institutional and political constraints on oversight; resources available to legislatures for oversight and the extent to which they were used; and motivations of legislators in monitoring contracts for education reform.

The first section of this chapter describes oversight strategies that the six sample states used to monitor education reform, and assesses the role of the political context in shaping the strategies. The second section assesses the influence of political factors on the motivations of legislators to conduct oversight. The concluding section assesses whether the current system of oversight by legislatures is sufficient, and discusses an alternative that is outside the political legislative arena.

1. Oversight Strategies and State Education Reform

States use both formal and informal strategies for legislative oversight. Formal methods include committee hearings or meetings, while informal oversight is performed through casework, telephone calls and other informal contacts.

Formal Strategies

There are three formal strategies that legislatures have used to enhance the likelihood and success of oversight activities: 1) establishing oversight committees to monitor implementation; 2) mandating evaluation and reporting requirements in legislation; and 3) specifying a schedule for oversight through either reauthorization or sunset clauses. In the six states studied, all of these formal strategies were used to some extent.

Three states—Arizona, Florida and Pennsylvania—established special oversight committees. Pennsylvania used the conventional approach of setting up a temporary subcommittee to oversee the impact of higher academic standards on vocational education students. Oversight strategies in the other two states were more unusual.

Arizona's career ladder legislation created a joint legislative committee to implement as well as monitor the program, largely because the legislature was dissatisfied with the department of education's management of earlier reforms. Legislating more detailed instructions to the department was not an option, in part because of the strong tradition of local control in the state. The legislature, at the time the legislation was passed, also was uncertain how a career ladder program should be implemented statewide, and therefore opted to test the program with a few districts on a pilot basis, vesting itself with oversight responsibility. The law gave local implementors a great deal of flexibility to pursue their own career ladder models. By funding a few districts and studying the success of their programs, the legislature would be able to refine its policy choice over time and to make more informed decisions about possible statewide career ladder legislation. In the short term, the joint committee (rather than the department) had control over and direct access to information about implementation, which enhanced the legislature's ability to monitor during the pilot test. In addition, with legislators serving as program field monitors, there was the political boon for committee members of frequent constituency contact.

The Florida legislature, which has a similar history of poor relations with the department of education in its 1983 education reform legislation, established the Florida Quality Instructional Incentives Council to oversee implementation of the reforms. With this strategy the Florida legislature, as did Arizona's, consolidated control over implementation into one body. The council, whose members included legislators as well as representatives of the business community appointed by the governor, helped improve executive branch cooperation and awarded a monitoring role to the interest group that had been most supportive of the reforms. Shared responsibility probably also reduced the time most legislators had to devote to oversight. The Florida legislature had access to the council through its members, but, in contrast to Arizona's experience, it was not a drain on resources: the legislature provided the council with its own staff.

Four states included reporting requirements in their legislative oversight strategies, forcing agencies to provide information about implementation on a timely basis that can be used to audit and correct agency performance. This strategy was used not only in Arizona and Florida, where reports were required from the two oversight bodies, but in Georgia and Minnesota as well. Georgia used the traditional approach of requiring quarterly progress reports from the state department of education.

The Minnesota legislature typically requires many reports from executive agencies, and terms in its legislative contracts for education reform were more comprehensive than most. Local control is strong in Minnesota, and the legislature prefers to delegate implementation authority to the local level. Report requirements are politically acceptable control mechanisms; as in Arizona, control through legislated directives usually is not. In addition to a requirement for independent evaluations, the enabling legislation in Minnesota specified program goals to be evaluated, the type of information required in reports, and the date information was due to the legislature.

The Arizona and Florida legislatures tapped sources other than implementing agencies for information. These independent evaluations, in effect, substituted for direct knowledge of agency performance, much as stock market evaluations of a company's profitability or the threat of takeovers is used to assess performance in the private sector (Moe 1984). Northern Arizona University was appointed by the legislature to evaluate the career ladder program, with a report due in 1989 when the legislation expired. The Florida legislature initially relied on the Quality Instructional Incentives Council for implementation information; later the legislature ordered the department of education to commission studies of reform programs from independent evaluators.

In the six states studied, evaluation reports were mandated and special oversight units were established by the legislation with the intent that legislators would "patrol" for violations during implementation.[2] A few state legislatures, with a history of less than cooperative relations with the executive, incorporated into implementation contracts provisions that expanded the legislature's role during implementation and imposed reporting requirements on agencies. This allowed legislatures to survey implementation activities with the aim of discouraging violations of legislative intent and detecting and rectifying those that occurred (Wohlstetter 1990).

In writing legislation for education reforms, legislatures also could have exerted control over agencies by specifying implementation schedules, through either reauthorization or sunset clauses. The value of these mechanisms is that evaluation is automatic; legislators do not have to call for a review, nor do they have to persuade colleagues that a review is warranted. Arizona, which authorized the five-year pilot test for its career ladder program, was the only state in the sample that used these mechanisms.

Underlying the formal strategies adopted by the states studied was the inextricable link between oversight and politics. During interviews, legislators and staff stressed the political goals of oversight, more than the importance of oversight as an accountability tool. Oversight strategies apparently were not often formulated with the intent of controlling implementors. Furthermore, in weighing various approaches to oversight, legislators and staff said they considered which approach "made the most political sense"; other criteria, such as efficiency or rationality, were seldom used. In Pennsylvania, for example, the temporary oversight subcommittee was established so that the chair of the education committee would not have to attend the field hearings, which were time-consuming and of little interest to him. Thus, oversight in the present study appeared to be used often as a political strategy.

Informal Strategies

The six states relied on various informal mechanisms as well in overseeing educational policy. Informal oversight strategies generally are ad hoc and reactive, such as when legislators hear complaints from individual constituents or interest groups that implementation harms them in some way. Casework conducted through telephone calls or letters to the implementing agency is a common informal oversight tool. Legislators often act alone in conducting informal oversight, as contrasted with formal strategies, such as committee hearings.

State departments of education were the main target of oversight efforts in Arizona and California, where school districts and lobbyists complained that they were being harmed by state policy. When legislative staff telephoned the department of education, they discovered that department staff had strayed from legislative intent and were implementing their own policies. In Arizona the legislature had intended that the department of education establish minimum competency levels in essential subjects, allowing local districts to set their own standards within state department guidelines. Instead, the state department planned to issue skill lists for all subject areas, with statewide standards for each. When districts heard about the plan, they flooded legislators with phone calls and letters. The original sponsor of the legislation and her staff quickly arranged a meeting with the state department of education and informally a compromise was worked out.

In California alarms were sounded by constituents when the department of education began to implement Cash-for-CAP, a student assessment program, statewide instead of on a pilot basis as intended by the legislature. Cash-for-CAP, which subsequently was vetoed by the governor in 1987, awarded individual high schools cash bonuses based on gains in test scores by twelfth graders. Education lobbyists also charged that local implementation was contrary to the spirit of the law: some districts reclassified twelfth graders as eleventh graders to improve school scores. Appropriations committee members briefly considered terminating the program but, according to legislative staff, ultimately opted for a milder fiscal sanction since all legislators had constituents benefiting from the program.

In Pennsylvania, where the state board of education is allowed to make law, two reforms, one increasing academic requirements for vocational students and the other imposing continuing education requirements on teachers, were perceived as harmful by the affected parties—vocational education teachers and teacher unions. A committee staff member summed up the politics this way:

> The Pennsylvania legislature is an appeals forum. When the executive branch or any agency does something constituents don't like, their appeal is to the legislature—fix it, help us out.

The legislative education committee resolved the first problem through informal meetings with the state board and the second by repealing the board's ruling.

Legislation was often the target of complaints in Florida, Georgia, and Minnesota. Constituents telephoned their legislators with complaints, identified areas in need of repair, and proposed solutions. Through the process of oversight, implementation contracts for education reforms were refined and elaborated. In Georgia, where an education funding bill had been rushed through the assembly and weights in the funding formula had been miscalculated, complaints from special education groups led legislators to repair the legislation. Reforms in Florida and Minnesota had been controversial from the beginning, and during implementation, affected interest groups were on the lookout for problems that might justify repeal. In Minnesota alarms were sounded by school districts, and the department of education, in support of the districts, tried to discourage students from leaving high school to attending a community college or vocational center. Legislators held hearings around the state to solicit information, and, based also on findings of the mandated preliminary evaluation report, amendments were introduced in the next legislative session to rectify some of the problems. In Florida alarms were sounded by teacher unions, which pointed out weaknesses in administration of the implementation contract by the department of education. Although proviso language requiring an evaluation subsequently was inserted in the appropriations bill, continued complaints from unions and negative press publicity, according to committee staff, led legislators to phase out the program, which was replaced with a more flexible (and politically acceptable) program that allowed greater local participation.

In sum, informal strategies where legislatures responded to alarms or complaints from constituents was the predominant form of oversight used by legislatures in monitoring education reforms. Oversight was selective, usually triggered by complaints from constituents who voluntarily monitored policy implementation, augmenting the resources of part-time legislators. Legislatures spent less time on oversight because constituents assumed the time-consuming task of monitoring implementation. By waiting for alarms to sound, legislators also increased the political benefits of oversight: they received credit from constituents for intervening to investigate the causes of complaints.

Contrary to expectations, legislative staff generally played minor roles in triggering oversight of education reforms. Across the six states, staff spent more time confirming problems and sifting through complaints from outside sources to help legislators avoid false alarms. Efforts to modernize legislatures by increasing staff have proven beneficial in many ways to oversight; nevertheless, legislative staff usually were not the ones discovering or uncovering violations during implementation.

2. Motivations for Oversight

Political scientists have interpreted legislative behavior by analyzing members' goal orientations. Prior research at the federal level has found that the committee assignments members seek depend upon whether members' goals are oriented toward the district, good public policy or gaining prestige within the legislature (Fenno 1973; Bullock 1976; Smith and Deering 1983). For example, the House Education and Labor Committee appeals to congressmen for district reasons—all congressmen have schools in their districts—and also is attractive for policy reasons (but less so in recent years); on the other hand, desire for prestige attracts congressmen to the House Appropriations Committee because of its control over money (see Table 4, Smith and Deering 1983).

Results from this study suggest the three motives—constituency service, influence in the legislation and good public policy—also explain why legislators engaged in oversight and furthermore, that legislative oversight behavior differed across the three motivation orientations.[3] Smith and Deering in their 1983 study of freshmen in the U.S. House of Representatives found that district-oriented motivations (including constituency service and re-election) were the most commonly mentioned of the three, followed closely by policy and distantly by prestige. Constituency service motives also were most frequently mentioned by overseers of education reforms, followed by an interest in gaining influence in the legislature and lastly, by policy motives. The oversight behavior associated with these three motivation orientations is discussed below.

Constituency Service

Legislators in the six sample states often paired oversight with constituency service, i.e., dealing with constituents' complaints and problems. This is an offshoot of the legislator's role as ombudsman, which has become increasingly popular (Goodman et al. 1986). When individual citizens or organized interest groups who were negatively affected by education reforms reported potential implementation problems, legislators responded with oversight, thus reaping the political benefits of addressing complaints from potential supporters.

Constituency service was an important goal of legislators in Pennsylvania, Arizona, and Georgia. In Pennsylvania, vocational education teachers and directors telephoned legislators to voice concern about the State Board of Education's new academic requirements, arguing that they made graduation difficult for vocational education students. Teacher unions were angry with another new board policy that required their members who had Masters' degrees to take six credits of continuing education every five years.[4] In both instances, the Senate Education Committee used formal oversight strategies to investigate the cause of constituents' complaints.

With the new continuing education requirements, the committee led the fight to have the State Board of Education rule statutorily repealed. According to Senate staff, it would have been difficult for the committee to garner legislative support for an education bill with specific program provisions, so they waited until June when the omnibus education bill was considered and added the repeal. The process was quick and there was no floor debate; the details were worked out by the conference committee. In responding to constituents' concerns, the senators on the education committee won credit from the teacher unions, and, equally important, they avoided having to cash in the political chits that a separate bill likely would have required.

With Pennsylvania's new academic requirements, the Senate Education Committee created a temporary subcommittee whose sole mission was to investigate the effects of increased high school graduation requirements on vocational education students. Without policy development responsibility, the subcommittee devoted nearly all its time to oversight, conducting hearings around the state and meeting with constituents and interest groups. Subcommittee staff subsequently wrote an options paper, with draft legislation, but oversight was accomplished behind the scenes by legislative staff through negotiations with department of education officials, who advised the board. Ultimately, the board amended the rule and interest groups were reassured that legislators were on their side.

The formal oversight strategy of Arizona's joint career ladder committee, like the temporary subcommittee's in Pennsylvania, provided monitoring services to the legislature and created public relations opportunities for legislators: members of the committee were responsible for visiting several local districts, usually including their own, to monitor implementation. Legislative monitors, for example, discovered early that some districts, contrary to intent, continued to use traditional salary schedules for teacher compensation decisions. The joint committee called a meeting with representatives of local districts, and a revised policy statement was issued to clarify legislative intent. According to committee staff, oversight in this instance improved relations between most participating school districts and the joint legislative committee, which districts at first thought was trying to change the rules midway through implementation.

Georgia's Quality Basic Education (QBE) Act was closely tracked by special education groups, whose attention was drawn by promises from the legislature of increased funding. During implementation, special education groups complained that their constituents received less money under QBE than in previous years. The legislature, lacking the benefit of strong staff resources, apparently had miscalculated the weights in QBE's funding formula for special education. Objections from interest groups identified the area in need of repair and led legislators to correct the formula, thereby reassuring constituents of the legislature's intent to increase funding for special education.

In sum, legislators with an orientation toward constituency service used formal, visible oversight methods to publicize their efforts among potential supporters. Often times oversight included trips for legislators to home districts where monitoring combined with constituency service. Legislators focused on overseeing the implementation contracts that negatively affected their constituents and usually conducted oversight in formal hearings, which could be easily seen by or reported to voters. Oversight under such circumstances often was conducted along with policy development activities to gain the political rewards of passing new legislation.

When legislators were motivated by constituency service and used formal oversight strategies, they often reduced the time involved in monitoring by relying on interested citizens to signal potential problems. As a result, legislators were able to spend less time on oversight (leaving more time for other activities) or to spend more time on oversight activities with greater political payoffs, such as holding hearings in response to complaints from potential supporters.

> Justly or unjustly, time spent putting out visible fires gains one more credit than the same time spent sniffing for smoke (McCubbins and Schwartz 1984, p. 168).

Outside monitors also helped ease the monitoring burden for legislative staff, an important benefit to states such as Arizona and Georgia where staff resources are weak.[5]

Influence in the Legislature

Success of education reforms was directly tied to the political agendas and self-interests of their legislative sponsors or champions. Thus, legislative champions were active overseers in the states studied, often intervening to repair the legislation they helped to create. Equipped with staff resources (all held leadership positions), these individuals actively monitored implementation to protect against opposition and to discover whether the education reforms were producing the changes they had anticipated.

Legislators in the sample states championed Arizona's eighth and twelfth grade competency testing initiative, California's mentor teacher program, and Florida's RAISE legislation, which extended the instructional day and increased requirements for high school graduation. During policy implementation, the champions became the overseers and fixers of these reforms. Oversight produced political benefits, namely helping the champions protect or enhance their reputations in the legislature.

The RAISE legislation in Florida was championed by a senior senator who served as education committee chair. RAISE, which increased high school graduation requirements and extended the instructional day, had been opposed initially by many school districts and teacher organizations, so there was a possibility that the reforms would be sabotaged by local implementors. The senator wanted to make certain that the reforms were successfully underway before he retired. According to committee staff, "They are his legacy." Informal monitoring by staff through telephone calls to constituents and field visits to schools helped the senator head off attempts by the opposition to change the reforms and, in the process, helped protect his reputation. The success of the reforms, and the political saliency of his involvement in oversight actions, are perhaps best judged by the fact that the legislative champion was subsequently elected president of the Florida State Senate.

In Arizona and California, education reform champions were politically ambitious, and saw reforms, providing nothing disastrous happened during implementation, as vehicles for building reputations. The champion of California's mentor teacher program was a rising star who had moved from the Assembly to the Senate just prior to the time he sponsored the reform. As a staff member to the senator explained:

> There was a lot of opposition to the mentor teacher program when it was passed and we didn't want anything coming back to haunt the Senator. His name is closely tied to the program, so he'll get the blame if anything goes wrong.

Legislators need to protect their reputations, and not following up on something can be more damaging than failing to move on to the next issue. Staff for this legislative champion held several informal meetings in the field with teachers and other school district representatives to collect information about the program's impact on mentor teachers and non-mentors, too. The champion of the mentor teacher program is now considered the Senate's education expert, and in 1988 he ran for the U.S. House of Representatives but did not win the election.

Arizona's champion of competency testing for eighth and twelfth graders also kept a continuous watch over implementation while she was chair of the Senate Education Committee. The Arizona Legislature has no formal rule review power, but, through telephone calls and letters, this champion guided and prodded the State Department of Education into developing rules that more closely resembled her intent. Unfortunately, once the senator was elected majority whip in 1985, good politics became more than education, her interests broadened, and monitoring of the reform stopped. In 1986, she resigned from the legislature to run for the state-wide office of superintendent of public instruction.

Thus, across the states legislators concerned with protecting or enhancing their own reputations and gaining influence in the legislature (i.e., with a prestige motivation) tended to use more informal oversight methods to detect problems during implementation. There were frequent meetings and telephone calls with program staff in the departments of education. Occasionally also, champions or legislative staff made visits to local school districts. Informal methods, argued the champions, were easier to schedule and less time-consuming than formal methods of review, such as oversight hearings. Several champions speculated that, without evidence of a problem, there would have been little interest in instituting a formal oversight strategy. The champions probably would have had difficulty getting a committee quorum during the session, when schedules were tight and new legislation was given priority, or during the interim, when many members were busy in other occupations. Off-the-record meetings, according to the champions, also were "less embarrassing" for department staff than formal committee hearings, for example, so there tended to be more honesty, more information exchanged, and more of a willingness to build a consensus. Legislative champions often fine-tuned or repaired reforms through means other than passing new legislation, a tactic that reduced the time involved in program fixing.

Good Public Policy

Recent research on legislators' goals at federal and state levels has shown that the importance of policy motivations has diminished since Fenno's 1973 study, *Congressmen in Committees*. In the early 1980s, policy motivations were not very important in committee preferences either to freshmen in the U.S. House of Representatives (Smith and Deering 1983), or to state legislators in Ohio (Weisberg et al. 1982; Goodman et al. 1986). In this study, policy motives for oversight actions were reported by legislators and their staffs considerably less often than constituency service or influence; nevertheless, some oversight action was initiated to improve education policy.

The legislative champion in Minnesota staked out a career in the legislature changing service delivery systems, first in the juvenile justice area and later in education. The Postsecondary Enrollment Options Act (PSEO), part of the Minnesota education reform which gives eleventh and twelfth grade students the option of attending postsecondary institutions, was her effort to change the education service delivery system. With a vested interest in insuring that this act changed service delivery, she spent considerable time in close communication with state depart-

ment of education staff. For example, she assigned legislative staff to
work with the department in developing PSEO guidelines, which ultimately were issued as "a cooperative effort on the part of . . . legislative
staff and state agencies." Monitoring usually was conducted through
informal meetings and telephone calls, in part because the legislator
was minority leader in the House and had control over the deployment
of substantial staff resources.

To minimize the constraint of being a part-time legislator, the representative, by her own account, took advantage of any opportunity to
further the success of PSEO. For example, when Minnesota's Legislative
Commission on Public Education held hearings around the state "to get
a feel for the public's educational concerns and to float some trial bal-
loons, I asked at every single meeting what people were doing to implement PSEO." School districts complained that students made the decision to attend a postsecondary school arbitrarily and with little notice to
districts; that some students dropped out of postsecondary schools after
several weeks and wanted to return to high school; and that estimating
the number of sections to offer and teachers to hire was difficult since
student enrollments were not stable. These glitches all needed fixing to
make PSEO work. The legislative champion, working with the department of education, added deadlines requiring that students notify districts in spring of their intent to participate and provisions for counseling
students to help them make more thoughtful decisions.

Improving public policy was the main goal of this legislator, and
in its pursuit she was willing to make some political sacrifices:

> If you were to run a balance sheet on PSEO, it cost me more than it
> helped me politically. I had to lay out a lot of chits to accomplish
> what I did. But that's okay. I happen to believe PSEO is a major
> change in the structure of the delivery system.

In the pursuit of good public policy, sometimes comprehensive
bills are enacted hastily to take advantage of a favorable political climate. After the session during the interim, legislators and legislative
staff turn their attention to technical revisions and adjustments in order
to insure good public policy. Georgia's large, comprehensive education
reform provides an example.

Oversight of Georgia's Quality Basic Education Act was needed to
clean up unfinished business. The original bill, with a strong push from
the governor, was rushed through the General Assembly and passed
both houses unanimously. At the time of passage, some things were
allowed to slide (in order to get the vote) with the expectation that

repairs could be made the following year. As one staff member explained:

> From the day QBE was first adopted, there were people making their shopping lists of things they felt needed to be refined. The Governor and General Assembly wanted to get the major elements into the bill and worry about fine-tuning later on. So we all knew there was a tremendous amount of fine-tuning that needed to be done.

Many of the repairs were technical changes—correcting capitalization errors, clarifying requirements for program eligibility, and closing spending loopholes.

Most notable was the expediency of the QBE revision process, which took into account the General Assembly's short session and the time constraints of legislators. At the governor's initiative, a "revision group" was formed with staff representatives from the House, the Senate, and the executive. The group met mostly during the interim and operated consensually—all proposed amendments were approved unanimously or deleted. Consequently, the revision bill introduced in the General Assembly had the support of all key policymakers and there was little controversy, which lessened the time legislators spent in hearings or debate. Sharing responsibility with the executive also reduced the time most legislators had to devote to monitoring and oversight.

3. Conclusions and Implications

The aim of this research was to discover and analyze both the oversight strategies that state policymakers employed and the motives that compelled their oversight efforts with recent state education reforms. Oversight in this study was conceived of as the means by which state legislatures could monitor and control contracts for education reforms with implementing agencies.

Legislatures in the study sample used different styles, including formal and informal methods, to oversee state education reforms. Formal methods, such as oversight committees and evaluation requirements, tended to be written *a priori* into implementation contracts. Informal methods, on the other hand, were more often reactive, in response to constituent complaints about implementation, for instance. The legislators and legislative staff interviewed also reported different motivations for engaging in oversight. Oversight was viewed frequently as a way to serve constituents; less often, legislators used oversight to help them gain influence in the legislature, or strengthen education policy.

Finally, the results from this study suggest an interesting relationship between style of oversight—formal or informal—and motivation. When the motive was constituency service, formal methods tended to be used. Legislators concerned with influence in the legislature frequently engaged in informal oversight to protect or enhance their reputations. But when good public policy was the main motive, both styles of oversight were used to push the reforms to be implemented faithfully.

How legislatures conducted oversight and why it occurred appeared linked inextricably with politics. Oversight strategies, both formal and informal, were designed in ways that minimized time commitments and maximized political benefits for legislators. The states preferred having education specialists (e.g., legislative champions) act on behalf of the legislature. Oversight was selective, focusing on reports of possible violations from constituents and interest groups. Finally, legislators in the six states mixed quick, informal monitoring, such as communicating directly with department of education personnel, with formal methods (committee hearings) that had greater political payoffs.

Legislative motives for conducting oversight also were driven largely by politics. The two politically-oriented motives—constituency service and gaining influence—were cited most often as reasons for engaging in oversight. In addition, during interviews legislators and legislative staff stressed the political reasons for oversight, not the importance of oversight as an accountability tool. For instance, of primary interest to legislators was fashioning a timely response to constituents' complaints; whether the complaints were accurate or valid was a secondary concern.

The conclusion that emerges from this six state study is that political considerations are at least as important in shaping oversight behavior as accountability concerns. Nevertheless, the reform policies in the six states benefited considerably from oversight.

Legislators enforced compliance and agencies were forced to adhere to legislative intent. Subsequently, legislators were able to judge whether the reforms were viable. There was little consensus on the single best approach to improving the education system, and many states were experimenting. Oversight helped to ensure that implementation was a true test of legislative ideas. Oversight also gave legislators opportunities to consider whether contracts for education reforms should be altered in response to new knowledge or to problems encountered in implementation. Acts of legislation did not always reflect well-defined goals, in part because public advocacy made resolving policy issues through legislation increasingly difficult. Ineffective or unpopular legislative decisions were changed later by oversight actions, and reform polices were improved.

Notwithstanding the benefits from oversight to education reforms, there is the question of whether oversight, as currently conducted in the legislative arena, relying heavily on anecdotes, and driven largely by politics, is good enough. The accountability system arguably is sufficient with the education reforms studied here, because they were easy to implement and required no major changes in behavior. Indeed, implementation analysts (see Fuhrman, Clune, and Elmore, chapter 11) saw those reforms as simple, compliant reforms that focused on shoring up a good system to make it better.

Reforms since the mid-1980s that focus, for instance, on higher-order thinking skills in curriculum or school restructuring or parental choice, arguably are tougher to implement than their predecessors. Like the War on Poverty programs of the 1960s, education reforms of the 1990s may require more formal accountability structures. South Carolina offers one interesting option.

The South Carolina model is a formal oversight strategy which features a three-prong approach. At the hub of the model, as adopted in the South Carolina Education Improvement Act of 1984 and amended in 1989, is the Business-Education Subcommittee, a group composed mostly of business and education leaders.[6] "Our purpose," explained the subcommittee's executive director, "is to be an independent body that carefully monitors and produces credible reports on the process and results of program implementation." In addition, the subcommittee serves as "adviser" to a select legislative committee, also established by the 1984 Act, that monitors educational progress, and recommends program and budget proposals to the legislature. The third prong of the oversight strategy is a specially-created division of public accountability in the department of education that collects assessment data and prepares annual reports for both the committee and the select committee.

In conclusion, there needs to be more experimentation and further study of alternative oversight strategies that are outside (but coordinated with) the legislative arena. The status of business and other community representatives, as taxpayers and consumers of public services, suggests that their influence on policy implementation is at least as proper as that of legislators with their legal-constitutional status as overseers. Both parties represent different but limited interests. Effective policy implementation, therefore, probably requires active monitoring by all of these groups.

Chapter 16

New Patterns of Education Policy Implementation
and Challenges for the 1990s

Allan R. Odden

Local response to state or federal government policy initiative changed dramatically in the twenty-five years after 1965. Local resistance to top-down policy initiative and lack of capacity and will, characteristics of local implementation response in the late 1960s and early 1970s, gave way in nearly all instances to local support and compliant implementation. By the early 1980s, the redistributive categorical programs for special student groups, the dominant type of state and federal initiative during the 1960s and 1970s, essentially were implemented (Peterson, Rabe, and Wong, chapter 4; Moore et al., chapter 5; and Knapp et al., chapter 6). Today the programs have been stripped of their overambitious goals (of reducing poverty for example) and now attempt to improve educational achievement for eligible students. Local, state, and federal support for their purposes, rules, regulations, and, to a substantial degree, their monitoring systems is evident. It simply is inaccurate to assert that top-down initiated programs did not change local behavior; these programs have been implemented and in compliance with accompanying requirements.

Further, those who argued that the early 1980s education reforms would not be implemented, largely because they were top-down, i.e., state and not locally initiated, were proven to be too pessimistic. As chapter 11 and other research (Odden and Marsh 1987; Goertz 1988) show, the developmental education reforms of the early 1980s, what many call "Wave I" reforms, enjoyed swift and positive local implementation response. By the mid-1980s, these comprehensive policy initiatives, even though characterized as restoring traditional notions of good schooling, i. e., firming up the old system, nevertheless changed local education behavior.

States then moved on and began to address even more complex strategies for improving local school systems including: 1) overhauling the entire school curriculum to emphasize active learning and acquisition of thinking and problem solving skills; 2) changing pre-service, entry and inservice teacher activities to transform teaching into a full-fledged profession; and 3) restructuring school organization and governance so that professionalized teachers could implement a thinking curriculum with the goal of raising the achievement of 80 percent of students to a level only 20 percent achieved in the 1980s. If the previous implementation findings were predictors, these policies too would enjoy quick implementation. Indeed, Armstrong et al. (1988) showed that several state curriculum reform initiatives had quickly penetrated school district boundaries and resulted in changed district curriculum programs.

But the news was not all good. First, claiming that categorical programs for special pupil populations were implemented was not the same as claiming that they were effective—that they worked. Indeed, there was substantial evidence that while the 1970s categorical programs had been implemented, their impact on student performance was insufficient (Odden, chapter 7). Further, there was growing evidence that the early 1980s education reforms, while implemented as designed by state political and business leaders, were not producing dramatic enough student performance increases (Fuhrman, Firestone, and Kirst 1989). While funding increased 26 percent in real terms during the 1980s (Odden 1990) and student academic course enrollments in mathematics, science, and history increased by more than 25 percent (a key reform goal), student test scores increased only marginally. Thus, the early 1980s "Wave 1" education reforms looked like they were joining the "achilles heel" of categorical programs—namely, having at best a modest impact on students performance. While no definitive studies of the student impact of 1980s curriculum reform had been conducted, the legacy of the post-Sputnik curriculum reforms suggested that impact might be less than modest (Atkin and House 1981), although the early Marsh and Odden (chapter 12) findings provided some evidence for optimism.

What then has been learned from implementation research? What still needs to be learned? In simple terms, one lesson learned is that state policy initiative can change important dimensions of local behavior. It is too simplistic to argue that top-down reforms have no local impact; the research evidence countering this claim is broad and deep (chapters 3, 4, 5, 6, 11, and 12). Many of the critical macro-implementation (Berman 1978) puzzles have been resolved. But, to be cynical, another lesson learned is that the new local behavior may not make any, or to be kinder, much difference on student performance.

Arguably, the modest student impact of both the 1960s and 1970s categorical programs and the early "Wave I" education reforms could be traced to both program design and process flaws—that neither effective programs nor effective micro-implementation processes were deployed. Indeed, many (Goodlad 1983; Boyer 1983; and Sizer 1984) argued that the early "Wave I" education reforms were unlikely to produce dramatic changes in student performance; firming up the "old system," they argued, was a flawed strategy because the "old system" was inadequate for meeting today's demands. Further, a change strategy that relied heavily on state and district leadership rather than directly enhancing professional expertise in classrooms and schools, ultimately was limited (McLaughlin, chapter 8, for example). Perhaps newly designed programs and more effective local change processes would produce larger student performance gains.

In short, while there have been great advances in knowledge of local response to state (or federal) policy initiative, the 1990s education reform challenge still is to design and implement in schools and classrooms education programs that substantially improve student performance. This challenge means that attention needs to be given both to the substance of the reform programs and to the local change, i.e., micro-implementation processes.

Drawing primarily on the studies reported in the previous four chapters, the remainder of this chapter begins to address this challenge. This chapter cannot analyze program effectiveness in depth and thus assumes that many proposals on current curriculum, the teaching profession, and school restructuring are the types of programs needed to improve dramatically student performance. This chapter, then, focuses on understanding the critical elements of the local change process for putting these programs in place. It seeks to answer two questions:

1. What are the critical elements of the local change process needed to implement in schools and classrooms a thinking oriented curriculum, more professional notions of teaching and restructured schools?

2. What roles can state policies play in these education imperatives? Can state policies impact either the content of local curriculum, teaching and school restructuring or the process of local change, and if so, how?

Section one quickly summarizes the key macro-implementation findings for "Wave I" education reforms and answers several key questions that still surround them. Why was local response so swift? Why was there such a lack of local resistance to these state initiated and federally supported policies which few local education leaders helped to create? Why did many districts move beyond even the strenuous new standards promulgated by the state?

The chapter then moves to analysis of the micro-implementation, or local change process used to implement education reforms as well as curriculum, the teaching profession and school restructuring policies. Section two synthesizes mid-1980s understandings of the local, i.e., micro-implementation/change process. These conventional understandings included important modifications to the seminal Rand Change Agent study (McLaughlin, chapter 8). This synthesis, drawn from post-1978 studies of curriculum change (Huberman and Miles 1984; Hall and Hord 1987, for example), reinforces the notion that many successful change efforts were characterized by district (i.e., top-down) initiation and coordination, with teacher involvement primarily in the post-adoption implementation phases. These phases, when successful, were accompanied by substantial assistance to teachers in classrooms and district pressure to progress to full, complete program implementation.

Drawing upon Odden and Marsh (1987) and Marsh and Odden (forthcoming), section 3 discusses how these understandings of local change "worked" for the "Wave I" education reforms of the early 1980s. This section also summarizes how different elements of states' "Wave I" education reforms impacted both the substantive and process dimensions of local response, thus showing how state policies can affect both the content of local system improvement as well as the local change processes used to implement them.

In section four, local change processes and roles of state policies are used to analyze the three studies reported in chapters 12, 13, and 14 on efforts to change dramatically the curriculum program, to transform teaching into a profession and to restructure schools. These are the substantive strategies now commonly accepted as the means for creating the system changes needed to bring 80 percent of the students to a performance level attained only by 20 percent today. This section shows how these three studies provide new findings about effective elements of the local change process when the objective is dramatic restructuring of curriculum, teaching and school organization, as well as new findings about how state policy can effectively impact both the substance and processes of local education system reform.

1. Education Reform Implementation[1]

Despite skepticism, there was widespread evidence of swift response to the early 1980s "Wave I" education reform initiatives. In 1983, the *Nation at Risk* report called for increasing high school graduation requirements, expanding student testing and toughening requirements for entering the teaching profession. By 1986–87, forty-two states had increased high school graduation requirements, forty-four states required student testing for minimum academic competencies, and thirty-eight states required new teachers to pass a state, standardized test before entering a teacher education program and/or before becoming certified to teach (Goertz 1988). This response was greater than even the diffusion of the 1970s state education initiatives in school finance and collective bargaining, and far exceeded the conventional political science notions that it takes twenty-four years for a new innovation to be diffused across half the states, and upwards of thirty-one years to impact 75 percent of the states (McDonnell and Fuhrman 1986).

Other studies found that these requirements changed student enrollments in academic courses. In a study of Arizona, California, Florida, Georgia, Minnesota and Pennsylvania, Clune (1988) found that within two years after the states' reforms were enacted, all local districts had implemented the increased high school requirements. As a result, about 27 percent of students took an extra mathematics course and 34 percent an extra science course. Many students also took new or added courses in history. The study concluded that the new courses were better than the previous courses, that the course changes probably increased average student academic achievement and probably did not raise the dropout rate or hurt at-risk students. Similar results were found by many California studies (Grossman et al. 1985; Odden and Marsh 1987; PACE 1988).

Other studies analyzed implementation of the entire array of states' early 1980s education reforms. The Center for Policy Research in Education (CPRE) analyzed documents and interviewed state and local education policymakers in fifty-nine schools in twenty-four districts in six states between April 1986 and June 1987 (Fuhrman, Clune, and Elmore 1988). Synthesizing earlier implementation research, they made several predictions about local implementation behaviors. Their findings countered most of their major predictions. They predicted that local response would vary, with some districts refusing to comply, others complying fully, and most "adapting" reforms to local goals and agendas. They also predicted that local educators would more readily adopt policies that matched local capacity, i.e., technical expertise. Instead, they found that local response was remarkably uniform, with little apparent local resistance. All districts and schools essentially implemented the key elements of the states' reform programs. There was little adaptation. While increasing student standards (like increasing high school graduation requirement and adding more traditional academic courses) matched local expertise more than did creating new roles for teachers under career ladder or mentor teacher programs (which experienced more initial implementation snags), all programs were quickly implemented in line with rules, regulations and state intent. Two California studies reached similar conclusions (Kaye 1985; Odden and Marsh 1987).

CPRE predicted that there would be little short term response, that it would take time for local educators to transform reform programs into local practice. Surprisingly, they found that local response was swift. The reform programs were implemented in the short term. It did not take several years to transform reform programs into local practice.

They predicted that the reforms themselves and local response would be more symbolic than substantive and that local educators would give more an appearance of change than meaningful change in students' experiences. But they found that local response was substantive and not just symbolic. Many districts had begun to revamp local curriculum and instruction programs before state education reform began; indeed the study found a secular trend for centralizing curriculum at the district level and aligning curriculum objectives, texts, tests, teacher evaluation and other mechanisms. PACE (Odden and Marsh 1987) found this same phenomenon in California.

CPRE predicted that implementation success would be enhanced when reform programs sent clear signals about policy intent. But they found that policy clarity was less critical than predicted. While some policies appeared more straightforward than others (increased student standards, for example), all policies had ambiguities and multiple meanings. Local districts coped nevertheless, responding to the spirit of nearly all policy elements. Local education leaders were able to take the various and disparate components of state education reform policies and weave them into an integrated local vision of new curriculum and instruction policy. Again, Odden and Marsh (1987) found that local educators were able to integrate the disparate elements of California's reforms into a coherent new view of curriculum and teaching.

Finally, CPRE predicted that local ownership would depend on the degree to which local educators were involved in the policymaking process, that low involvement would lead to little ownership and that little ownership would produce contentious implementation processes. But, they found that local involvement in the policy development process was less critical than predicted. In nearly all states and at both the state and local levels, educators rarely were involved in the reform development activities, but were active in designing policy responses to reform programs. The reforms themselves seemed to invigorate educator engagement in curriculum and instruction change. Moreover, there was widespread evidence that local and state educators, including teacher unions, were working hard to make reforms "work." Educators saw the reform programs, especially the new funding that accompanied most of them, creating opportunities to accomplish many of their own objectives.

Thus, reform legitimated local initiative. Rather than resistance (predicted by many), local response was characterized more by "strategic interaction" with state reform direction, both in responding to and affecting the content of state policy locally. Indeed, the study found that many districts who were "active users" of reform (Firestone 1989), i.e., had begun reform initiatives before state programs were enacted and went beyond several state standards and requirements.

Why These Results Should Not Be So Surprising

Despite previous implementation research and acknowledging significant differences across the states, the above study findings of swift, positive and in several instances enthusiastic local response to state education reform initiatives need not have been so surprising. First, as Yudof (1984) noted, the education system responds (swiftly) when there is a consensus for educational change on the part of political leaders outside the education system. And as McDonnell and Fuhrman (1986) argued, there not only was a consensus among the political elites for action, but also there was a consensus both about the kinds of changes needed and the need to act "immediately."

Second, while taking many forms across the country, the general goals of the early 1980s, "Wave I" state education reforms were to increase traditional notions of student achievement in academic subjects by improving the traditional curriculum and instruction program in classrooms, schools and school districts. To greater or lessor degree, this focus on curriculum and instruction has always been the primary emphasis of local educators. In other words, education reform reinforced local will to work on curriculum and instruction.

To use Peterson, Rabe, and Wong's typology (1986), education reform was a developmental rather than redistributive program. Developmental programs are state or federal initiatives in areas in which local governments (school districts in the case of education) are already involved—curriculum and instruction for education. Though state initiated, education reform nevertheless reinforced and bolstered—in the main—the substantive foci on which local educators already were working. While there obviously were several differences between local foci on curriculum and instruction and state initiatives, the fact remains that both levels of government targeted the same issue for action. Further, Peterson, Rabe, and Wong (1986) show, from analysis of earlier federal programs, that developmental programs not only get implemented less contentiously but also more quickly.

By contrast, redistributive programs—the bulk of education programs during the 1960s and 1970s—generally require local educators to focus on issues to which they had not been giving sufficient attention—desegregation, compensatory education, bilingual education, etc. At least in part because of this redirective nature, redistributive programs have a much more contentious implementation process and take longer to "put into place." Since most of the "conventional wisdom" about education policy implementation was drawn from research on the early years of redistributive policy implementation, when local resistance was strongest, it was inappropriate to apply it to the more developmental education reform initiatives.

Third and related, Murphy et al. (1985) have noted that while the local school is the unit of organizational change, the local district together with the state are the units of system change. Systems can identify the substantive direction in which local units (like schools) must move while allowing sites to determine specifically how to move in those directions. State education reform is an example, they argued, of system direction setting.

Fourth, CPRE and PACE found that many local educators appeared to have the technical expertise to make the changes implied by state education reform—the competence was there. Further, as just noted, the will was there—districts tended to be proactive rather than reactive to state education reform initiative, seizing state policy components both to bolster local visions and to help with the difficulties of the implementation process. If local response to new state (and federal) programs in the previous decades faltered on lack of capacity and will, in the 1980s, state education reform initiatives appeared to coincide with the local will and required capacity to implement. In short, top level state (and to some degree federal) policy initiative could impact local districts and schools.

2. The Elements of the Successful
Local Change/Implementation Process

Penetrating district boundaries, however, is only the first local step in the implementation process. Complete implementation requires the new policies to penetrate schools and classrooms as well. Further, significant change in classroom practice is needed in order to claim that full implementation has occurred. Altering classroom practice is produced through a more local, micro-implementation process usually referred to as the local change process.

In the mid-1980s, a rough consensus began to emerge about the key elements of the local change process. This consensus about how to produce change in classroom behaviors provided a new optimism about the potential success of major curriculum and instruction change, the ostensible objective of the evolving education reform agenda. The overviews of Fullan (1985), the Dessimination Study Supporting Local School Improvement (DESSI) study by Crandall and Associates (1982), Huberman and Miles (1984), Crandall, Eiseman, and Louis (1986), Odden and Marsh (1989) and McLaughlin (chapter 8) identified remarkably similar key factors associated with an effective local implementation change process. Eight factors seemed to be critical.

1. Ambitious efforts were better. Ambitious efforts had more impact on classroom change than did either narrowly focused projects or projects to change the entire local education structure. Ambitious efforts also were effective in stimulating teacher interest, engagement and involvement.

2. The micro-implementation/change process was key. The specific change processes were more important than the type of change pursued, geographical location or ethnic characteristics of districts or schools. How a change effort was conducted was more important than what it was, where it was attempted or for whom it was attempted.

3. High quality, proven effective programs worked better. Research-based programs with a track record of success produced more outcome success than locally created programs. This finding was somewhat different from the Rand conclusion that local, teacher developed materials were important. Subsequent studies (Huberman and Miles 1984) showed that externally developed programs that had been shown by research to be effective for a particular problem could be "exported" to other districts and, perhaps with modest tailoring at the margins to the new local context, could be effective in the new setting. Indeed, one risk local program development takes is in creating a program that does not work.

4. Top-down initiation could work. While the Rand study suggested that bottom-up initiation seemed to work better, Huberman and Miles (1984), for example, showed that top-down initiated efforts not only could work, but actually were successful in more instances than bottom-up initiated change efforts. Yin and White (1984) also found that top-down initiated efforts to install micro-computer systems reached more advanced implementation stages than did bottom-up initiated efforts. It seemed that top administrators more often were able to involve teachers and obtain their commitment than were teachers able to involve top administrator and obtain their commitment, and both administrator and teacher commitment were needed for implementation success. Top-down success was conditional, though. Top-down "worked" only if a proven effective program was adopted, if top adoption was followed by teacher involvement in designing implementation strategies, and if intensive ongoing assistance was provided to teachers in classrooms and schools (see also Fullan 1985 and Purkey and Smith 1985).

These post-Rand findings seemed to sanction a new role for district initiation, leadership and orchestration of curriculum change efforts. Indeed, most previous research seemed to imply that only bottom-up teacher initiated change would be successful. Beginning with the DESSI study, district leadership and direction were resurrected, to overstate the case, as a key factor in successful change efforts. These findings, it turned out, emboldened district leaders across the country who saw from this research a more pro-active role for administrative leadership.

5. Central office support and commitment, as well as site administrator support, commitment and knowledge were needed. These factors are somewhat different from initiation, leadership and orchestration. Nearly all studies found that administration commitment at the beginning, during the process of implementation, and when complete implementation occurred was important for successful implementation and institutionalization. Administrators pass new policies (which can support the change effort), allocate money, time, and personnel resources, schedule activities and conduct an entire array of administrative functions that can help or hinder the change process. Without district and site administrator support throughout the change effort, successful implementation was hindered.

6. Teacher participation, especially in designing implementation strategies, mattered. Teacher involvement usually occurred through a variety of "cross-role" teams of teachers, site administrators, central office curriculum staff and central office line staff. Teacher involvement helped engage teachers in the overall change effort, provided key teacher input into designing the specific implementa-

tion strategies that would be used, and helped to develop teacher commitment to the change effort.

7. Extensive, intensive, ongoing training and classroom specific assistance for learning new instructional strategies was critical. At the initial stages, training emphasized awareness or some specific component of new knowledge or expertise needed for implementation. Ongoing assistance included a variety of actions such as concrete, teacher specific help, classroom assistance from local staff, teacher observation of similar efforts in different classrooms, schools or districts, and regular project meetings to sort out practical problems. Assistance also included coaching with feedback, a key to successful classroom change (Joyce and Showers 1988). Ongoing assistance was the *sina qua non* for effective implementation when change in classroom practice was needed to put a new program into place. All studies, including Rand and post-Rand studies, documented the importance of this factor.

8. Teacher commitment also was critical. Few successful change efforts reached advanced stages unless teacher commitment to the project was developed. The Rand study concluded that teacher commitment must be built "up-front," before implementation began by involving teachers in identifying the change focus, in selecting the change program and in developing materials. The argument was that this initial involvement developed teacher commitment to the change program itself. Guskey (1986) and Huberman and Miles (1984) challenged that conclusion. This and other post-Rand research found that teacher commitment often emerged at the end of the implementation cycle when teachers gained mastery over the professional expertise needed to implement the new program and saw that the program improved student performance. This research suggested that teacher commitment came after mastery and after teachers saw that the program "worked" (see also McLaughlin, chapter 8).

While the findings seemed in conflict, they differed only at the margins. First, all studies identified teacher commitment as necessary to successful educational change efforts. At the time of the Rand study, there were very few high quality, proven effective programs so teacher up-front involvement in identifying topics to work on and in developing materials was crucial to initiating change efforts. But Rand also found that teacher skills mastery and positive program effects on students were necessary for complete implementation and institutionalization.

There also were two different kinds of commitment: commitment to try the new program and commitment to the new program. Commitment to try needed to be developed up-front; without it, teachers would not become engaged in trying to implement the program. This type of commitment was probably built through awareness sessions on what the program was and in responding to teachers' personal concerns about how the program might affect them individually. Commitment to the program usually emerged at the end of the implementation process as teachers developed the expertise needed to implement the new program and saw that it, indeed, resolved the problem to which it was applied, i.e., that it "worked."

Odden and Marsh (1989) suggested that these factors should form a minimum focus for analyzing the micro-implementation process of the evolving education reform agenda. McLaughlin (chapter 8) raised two other issues concerning aspects of effective local implementation practices. First, she recommended less of a focus on policy implementation per se, which had been the traditional focus, and more of a focus on actions—from whatever source—designed to improve classroom practice, the behavioral change that must occur before most educational innovations (such as curriculum reform) can be effective. Thus, she suggested analyzing the array of strategies that could improve teacher professional expertise, including how administrators managed opportunities for teacher professional growth. In other places (McLaughlin and Yee 1988), she reinforced this notion by arguing that professional growth opportunities were major incentives for professional oriented teachers.

Second, McLaughlin suggested that infiltrating teacher professional networks might be a powerful strategy for accomplishing the goal of enhancing classroom practice. She hinted that the usual formal mechanisms of district or county staff development, training related to policy implementation, etc. often are unconnected to the formal and informal networks in which teachers participate on a day-to-day basis and from which they develop professional norms focused on expanding professional expertise. She argued that getting inside these networks, whether they are the department structures of secondary schools, informal activities from participating in such projects as the Bay Area Writing Project or the Puget Sound program, or activities such as publishers workshops on *Math Their Way,* offer high potential for enhancing teachers professional classroom practice and expertise.

3. Micro-Implementation of Education Reform

Odden and Marsh (1987) and Marsh and Odden (forthcoming) used the above eight factors to analyze local change strategies for seventeen secondary schools implementing California's comprehensive, "Wave I," education reform. They found that all but one school mounted an effective local implementation process that included these eight factors. Except for two sites, the district initiated reform action and adopted the key elements of the reform program, usually incorporating all key elements of the state's education reform package. The reform vision was characterized by more academic curriculum, more requirements, higher standards, and tougher discipline, hallmarks of the state's policies. This combination of state and district action clearly characterized the initiation process as top-down in nature.

Each district then used some form of cross role team involving teachers, department chairs, site administrators and district staff to coordinate the implementation process. Cross-role teams blended top-down initiation with bottom-up participation in designing specific implementation strategies.

Site administrators and teachers received initial training to carry-out the reforms and undertook a variety of curriculum development activities. Coupled with administrator leadership, commitment, monitoring and pressure to implement, these initial trainings and curriculum development were found to be sufficient to implement the "Wave I" education reforms. Ongoing assistance was quite limited, and in many cases not necessary since teachers generally were not required to implement new strategies but to teach more academic courses, something for which they had been trained. For the "Wave I" reforms, the impetus was to teach, for example, more algebra and less general mathematics, not a new form of mathematics. Thus, teachers at most sites already had mastery of the expertise needed for the limited demands of the early education reforms. Almost all sites, moreover, were able to generate teacher engagement in the process.

Odden and Marsh (forthcoming) further found that these micro-implementation strategies produced significant outcomes. They analyzed the relationship between the strength of the above eight factors and both the level of student performance gains and the organizational capacity to manage the change process. They found that the stronger the schools and districts were ranked on the eight key change variables, the more they produced both in terms of student academic achievement and in terms of organizational capacity to implement major change.

In short, their analysis showed that a top-down initiated and orchestrated change process worked quite well for implementing California's ambitious "Wave I" reforms. Firestone (1989) found similar results in the six states CPRE studied:

1. Local educators knew how to "read" new state policies and design appropriate local programs—twenty-five years of responding to state and federal initiatives had enhanced local program development capacity.

2. Local leadership counted and top-down initiation worked. Local educators took the disparate state curriculum and instruction policies involved in California's (and most states' "Wave I" reforms) and wove them into a cohesive local system vision of good schooling, i.e., local leaders developed the integrated vision of curriculum and instruction and were "aided and abetted" by the signals and reform policy pieces from the state.

3. All local actors needed to be involved in implementation. While top-down initiative characterized local response at the adoption stage, wide involvement of teachers, site administrators and district curriculum coordinators characterized more effective implementation processes. Teacher and site administrator engagement in the technical decision-making of how to put education reform "in place" was a key factor in aligning the school vision with the district vision and in tightening the coupling between the district office and the local school site.

4. Effective implementation included more teacher and site assistance. Training, staff development and a variety of technical assistance activities were expanded. While not as intensive as would be needed for major pedagogical change (which was not required for most of the "Wave I" reforms), the expansion of assistance activities was an important ingredient of education reform implementation.

5. Teacher support and engagement counted. Teacher support—especially considering that teachers were not involved in the design of the reform—was surprisingly strong. This could be a result of the developmental nature of education reform—after twenty-five years of focus on special-needs students, states were seeking to improve the regular curriculum and instruction program, the activity which consumed most of the time of most teachers. State policy was trying to improve what teachers cared about the most. Teacher support also was a by-product of involvement in the implementation process. Further education reforms were "ambitious" efforts, and ambitious efforts stimulate teacher interest.

Odden and Marsh also found substantial impacts of the various components of the state's education reform programs on both the substance of local reform as well as the local, within district implementation process. State policy elements of California's "Wave I" reforms shaped several dimensions of the local reform content. First, all sites increased high school graduation requirements, often beyond the new state requirements. Second, all sites increased the number of academic courses offered—a key reform goal—in high schools as well as middle schools. Third, as required by law, districts compared their existing curriculum programs to the state's new model curriculum standards and, though not required by law, began extensive modification in line with the new standards. Fourth, districts adopted new state textbook selection criteria, even for high school textbooks which was not required. Fifth, most districts focused their overall curriculum on the content included in the changing state student testing program, a strategic response but not a required one. In other words, various dimensions of state policies focused on the curriculum and instruction program, per se, were incorporated into district visions of reformed education systems.

Further, Marsh and Odden (forthcoming) found state policy impact on the local implementation process as well. They found several examples of the state funded Mentor Teacher Programs providing assistance both in designing local implementation strategies and in providing ongoing assistance to teachers. Expansion funds for the state's School Improvement Program often were used to purchase local staff development assistance, rather than for classroom teacher aides to help with clerical duties. Further, as the local response to the state mandate to "certify" all staff involved in teacher evaluation, most districts created new staff development for teachers primarily in direct instruction methods and for administrators primarily in supervision of direct instruction. Overall, this response seemed to improve both the content and process of the local instruction program. Finally, many districts used the new state "quality indicators" public reporting mechanisms to expand local accountability efforts and to align the overall curriculum and teaching program to the new curriculum objectives, textbook materials and test instruments. In short, state policies affected the local implementation process in several different ways.

These findings provided additional evidence that state policy initiation could have powerful effects. At least in California, a combination of state policy initiatives involved in the early 1980s education reforms not only were quickly and substantively implemented, but impacted importantly the content of local system improvement and the local implementation processes mounted to engender change in classroom and school practice. These, indeed, are major impacts.

4. Implementing Curriculum, Teacher, and
School Structure Change

While education reform macro- and micro-implementation proceeded surprisingly smoothly for the early 1980s education reform, implementing bolder reforms to install a thinking skills oriented curriculum, to alter teaching and transform it into a full profession, and to restructure schools as organizations had a rougher ride. This section summarizes important pieces of the implementation puzzles that need to be completed in the 1990s if the hopes for dramatic improvements in the American education systems are to be realized.

Implementing Curriculum Reform

The Marsh and Odden (chapter 12) curriculum reform study adds several new dimensions to understanding local implementation when the change goal entails substantial new knowledge and expertise, such as major curriculum change. Their study was one of the first 1980s curriculum reform implementation studies and their findings were different from the post-Sputnik, NSF mathematics and science curriculum change studies which concluded that little had changed overall and that much of what changed in the short term reverted to previous practice over the long term (Atkin and House 1981 and Ravitch 1984). Marsh and Odden's study offers some optimism for the curriculum change efforts that are likely to continue throughout the 1990s, i.e., for changing the content of school curricula, for developing a thinking rather than basic or rote skills orientation, and for enhancing what teachers know and are able to do so that they can implement this curriculum successfully in the classroom.

California's 1980s curriculum initiatives are viewed as representative of the types of curriculum change needed to teach students how to learn content more in depth and how to use content knowledge to analyze issues and problems within and across content domains. The California science and mathematics curriculum frameworks specifically entailed a new vision of the content focus in these areas as well as an explicit focus on teaching thinking, problem solving and analysis of public problems (such as acid rain) with this content knowledge. The frameworks required teachers to learn new knowledge in both mathematics and science as well as a host of new pedagogical strategies. For example, the mathematics framework emphasized development of quantitative concepts such as numberness, quantity, measurement, probability and statistics through using manipulative materials for early elementary students, rather than the traditional emphasis on the basic mathematics algorithms. To implement successfully these substantial curriculum changes required large changes in what California teachers knew and were able to do.

In addition to the curriculum frameworks, California also launched a series of related efforts including changes in textbook adoption criteria and processes, focusing its School Improvement Program (see Marsh and Bowman 1989) on implementing good school curriculum (including science and mathematics), providing Mentor Teachers who could both develop new curriculum units and work with other teachers in professional development activities, creating curriculum centers across the state to foster teacher engagement in new curriculum and teaching practices, and at the beginning of the 1990s, creating a statewide staff development program with curriculum change as a major focus. In short, California mounted a series of integrated state strategies designed to impact both the content of local science and mathematics curriculum as well as the curriculum change implementation process (Honig 1989).

Marsh and Odden (chapter 12) analyzed fourteen districts and elementary schools during the 1988–89 school year that were actively responding to these state signals to change their science and mathematics curriculum. The study objectives were: 1) to identify local implementation practices that were successful in getting these new curriculum visions implemented within schools and classrooms; and 2) to identify how state policies affected both the content of local mathematics and science change and the change processes used. The study included intensive fieldwork (all conducted by teachers and administrators who were advanced students in a doctoral program) in each of the fourteen districts and schools, including teacher classroom observation to at least partially document the extent of actual change in classroom practice.

The study investigated districts and schools making fundamental changes in two, not one, curriculum areas. Further, all schools were scheduled to begin changing their language arts curriculum the next year and their history/social science curriculum the year after. So the overall context was one of massive and fundamental curriculum change, not just changing one content area or installing one new major curriculum program.

In general, the study found substantial change in district, school and classroom practice. The California frameworks almost in their entirety became the new district mathematics and science curriculum vision. The schools took the broad frameworks and wove them into more specific new mathematics and science programs for the site; in some but not all instances, greater site specificity was aided by district curriculum scopes and sequences. Finally, there was substantial evidence of change in classroom practice: teachers covered new mathematics and science topics, used the new textbooks, in nearly all cases used a variety of manipulatives in mathematics and "hands-on" laboratory/project activities in science, and used new teaching strategies such as inquiry methods, cooperative learning, and teaching for understanding. The study was conducted too early in the implementation process (in the district's second or third year in most instances) to fully investigate teacher use, but the evidence of changed practice was impressive nevertheless. These outcomes provided evidence to suggest that the state curriculum initiatives had penetrated districts, schools and classrooms in substantial ways, far beyond what some had predicted about the efficacy of curriculum reforms (Kirst and Meister 1985).

To analyze the local implementation/change process the study adapted qualitative research methods (Miles and Huberman 1984) drawn primarily from studies of single curriculum and program change and analyzed several aspects of the eight local change factors discussed above. While one key finding from change research was that "top-down" administrator initiated and led curriculum change efforts could work, the Marsh and Odden curriculum implementation study suggests that a more complex implementation process seems to be successful for multiple and fundamental curriculum reforms. Several districts in their study used the district led and orchestrated model. These districts, however, became overloaded when they initiated implementation for the second curriculum area, usually mathematics. The typical response was to drop most district coordinated follow-through activities for the first curriculum area, usually science.[2] And it appeared in some cases that the district would abandon mathematics as they moved to language arts the next year. Since the importance of ongoing assistance and pressure-to-continue implementation was so critical for effective implementation, this pattern suggested that science change should have aborted and that mathematics change would soon abort. But in many districts that was not the result.

What Marsh and Odden found in these districts was that expert, lead teachers "took over" site implementation and continued the implementation process complete with intensive ongoing teacher assistance and pressure to move towards full implementation. These teachers usually were individuals who had participated actively in an "antecedent" implementation phase during which they became aware of the new approach to curriculum, learned to use many "packaged materials" that had been developed to implement these new curriculum notions, learned new pedagogical strategies to teach the new curriculum, and began nudging the site and district to move in these new curriculum directions.

Teachers gained these new skills through participation in activities of several of what McLaughlin (chapter 8) calls professional networks, including *Math Their Way* workshops, Cal Math Projects, California Lawrence Hall of Science programs, involvement in the state's School Improvement Program's locally run Program Quality Reviews, and a host of other formal and informal projects/activities/networks that had developed to focus on new approaches to mathematics and science. To a substantial degree, involvement in these professional activities—some sponsored by the state (Cal Math, SIP PQRs, Lawrence Hall of Science, curriculum framework and textbook adoption committees), some sponsored by publishers (*Math Their Way*), and others sponsored by local networks—produced a strong, but informally coupled professional network of science and mathematics teacher experts at several schools who were able to continue the implementation process by providing appropriate teacher assistance, usually classroom specific, and collegial pressure to "get the new program fully in place." The antecedent phase built teacher professional knowledge and expertise critical for developing a professional site culture of what good science and mathematics curriculum was. Thus, when the district moved onto adoption of the next curriculum content vision, sites were not just "left on their own." A professional site culture "took over" and continued a collegial, expertise driven, teacher led curriculum change process.

This implementation process was very different from what had emerged as the new understandings about the efficacy of district led and orchestrated change efforts, even for education reform. Marsh and Odden, nevertheless, found important district leadership roles in the new curriculum change process. Districts, seemingly successfully, played strong leadership roles in adopting a new district vision of science and mathematics curriculum. Their new goals usually included all the key goals of the new state frameworks. Most districts followed these steps with districtwide adoption of new instructional materials that all schools were expected to use. Finally, most districts felt that the ongoing changes in the state's assessment program which aligned new tests with the state frameworks would, by the 1991–92 school year, provide good quality information on student achievement in the new curriculum areas.

Most districts developed cross-role teams of teachers, site administrators and central office curriculum coordinators to adopt new curriculum and textbooks, as well as to organize the implementation process. In most instances, the teachers who had become content experts in the antecedent phase played lead roles on these committees. Further, in several districts, these teacher experts assumed formal roles as district mathematics or science coordinator, Mentor teacher or site lead teachers during implementation. In other districts, moreover, the teacher experts assumed informal authority in the school for orchestrating the site implementation process.

At the district adoption stage, then, the curriculum change urgings that had been provided by the expert teachers became supported by the state curriculum frameworks, new textbook adoption criteria, SIP PQRs, and other state initiatives. In other words, state policies helped the district synthesize, integrate and formalize a new notion of school mathematics and science curriculum, that undergirded a bottom-up professional pressure for major curriculum change that had evolved out of the antecedent phase. Put differently, at the adoption phase, the bureaucratic culture of the district which is dominated by line administrators was able to mobilize and enpower the professional culture which was dominated by expert mathematics and science teachers to produce a new, district wide mathematics and science curriculum vision. Without the professional culture development that occurred during the antecedent stage or the notions of good curriculum contained in the state curriculum frameworks (which mobilized the bureaucratic culture), the symbiotic interaction between the bureaucratic and professional cultures might not have occurred.

State policy initiatives also played several important roles. At the antecedent phase, programs such as Cal Math (and now Cal Lit and Cal Writing), Lawrence Hall of Science, School Improvement and today the Mentor Teacher Program and the New Staff Development Program helped develop lead teacher experts in a curriculum content area who provided pressure for change from the classroom and site. At the adoption phase, state policies such as the new curriculum frameworks, new textbook adoption criteria and revised student assessment program outlined a comprehensive view of new curriculum that districts adopted as a new system approach. At the implementation phase, state policies such as SIP (when the funds were used to purchase technical assistance), Mentor Teachers, and staff development, for example, provided the site resources needed by the variety of site professional content experts to continue a vigorous implementation process. The comprehensive set of state policies and programs seemed to help at all implementation stages.

This new pattern of local implementation led and carried by lead teacher experts should not be understood as a precisely planned and formally coordinated set of activities at the site level. The metaphor of simultaneous tight/loose applies, with tight goals and objectives from the district, i.e., from the top of the local education system, but looser, though intensively professional implementation at the site and classroom. Few schools had formal, comprehensive, written implementation plans. Integration and coordination occurred, however, but through intensive, collegial interaction especially among the lead teacher experts over issues, problems and activities needed to get the new science and mathematics curriculum "in place." For these teacher-led professional activities, there were no formal "site councils" who had the authority to make decisions, there generally was no formal "shared decision-making" program, and usually the decision-making was not among all faculty at the school—all teachers were not equal. Leadership was provided by and deference given to those with professional expertise, to those individuals who were the mathematics and science experts. While schoolwide consultation was the norm, decisions were made by the experts.

Thus, a professional-collegial model based on expertise emerged from their study. Major curriculum change was possible but required site teacher leaders with clout who could provide signals about what constituted good mathematics (or science) curriculum, who had access to resources and who had authority to command attention. What emerged was a knowledge and expertise-based notion of leadership, a leadership style based on what teachers knew and were able to to. What also emerged was that this type of process empowered the professional teacher expert, informally through leadership channels in the school and formally through such leadership channels as becoming a Mentor Teacher, a site resource or lead teacher, or a central office curriculum coordinator.

These findings provide new insights into mechanisms that can substantially enhance teacher professional knowledge and expertise, which as McLaughlin states in chapter 8, is the key to improving system effectiveness. The Marsh and Odden findings also undergird the importance of how "infiltrating" the formal and informal teacher professional networks can become powerful strategies for dramatically improving the expertise of teachers and for dramatically changing curriculum. Indeed, their findings suggest that districts will not be able to lead and coordinate the 1990s goals of restructuring the curriculum, teaching and school organizations, unless their adopted visions are "taken over" by site-based professional teacher leaders who manage the intensive change process at the site. The study shows that what teachers "know and are able to do" is what is critical for fundamental system improvements, at least in curriculum reform, and that while both state policies and district leadership are important and can help the process, developing, enabling and empowering professional teacher expertise seem to be the most efficacious routes to the changes the country experts of its education system in the 1990s.

Finally, these positive findings need to be somewhat conditioned by the more pessimistic findings of Cohen (1990) as the difficulties of developing in depth the knowledge and skills needed to teach the new mathematics and science curriculum. The good news documented by Marsh and Odden is that the will is there; the distressing news documented by Cohen is that it will take substantial time and perhaps the recruitment of more able individuals into teaching to put these ambitious new curricula fully into place in the classroom.

Implementing Teacher Professionalism Proposals

McDonnell's (chapter 13) analysis of the implementation of teacher professionalism proposals raises several issues, but two are key for the education policy implementation issues in the 1990s that are suggested by the preceding chapters. The first is that because teacher professionalism, at one basic level, means "turning over" to teachers control of several aspects of local education systems, the idea of teacher professionalism itself confronts the historic tradition of lay control in education. McDonnell shows how this fundamental conflict created fatal implementation problems for teacher professionalism programs in some states and will continue to plague wholesale pursuit of this educational objective. Many state and local political leaders were unwilling to turn over control to teachers when they were unhappy with student achievement and want teachers to know and be able to do more. Accommodating these opposite pulls between professional and political control, i.e., reconciling the twin pulls of local will, is a paramount objective if policies enhancing the professional nature of teaching will progress in the future. Her short-term suggestion is to proceed vigorously with proposals for which there is agreement by both the proponents of professionalism and the proponents of political control.

The second is that McDonnell shows how many aspects of teacher professionalism proposals exceed current capacity, i.e., know-how, for implementation. The technology, or knowledge and expertise, for example, for ensuring professional standards for entry into the profession, for evaluating teachers validly and fairly for career advancement, for assessing accurately what teachers know and are able to do, and for reorganizing the work of teachers in more meaningful and "professional" ways is simply vastly underdeveloped. Thus, teacher professionalism proposals, which are the proposals that have encountered the most serious implementation difficulties, face the twin dilemmas of lack of local will and capacity, and thus have produced the most strenuous implementation experiences.

McDonnell's substantive points, however, show that the Janusfaced problem of local will is more complex than, simply, that some individuals do not want to implement teacher professionalism proposals, as was the case for most initial response to desegregation proposals. Teacher professionalism proposals raise the issue of who ultimately controls the schools: professional teachers (since the professionals have the control in other professions) or political leaders or members of boards of education, those who traditionally have held control. Just as an accommodation between local, state and federal control was worked out over time for the redistributive categorical programs of the 1960s and 1970s so also must an accommodation be worked out for teacher professionalism proposals, but this time a new actor—teacher professionals themselves—will become part of the equation.

Finally, an interesting aspect of McDonnell's suggestions for moving forward on the capacity side of the the teacher professionalism agenda is her call for capacity building programs, including especially professional staff development activities, which have not to date been been central elements of these policies. The National Board for Professional Teaching Standards (1989), an outgrowth of the Carnegie teacher professionalism proposals (1986), is the boldest attempt to identify an assessment mechanism that can identify what the best experienced teachers know and are able to do. But McDonnell's suggests that teachers' knowledge and expertise per se needs to be substantially enhanced through intensive, professional teacher staff development.

This conclusion, thus, joins the conclusions of both Marsh and Odden (chapter 12) and McLaughlin (chapter 8) that one key to future education system improvements is dramatically enhancing teacher's professional expertise. The Marsh and Odden study, as argued above, moreover, shows how this notion, especially when it is linked to major curriculum reform, supports broader notions of teacher professionalism such as teacher empowerment, teacher leadership and teacher control. These conclusions provide the outlines for an argument that when teachers know and are able to do more, and this expertise results in dramatically improved student performance, the strength of control pressures outside the profession could wane.

Implementing School Restructuring Proposals

Marsh and Crocker's study (chapter 14) of middle school restructuring provides solid beginning knowledge about effective processes for restructuring secondary schools, specifically middle schools, and the roles various state policies can play both in stimulating a restructured school vision and in enhancing local change processes for putting the vision into place. Marsh and Crocker analyzed eight California schools actively working to implement a middle school vision. They analyzed the degree to which and how these schools implemented the middle school vision outlined in the Superintendent's Middle Grade Task Force report entitled *Caught in the Middle* (1987), which synthesized the best thinking about twenty-two key elements of a quality middle school. Marsh and Crocker also analyzed how California's School Improvement Program assisted these schools in implementing this complex vision of school restructuring. Their sample included only activist middle schools, i.e., schools that had begun to restructure towards the middle school vision even before the impetus of the state report. Thus, their findings provide insights into how some of the "best" and "most interested" schools were able to implement dramatic school restructuring.

Caught in the Middle identified five major components for middle school restructuring: 1) a core curriculum focused on thinking and problem solving, application to real life issues, and delivered with new instructional methods including cooperative learning; 2) five elements focused on important developmental needs of young adolescents; 3) a series of organizational and structural changes from school culture to new student assessments; 4) changes in teaching and administration; and 5) community and parent involvement. The vision, thus, included major curriculum restructuring, a renewed emphasis on specific development issues for young teenagers, and deep changes in the organizational and structural dimensions of the school. In total, the report identified twenty-two elements of an effective middle school, most of which did not exist in most schools.

Marsh and Crocker found that each school produced substantial change in several of the individual elements, but only modest success in implementing all twenty-two elements. Even though these schools were among the most active and energetic, had knowledgeable and strong leadership and had numerous capable staff, they had difficulty making deep, substantial curriculum and organizational changes. In other words, Marsh and Crocker found that restructuring middle schools was tough. This finding "squares" with the Rand Change Agent study finding that systemwide change is particularly difficult (McLaughlin, chapter 8). Even though concluding that only modest implementation of the entire middle school vision occurred, the substantial change that Marsh and Crocker found shows that several dimensions of school restructuring can be accomplished but that full school restructuring is probably more complicated and will take much longer than most have assumed.

Marsh and Crocker identified several key change processes variables that reflected the general change literature (Huberman and Miles 1984), but two require specific mention. First, each school had a very strong principal who had a comprehensive middle school vision (usually bolstered by *Caught in the Middle*), had good working relationships with the faculty, and knew how to mobilize resources to support a change process that moved the school forward towards implementing the middle school vision. Further, most of the principals had been involved in regional networks of administrators and teachers concerned about middle school issues. These principals were able to articulate the vision and able to provide ongoing leadership and commitment over several years to get the vision put into place.

Second, lead, expert teachers played critical roles in implementing the twenty-two program elements that constituted the core of the middle school vision. In many ways, the development and roles of these teachers were similar to the findings discussed above for mathematics and science implementation. Lead teachers were created and nurtured, they were not born. Through a variety of local teacher networks that grew out of involvement primarily in curriculum projects such as Cal Lit and Cal Writing, lead expert teachers over a two to three year time span developed the expertise—the capacity—to teach a restructured curriculum in a specific content area, such as language arts or mathematics, gained proficiency by implementing these new curriculum strategies in their classrooms and then began to work with other teachers in their departments to do the same.

Again, the development function often occurred in an antecedent phase prior to the school's formally adopting the middle school vision. After adoption then, these lead teachers often became involved with the principal in helping to implement the overall middle school vision, as well as became Mentor Teachers or assumed other formal roles to work with teachers in their department to change the curriculum within the entire department. While only a few schools were able to restructure the curriculum in entire departments, and while several of the twenty-two middle school elements were not supported by regional networks that developed teacher expertise (and thus were only partially implemented), in all schools lead teachers played the most critical roles in getting different curriculum elements fully implemented. Indeed, in most schools, principals "turned over" to teacher teams implementation responsibility for most of the individual twenty-two program elements.

These findings again reinforce the notion of the power of formal and informal professional networks—both for principals and teachers—in getting deep change in classroom and school practice. These findings for secondary school restructuring not only parallel those for mathematics and science curriculum restructuring, but also provide empirical evidence for the importance of ongoing face-to-face contacts and social networks for disseminating new professional practices (McLaughlin, chapter 8; and House 1974).

Marsh and Crocker also found several important roles for state policy initiatives both in defining the substance of middle school restructuring and in assisting the local change processes. First, the state *Caught in the Middle* report helped all schools comprehensively articulate a middle school vision that included major curriculum change linked to developmental needs of young adolescents linked to needed changes in school organization and structure. While most schools had begun to move towards a middle school model before dissemination of the state report, the report itself reinforced the school's directions and layed out the comprehensive set of issues that needed to be addressed to implement fully a middle school restructuring. Further, once it was published, *Caught in the Middle* became the school vision, just as for mathematics and science, the state curriculum frameworks became the district's new curriculum vision.

Second, California's School Improvement Program (SIP) played several critical roles. To begin, it provided a schoolwide planning process, that within one large cross-role school committee, incorporated all the major elements of the middle school vision and consolidated them into an organization-wide school restructuring agenda. Next, and very importantly, it provided the discretionary resources for teachers to attend summer workshops and other outside staff development activities that got them involved in external networks of teachers working on various elements related to the middle school curriculum and organizational vision. Third, SIP created a school-wide cross-role team—the school site council—charged with engaging in an ongoing planning process; this team became the entity that consolidated several of the middle school activities into a schoolwide plan. Finally, the SIP Program Quality Review (the SIP assessment mechanism) undergirded the school's attempts to implement the overall core elements of the middle vision. In these many ways, SIP and *Caught in the Middle* worked together. The latter detailed and gave research support to the vision. The former provided teacher involvement through a schoolwide planning process, the slack resources needed to support capacity building activities, and a formative evaluation process to help the school "stay the course."

Third, the state curriculum frameworks, which reinforced the core curriculum changes involved in the curriculum elements of the middle school vision, added further district and school pressure to continue major curriculum reform. Fourth, as mentioned above, the state's Mentor Teacher Program provided opportunities for lead, expert teachers to assume formal positions for providing ongoing technical assistance and support to other teachers, with sanction from the school and district. Finally, the state's new eighth grade student assessment program, which tested students in mathematics, science, language arts, history and writing areas that were tightly aligned with the state's curriculum frameworks, functioned as an additional accountability and evaluation mechanism that provided data on the student impact of implementing the new middle school curriculum. In other words, a variety of state policies contributed positively both to the substance of the middle school vision in each school studied as well as to a number of important local change process variables.

4. Conclusions and Implications

Several conclusions and implications flow from the above discussion in this chapter as well as the issues discussed in the preceding chapters. First, state and federal government initiative can affect local behavior. The 1960s and 1970s categorical, redistribution programs, the early 1980s "Wave I" education reforms, and the late 1980s reforms to restructure curriculum, teaching and schools have all experienced substantial implementation in local schools and districts. While implementation of many of the more complex dimensions of the late 1980s reforms have proven more difficult than expected, local response to implement has been swift and enthusiastic in many cases, and local education leaders continue to work on advancing implementation further. The swift and substantive response to the 1980s education reforms reflect, to some degree, the developmental nature of these policy initiatives. In short, evidence is wide and deep that governmental initiative does not just lead to conflict, resistance and bargaining; accommodation, cooperation and strategic interaction to improve the American education system is more descriptive of conditions today.

Second, a key policy focus at all governmental levels is to insure that programs are designed to have substantial impacts on all students' achievement. While the categorical programs of the 1960s and 1970s have been implemented, their impact on student achievement is minimal. Further, the early 1980s education reforms also have not produced sufficient impacts on student performance. It is hoped that the proposals for curriculum restructuring, as evidenced in the evolving California state curriculum frameworks, as well as proposals to restructure teaching into a full profession, and general proposals to restructure schools to allow professional teachers to deliver a thinking skills oriented curriculum, are on the right track for producing more than incremental changes in student performance. Analysts will need to track the impacts of these strategies to insure that what is being implemented locally has the power to make dramatic improvements in all students' achievement. The findings from the 1980s education reform implementation research show, moreover, that state policy can impact the important technical core of curriculum and teaching.

Third, recent implementation research confirms the understanding of many about the nature of the local educational change process. Ambitious efforts continue to produce more change than narrowly focused efforts, and school restructuring, i.e., really ambitious efforts, today shows some promise for producing substantial change as well. District and site leadership is important, both in the initial, middle and advanced implementation stages. Teacher involvement in designing and implementing change activities is still important. Ongoing, follow-through assistance to teachers in schools and classrooms is still the *sine qua non* for producing change in classroom practices. Teacher commitment and effort are critical; without effort and commitment, change rarely occurs, but commitment can emerge at the end of the implementation process rather than at the beginning.

Fourth, there seem to be some important new elements to effective local change processes when fundamental and multiple curriculum change or school restructuring are the goals. For these efforts, district led and orchestrated change efforts are insufficient. Teachers must play more central, leadership roles. A new antecedent implementation phase emerged from both studies of curriculum and school restructuring. In the antecedent phase, teacher capacity is developed for implementing more complex education reform goals. Also in the antecedent phase, the professional expertise of those who become lead teachers is developed. Through involvement in a variety of professional development opportunities, teachers learn about, for example, new curriculum notions, become aware of instructional packages that can be used to teach the new curriculum, develop the content knowledge and pedagogical expertise to teach the new curriculum in their classrooms, and interact over several years with other teachers in formal and informal networks created to foster a collegial culture to continue to refine and master new practices.

Lead teachers then often become involved at the site and district levels when they move to adopt new notions of curriculum or even more grandiose notions of school restructuring. At this stage, the bottom-up urgings of the professional culture of lead teachers to move the system in these new directions obtain official sanction by the district and site bureaucratic culture through formal adoption of new curriculum and school visions. At the implementation stage, action reverts to the site and professional, expert lead teachers; lead teachers often provide the important ongoing technical assistance and support functions which are critically necessary to produce significant change in teacher classroom practice. All three notions—the antecedent phase, the power of formal and informal teacher networks to sustain the development and schoolwide deployment of lead teachers, and the importance of lead teachers and the key role they play in providing ongoing assistance—are new and important findings.

These results provide more complexity to the debate between bottom-up versus top-down initiated reform; both are important. During the antecedent stage, the efforts are bottom-up by teacher participation in professional development networks. At the district and site adoption stage, the locus shifts to the top where formal action, usually with teacher (often lead teacher) involvement, is taken to sanction a new direction in curriculum or school organization and structure. Then the action shifts back to the bottom—to the site—where lead teachers play the critical roles during advanced implementation activities.

Fifth, more focused notions of teacher professionalism and teacher empowerment emerge from the late 1980s implementation studies. Teacher professionalism becomes strongly linked to curriculum and instructional expertise and is reinforced through participation in ongoing collegial networks that support a professional notion of what good curriculum, pedagogy or school organizations are. While this notion of professionalism ultimately includes control, power and leadership, these flow from expertise and are ceded, if you will, to expert teachers. Expert teachers become the leaders and have power because of their expanded professional expertise.

Sixth, the studies show that a variety of state policy initiatives have potential to affect both the substance of local education reforms as well as the processes of putting them into place. At the antecedent stages, state funded professional development projects such as Cal Lit, Cal Writing and Cal Math projects over time produced many lead, expert teachers and consciously involved these teachers in ongoing networks of teachers from other schools and districts. State Department of Education and County regional awareness workshops played similar roles and often produced additional networks of professionals actively interacting for the purpose of learning new strategies and changing classroom and school practice. At the adoption stage, California's curriculum frameworks were major factors in shaping new district visions of good mathematics and science curriculum, and its *Caught in the Middle* report played a similarly influential role in shaping site's restructured school visions. These state documents consolidated the vision of curriculum or school structure and reinforced bottom-up pressures that had been provided by lead teachers pushing for change. These efforts were complemented by California's new textbook selection criteria and revised instructional materials selection process. Finally, at the implementation and evaluation stages, state school improvement programs, Mentor Teachers, state staff development programs, program quality review documents and a state assessment program linked strongly to the curriculum vision both provided resources for the ongoing supports that are critical to successful change efforts, as well as provided pressure to continue to move towards complete implementation. In short, the studies show that state policies, rather than simply hindering local education reform goals, can play a variety of critical and helpful roles at all stages of the implementation/change process.

Seventh, Wohlstetter's sober findings that state legislative oversight of education reform, while expanding, is more political to broaden influence than substantive to insure accountability might not be so problematic if the future strategy for deep reform continues to entail dramatic improvements in professional teacher expertise. Teachers have the ultimate control over policy when they enter the classroom to teach. If the antecedent teacher development strategies found in chapters 12 and 14 are as powerful as found in these studies, and are expanded, the teacher professional culture can—and rightfully so—obviate the need for legislative oversight. Only time will tell whether the evolving new and professional roles for teachers found in the California curriculum and middle school restructuring studies include powerful, site-based professional-driven teacher roles in accountability as well.

The 1990s probably will continue to witness evolution of policy strategies designed to dramatically improve the student impact of the American education system. Indeed, President George Bush and the nation's governors in early 1990 set high education goals for student performance in mathematics, science, reading, writing, history, and geography and seek to have U.S. students be the best in the world in mathematics and science. Thus, implementation research in the 1990s likely will focus on the appropriate design of policies to accomplish these goals, effective implementation strategies to put them into place, and program design and implementation activities needed to insure that all students—minorities (which are growing in numbers) and non-minorities, limited-English-proficient (which also are growing in numbers) as well as English-proficient, poor (about one in every four students comes from a family {where at least one person works full time in the majority of cases} with an income below the poverty level) and nonpoor, girls (especially in mathematics, science, and technology) and boys—benefit from these bold attempts to improve the overall American education system.

Notes

Chapter 2

1. A variety of means were used to gather the information for this study. Interviews were conducted in the USOE, in the Massachusetts Department of Education and at the local level. Other information was gathered through reports, Congressional hearings, questionnaires, correspondence, conversations, memoranda, and, or course, a reading of the general literature. In addition, some of the material is based on my personal experience with the program, gained while working for the Department of Health, Education, and Welfare between 1964 and 1969.

2. My discussion of Title I is limited to programs administered at the local level by the public schools. Title I also provides support for the handicapped, for institutionally neglected or delinquent children, for Indian children, and children of migrants.

3. This comment is not meant as a criticism of the Title I formula. When it was being developed in the fall of 1964, a major concern was a politically acceptable way to distribute funds. The formula met this criterion since funds were concentrated in key Congressional districts in urban areas and poor rural sections of the South. Also the formula allowed the Administration to come up with estimates, prior to Congressional action, showing each Congressman how much his district would receive if the proposal passed. The formula's effect on bargaining during implementation may be viewed as an unanticipated consequence.

4. In the early days of the program, the Divison of Program Operations (later the Division of Compensatory Education) approached its authorized personnel strength of 82 (including professional and clerical staff) (Bailey and Mosher 1968) but subsequently dwindled.

5. Interview with Benjamin Rice, Midwest and Eastern Regional Representative, Division of Compensatory Education, USOE.

6. Estimates supplied by Holly Knox, Office of Legislation, USOE.

7. Interview with Terry Lynch, area desk officer, Division of Compensatory Education, USOE.

8. Most important decisions made by USOE are the products of bargaining among persons holding different points of view. The decision to push for legislation was not an exception to this general rule.

9. See Section 415 of Title IV of Public Law 90–247 as amended by Public Law 91–230.

10. Interview with John F. Hughes, former Director of the Division of Compensatory Education, USOE. He stated that Commissioner Keppel was under political pressure to cut back on the guidelines.

11. Interviews with Robert L. Jeffrey, Senior Supervisor in Education and Massachusetts Department of Education Title I Director.

12. Estimates provided by Robert L. Jeffrey, Senior Supervisor in Education and Massachusetts Department of Education Title I Director.

13. 20 U.S.C. 241e.

14. As an example of the type of local evaluation reports the state receives from participating districts, I analyzed the fiscal year 1968 annual report of the public schools for one community in the Metropolitan Boston area. The school system's evaluation of its reading program concludes that the overall effect of Title I has been a positive one, citing the fact that fourth-grade Title I children went from five months behind non-Title I children in September 1967 to four months behind in June 1968 on a standardized reading test. Examination of the supporting data indicate that the gap did close. The report, however, failed to point out the reason: the non-Title I group regressed two months in reading during the year, while the Title I group fell back only one month. Although the net result may be a closing of the gap, these data hardly support the conclusion of positive benefits under Title I.

During the 1968 fiscal year, the Department had only two full-time staff supervisors, plus three part-time specialists to cover all phases of some 460 separate Title I projects. Discrepancies and inaccuracies like the one above simply could not be picked up. Thus, we find school districts with the natural desire, as well as the political necessity, to show the success of their program, and virtually no follow-up analysis by the Department of the data submitted to them.

Chapter 4

1. Still other federal provisions helped govern the design and operation of compensatory education at the local level. Under concentration of services, school districts were required to channel federal aid to schools with a higher proportion of poor students before spending money on schools with a lower proportion. Needs assessment directed districts to identify all educationally disadvantaged children in low-income areas and to design a program to meet the needs of these children. To avoid program duplication, local authorities were encouraged to coordinate compensatory instruction with other federal and state programs.

2. Memorandum, U.S. Department of Education, Assistant Secretary for Elementary and Secondary Education, to David W. Hornbeck, Superintendent of Schools, State Department of Education, Maryland, "Enclosure No. 1," July 29, 1981.

Chapter 5

1. In 1960, Morton Grodzins wrote his now-famous critique in which he argued that American federalism no longer resembled a "three-layer cake" where functions were neatly divided into federal, state, and local activities. Rather, federalism was more like the "rainbow of marble cake" in which the activities were inextricably mixed.

2. This study was part of a larger research program mandated by P.L. 95–561 (Section 1203), the Education Amendments of 1978, to examine how public and private elementary and secondary education is financed, and what role the federal government should play in the process. The School Finance Project (SFP), established to implement this mandate, commissioned three field-based studies: this study, a study of cumulative effects of federal and state programs on school districts and schools conducted by SRI International, and a study analyzing alternative state programs for special pupil populations undertaken by Decision Resources.

3. For example, the extent to which a service provider must provide access or additional special services to make access meaningful varies among programs prohibiting racial/sex discrimination and programs prohibiting discrimination against handicapped and limited English speaking students.

4. As an illustration, Reisner (1981) proposes several options for merging major federal education programs currently in existence.

5. Clune (1982, p. 1) notes, "The deregulation thesis in education may be briefly stated as follows: it is possible to reduce the number and intensity of legal obligations on educational organizations without decreasing the quantity or quality of education in any respect."

6. Levin (1982, p. 455) suggests, "A reading of at least some of the regulations attached to federal categorical grant programs for disadvantaged, bilingual and handicapped students will suggest that the benefits in terms of contributions to equity are probably less than the costs of compliance and enforcement."

7. Murphy (1981, p. 13) notes, "Anecdotal evidence suggests . . . that a fair amount of differentiation takes place informally."

8. Elmore (1981) proposes a differential states' assumption strategy that requires all states to meet uniform guarantees. Beyond this minimum, states which assume responsibility for federal requirements would develop their own

policies and procedures in specified areas to ensure adequate services. Other states would follow federally mandated program requirements.

9. Noteworthy are similar recent findings at the district level that "contrary to current claims of excessive red-tape and misplaced priorities, the major elementary and secondary education programs were by 1980 well integrated into the American system of education" (Rabe and Peterson 1983, p. 2).

Chapter 6

1. P.L., pp. 95–561 (Section 1203), The Education Amendments of 1978.

2. The reader is referred to our review of pertinent prior research (Knapp et al. 1982).

3. California, Florida, Louisiana, Massachusetts, Missouri, New Mexico, Ohio, Wyoming.

Chapter 8

1. This chapter is based on an invited address given at the April 1989 AERA meeting in San Francisco. Gary Griffin, Program Chair for the convention, had both the idea for the address—a revisitation of the Rand Change Agent study—and the persistence to persuade me to do it. Ann Lieberman, as Session Chair, provided wonderful context for and introduction to the talk as well as comments on this written version. Feedback from Stanford colleagues Larry Cuban, Kim Ford, Joan Talbert and David Tyack contributed helpful direction for clarification and elaboration. The OERI Center for Research on the Context of Secondary School Teaching, Stanford University supported the preparation of the paper.

2. Mary Metz of the University of Wisconsin adds the important caveat that while it is difficult to mandate what matters, "*what* you mandate matters."

3. Reported under the general title A Study of Dissemination Efforts Supporting School Improvement, (Crandall 1982), the Dessi study examined a national sample of the next generation of change agent projects.

4. One way to view the effective implementation strategies identified by the Change Agent study is that they all functioned to enable teacher's efforts to change classroom practices and learn new, more effective ways of operating.

Chapter 9

1. A more extensive treatment of institutional choice issues is contained in Clune (1987).

2. In common language, mandates are often called regulations, or regulatory policy. This terminology is somewhat confusing because, as we shall see, "regulations" are also used to describe the conditions attached to inducements, which are significantly different in their pure form from mandates.

3. For the purposes of this discussion, we are assuming that the initial decision to act on a policy problem has already been made; that the governmental level (federal, state, or local) and decision-making institution (e.g., legislature vs. judiciary) have been decided; and that policy choices are shaped in a system of multiple actors with competing interests.

This initial determination about which problems are placed on public agendas and which institutions and individuals actually make decisions are critical in shaping policy outcomes (e.g., see Schattschneider 1960). For example, having the state legislature select criteria for teacher compensation would likely result in very different policy than if local districts resolved the issue at the collective bargaining table.

Our analysis complements other research which focuses on these agenda-setting and institutional choice concerns by taking the process one step further and examining subsequent decisions about which policy instruments to use. As we indicate in a later section, the choice of a policy instrument is certainly constrained by who does the choosing, but we would also argue that it remains a relevant concept, regardless of who the policymaker is.

4. As we shall see in the next section, however, the resources and constraints inherent in the political system often modify these initial preferences.

5. Past policies not only constrain the choice of instruments, but they can also limit the impact of any given instrument. When policymakers decide to use a particular instrument, it is added to ones already operating in a policy area. Consequently, the marginal effect of the new instrument depends on how it interacts with existing instruments. Only in very rare cases is any single policy or instrument so comprehensive that it can completely negate the effect of past policies.

6. The idea of examining policy instruments, used in combination with one another as part of an overall policy strategy, is particularly appropriate for examining state education reform. In several states such as Georgia and South Carolina, state policymakers saw themselves as working to improve the entire educational system with an array of different instruments. However, in states that have taken a more incremental approach to education reform (e.g., Arizona and Pennsylvania), policymakers have directed this attention to only one aspect of the system at a time, and typically used one instrument at a time. An analytical framework that allows for the analysis of policy instruments singly and in combination can capture both these philosophies and approaches to education reform.

Chapter 10

1. As an example, Rosenbaum's analysis of Wetlands Regulation frames

implementation outcomes in terms of two statutory features: specificity and enforceability. He argues that ". . . the enforceability of a law must be assessed in terms of the balance between the amount of behavioral change required and the stringency of mechanisms established to secure bureaucratic cooperation and stimulate public compliance" (1980, p. 578).

2. Thanks to Sheldon White for this point.

Chapter 11

1. For a very recent summary of research on policy implementation, see McLaughlin (1987). Earlier research and reviews include Bardach (1977), Berman and McLaughlin (1978), Elmore (1978), Sabatier and Mazmanian (1980), and Van Meter and Van Horn (1975).

2. See Odden and Marsh (1987) for a study of California reform that reaches the same conclusion based on a larger local sample than CPRE's in that state.

3. To a number of reform critics the student standards reforms are merely marginal adjustments that do not penetrate the core of the teacher-centered classroom (see, for example, Cohen 1987; Cuban 1984, 1988). These analysts would probably relate ease of compliance to the conformance of the reforms to existing structures—that is, the reforms were quickly implemented as much because they were peripheral as because they were easy to understand.

4. We are indebted to our colleague Marshall Smith of Stanford University for making this point.

Chapter 13

1. The research reported in this chapter was sponsored by the Center for Policy Research in Education (CPRE) through a grant from the U.S. Department of Education and by the Center for the Study of the Teaching Profession (CSTP) through a grant from the Southwestern Bell Foundation. A more extensive version of this work has been published as The Dilemma of Teacher Policy, Santa Monica, CA: The RAND Corporation. The opinions expressed are those of the author, not of the sponsoring institutions.

2. This study is based on field interview data collected between May 1986 and June 1987 in nineteen local districts and fifty schools in the five states. These data include over 600 interviews with state policymakers, interest group representatives, local district officials, principals, and classroom teachers. They were collected by researchers at RAND, Rutgers University, and the University of Wisconsin-Madison. Other projects, based on these data, focus on student standards, teachers unions and school reform, educational technology, and efforts to monitor educational progress.

Chapter 15

1. The study was conducted while the author was a postdoctoral fellow with the Center for Policy Research in Education (CPRE) at The RAND Corporation. CPRE, which is funded by the U.S. Department of Education, is a consortium of Rutgers University, Michigan State University, Stanford University and the University of Wisconsin-Madison. The views expressed here are those of the author, not of the sponsoring institutions.

2. McCubbins and Schwartz (1984) in their study of congressional oversight of regulatory agencies coined the terms "police-patrol" oversight and "fire-alarm" oversight. The term police-patrol oversight refers to active monitoring to detect violations as opposed to fire-alarm oversight which refers to reactive responses to alarms from outsiders.

3. The motivations of legislators to undertake oversight were identified by asking legislators and their staffs why oversight was conducted and what the benefits of oversight were to individual legislators and to the legislature.

4. The Pennsylvania Legislature delegates broad discretion for policy-making to the State Board of Education and so the board, not the legislature, has been the initiator of education reforms.

5. Staffing for standing committees in Georgia is centralized in each chamber, and staff work for more than one committee. This system also is used by the House and Senate Appropriations Committees in Arizona, which are staffed by the Joint Legislative Budget Committee. Arizona's education committees have very small staffs (two each in the House and Senate); and the Senate's senior staffer doubles as project director for the career ladder program and staff to the joint committee responsible for overseeing implementation of the program.

6. The group is a subcommittee of the Business-Education Partnership for Excellence in Education whose original members were appointed by the governor in the early 1980s to develop a plan for education reform, which became the South Carolina Education Improvement Act of 1984. Of the twenty members on the subcommittee, ten are from the business and civic communities, six are educators, and four are legislators.

Chapter 16

1. This section draws from Odden and Marsh 1990.

2. Since the science curriculum framework was adopted two years before the mathematics framework, most districts began science curriculum implementation before mathematics.

References

Aberback, Joel D. "Changes in Congressional Oversight," *American Behavioral Scientist,* vol. 22, 1979, pp. 493–515.

Advisory Commission on Intergovernmental Relations. *Categorical Grants: Their Role and Design,* A–52, Washington, D.C.: Advisory Commission on Intergovernmental Relations, 1977.

Allington, Richard L. and Anne McGill-Franzen. "School Response to Reading Failure: Instruction for Chapter 1 and Special Education Students in Grades Two, Four and Eight," *Elementary School Journal,* vol. 89, no. 5, May 1989, pp. 529–542.

Allison, Graham T. *Bureaucracy and Policy: Conceptual Models and the Cuban Missile Crisis,* Boston: Little, Brown and Co., 1971.

Amendments to the Elementary and Secondary Education Act of 1965, 84 Stat. 124, Title I, sec.109 (a).

Anderson, Beverly, Allan Odden, Eleanor Farrar, Susan Fuhrman, Alan Davis, Eugene Huddle, Jane Armstrong, and Patty Flakes-Mosqueda. "State Strategies to Support Local School Improvement," *Knowledge: Creation, Diffusion, Utilization,* vol. 9, no. 1, 1987, pp. 42–86.

Applebee, Arthur N., Judith A. Langer, and Ina V. Mullis. *Crossroads in American Education,* Princeton, N.J.: Educational Testing Service, 1989.

Archombault, Francis. "Instructional Setting: Key Issue or Bogus Concern," Paper presented before the Conference on Effect of Alternative Designs in Compensatory Education, Washington, D.C.: June 1986.

Armstrong, Jane, Alan Davis, Allan Odden, and J. Gallegher. *The Impact of State Policies on Improving Science Curriculum,* Denver, CO: Education Commission of the States, 1988.

Atkin, Myron and Ernest House. "The Federal Role in Curriculum Development: 1950–1980," *Educational Evaluation and Policy Analysis,* vol. 3, no. 5, September–October 1981, pp. 5–36.

Bailey, Stephen K. and Edith K. Mosher. ESEA: *The Office of Education Administers a Law,* Syracuse, N.Y.: Syracuse University Press, 1968.

Baker, Keith A. and Adriana A. DeKanter. *Bilingual Education,* Lexington, Mass.: Lexington Books, 1983.

Barber, Bernard. "Some Problem in the Sociology of Professions," in Kenneth S. Lynn, ed., *The Professions in America,* Boston: Houghton-Mifflin, 1965, pp. 15–34.

Bardach, Eugene. *The Implementation Game: What Happens after a Bill Becomes a Law,* Cambridge, Mass.: Massachusetts Institute of Technology Press, 1977.

Bardach, Eugene and R. Kagan. *Going by the Book: The Problem of Regulatory Unreasonableness,* Philadelphia, PA: Temple University Press, 1982.

Bardach, Eugene. *Implementation Studies and the Study of Implements,* Paper presented to the 1980 Annual Meeting of the American Political Science Association, Washington, DC., 1980.

Barnett, Stephen W. "Benefit-Cost Analysis of the Perry Preschool Program and Its Policy Implications," *Educational Evaluation and Policy Analysis,* vol. 7, no. 4, Winter 1985, pp. 333–342.

Barro, Stephen M. "Federal Education Goals and Policy Instruments: An Assessment of the 'Strings' Attached to Categorical Grants in Education," in Michael Timpane, ed., *The Federal Interest in Financing Schools,* Santa Monica, Calif.: The Rand Corporation, 1978.

Barro, Stephen. *The Impact of Inter-governmental Aid on Public School Spending,* Unpublished doctoral dissertation, Stanford University, 1974.

Beer, Samuel H. and Richard E.Barringer, editors. *The State and the Poor,* Cambridge: Winthrop Publishers, 1970.

Behn, Robert. "Policy Analysis and Policy Politics," *Policy Analysis,* vol. 7, Spring 1981, pp. 199–226.

Bell, Terrel H. Memorandum from the U.S. Office of Education Acting Commissioner to Chief State School Officers, October 5, 1970b.

Bell, Terrel H. Memorandum from the U.S. Office of Education Acting Commissioner to Chief State School Officers, October 30, 1970c.

Bell, Terrel H. Memorandum from the U.S. Office of Education Acting Commissioner to Chief State School Officers, September 15, 1970a.

Bellamy, G. Thomas. *The Mission of Special Education,* Washington, D.C.: U.S. Department of Education, 1988.

Bendiner, Robert. *Obstacle Course on Capitol Hill,* New York: McGraw Hill Book Company, 1964.

Berman, Paul. "Thinking about programmed and adaptive implementation: Matching strategies to situations," Paper presented to Institute for Educational Finance and Governance Law Seminar, San Francisco, Calif., February 29, 1980.

Berman, Paul and Milbrey Wallin McLaughlin, *Federal Programs Supporting Educational Change, Vol. V: Executive Summary*, Santa Monica, CA.: The Rand Corporation, 1975d.

Berman, Paul and Milbrey Wallin McLaughlin. *Federal Programs Supporting Educational Change, Vol. I: A Model of Educational Change*, Santa Monica, CA.: The Rand Corporation, 1974.

Berman, Paul and Milbrey Wallin McLaughlin. *Federal Programs Supporting Educational Change, Vol. II: Factors Affecting Change Agent Projects*, Santa Monica, CA.: The Rand Corporation, 1975a.

Berman, Paul and Milbrey Wallin McLaughlin. *Federal Programs Supporting Educational Change, Vol. III: The Process of Change*, Santa Monica, CA.: The Rand Corporation, 1975b.

Berman, Paul and Milbrey Wallin McLaughlin. *Federal Programs Supporting Educational Change, Vol. IV: The Findings in Review*, Santa Monica, CA.: The Rand Corporation, 1975c.

Berman, Paul and Milbrey Wallin McLaughlin. *Federal Programs Supporting Educational Change, Vol. VI: Implementing and Sustaining Title VII Bilingual Projects*, Santa Monica, CA.: The Rand Corporation, 1977a.

Berman, Paul and Milbrey Wallin McLaughlin. *Federal Programs Supporting Educational Change, Vol. VII: Factors Affecting Implementation and Continuation*, Santa Monica, CA.: The Rand Corporation, 1977b.

Berman, Paul and Milbrey Wallin McLaughlin. *Federal Programs Supporting Educational Change, Vol. VIII: Implementing and Sustaining Innovations*, Santa Monica, CA.: The Rand Corporation, 1978.

Berman, Paul, Thomas Gjelten, Katherine Csezak, JoAnn Izu, and David D. Marsh. *Improving School Improvement: The Final Report of the Statewide Study of the California School Improvement Program, Vol. II: Findings*, Berkeley, CA: Berman, Weiler & Associates, 1984.

Berman, Paul. "The Study of Macro- and Micro-Implementation," *Public Policy*, vol. 26, no. 2, Spring 1978, pp. 157–184.

Berman, Paul. "Thinking about Programmed and Adaptive Implementation: Matching Strategies to Situations," Paper presented to Institute for Educational Finance and Governance Law Seminar, San Francisco, Calif., February 29, 1980.

Bibby, John F. "Congress' Neglected Function," in *Republican Papers*, New York: Praeger, 1968.

Birman, Beatrice, Martin Orland, Richard Jung, Ronald Anson, and Gilbert Garcia. *The Current Operations of Chapter 1 Programs,* Washington, D.C.: U.S. Department of Education, Office of Educational Research and Improvement, 1987.

Blau, Peter M. and W. R. Scott. *Formal Organizations: A Comparative Approach,* San Francisco: Chandler Publishing Co., 1962.

Bongiovanni, Lawrence M. Memorandum from the Director of the Bureau of Elementary and Secondary Education, Massachusetts Department of Education to Superintendents of Schools and ESEA Title I Directors, June 26, 1970.

Boreham, Paul. "Intermination: Professional Knowledge, Organization and Control," *Sociological Review,* vol. 32, 1983, pp. 693–718.

Bosworth, Barry P. *Tax Incentives and Economic Growth,* Washington, DC: The Brookings Institution, 1984.

Boyd, William. "Public Education's Last Hurrah?: Schizophrenia, Amnesia, and Ignorance in School Politics," *Educational Evaluation and Policy Analysis,* vol. 9. no. 2, Summer 1987, pp. 85–100.

Boyer, Ernest. *High School,* New York: Harper and Row, 1983.

Bredderman, Theodore. "Effects of Activity-Based Elementary Science on Student Outcomes: A Quantitative Synthesis," *Review of Educational Research,* vol. 53, no. 4, 1973, pp. 499–518.

Brophy, Jere E. and Thomas L. Good. "Teacher Behavior and Student Achievement," in Merlin C. Wittrock, ed., *Handbook of Research on Teaching,* New York: Macmillian, 1986, pp. 328–375.

Brown, David S. and Edward E. Rosendahl. "A Summary of Findings Extracted from the Preliminary Report Entitled, Education of the Disadvantaged, Fiscal Year 1969," Washington: Bureau of Elementary and Secondary Education, USOE, July 1970.

Buckley, James A. "A Study of the Professional Staffs of the New England State Departments of Education," Unpublished special qualifying paper, Harvard Graduate School of Education, 1969.

Bullock, Charles S., III. "Motivations for U.S. Congressional Committee Preferences: Freshman of the 92nd Congress," *Legislative Studies Quarterly,* vol. 1, 1976, pp. 201–212.

Burns, Thomas J. Memorandum from the U.S. Office of Education Acting Associate Commissioner for Elementary and Secondary Education to Chief State School Officers, August 14, 1970.

Carnegie Forum on Education and the Economy. *A Nation Prepared: Teachers for the 21st Century,* The Report of the Task Force on Teaching as a Profession, New York: Carnegie Forum on Education and the Economy, 1986.

Carter, Lavnor F. "The Sustaining Effects Study of Compensatory and Elementary Education," *Educational Researcher*, vol. 13, no. 7, 1984, pp. 4–13.

Center for Education Statistics. *The Condition of Education: A Statistical Report*. Washington, D.C.: Office of Educational Research and Improvement, U.S. Department of Education, 1987.

Center for National Policy. *Educating Our Citizens: The Search for Excellence, Alternatives for the 1980s*, no. 9, Washington, D.C.: Center for National Policy, 1983.

Center for Policy Research in Education. "Graduating from High School: New Standards in the States," *CPRE Policy Briefs*, New Brunswick, N.J.: Rutgers University, 1989.

Chubb, John E. "The Political Economy of Federalism," *American Political Science Review*, vol. 79, no. 4, December 1985, pp. 994–1015.

Clark, David L. and Terry A. Astuto. *The Significance and Permanence of Changes in Federal Educational Policy 1980–88*, Bloomington, Ind.: Policy Studies Center of the University Council for Educational Administration, 1986.

Clune, William H. "Institutional Choice as a Theoretical Framework for Research on Educational Policy," *Educational Evaluation and Policy Analysis*, vol. 9, 1987, pp. 117–132.

Clune, William H., III. "The Deregulation Critique of the Federal Role in Education," Working Paper No. 332, Madison, Wisconsin Center for Education Research, 1982.

Clune, William. "Educational Reform: The Effects of Graduation Requirements and Other Student Standards," New Brunswick, N.J.: Center for Policy Research in Education. Rutgers University, 1988.

Clune, William. "Institutional Choice as a Theoretical Framework for Research on Educational Policymaking," *Educational Evaluation and Policy Analysis*, vol. 9, no. 2, 1987, pp. 117–132.

Clune, William. *The Implementation and Effects of High School GraduationRequirements: First Steps Toward Curricular Reform*, New Brunswick, N.J.: Rutgers University, Center for Policy Research in Education, 1988.

Cohen, David K. "Policy and Organization: The Impact of State and Federal Education Policy on School Governance," *Harvard Educational Review*, vol. 52, no. 4, November 1982, pp. 474–499.

Cohen, David K. and Tyll Van Geel. "Public Education," in Samuel H. Beer and Richard E. Barringer, eds., *The State and the Poor*, Cambridge: Winthrop Publishers, 1970.

Cohen, David. "Educational Technology, Policy and Practice," *Educational Evaluation and Policy Analysis,* vol. 9, 1987, pp. 153–170.

Cohen, David. "A Revolution in One Classroom: The Case of Mrs. Oublier," *Educational Evaluation and Policy Analysis,* vol. 12, no. 3, Fall 1990, pp. 327–346.

Cohen, Michael. "Instructional, Management and Social Conditions in Effective Schools," in Allan Odden and L. Dean Webb, eds., *School Finance and School Improvement: Linkages for 1980s,* Cambridge, Mass.: Ballinger, 1983, pp. 17–50.

Commission on the Organization of the Executive Branch of the Government. "Federal State Relations," *A Report to the Congress,* Washington, D.C.: Government Printing Office, 1949.

Commonwealth of Massachusets. *Report of the Special Commission Established to Make an Investigation and Study Relative to Improving and Extending Educational Facilities in the Commonwealth,* House Document No. 4300, June 1965.

Conference Board of the Mathematical Sciences. *New Goals for Mathematical Sciences Education,* Report of a conference sponsored by the Conference Board of the Mathematical Sciences, Washington, D.C.: The Conference Board of the Mathematical Sciences, 1983b.

Conference Board of the Mathematical Sciences. *The Mathematical Sciences Curriculum K–12: What Is Still Fundamental and What Is Not,* Washington, D.C.: National Science Foundation, 1983a.

Congressional Budget Office. *Trends in Educational Achievement,* Washington, D.C.: Congressional Budget Office, 1986.

Cooley, William W. "Effectiveness of Compensatory Education," *Educational Leadership,* vol. 3, January 1981, pp. 298–301.

Craig, Steven G. and Robert P. Inman. "Federal Aid and Public Education: An Empirical Look at the New Fiscal Federalism," *Review of Economics and Statistics,* vol. 64, November 1982, pp. 541–552.

Crandall, David and Associates. *A Study of Dissemination Efforts Supporting School Improvement, Volumes 1–10,* Andover, MA: 1982.

Crandall, David P. , Jeffrey Eiseman and Karen S. Louis. "Strategic Planning Issues that Bear on the Success of School Improvement Efforts," *Educational Administration Quarterly,* vol. 22, no. 3, 1986, pp. 21–53.

Cremin, Lawrence. *The Genius of American Education,* New York: Vintage Books, 1965.

Crocker, Patricia. "California's School Improvement Program: Policy Implications for a Developmental Approach," Unpublished doctoral dissertation, University of Southern California, 1989.

Cronbach, Lee J. *Designing Evaluations of Educational and Social Programs,* San Francisco: Jossey-Bass, 1982.

Cronin, Joseph. "The Federal Takeover: Should the Junior Partner Run the Firm?" in S. Halperin, ed., *Federalism at the Crossroads: Improving Educational Policymaking,* Washington, D.C.: Institute for Educational Leadership, 1976.

Crozier, Michel. *The Bureaucratic Phenomenon,* Chicago: The University of Chicago Press, 1964.

Cuban, Larry. *How Teachers Taught,* New York: Longman, 1984.

Cuban, Larry, "Transforming the Frog Into a Prince: Effective Schools Research, Policy and Practice at the District Level," *Harvard Educational Review,* vol. 54, no. 2, May 1984a, pp. 129–151.

Cuban, Larry, "School Reform by Remote Control: S.B. 813 in California," *Phi Delta Kappan,* vol. 66, no. 3, 1984b, pp. 213–215.

Cuban, Larry. "A Fundamental Puzzle of School Reform," *Phi Delta Kappan,* vol. 69, 1988, pp. 340–344.

Cummins, James. *Empowering Language Minority Students,* Sacramento, Calif.: California Association for Bilingual Education, 1989.

Cusick, P. A. *The School Reform Movement's Impact on School Dropout and Retention Efforts,* East Lansing, Mich.: Michigan State University, 1984.

Cyert, Richard M. and James March. *A Behavioral Theory of the Firm,* Englewood Cliffs, N.J.: Prentice Hall, 1963.

Dahl, Robert A. *Dilemmas of Pluralist Democracy: Autonomy vs. Control,* New Haven: Yale University Press, 1982.

Darling-Hammond, Linda and Barnett Berry. *The Evolution of Teacher Policy,* Prepared for the Center for Policy Research in Education, Santa Monica, Calif.: RAND Corporation, 1988.

Darling-Hammond, Linda. *Beyond the Commission Reports: The Coming Crisis in Teaching,* Santa Monica, CA: The RAND Corporation, 1984.

David, Jane L. *Restructuring in Progress: Lessons from Pioneering Districts,* Washington, DC: National Governors' Association, 1989a.

David, Jane L. "Synthesis of Research on School-Based Management," *Educational Leadership,* vol. 48, 1989b, pp. 45–53.

Demerest, Elizabeth. "The HEW Sanction Study: Enforcement Policy in Title I ESEA: Analysis and Recommendations," Unpublished Office of Education document, Washington, D.C.: U.S. Department of Education, 1977.

Denham, Carolyn and Ann Lieberman. *Time to Learn*, Washington, DC: The National Institute of Education, U.S. Department of Education, 1980.

Derthick, Martha and P. J. Quirk. *The Politics of Deregulation*, Washington: Brookings Institution, 1985.

Derthick, Martha. *The Influence of Federal Grants*, Cambridge: Harvard University Press, 1970.

Derthick, Martha. "Washington: Angry Citizens and an Ambitious Plan," in Walter Williams and Richard Elmore, eds., *Social Program Implementation*, New York: Academic Press, 1976.

Dery, David. *Problem Definition in Policy Analysis*, Lawrence, Kansas: University Press, 1984.

Dougherty, Van and Allan Odden. *State School Improvement Programs*, Denver, Colo.: Education Commission of the States, 1982.

Downs, Anthony. *An Economic Theory of Democracy*, New York: Harper, 1957.

Doyle, Denis P. and Chester E. Finn, Jr. "American Schools and the Future of Local Control," *The Public Interest*, vol. 77, Fall 1984, pp. 77–95.

Duane, Edward A. and William Bridgeland. "Power Differentiation among Educational Interest Groups," Unpublished paper, Michigan University, 1979.

Eckstein, H. "Case Studies in Political Science," in F. I. Greenstein and Nelson W. Polsby, eds., *Handbook of Political Science*, vol. 7, Reading, Mass.: Addison Wesley, 1975.

Edelman, Marian. *The Symbolic Use of Politics*, Urbana, Il.: University of Illinois Press, 1964.

Edwards, George C. *Public Policy Implementation*, Greenwid, CT: JAI Press, 1980.

Elazar, Daniel J. *American Federalism: A View from the States*, New York: Harper & Row, 1973.

Elazar, Daniel J. *American Federalism: A View from the States*, New York: Thomas Y. Crowell Company, 1966.

Elementary and Secondary Education Act of 1985, 79 Stat. 32, Title I, sec. 207 (c) (2).

Elmore, Richard and Milbrey McLaughlin. "Strategic Choice in Federal Policy: The Compliance-Assistance Trade-off," in Ann Lieberman and Milbrey McLaughlin, eds., *Policymaking in Education*. Chicago: Chicago University Press, 1981, pp. 159–194.

Elmore, Richard and Milbrey McLaughlin. "The Federal Role in Education:

Learning From Experience," *Education and Urban Society*. vol. 15, no. 3, May 1983, pp. 309–330.

Elmore, Richard F. "Differential Treatment of States in Federal Education Policy," Prepared for the School Finance Project, Washington, D.C.: U.S. Department of Education, 1981.

Elmore, Richard F. "Organizational Models of Social Program Implementation," *Public Policy,* vol. 26, 1978, pp. 209–217.

Elmore, Richard F. and Milbrey W. McLaughlin. "Rethinking the Federal Role in Education," Prepared for the School Finance Project, Washington, D.C.: U.S. Department of Education, 1981.

Elmore, Richard F. and Milbrey Wallin McLaughlin. *Steady Work: Policy, Practice and Reform of American Education,* Santa Monica, CA: The Rand Corporation, February 1988.

Elmore, Richard F. *Policy Analysis as the Study of Implements,* Paper prepared for the annual meeting of the Western Political Science Association, Las Vegas, NV, March 1985.

Elmore, Richard F. "The Problem of Quality in Chapter 1," in Denis P. Doyle and Bruce S. Cooper, eds., *Federal Aid to the Disadvantaged: What Future for Chapter 1?,* Philadelphia: The Falmer Press, 1988, pp. 167–180.

Elmore, Richard. "Lessons from Follow Through," *Policy Analysis,* vol. 1, Summer 1977, pp. 549–584.

Elmore, Richard. "Backward Mapping: Implementation Research and Policy Decisions," *Political Science Quarterly,* vol. 94, no. 4, Winter 1979–80, pp. 601–616.

Elmore, Richard. "Organizational Models of Social Program Implementation," in Dale Mann, ed., *Making Change Happen,* New York: Teachers College Press, 1978.

Epstein, Joyce. "School Policy and Parent Involvement: Research Results," *Educational Horizons,* Winter 1984, pp. 70–72.

Farrar, Eleanor and Mary Ann Milsap. *State and Local Implementation of Chapter 1,* Cambridge, Mass.: Abt Associates, 1986.

Farrar, Eleanor, J. E. DeSanctis, and David K. Cohen. "The Lawn Party: The Evolution of Federal Programs in Local Settings," *Phi Delta Kappan,* vol. 62, no. 3, October 1980, pp. 167–171.

Feldstein, Martin, "The Effect of a Differential Add-On Grant: Title I and Local Education Spending," *Journal of Human Resources,* vol. 13, Fall 1978, pp. 443–458.

Fenno, Richard F., Jr. *Congressmen in Committee,* Boston: Little, Brown and Company, 1973.

Fiorina, Morris P. *Representatives, Roll Calls, and Constituencies*, Lexington, MA: Lexington Books, D.C. Heath, 1974.

Firestone, William. "Using Reform: Conceptualizing District Initiative," *Educational Evaluation and Policy Analysis*, vol. 11, no. 2, 1989, pp. 151–164.

Friedson, Elliot. "Professionalization and the Organization of Middle Class Labour in Post-Industrial Society". In P. Halmas, ed., *Professionalization and Social Change, Sociological Review Monograph 20*, Keele, England: University of Keele, 1973, pp. 47–59.

Fuhrman, Susan, William Clune and Richard Elmore. "Research on Education Reform: Lessons on Implementation of Policy," *Teachers College Record*, vol. 90, no. 2, Winter 1988, pp. 237–258.

Fuhrman, Susan, William Firestone, and Michael Kirst. *The Progress of Reform: An Appraisal of State Education Initiatives*, New Brunswick, N.J.: Rutgers University, Center for Policy Research in Education, 1989.

Fullan, Michael G., Barrie Bennett, and Carol Rolheiser-Bennett. "Linking Classroom and School Improvement," Invited Address, American Educational Research Association,1989, pp. 3–4.

Fullan, Michael. "Performance Appraisal and Curriculum Implementation Research," Manuscript for the Conference on Performance Appraisal for Effective Schooling, Ontario Institute for Studies in Education, Toronto, February 1986.

Fullan, Michael. "Change Processes and Strategies at the Local Level," *The Elementary School Journal*, vol. 85, no. 3, January 1985, pp. 391–422.

Fullan, Michael. "Change Processes in Secondary Schools: Towards a More Fundamental Agenda," Paper prepared for the Teacher Context Center, Stanford University, Palo Alto, California, 1988.

Fullan, Michael. *The Meaning of Educational Change*, New York: Teachers College Press, 1982.

Gabriel, Rory M., Beverly L. Anderson, G. Benson, S. Gordon, R. Hill, J. Pfannenstiel, and Robert M. Stonehill. *Studying the Sustained Achievement of Chapter 1 Students*, Washington, DC: U.S. Department of Education, 1985.

Gallup, Alec M. and Stanley M. Elam. "The 20th Annual Gallup Poll of the Public's Attitudes Toward the Public Schools," *Phi Delta Kappan*, vol. 70, no. 1, September 1988, pp. 33–46.

Gartner, Alan and Dorothy Kerzner Lipsky. "Beyond Special Education: Toward a Quality System for All Students," *Harvard Educational Review*, vol. 57, no. 4, November 1987, pp. 367–395.

Gartner, Alan and Dorothy Kerzner Lipsky. "The Yoke of Special Education: How to Break It," Rochester, N.Y.: National Center on Education and the Economy, 1989.

Gibson, John S. *The Massachusetts Department of Edcuation: Proposals for Progress in the 70's, Final Report,* Tufts University, September 1970.

Glass, Gene. *Education of the Disadvantaged: An Evaluation Report for Title I, Elementary and Secondary Education Act of Fiscal Year 1969,* Boulder, CO.: University of Colorado, 1970.

Goertz, Margaret E. *State Educational Standards in the 50 States: An Update,* Princeton, New Jersey: Educational Testing Service, March 1988.

Goettel, Robert. "Financial Assistance to National Target Groups: The ESEA Tidal (sic) I Experience," in M. Timpane, ed., *The Federal Interest in Financing Schooling,* Cambridge, Mass.: Ballinger, 1978.

Good, Thomas, D. Grouws and T. Beckerman. "Curriculum Pacing: Some Empirical Data in Mathematics," *Journal of Curriculum Studies,* vol. 10, 1978, pp. 75–81.

Goodlad, John. *A Place Called School,* New York: McGraw-Hill, 1983.

Goodman, Marshall R., Delora S. Gross, Thomas A. Boyd, and Herbert F. Weisberg. "State Legislator Goal Orientations: An Examination," *Policy,* vol. 18, no. 4, 1986, pp. 707–719.

Gramlich, Edward M. "Intergovernmental Grants: A Review of the Empirical Literature," in W. E. Oates, ed., *The Political Economy of Fiscal Federalism,* Lexington, MA: Lexington Books, 1977.

Graves, Donald. *Writing: Teachers and Children at Work,* Portsmouth, N.H.: Heinemann, 1983.

Grodzins, Morton. "The Federal System," in *Report of the President's Commission on National Goals and Chapters Submitted for the Consideration of the Commission Goals for Americans: Programs for Action in the Sixties,* New York: Prentice-Hall, 1960.

Grodzins, Morton. *The American System: A New View of Government in the United States,* Chicago: Rand McNally and Company, 1966.

Grossman, Pam, Michael Kirst, Worku Negash, and Jackie Schmidt-Posner. *Curricular Change in California Comprehensive High Schools: 1982–83 to 1984–85,* Berkeley, Calif.: University of California, PACE, 1985.

Grubb, Norton. "Young Children Face the State: Issues and Options for Early Childhood Programs," *American Journal of Education,* vol. 97, no. 4, August 1989, pp. 358–397.

Gruber, Judith E. *Controlling Bureaucracies: Dilemmas in Democratic Governance,* Berkeley: University of California Press, 1987.

Guskey, Thomas. "Staff Development and the Process of Teacher Change," *Educational Researcher,* vol. 15, no. 5, 1986, pp. 5–12.

Guthrie, James W. "The 1965 ESEA: The National Politics of Educational Reform," Unpublished dissertation, Stanford University, 1967.

Hall, Eugene and Shirley Hord. *Change in Schools,* Albany, N.Y.: State University of New York Press, 1987.

Halperin, Samuel. "The Elementary and Secondary Education Act: 5 Years Later," *Congressional Record,* September 9, 1970, H. 8492.

Hamm, Keith E. and Roby D. Robertson. "Factors Influencing the Adoption of New Methods of Legislative Oversight in the U.S. States," *Legislative Studies Quarterly,* vol. 6, no. 1, February 1981, pp. 133–150.

Hargrove, Erwin C. *Strategies for Implementation of Federal Educational Policies: Compliance vs. Incentives,* Prepared for the School Finance Project, Washington, D.C.: U.S. Department of Education, 1981.

Hargrove, Erwin. "The Search for Implementation Theory," in Richard J. Keckhauser and Derek Leebaert, eds., *What Role For Government?,* Durham, N.C.: Duke University Press, 1983.

Hastings, Anne H. "The Block Grant Record: Lessons from Experience," *Phi Delta Kappan,* no. 63, no. 5, January 1982, pp. 330–332.

Hawkridge, D. *A Study of Selected Exemplary Programs for the Education of Disadvantaged Children, Parts I and II,* Final Report No. 08 9013 for Office of Education, Palo Alto, Calif.: American Institutes for Research, 1968, (Mimeo).

Heclo, Hugh. *A Government of Strangers: Executive Politics in Washington,* Washington, D.C.: Brookings, 1977.

Hill, Paul T. *Enforcement and Informal Pressure in the Management of Federal Categorical Programs in Education,* Prepared for the Office of the HEW Assistant Secretary for Education, Santa Monica, CA: Rand Corporation, 1979.

Hochschild, Jennifer L. *The New American Dilemma: Liberal Democracy and School Desegregation,* New Haven: Yale University Press, 1984.

Honig, Bill. "California's Experience with Textbook Improvement," *Educational Policy,* vol. 3, no. 2, June 1989, pp. 125–136.

House, Ernest. *The Politics of Educational Innovation,* Berkeley, CA: McCutchan, 1974.

Howe, Harold II. Letter from the U.S. Commissioner of Education, Septermber 18, 1970.

Howe, Harold II. Memorandum from the U.S. Office of Education Commissioner to Chief State School Officers, July 2, 1968b.

Howe, Harold II. Memorandum from the U.S. Office of Education Commissioner to Chief State School Officers, July 19, 1968c.

Howe, Harold II. Memorandum from the U.S. Office of Education Commissioner to Chief State School Officers, March 18, 1968a.

Howe, Harold II. Memorandum from the U.S. Office of Education Commissioner to Chief State School Officers, November 20, 1968d.

Huberman, Michael and Matthew Miles. *Innovation Up Close: How School Improvement Works*, New York: Plenum,1984.

Huefner, Dixie Snow. "The Counseling Teacher Model: Risks and Opportunities," *Exceptional Children*, vol. 54, no. 5, 1988, pp. 403–414.

Hueftle, S. J., S. J. Rakow, and W. W. Welch. *Images of Science: A Summary of Results from the 1981–82 National Assessment in Science*, Minneapolis, MN: Minnesota Research and Evaluation Center, 1983.

Hughes John F. and Anne O. Hughes. *Equal Education: A New National Strategy*, Bloomington, Ind.: Indiana University Press, 1972.

Hughes, John F. Memorandum from the Director of Compensatory Education, USOE, to Chief State School Officers, April 14, 1967.

Ingram, Helen. "Implementation: Finding a Way Through the Studies," in Aaron Wildavsky and L. Lynn, eds., *Public Administration: The State of the Field*, in press.

Ingram, Helen. "Policy Implementation Through Bargaining: The Case of Federal Grants-In-Aid," *Public Policy*, vol. 25, no. 4, Fall 1977, pp. 499–526.

Jacobsen, Willard. *Analyses and Comparison of Science Curricula in Japan and the United States*, The International Association for Evaluation of Educational Achievement (IEA), New York: Teachers College, Columbia University, 1986.

Jeffrey, Robert L. Memorandum requested by the Director of the Division of Elementary and Secondary Education, Massachusetts Department of Education , December, 1969.

Johnson, Robert W. and R. E. O'Connor. "Intra-Agency Limitations on Policy Implementation: You Can't Always Get What You Want, But Sometimes You Get What You Need," *Administration and Society*, vol. 11, no. 2, August 1979, pp. 193–215.

Johnston, William. *Workforce 2000*, Indianapolis, IN: The Hudson Institute, 1987.

Jordan, Daniel C. and Kathryn Spiess. *Compensatory Education in Massachusetts: An Evaluation with Recommendations*, School of Education, University of Massachusetts, 1970.

Joyce, Bruce and Beverly Showers. *Student Achievement Through Staff Development,* New York: Longman, 1988.

Jung, Richard and Michael Kirst. "Beyond Mutual Adaptation, Into the Bully Pulpit: Recent Research on the Federal Role in Education," *Education Administration Quarterly,* vol. 22, no. 3, Summer 1986, pp. 80–109.

Kagan, Spencer. "Cooperative Learning and Socio-Cultural Factors in Schooling," in *Beyond Language: Social and Cultural Factors in Schooling Language Minority Students,* Los Angeles: Evaluation, Dissemination and Assessment Center, California State University, Los Angeles, 1986.

Kaiser, Fred. "Oversight of Foreign Policy: The U.S. House Committee on International Relations," *Legislative Studies Quarterly, II,* August 1977, pp. 255–279.

Karweit, Nancy. *Effective Preschool Programs for Children At Risk,* Baltimore, MD: John Hopkins University, Center for Research on Elementary and Middle Schools, 1987.

Karweit, Nancy. "Time and Learning: A Review," in Robert Slavin, ed., *School and Classroom Organization,* Hillsdale, N.J.: Lawrence Erlbaum Associates, 1989, pp. 69–95.

Kaufman, Herbert. *Politics and Policies in State and Local Governments,* Englewood Cliffs, New Jersey: Prentice-Hall, Inc., 1963.

Kaye, Loren. *Making the Grade? Assesing School District Progress on SB 813.* Sacramento, Calif.: California Tax Foundation, 1985.

Kelman, S., "Why Public Ideas Matter," in Robert B. Reich, ed., *The Power of Public Ideas,* Cambridge, MA: Ballinger Publishing Company, 1988, pp. 31–53.

Kennedy, Mary M., Beatrice F. Birman, and Randy E. Demaline. *The Effectiveness of Chapter 1 Services,* Washington, D.C.: U.S. Department of Education, Office of Educational Research and Improvement, 1986.

Kenoyer, Charles E. et al. *The Effects of Discontinuing Compensatory-Education Services,* Technical Report 11 from the Study of the Sustaining Effects of Compensatory Education on Basic Skills, Santa Monica, California: System Development Corporation, 1981.

Kimbrough, Jackie and Paul T. Hill. *The Aggregate Effects of Federal Education Programs,* Santa Monica, CA: The Rand Corp, 1981.

Kingdon, John W. *Agendas, Alternatives, and Public Policies,* Boston, MA: Little, Brown, 1984.

Kingdon, John W. "Ideas, Politics and Public Policies," Paper presented at the 1988 Meeting of American Political Science Association, Washington, D.C.: September 1988.

Kirst, Michael and Gail Meister. "Turbulence in American Secondary Schools: What Reforms Last?" *Curriculum Inquiry,* vol. 15, no. 2, 1985, pp. 169–185.

Kirst, Michael and Richard Jung. "The Utility of a Longitudinal Approach in Assessing Implementation," *Educational Evaluation and Policy Analysis,* vol. 2, no. 5, September–October 1980, pp. 17–34.

Kirst, Michael W. "The Federal Role and Chapter 1: Rethinking Some Basic Assumptions," in D. Doyle, J. Michie and B. Williams, eds., *Policy Options for the Future of Compensatory Education: Conference Papers,* Washington, D.C.: Research and Evaluation Associates, 1987, pp. 89–105.

Kirst, Michael. "Recent State Education Reform in the United States: Looking Backward and Forward," *Educational Administration Quarterly,* vol. 2, no. 5, 1988, pp. 17–34.

Kirst, Michael. "State Policy in an Era of Transition," *Education and Urban Society,* vol.16, no. 2, 1984, pp. 225–237.

Kirst, Michael. "The Federal Role and Chapter 1: Rethinking Some Basic Assumptions," in Denis P. Doyle and Bruce S. Cooper, eds., *Federal Aid to the Disadvantaged: What Future for Chapter 1?,* Philadelphia: The Falmer Press, 1988, pp. 97–115.

Klein, Frances, Kenneth Tye, and Julia Wright. "A Study of Schooling: Curriculum," *Phi Delta Kappan,* vol. 61, no. 4, 1979, pp. 244–248.

Knapp, Michael S., Jane L. David, C. R. Finnan, and Marion S. Stearns. "Assessing the Cumulative Effects of Federal Education Policies at the Local Level: A Review of an Emerging Policy Research Literature," A paper presented at the American Educational Research Association annual meeting, New York (March 1982).

Knapp, Michael, Maria Stearns, Brenda Trunbull, Jane David, and Susan Peterson. *Cumulative Effects of Federal Education Policies on Schools and Districts,* Menlo Park, CA: SRI International, 1983.

Krashen, Stephen and Douglas Biber. *On Course: Bilingual Education's Success in California,* Sacramento, CA.: California Association for Bilingual Education, 1988.

Lawyer's Committee for Civil Rights Under Law. *An Analysis of the Legal Framework for State Administration of Title I of the Elementary and Secondary Education Act of 1965,* Washington, D.C.:Lawyer's Committee for Civil Rights Under the Law, 1977.

Leinhardt, G. and A. Pallay. "Restrictive Educational Settings: Exile or Haven?" *Reveiw of Educational Research,* vol. 52, no. 4, pp. 557–578.

Lerner, A. W. "Ambiguity and Organizational Analysis: The Consequences of Micro Versus Macro Conceptualization," *Administration and Society,* February 1986.

Levin, Henry M. "Federal Grants and Educational Equity," *Harvard Educational Review,* vol. 52, no. 4, November 1982, pp. 444–459.

Levin, Henry, David Leitner, and Gail Meister. "Cost Effectiveness of Computer Assisted Instruction," *Evaluation Review,* vol. 11, no. 1, February 1987, pp. 50–72.

Levin, Henry, "Education and Earnings of Blacks and the Brown Decision," in Michael Namorato, ed., *Have We Overcome? Race Relations Since Brown,* Mississippi: University of Mississippi Press, 1979, pp. 79–120.

Levin, Henry. "A Decade of Policy Development in Improving Education Training for Low Income Populations," In R. Haveman, ed., *A Decade of Federal Anti-Poverty Policy: Achievements, Failures, and Lessons,* New York: Academic Press, 1977.

Lindblom, Charles and D. Braybrooke. *A Srategy of Decisions,* New York: Free Press, 1963.

Lindblom, Charles. "The Science of Muddling Through," *Public Administration Review,* vol. 19, no. 1, Spring 1959, pp. 79–88.

Lipsky, Dorothy Kerzner and Alan Gartner. *Beyond Separate Education: Quality Education for All,* Baltimore, Md.: Paul H. Brookes Publishing Co., 1989.

Lowi, Theodore J. *The End of Liberalism,* 2nd ed., Washington, D.C.:Norton, 1979.

Lowi, Theodore. *The End of Liberalism,* New York: W.W. Norton & Co., 1969.

Lynn, Laurence E., Jr. *Managing the Public's Business,* New York: Basic Books, 1981.

MacRae, Duncan, Jr. and J. A. Wilde. *Policy Analysis for Public Decisions,* North Scituate, MA: Duxbury Press, 1979.

MacRae, Duncan, Jr. *Policy Indicators: Links Between Social Science and Public Debate,* Chapel Hill: The University of North Carolina Press, 1985.

Madden, Nancy A. and Robert E. Slavin. "Effective Pullout Programs for Students At Risk," in Robert E. Slavin, Nancy Karweit and Nancy Madden, ed., *Effective Programs for Students At Risk,* Needham Heights, MA.: Allyn and Bacon, 1989, pp. 52–74.

Madden, Nancy and Robert E. Slavin. "Mainstreaming Students with Mild Handicaps: Academic and Social Outcomes," *Review of Educational Research,* vol. 53, 1983, pp. 519–569.

Madden, Nancy, Robert Slavin, Nancy Karweit, and Barbara Livermon, "Restructuring the Urban Elementary School," *Educational Leadership*, vol. 46, no. 5, February 1989, pp. 14–20.

Majone, Giandormenico and Aaron Wildavsky. "Implementation as Evolution," *Policy Studies Review Annual*, vol. 2, 1977, pp. 103–117.

Majone, Giandormenico. *Evidence Argument and Persuasion in the Policy Process*, New Haven: Yale University Press, 1989.

Malen, Betty and Rodney Ogawa. "Professional-Patron Influence on Site-Based Governance Councils: A Confounding Case Study," *Educational Evaluation and Policy Analysis*, vol. 10, no.4, 1988, pp. 251–270.

March, James. *Footnotes to Organizational Change*, Project Report No. 80–A6, Stanford, Calif.: Institute for Research on Educational Finance and Governance, 1980.

Marcus, A. "Environmental Protections Agency," in James Q. Wilson, ed., *The Politics of Regulation*, New York: Basic Books, 1980, pp. 267–303.

Marsh, David and Gregory Bowman. "Top-Down versus Bottom-Up Reform," *Educational Policy*, vol. 3, no. 3, September 1989, pp. 195–216.

Marsh, David D. and Allan Odden. "Key Factors Associated with the Effective Implementation and Impact of California's Education Reform," *International Journal of Qualitative Studies in Education*, forthcoming.

Marsh, David D. and Allan R. Odden. "Policy Implementation and Current Curriculum Reform: An Analysis of the Implementation of the California Mathematics and Science Curriculum Frameworks," In Allan R. Odden, ed., *Educational Policy Implementation*, Albany, New York: State University of New York Press, 1990.

Marsh, David D. and Allan R. Odden. *The USC Study of Mathematics and Science Curriculum Implementation: Training Seminar Materials*, Los Angeles, CA: University of Southern California, 1988.

Marsh, David D. and Gregory Bowman. *Building Better Secondary Schools: A Comparison of School Improvement and School Reform Strategies in California*, A paper presented at the annual meeting of the American Educational Research Association in New Orleans, April 1988.

Marsh, David D. "Curriculum Change Strategies in Secondary Schools: An Extension of the California School Improvement Study," Paper presented at the annual meeting of the American Educational Research Association in Washington, D.C., April 1987.

Marsh, David D., Eleanor Brown, Patricia Crocker, and Howard Lewis. *Building Effective Middle Schools: A Study of Middle School Implementation in California Schools*, Los Angeles: University of Southern California, 1988.

Marsh, David D., Eleanor Brown, Patricia Crocker, and Howard Lewis. "Helping Middle Schools Improve: A Study of Middle School Implementation in California," *California ASCD Journal,* vol. 2, no.3, 1989, pp. 14–22.

Martin, Ruby and Phyllis McClure. *Title I of ESEA: Is It Helping Poor Children?,* Washington, D.C.: Washington Research Project of the Southern Center for Studies in Public Policy and the NAACP Legal Defense of Education Fund, Inc., 1969.

Mathis, Nancy. "Florida Incentive Pay Experiment Dies Quietly." *Education Week.* June 22, 1988, p. 11.

May, Peter J. "Politics and Policy Analysis," *Political Science Quarterly,* vol. 101, 1986, pp. 109–125.

Mayhew, David R. *Congress: The Electoral Connection,* New Haven: Yale University Press, 1974.

Mazmanian, Daniel A. and Paul A. Sabatier. *Implementation and Public Policy,* Glenview, IL: Scott, Foresman and Company, 1983.

McCubbins, Matthew D. and Thomas Schwartz. "Congressional Oversight Overlooked: Police Patrols Versus Fire Alarms," *American Journal of Political Science,* vol. 28, no.1, 1984, pp. 165–179.

McDill, Edward L., Gary Natriello, and Aaron M. Pallas. "Raising Standards and Retaining Students: The Impact of the Reform Recommendation on Potential Dropouts," Report 358. Center for Social Organization of Schools, Baltimore, MD.: Johns Hopkins University Press, 1985.

McDonnell, Lorraine and Susan Fuhrman. "The Political Context of Reform," in Van Mueller and Mary McKeown, eds., *The Fiscal, Leagal, and Political Aspects of State Reform of Elementary and Secondary Education,* Cambridge, Mass.: Ballinger, 1986, pp. 43–64.

McDonnell, Lorraine M. and Anthony Pascal. *Teacher Unions and Educational Reform,* Santa Monica, CA: The RAND Corporation, 1988.

McDonnell, Lorraine M. and Milbrey W. McLaughlin. *Program Consolidation and the State Role in ESEA Title IV,* Santa Monica, CA: The RAND Corporation, 1980.

McDonnell, Lorraine M. and Richard F. Elmore. "Getting the Job Done: Alternative Policy Instruments," *Educational Evaluation and Policy Analysis,* vol. 9, no. 2, 1987, pp. 133–152.

McKean, R. N. "Enforcement Costs in Environmental and Safety Regulation," *Policy Analysis,* vol. 6, Summer 1980, pp. 269–287.

McKnight, Curtis C., F. J. Crosswhite, J. A. Dossey, E. Kifer, J. O. Swafford, K. J. Travers, and T. J. Cooney. *The Underachieving Curriculum: Assessing U.S. School Mathematics from an Internation Perspective,* Champaign, IL: Stipes Publishing Co., 1987.

McLaughlin, Milbrey W. *Evaluation and Reform: The Case of ESEA, Title I,* Cambridge, Mass.: Ballinger, 1975.

McLaughlin, Milbrey W. "Implementation as Mutual Adaptation: Change in Classroom Organization," *Teachers College Press,* vol. 77, no. 3, February 1976, pp. 339–351.

McLaughlin, Milbrey W. "Implementation of ESEA, Title I: A Problem of Compliance," in D. Mann, ed., *Making Change Happen,* New York: Teachers College Press, 1978.

McLaughlin, Milbrey W., Patrick M. Shields, and Dale J. Rezabek. *State and Local Response to Chapter 1 of the Education Consolidation and Improvement Act,* no. 85–A6, Stanford, CA: Institute for Research on Educational Finance and Governance, School of Education, Stanford University, 1985.

McLaughlin, Milbrey W. "Learning from Experience: Lessons from Policy Implementation," *Educational Evaluation and Policy Analysis,* vol. 9, no. 2, 1987, pp. 171–178.

McLaughlin, Milbrey W. and David D. Marsh. "Staff Development and School Change," *Teachers College Record,* vol. 80, no. 1, 1978, pp. 69–94.

McLaughlin, Milbrey W. and P. Shields. "Parent Involvement in Compensatory Education: Lessons for Policy, Paper for the Conference for Alternative Designs in Compensatory Education," Washington, DC, June 1986.

McLaughlin, Milbrey W. and R. S. Pfeifer. *Teacher Evaluation: Learning for Improvement and Accountability,* New York: Teachers College Press, 1988.

McLaughlin, Milbrey W. and Sylvia Yee. "School as a Place to Have A Career," in Ann Libberman, ed., *Developing the Case for a Professional Culture,* New York: Teachers College Record, 1988, pp. 23–44.

McMahon, Jane M. *Factors Related to Successful Implementation of New Mathematics and Science Curriculum Programs in California,* Unpublished dissertation, University of Southern California, 1990.

Meranto, Philip. *The Politics of Federal Aid to Education in 1965,* Syracuse: Syracuse University Press, 1967.

"Metropolitan Life Survey of the American Teacher 1986." New York: Metropolitan Life Insurance Company, 1987.

Meyer, John and Brian Rowan. "Institutional Organizations: Formal Structure as Myth and Ceremony," *American Journal of Sociology,* vol. 83, September 1977, pp. 340–363.

Meyer, John. *The Impact of the Centralization of Educational Funding on State and Local Organizational Governance,* Project Report No. 79–C5, Stanford, Ca.: Institute for Research on Educational Finance and Governance, 1979.

Miles, Matthew and A. Michael Huberman. *Qualitative Data Analysis,* Beverly Hills, Calif.: Sage, 1984.

Milward, H. Brinton, Katheryn G. Denhardt, Robert E. Rucker, and Thomas L. Thomas. "Implementing Affirmative Action and Organizational Compliance: The Case of Universities," *Administration and Society,* vol. 15, no. 3, November 1983, pp. 363–384.

Mitnick, B. M. *The Political Economy of Regulation,* New York: Columbia University Press, 1980.

Moe, Terry M. "The New Economics of Organization," *American Journal of Political Science,* vol. 28, no. 4, 1984, pp. 739–777.

Montjoy, Robert S. and Lawrence J. O'Toole. "Toward a Theory of Policy Implementation: An Organizational Perspective," *Public Administration Review,* September/October 1979, pp. 465–476.

Moore, Mary T., Margaret Goertz, Terry Hartle, Harold Winslow, Jane David, Jane Sojogren, Brenda Turnbull, Richard Coley, and Richard Holland. *The Interaction of Federal and Related State Education Programs,* Executive Summary, Princeton, N.J.: Educational Testing Service, 1983.

Moynihan, Daniel P. *Maximum Feasible Misunderstanding,* New York: The Free Press, 1969.

Mundell, Alice. *Resource Distribution Inside School Districts,* Lexington, Mass.: Lexington Books, 1975.

Munger, Frank J. and Richard F. Fenno, Jr. *National Politics and Federal Aid to Education,* Syracuse: Syracuse University Press, 1962.

Murphy, Jerome T. *Differential Treatment of the States: A Good Idea or Wishful Thinking?,* Prepared for the School Finance Project, Washington, DC: U.S. Department of Education, 1981.

Murphy, Jerome T. "Title I of ESEA: The Politics of Implementing Federal Education Reform," *Harvard Educational Review,* vol. 41, February 1971, pp. 35–63.

Murphy, Jerome. "The Educational Bureaucracies Implement Novel policy: The Politics of Title I ESEA, 1965, 1965–72," in A. Sindler, ed., *Policy and Politics in America,* Boston: Little, Brown, 1973.

Murphy, Joseph, Phillip Hallinger, and Richard Mesa. "School Effectiveness: Checking Progress and Assumptions, and Developing a Role for State and Federal Government," *Teachers College Record,* vol. 86, no.4, Summer 1985, pp. 615–641.

Murphy, Joseph. "The Educational Reform Movement of the 1980's: A Comprehensive Analysis," in Joseph Murphy, ed., *The Reform of American Public Education in the 1980's: Perspectives and Cases*, Berkeley, CA: McCutchan, 1990a.

Murphy, Joseph. *The Reform of American Public Education in the 1980s: Perspectives and Cases*, Berkeley, CA: McCutchan, 1990b.

National Assessment of Educational Progress. *Crossroads in American Education*, Princeton, New Jersey: Educational Testing Service, 1989.

National Board for Professional Teaching Standards. *Toward High and Rigorous Standards for the Teaching Profession*, Detroit, Mich.: National Board for Professional Teaching Standards, 1989.

National Commission on Excellence in Education. *A Nation at Risk: The Imperative for Educational Reform*, Washington, D.C.: U.S. Government Printing Office, 1983.

National Council of Teachers of Mathematics. *Curriculum and Evaluation Standards*, Working draft, Reston, VA: National Council of Teachers of Mathematics, 1987.

National Council on Science and Technology Education. *What Science Is Most Worth Knowing*, Working draft, Washington, D.C.: American Association for the Advancement of Science, 1987.

National Institute of Education. *Administration of Compensatory Education*, Washington, D.C.: U.S. Government Printing Office, 1977.

National School Public Relations Association. "Education U.S.A., Washington Monitor," September 28, 1970.

National Science Board Commission on Precollege Education in Mathematics, Science, and Technology. *Educating Americans for the 21st Century: A Plan of Action for Improving the Mathematics, Science, and Technology Education for All American Elementary and Secondary Students So that Their Achievement Is the Best in the World by 1995*, Washington, D.C.: National Science Foundation, 1983.

Nelson, Barbara J. "Setting the Public Agenda: The Case of Child Abuse," in Judith V. May and Aaron Wildavsky, eds., *The Policy Cycle*, Beverly Hills, CA: Sage, 1978, pp. 17–41.

Neustadt, Richard E. *Presidential Power*, New York: New American Library, 1960.

Niskanen, William A., *Bureaucracy and Representative Government*, Chicago: Rand McNally, 1971.

"O.E. Collecting Misspent Title I Funds." *Education Daily*, January 1980, pp. 4–5.

Odden, Allan and David Marsh. "How Comprehensive Education Reform Can Improve Secondary Schools," *Phi Delta Kappan,* vol. 69, no. 7, April 1988.

Odden, Allan and David Marsh. *How State Education Reform Can Improve Secondary Schools, Vol. I and II,* Berkeley, Calif.: University of California, Policy Analysis for California Education (PACE), 1987.

Odden, Allan and David Marsh. "Local Response to the 1980s State Education Reforms: New Patterns of Local/State Interaction," in Joseph Murphy, ed., *The Reform of American Education in the 1980s: Perspectives and Cases,* Berkeley, Ca.: McCutchan, 1990.

Odden, Allan and David Marsh. "State Education Reform Implementation: A Framework for Analysis," in Jane Hannaway and Robert Crowson, eds., *The Politics of Reform and School Administration,* Philadelphia: Falmer Press, 1989.

Odden, Allan and Eleanor Odden. "Education Reform, School Improvement, and State Policy," *Educational Leadership,* vol. 42, no. 2, 1984, pp. 13–19.

Odden, Allan, C. Kent McGuire, and Grace Belsches-Simmons. *School Finance Reform in the States, 1983,* Denver, Colo.: Education Commission of the States, 1983.

Odden, Allan. "The Economics of Financing Education Excellence," Paper presented at the American Educational Research Association, Washington, D.C., April 20, 1987.

Odden, Allan. "Class Size and Student Achievement: Research-Based Policy Alternatives," *Educational Evaluation and Policy Analysis,* vol. 12, no. 2, Summer 1990, pp. 213–227.

Odden, Allan. "How Fiscal Accountability and Program Quality Can Be Insured for Chapter 1," in Denis P. Doyle and Bruce S. Cooper, eds., *Federal Aid to the Disadvantaged,* Philadelphia: The Falmer Press, 1988, pp. 181–204.

Ogul, Morris S. *Congress Oversees the Bureaucracy: Studies in Legislative Supervision,* Pittsburgh: University of Pittsburgh Press, 1976.

Olson, Lynn. "Florida Lawmakers Raise Teacher Pay," *Education Week,* June 17, 1987, p. 9.

Owen, John D. "The Distribution of Educational Resources in Large American Cities," *Journal of Human Resources,* vol.7, no. 1, 1972, pp. 26–38.

Peterson, Paul, Barry Rabe, and Kenneth Wong. *When Federalism Works,* Washington, D.C.: The Brookings Institution, 1986.

Peterson, Paul. "Did the Education Commissions Say Anything?" *The Brookings Review,* 1983, pp. 3–11.

Peterson, Penelope and Michelle Comeaux. "Assessing the Teacher as a Reflective Professional: New Perspectives on Teacher Evaluation," In A. Woolfolk, ed., *The Graduate Preparation of Teachers*, Englewood Cliffs, N.J.: Prentice Hall, 1988.

Peterson, Penelope L. "Selecting Students and Services for Compensatory Education: Lessons from Aptitude-Treatment Interaction Research," Paper prepared for the Conference on Effect of Alternative Designs in Compensatory Education, Washington, D.C.: June 1986.

Peterson, Penelope, "Alternatives to Student Retention: New Images of the Learner, the Teacher and Classroom Learning," in Lorrie A. Shepard and Mary Lee Smith eds., *Flunking Grades: Research and Policies on Retention,* Philadelphia: The Falmer Press, 1989, pp. 174–201.

Picariello, H. "Evaluation of Title I," Washington, D.C.: U.S. Office of Program, Planning, and Evaluation, 1969. (Mimeo).

Pitkin, Hannah F. *The Concept of Representation,* Berkeley: University of California Press, 1967.

Pogrow, Stanley. "A Socratic Approach to Using Computers with At-Risk Students," *Educational Leadership,* vol. 47, no. 5, February 1990, pp. 61–67.

Pogrow, Stanley. "A Thinking Skills Approach to Enhance the Performance of At-Risk Students: Experience from the HOTS Program," *Educational Leadership,* vol. 47, no. 7, pp. 79–85.

Policy Analysis for California Education (PACE). *Conditions of Education in California 1988,* Berkeley, CA: University of California, PACE, 1988.

Policy Analysis for California Education (PACE). *Conditions of Education in California, 1985,* Berkeley, CA: PACE, School of Education, University of California, 1985.

Pollen, H. "Study of the Audit Resolution Process in the U.S. Office of Education," Unpublished internal Office of Education document, August 1975.

Pressman, Jeffery and Aaron Wildavsky. *Implementation,* Berkeley, CA: University of California Press, 1973.

Pressman, Jeffrey and Aaron Wildavsky. *How Great Expectations in Washington are Dashed in Oakland, or Why It's Amazing that Federal Programs Work at All,* Berkeley: University of California, 1973.

Pressman, Jeffrey L. and Aaron Wildavsky. *Implementation,* 3rd ed., Berkeley: University of California Press, 1984.

Puleo, Vincent T. "A Review and Critique of Research on Full-Day Kindergarten," *Elementary School Journal,* vol. 88, no. 4, March 1988, pp. 425–439.

Purkey, Stewart and Marshall Smith. "The District Policy Implications of the Effective Schools Literature," *The Elementary School Journal,* vol. 85, no. 3, January 1985, pp. 353–388.

Purkey, Stuart C. and Marshall S. Smith. "Effective Schools: A Review," *Elementary Schools Journal,* vol. 83, no. 4, March 1983, pp. 427–452.

Rabe, Barry G. and Paul E. Peterson. "Educational Policy Implementation: Are Block Grant Proposals Based On Out of Date Research?" *Issues in Education,* vol. 1, no. 1, Spring 1983.

Raizen, Senta A. and Lyle V. Jones, eds. *Indicators of Precollege Education in Science and Mathematics: A Preliminary Review,* Washington, D.C.: National Academy Press, 1985.

Ravitch, Diane, *The Troubled Crusade,* New York: Basic Books, 1984.

Rawson, G. E. "Organizational Goals and Their Impact on the Policy Implementation Process," *Policy Studies Journal,* vol. 8, no. 7, 1980, pp. 1109–1118.

Reich, Robert B., ed. *The Power of Public Ideas,* Cambridge, MA: Ballinger Publishing Company, 1988.

Reisner, Elliot. *Delivery of Educational Services to Federally Identified Target Groups: A Comparison and Analysis of Current Approaches,* Prepared for the School Finance Project, Washington, DC: U.S. Department of Education, 1981.

Resnick, Daniel P. and Lauren B. Resnick. "The Nature of Literacy: An Historical Exploration," *Harvard Educational Review,* vol. 47, 1977, pp. 370–385.

Resnick, Lauren. *Education and Learning to Think,* Washington, D.C.: National Academy Press, 1987.

Ripley, Randall B. and Grace A. Franklin. *Bureaucracy and Policy Implementation,* Homewood, IL: Dorsey Press, 1982.

Rivlin, Alice M. *Systematic Thinking for Social Action,* Washington, D.C.: Brookings, 1971.

Romberg, Thomas A. and Thomas P. Carpenter. "Research on Teaching and Learning Mathematics: Two Disciplines of Scientific Inquiry," in Merlin C. Wittrock, ed., *Handbook of Research on Teaching,* 3rd edition, New York: Macmillan, 1986, pp. 850–873.

Romberg, Thomas A. *Changes in School Mathematics: Curricular Changes, Instructional Changes, and Indicators of Changes,* New Brunswick, N.J.: Center for Policy Research in Education, Rutgers, The State University of New Jersey, September 1988.

Romberg, Thomas A. *School Mathematics: Options for the 1990s,* Chairman's report of a conference, Washington, D.C.: U.S. Government Printing Office, 1984.

Rosenbaum, N. "Statutory Structure and Policy Implementation: The Case of Wetlands Regulation," *Policy Studies Journal,* vol. 8, no. 4, 1980, pp. 575–596.

Rosenshine, Barak and Robert Stevens. "Teaching Functions," in Merlin C. Wittrock, ed., *Handbook of Research on Teaching,* New York: Macmillian, 1986, pp. 376–391.

Rosenthal, Alan. "Legislative Behavior and Legislative Oversight," *Legislative Studies Quarterly,* vol. 6, no. 1,1981, pp. 115–131.

Rosica, Thomas. "Reaction Paper to Student-to-Instructor Ratios," Paper presented before the Conference on Effect of Alternative Designs in Compensatory Education, Washington, D.C.: June 1986.

Rowan, Brian and Larry F. Guthrie. "The Quality of Chapter 1 Instruction: Results from a Study of Twenty-Four Schools," in Robert E. Slavin, Nancy Karweit and Nancy Madden, eds., *Effective Programs for Students At Risk,* Needham Heights, Ma.: Allyn and Bacon, 1989, pp. 195–219.

Sabatier, Paul A. "Top-Down and Bottom-Up Approaches to Implementation Research: A Critical Analysis and Suggested Synthesis," *Journal of Public Policy,* vol. 6, no.1, January 1986, pp. 21–48.

Sabatier, Paul and Daniel Mazmanian. *The Implementation of Regulatory Policy: A Framework of Analysis,* No. 39, Research reports of the Institute for Governmental Affairs, Davis, Calif.: University of California Press, 1979.

Sabatier, Paul and Daniel Mazmanian. "The Implementation of Public Policy: A Framework of Analysis," *Policy Studies Journal,* vol. 8, no. 4, 1980, pp. 538–560.

Sabatier, Paul and Daniel Mazmanian. "The Conditions of Effective Implementation: A Guide to Accomplishing Policy Objectives," *Policy Analysis,* vol. 5, no. 5, Fall 1979, pp. 481–504.

Salamon, Lester M. "Rethinking Public Management: Third Party Government and the Changing Forms of Government Action," *Public Policy,* vol. 29, 1981, pp. 255–275.

Salamon, Lester. "The Time Dimension in Policy Evaluation: The Case of New Deal Land-Reform Experiments," *Public Policy,* vol. 2, no. 1, 1979, pp. 129–183.

Sarason, Seymour. *The Culture of the School and the Problem of Change,* 2nd edition, Boston, MA: Allyn and Bacon, 1982.

Schattschneider, Elmer E. *The Semi-Sovereign People,* New York: Holt, Rinehart, Winston, 1960.

Scher, Seymour. "Conditions for Legislative Control," *Journal of Politics,* vol. 25, August 1963, pp. 525–661.

Schlechty, Phillip and Victor Vance. "Do Academically Able Teachers Leave Education? The North Carolina Case," *Phi Delta Kappan,* vol. 63, 1981, pp. 106–112.

Schoenfeld, Alan H., ed. *Cognitive Science and Mathematics Education,* Hillsdale, N.J.: Lawrence Erlbaum Associates, Inc., 1987.

Schultze, Charles L. *The Public Use of Private Interest,* Washington, DC: The Brookings Institution, 1977.

Sharkansky, Ira. *Routines of Politics,* New York: Van Nostrand Reinholt, 1970.

Shepsle, Kenneth A. and Barry R. Weingast. "Political Solutions to Market Problems," *The American Political Science Review,* vol. 78, 1984, pp. 417–434.

Sizer, Theodore. *Horace's Compromise,* Boston: Houghton-Mifflin, 1984.

Slavin, Robert E. and Nancy Madden. "Effective Classroom Programs for Students At Risk," in Robert E. Slavin, Nancy Karweit, and Nancy Madden, eds., *Effective Programs for Students At Risk,* Needham Heights, Ma.: Allyn and Bacon, 1989a, pp. 23–51.

Slavin, Robert and Nancy Madden. "What Works for Students At Risk: A Research Synthesis," *Educational Leadership,* vol. 46, no. 5, February 1989b, pp. 4–13.

Slavin, Robert, Nancy Karweit, and Nancy Madden. *Effective Programs for Students At Risk,* Needham Heights, Ma.: Allyn and Bacon, 1989.

Slavin, Robert. "Ability Grouping and Student Achievement in Elementary Schools: A Best Evidence Synthesis," *Review of Educational Research,* vol. 57, no. 3, Fall 1987, pp. 293–336.

Slavin, Robert. "Achievement Effects of Substantial Reductions in Class Size," in Robert Slavin, ed., *School and Classroom Organization,* Hillsdale, N.J.: Lawrence Erlbaum Associates, 1989, pp. 247–257.

Slavin, Robert. "Cooperative Learning and Student Achievement," in Robert Slavin, ed., *School and Classroom Organization,* Hillsdale, N.J.: Lawrence Erlbaum Associates, 1989, pp. 129–156.

Smith, James. *Curriculum Review, Improvement and Implementation,* Program Advisory 87/8–9, Sacramento, CA: California State Department of Education, 1987.

Smith, Marshall. *Informal Policy Recommendations about Mathematics and*

Science Reform, Stanford, CA: Office of the Dean, School of Education, Stanford University, August 1988.

Smith, Steven S. and Christopher J. Deering. "Changing Motives for Committee Preferences of New Members of the U.S. House," *Legislative Studies Quarterly,* vol. 8, no. 2, 1983, pp. 271–281.

Stanford Research International. *Research on the Effectiveness of Compensatory Education Programs: A Reanalysis of Data,* Final Report, Menlo Park, Calif., 1977a.

Stanford Research International. *Trends in Management of ESEA Title I: A Perspective from Compliance Reviews, Vol. I: Overview, Findings, and Conclusions,* Menlo Park, Calif., 1977b.

Starr, Paul. *The Social Transformation of American Medicine,* New York: Basic Books, 1982.

Stein, Mary Kay, Gaea Leinhardt, and William Bickel. "Instructional Issues for Teaching Students At Risk," in Robert Slavin, ed., *Effective Programs for Students At Risk,* Needham Heights, Ma.: Allyn and Bacon, 1989, pp. 145–194.

Stigler, G. J. "Theory of Economic Regulation," *Bell Journal of Economics and Management Science,* vol. 2, 1971, pp. 1–21.

Stoner, Floyd E. "The Implementation of Ambiguous Legislative Language: Title I of the Elementary and Secondary Education Act," Unpublished Doctoral Dissertation, University of Wisconsin-Madison, 1976.

Sullivan, Neil V. Memorandum form the Commissioner of Education of the Massachusetts Department of Education to Superintendents and ESEA Tile I Directors, October 23, 1970.

Sundquist, James L., ed. *On Fighting Poverty,* New York: Basic Books, Inc., 1969.

Superintendent's Middle Grade Task Force. *Caught in the Middle: Educational Reform for Young Adolescents in California Public Schools,* Sacramento, CA: California State Department of Education, 1987.

The Metropolitan Life Survey of the American Teacher 1986, New York: Metropolitan Life Insurance Company, 1987.

The NETWORK. *A Proposal for a National Center for the Improvement of Science Teaching and Learning,* Andover, MA: The NETWORK, 1987.

The Planar Corporation. *The Silken Purse: Legislative Recommendations for Title I of the Elementary and Secondary Eduction Act,* Washington, D.C.: Author, 1973.

Thompson, Dennis F. *Political Ethics and Public Office,* Cambridge: Harvard University Press, 1987.

Tikunoff, William, ed. *Compatibility of the SIBF Features with Other Research on Instruction for LEP Students,* San Francisco, Calif.: Far West Laboratory for Educational Research and Development, 1983.

Timar, Thomas and David Kirp. *Managing Educational Excellence,* Philadelphia: Falmer Press, 1988.

Tukey, John W. "The Future of Data Analysis," *Annals of Mathematical Statistics,* vol. 3, 1962, pp. 3–21.

Tullock, Gordon. *The Politics of Bureaucracy,* Washington, DC: Public Affairs Press, 1965.

Turnbull, Brenda J., Marshall S. Smith, and Alan L. Ginsburg. "Issues For a New Administration: The Federal Role in Education," *American Journal of Education,* August 1981, pp. 396–427.

U. S. Department of Health, Education, and Welfare, *The Audit Report on the Review of Comparability Data Under Title I of the Elementary and Secondary Education Act of 1965, School District of Baltimore City for the Period July 1, 1974 Through June 30, 1978,* Washington, D.C.: U.S. Department of Education, 1980.

U.S. Congress. House. General Subcommittee on Education. *Hearings on Aid to Elementary and Secondary Education.* 89th Congress, 1st sess., 1965, Report No. 146.

U.S. Department of Health, Education, and Wefare. *Report on Review of Grants Awarded to the Commonweath of Massachusetts Under Title I, Elementary and Secondary Education Act of 1965,* Washington, DC: HEW Audit Agency, January 23, 1969.

U.S. Office of Education. *Education of the Disadvantaged, an Evaluative Report on Title I Elementary and Secondary Education Act of 1965,* fiscal year 1968, Washington, DC: USOE, 1970.

Van Horn, Carl E. and Donald S. Van Meter. " The Implementation of Inter-Governmental Policy." in C. O. Jones and R. D. Thomas, eds., *Public Policy Making in a Federal System,* New York: Academic Press, 1976.

Van Meter, Donald S. and Carl E. Van Horn. "The Policy Implementation Process, a Conceptual Framework," *Administration and Society,* vol. 6, no. 4, 1975, pp. 445–488.

Viscusi, W. Kip and Richard J. Zeckhauser. "Optimal Studies With Incomplete Enforcement," *Public Policy,* vol. 27, no. 4, Fall 1979, pp. 437–456.

Wargo, Michael. *ESEA Title I: A Reanalysis and Synthesis of the Evidence,* Palo Alto, Calif.: American Institutes for Research, 1972.

Weatherford, Michael S. *Presidential Leadership in Economic Policymaking: The Interplay of Ideas and Self Interest,* Paper presented at the 1989

Annual Meeting of the American Political Science Association, Atlanta, August 1989.

Weatherly, Richard and Michael Lipsky. "Street-level Bureaucrats and Institutional Innovation: Implementing Special Education Reform," *Harvard Educational Review,* vol. 47, no. 2, May 1977, pp. 171–197.

Weaver, Timothy. *America's Teacher Quality Problem: Alternatives for Reform,* New York: Praeger, 1983.

Webb, Eugene, Donald T. Campbell, Richard D. Schwartz, and Lee Sechrest. *Unobtrusive Measures: Non-Active Research in the Social Sciences,* Chicago: Rand McNally, 1971.

Weiner, Roberta. *P.L. 94–142: Impact on the Schools.* Washington, D.C.: Capitol Publications, 1985.

Weisberg, Herbert, Thomas Boyd, Marshall Goodman, and Debra Gross. "Reelection and Constituency Service as State Legislator Goals: It's Just Part of the Job," Paper presented at the 1982 meeting of the American Political Science Association. Denver, CO., 1982.

Weiss, Janet A. and Judith E. Gruber. "Using Knowledge for Control in Fragmented Policy Arenas," *Journal of Policy Analysis and Management,* vol. 3, no. 2, 1984, pp. 225–247.

White, Richard T. and Richard P. Tisher. "Research on Natural Sciences," in Merlin C. Wittrock, ed., *Handbook of Research on Teaching,* 3rd edition, New York: Macmillan, 1986, pp. 874–905.

Wildavsky, Aaron. *A Comparative Theory of the Budgetary Process,* Boston: Little, Brown, 1975.

Wildavsky, Aaron. *Speaking Truth to Power: The Art and Craft of Policy Analysis,* Boston, MA: Little, Brown, 1979.

Wildavsky, Aaron. *The Politics of a Budgetary Process,* Boston: Little, Brown, 1974.

Williams, Walter. "Implementation Analysis and Assessment," in Walter Williams and Richard Elmore, eds., *Social Program Implementation,* New York: Academic Press, 1976.

Willig, Ann C. "Meta-Analysis of Studies on Bilingual Education," *Review of Educational Research,* vol. 55, no. 3, Fall 1985, pp. 269–318.

Wilson, William J. "The Urban Underclass in Advanced Industrial Society," in Paul E. Peterson, ed., *The New Reality,* Washington, D.C.: Brookings, 1985.

Wirt, Frederick and Michael Kirst. *Political and Social Foundations of Education,* Berkeley, Calif.: McCutchan, 1972.

Wisconsin Department of Public Instruction. *Information on the HEW Audit Agency Report of Audit 1968 Through 1973, The Milwaukee Public*

School System, Madison, Wisconsin: Wisconsin Department of Public Instruction, 1982.

Wise, Arthur E. *Legislated Learning,* Berkeley, CA: University of California Press, 1979.

Wise, Arthur, Linda Darling-Hammond, Milbrey McLaughlin, and Harriett Bernstein. *Teacher Evaluation: A Study of Effective Practices,* Santa Monica, CA: The Rand Corporation, 1984.

Wohlstetter, Priscilla. "The Politics of Legislative Evaluation: Fire-Alarm and Police Patrol as Oversight Procedures," *Evaluation Practice,* vol. 11, no. 1, February 1990, pp. 25–32.

Wolf, Richard M. *Achievement in America,* New York: Teachers College Press, 1977.

Yates, Douglas. *Bureaucratic Democracy: The Search for Democracy and Efficiency in American Government,* Cambridge, MA: Harvard University Press, 1982.

Yin, Robert and J. Lynne White. *Microcomputer Implementation in Schools.* Washington, D.C.: Cosmos Corporation, 1984.

Yin, Robert K. and Douglas Yates. *Street-Level Governments,* Lexington, MA: Lexington Books, 1975.

Yin, Robert. "Life Histories of Innovations: How New Practices Become Routinized," *Public Administration Review,* January/February 1981, pp. 21–28.

Yin, Robert. "Studying the Implementation of Public Programs," Paper prepared for Solar Energy Research Institute, Golden, Co., 1979.

Yudof, Mark. "Educational Policy Research and the New Consensus in the 1980s," *Phi Delta Kappan,* vol. 65, no. 7, March 1984, pp. 456–459.

Zald, Mayer N. and David Jacobs. "Compliance/Incentive Classifications of Organizations: Underlying Dimensions," *Administration and Society,* vol. 9, no. 4, February 1978, pp. 403–424.

Contributors

William Clune is Voss-Bascom Professor of Law and Professor, La Follette Institute of Public Affairs; Director, Wisconsin Unit, Center for Policy Research in Education; Co-Director, Wisconsin Center for Educational Policy; University of Wisconsin-Madison.

Patricia S. Crocker is Superintendent of Schools, Martinez Unified School District, California; Lecturer, California State University-Hayward.

Jane L. David is president of the Bay Area Research Group.

Richard F. Elmore is professor, Graduate School of Education; Harvard University.

Susan Fuhrman is professor, School of Education; Director, Center for Policy Research in Education, Eagleton Institute of Politics; Rutgers University.

Margaret E. Goertz is Executive Director; Education Policy Research Division; Educational Testing Service.

Terry Hartle is Education Staff Director, U.S. Senate Committee on Labor & Human Resources.

Richard Jung is Principal, John Burroughs School, St. Louis, Missouri; Adjunct-Faculty Member, Washington University and Maryville College.

Michael Kirst is professor of Education; Co-Director, Policy Analysis for California Education (PACE); Stanford University.

Michael S. Knapp is associate professor of Education Leadership and Policy Studies; College of Education, University of Washington.

David D. Marsh is professor, School of Education; Coordinator, California Coalition of Essential Schools; University of Southern California.

Lorraine M. McDonnell is Senior Political Scientist for The Rand Corporation.

Milbrey Wallin McLaughlin is professor of Education; Director, Center for Research on the Context of Secondary School Teaching; Stanford University.

Mary T. Moore is vice-president of Decision Resources Corporation.

Jerome T. Murphy is professor, Graduate School of Education, Harvard University.

Allan R. Odden is professor, School of Education; Co-Director, Policy Analysis for California Education (PACE); Director, Center for Research in Education Finance; University of Southern California.

Paul Peterson is professor of Government at Harvard University.

Susan M. Peterson was formerly with the Bay Area Research Group.

Marian S. Stearns is vice-president of SRI International.

Brenda J. Turnbull is vice-president of Policy Studies Associates.

Priscilla Wohlstetter is assistant professor of Politics and Policy, School of Education; University of Southern California.

Author Index

Subject Index